V

DATE DUE

Brodart Co.   Cat. # 55 137 001   Printed in USA

D1443514

TERRORISM
ON AMERICAN SOIL

TERRORISM
ON AMERICAN SOIL

*A Concise History of Plots and Perpetrators from
the Famous to the Forgotten*

JOSEPH T. McCANN

SENTIENT PUBLICATIONS

First Sentient Publications edition, 2006

Cover design by Kim Johansen, Black Dog Design
Book design by Timm Bryson and Nicholas Cummings
Cover photo—Wall Street bombing, 1920

Library of Congress Cataloging-in-Publication Data

McCann, Joseph T.
 Terrorism on American soil : a concise history of plots and perpetrators from the famous to the
forgotten / Joseph T. McCann.
     p. cm.
 Includes bibliographical references.
 ISBN 1-59181-049-3
 1. Terrorism--United States--History. I. Title.

HV6432.M388 2006
363.3250973--dc22

                                                    2006025471

Printed in the United States of America

10 9 8 7 6 5 4 3 2 1

SENTIENT PUBLICATIONS
A Limited Liability Company
1113 Spruce St.
Boulder, CO 80302
www.sentientpublications.com

CONTENTS

To my dear son, Ashton,
with loving hope that your generation will
see a future free of the kinds of tragedies
described in these pages.

INTRODUCTION

THE CATASTROPHIC ATTACKS OF SEPTEMBER 11, 2001 HAVE USHERED IN NOT only a new era of public awareness about the threat of terrorism, but also an increase in curiosity about what motivates terrorists and the ways in which they can be prevented from carrying out their horrific attacks. Many new terms and catchphrases have found their way into discussions about terrorism. Terms like *war on terror, axis of evil,* and *suicide bomber* are cited widely, but controversy rages on about what these terms mean and whether they accurately portray the true nature of terrorism. A common theme has emerged in discussions on how terrorism can be battled effectively—which is that terrorists and those they target are often engaged in a battle of ideas. Today, this battle is most clearly illustrated in the public statements that have gone back and forth between members of al-Qaeda and leaders in the West—particularly the United States and Great Britain.

A statement issued by Osama bin Laden in November 2002 is quite telling in demonstrating how the radical thinking of al-Qaeda and its sympathizers differs from the views of Westerners, particularly with respect to the legitimacy of political violence. The statement by bin Laden, which was broadcast on Al Jazeera television, provided justification for not only the September 11, 2001 attacks in New York and Washington, but also post-9/11 attacks in Bali, Yemen, and Kuwait against Australian, British, German, and French targets. As with all terrorist attacks carried out by al-Qaeda, bin Laden made clear that they were motivated by "zealous sons of Islam" who were defending their religion in accordance with what bin Laden and his followers believe to be ordered by God and his prophecies.[1]

A close reading of bin Laden's message reveals an important feature of his thinking and motivation. In referring to U.S. President George Bush as "the pharaoh of his age" who is part of a "criminal gang," bin Laden

claimed that Bush was responsible for mass killings in Iraq and for supporting Israel's use of aircraft to bomb people in Palestine.[2] While these claims
are not new, bin Laden went farther by including U.S. Secretary of Defense
Donald Rumsfeld, Vice-President Dick Cheney, and U.S. Secretary of State
Colin Powell as targets of his verbal attack. Bin Laden claimed that "Cheney
and Powell killed and destroyed in Baghdad more than Hulegu of the
Mongols."[3] By calling Cheney and Powell worse than Hulegu, bin Laden
was engaging in a form of name-calling that would likely befuddle a large
number of American citizens, who were no doubt the target audience the
al-Qaeda leader was hoping to reach with his message.

However, the reference to "Hulegu of the Mongols" is more than an
obscure comparison that makes for colorful hyperbole. The reference provides an important insight into the thinking and motivation of the terrorist
leader.

The individual referenced in bin Laden's message is Hulegu Kahn,
grandson of the infamous conqueror Genghis Khan who ruled over a vast
empire in the Far East. Three of Genghis Khan's grandsons took over their
grandfather's empire, with one ruling in China, another ruling in Mongolia,
and Hulegu overseeing the empire in Persia in what is currently Iran.[4] In
the thirteenth century, Hulegu Khan sought to expand his grandfather's
empire by conquering the Islamic domain and began with the caliphate in
Baghdad. To bin Laden, the destruction wrought by Hulegu Khan in the
Islamic world is an example of rulers in the non-Islamic world attacking
Islam.

What makes bin Laden's comparison of Cheney and Powell to Hulegu
Khan so intriguing is that it illustrates the significance that events from centuries ago hold in the minds of al-Qaeda and like-minded terrorists.
Moreover, it underscores the importance that historical events have in the
thinking and planning of terrorist activities. Indeed, one terrorism
researcher has said that "to study the history of terrorism should not be anything less than a *requirement* for understanding terrorism."[5]

Historical references are found throughout most of the public statements issued by bin Laden and his second-in-command, Ayman al-
Zawahiri, on behalf of al-Qaeda. These references stand in stark contrast to
many of the themes found in public statements made in the American
media and by U.S. government officials. For example, when discussing
whether we are having success in the war on terror, officials often point out
that we are indeed winning because there has not been an al-Qaeda-spon-

sored attack on American soil since 9/11 and many plots and attacks have been prevented. A careful review of the themes that run through public statements in the war on terror reveals an important difference between terrorist organizations and the people and governments they attack. That is, terrorists tend to think of the current conflict in terms of decades or centuries, whereas citizens in stable Western societies who are the victims of terrorism often think of the conflict in terms of months or years.

The United States is a relatively young nation compared to others in the world that have much longer heritage. In many places where terrorism has long been a concern—such as Ireland, the Middle East, Turkey, and various regions of Europe—many conflicts can be understood only against the background of historical events that led up to the present day conflict. The United States turned 225 years old right before the attacks of September 11, 2001, yet the history of terrorism in America provides an important context for understanding today's threats.

Within a span of only six years, the United States experienced the two deadliest terrorist attacks in its history. On April 19, 1995, a truck bomb detonated by Timothy McVeigh outside the federal building in Oklahoma City, Oklahoma, resulted in 168 fatalities, and the attacks of September 11, 2001 resulted in over 3,000 deaths. The fear and outrage following these acts, as well as the demand for punishment of those responsible, were certainly understandable. However, a popular but mistaken sentiment that emerged in the wake of Oklahoma City and 9/11 was that Americans were somehow no longer safe from terrorism in their homeland. Yet throughout its history the United States has experienced several terrorist attacks. Some are fresh in the minds of many, while others remain relatively unknown or have fallen into obscurity. Because of this mistaken perception that terrorism is a relatively new phenomenon in America, I have decided to examine acts of terrorism that have occurred on the domestic mainland of the United States, rather than attacks that have taken place against U.S. targets overseas, even though attacks on foreign soil can assist us in our understanding of the changing nature of terrorist threats.

As a psychologist and attorney with a long history of studying violent behavior and consulting in cases where there has been a threat of violence, I know that past behavior is a very potent (albeit imperfect) predictor of future behavior. For the last several years, I have also taught a course on psychological and legal issues in terrorism. Anyone who studies terrorism in any depth cannot help but come away with a healthy appreciation for the important role history plays in understanding the evolution of terrorist threats over time, the common themes that run through all forms of terrorist thinking and planning, and the lessons that can be learned by examining previous successes and failures.

In the pages that follow, I chronicle over three dozen cases of terrorist plots and attacks that have occurred on American soil since the end of the Civil War. The deadliest and most outrageous attacks are covered in detail, as are some obscure cases that never made headlines but that nevertheless provide interesting lessons on terrorist motivation, public reaction to terrorism, and other facets of political violence. The historical period I have chosen to cover begins with the Lincoln assassination at the end of the Civil War and ends with the attacks of 9/11 and the subsequent anthrax letters that marked a new era of danger—one characterized by terrorists who are able and willing to use weapons of mass destruction. Between these two points in American history lie a number of deadly attacks, historical "firsts," and unusual plots that have been carried out by a wide range of individuals and groups with differing political motives and views.

I have chosen to present this history in the format of case studies presented in chronological order. This format permits them to be read independently of each other so that the people involved and the detailed social and political context of each event can be appreciated. Although these case narratives can be read individually, when they are studied in chronological order, they describe an evolving history where common terrorist motives (e.g., anarchism, leftist groups) are found in different periods of history, and common themes (e.g., anti-government sentiments) re-emerge in subsequent years.

A few years ago, British agents conducted a raid on a London apartment where a suspected al-Qaeda operative was believed to have been living. Inside the apartment, agents found a copy of an al-Qaeda training manual that provided an opportunity to peer into the inner world of terrorist ideologies and methods.[6] The manual was organized around specific methods that terrorists use to attack their targets, including assassination, bombings, kidnapping, hijacking, shooting attacks, clandestine methods of avoiding detection, and bioterrorism. None of these methods for attacking innocent civilians and government targets are new. They were used by terrorist organizations operating long ago and continue to be used by groups operating throughout the world today.

Terrorism has existed for centuries. However, changes have occurred over time with respect to specific methods terrorists use, often as a result of innovation or technological advances. For example, the invention of dynamite brought about a new form of violence favored by anarchists in the late nineteenth century. The innovation of commercial air travel in the middle of the twentieth century brought about international hijackings as a major form of terrorist activity. The development of computer networks and the Internet in the latter part of the twentieth century has brought about cyberterrorism.

Political assassination has a history dating back centuries. In fact, the word assassination is derived from an Arabic form of the word hashish, or *hashshashin*, which has can be translated literally as "users of hashish."[7] The word "assassination" derives from the name given to members of a Shiite sect of Islam established in the eleventh century in an Asiatic region near the Caspian Sea that now consists of Syria and Iran. Members of this sect attempted to change political power with attacks on Sunni leaders in dramatic, public killings by plunging a dagger into the target with near certainty of capture. Although the name *hashshashin* was derived from the observation that the first assassins appeared to be under the influence of hashish, it is doubtful that this was true; in all probability, the first assassins carried out their missions with great passion that merely gave the appearance of intoxication.[8]

Still, the term assassination has come to denote the targeted killing of a government leader or official for political purposes. In the formative years of the United States, assassination was not considered to be a prominent concern; there was no Secret Service nor were extensive security measures taken to protect the President or other government officials. Since America was a new democracy that encouraged openness between the people and its leaders, access to government officials was fostered. The first attempt on the life of a U.S. president occurred several decades after the birth of the nation when a mentally ill individual believed Andrew Jackson owed him a debt and tried to shoot the President on the steps of the U.S. Capitol building. The Lincoln assassination was the first politically motivated killing of a U.S. president and thus constitutes a starting point for the cases I discuss in this book.

Throughout history, there have been both successful assassinations and unsuccessful attempts on presidents, a president-elect, presidential candidates, and public figures who are not government officials, but whose death might represent a political statement of sorts. Where the motivation for targeted killings is clearly political, these acts are rightfully considered terrorism, and I discuss them as they occur in the chronological sequence of events.[9]

Bombing represents another favored method of attack by terrorists that gained prominence among anarchists during the late nineteenth century. The use of explosives is common among all terrorist groups, regardless of organizational structure or motivation. Lone terrorists who operate without allegiance to a group (e.g., the Unabomber), diffuse terrorist groups without specific leaders (e.g., Earth Liberation Front), and hierarchical organizations with identified leaders (e.g., al-Qaeda) all use bombing as a means of attacking their targets. Among the advantages of using bombs are the ability to kill large numbers of people with relatively little cost, the ability for terrorists to escape by using timing devices, and high visibility or drama.[10]

Throughout American history, bombings have been carried out for a variety of reasons, and more recently the number of bombing incidents has increased. In 1989, the FBI reported 1,699 attempted or actual bombings, and by 1994, the number had risen to 3,163.[11] Of course, many bombings that occur in the United States are motivated by revenge, greed, or other criminal motives and do not necessarily constitute terrorism.

Other methods of attack are also chronicled, including mass shootings, kidnapping, hijackings, bioterrorist attacks, and sabotage. Each of these methods illustrates important features of terrorist violence that provide insight into terrorist thinking and motivation. Kidnapping and hijacking are similar in that they both involve the barricading of victims in a confined area to prevent their escape. Terrorists typically use hostages as leverage to negotiate political change, raise money for their cause through demands for ransom, or simply to make a public statement. As the events described in this book illustrate, some barricade incidents are relatively benign and result in no injury to the victims, but the events of 9/11 certainly suggest that hostage situations are becoming more lethal.[12]

The cases discussed in this book represent many of the deadliest and most dramatic terrorist attacks that have occurred on American soil. Yet I also present some of the more obscure and less publicized plots and attacks that nevertheless provide an opportunity to explore interesting facets of terrorist violence. Some readers may quibble with my decision to include certain incidents and to leave others out. My intention is not to provide encyclopedic coverage of all terrorist acts that have ever occurred in

America. Rather, I have selected cases that portray the vast range of methods (e.g., assassination, bombings, shootings, hijackings), perpetrators (e.g., lone individuals, diffuse groups or movements, and organized terrorist organizations), and group identifications (e.g., anarchism, Middle Eastern, domestic, nationalist-separatist) that have spurred these attacks. Some cases considered for inclusion—such as the downing of Egypt Air 990 by the flight's co-pilot shortly after takeoff on October 31, 1999—were ultimately left out because of lingering doubt about whether the incidents were actual terrorist incidents.[13]

This final point raises the question of what is actually meant by the term "terrorism." Many scholarly papers have been written about problems in defining terrorism. A universally accepted definition has been elusive. Major textbooks on terrorism discuss international conferences and summits that failed to make any advances toward a universal definition. The trite observation that defining terrorism is difficult because "one person's terrorist is another person's freedom fighter" does little to shed light on what terrorism is and how it can be defined for scientific study.

Despite these difficulties, some common themes have emerged in how terrorism is defined. Two researchers, Alex Schmid and Albert Jongman, conducted an empirical study of 109 definitions of terrorism and found that three themes were involved in over half of them.[14] The most prevalent was the use of violence or force (found in 84 percent); political motivation was the second most common element (65 percent); and fear or terror was the third most common element (51 percent). This study illustrated that terrorism tends to be defined by violent action that is motivated by political goals, but even these factors are not always agreed upon by terrorism researchers.

Definitions of terrorism are complicated by the fact that many forms of violent action—such as war, guerilla activity, and related forms of political violence—overlap with terrorism. Where formal warfare ends and insurgency or guerilla activity begins is sometimes unclear, and the boundary between insurgency and terrorism is also difficult to identify. Nevertheless, the boundary between war and terrorism can sometimes be identified. Thus, the attack on Pearl Harbor—even though it occurred on American soil—is rightfully considered an act of war rather than terrorism, and is therefore not covered in this book. Yet we are still left with the question of what constitutes terrorism.

There are many definitions from which to choose. The U.S. Department of Defense, Federal Bureau of Investigation, federal law, and the

U.S. Department of State all have their own definitions. While there is some overlap, each government agency has adopted a particular definition that suits its specific mission or goal. As a law enforcement agency, the FBI emphasizes the criminal nature of terrorism, whereas the U.S. Department of State, given its international mission, emphasizes subnational groups as perpetrators of terrorism. Other countries and international agencies have adopted their own definitions. For the purpose of this book, I rely on the FBI's definition of terrorism as a general guide. The FBI defines terrorism as "the unlawful use of force or violence against persons or property to intimidate or coerce a government, the civilian population, or any segment thereof, in furtherance of a political or social objective."[15] For a book covering terrorist acts on American soil, this definition is suitable because the FBI is responsible for investigating and preventing terrorist attacks within the United States. The FBI mission extends to both domestic and international threats, as well as to intelligence gathering for the purpose of preventing attacks. While some of the cases in this book were investigated or prosecuted at the local or state level—particularly some of the mass shootings—and were not necessarily viewed as acts of terrorism by the FBI, I believe they meet the definition of terrorism, and I have therefore included them.

During the twentieth century alone, there has been at least one act of terrorism in every decade. In some periods, several attacks occurred within a span of only a few years, and in a few instances, several attacks occurred within the same year. After chronicling terrorist acts, plots, and perpetrators that are both infamous and obscure, I will conclude by taking a look at observable trends and lessons to be learned. My hope is that in understanding our past we may successfully confront the challenges of the future.

LOST-CAUSE TERRORISM

THE ASSASSINATION OF ABRAHAM LINCOLN

Assassination has never changed the history of the world.
—Benjamin Disraeli[1]

TERRORISM IS A FORM OF COMMUNICATION THAT USES VIOLENT ACTIONS TO deliver a message. The amount of planning required to select a symbolic target, plot the method of attack, and time the attack highlights the fact that acts of terrorism are neither random nor impulsive. Some terrorist acts are carried out in pursuit of political change, others seek to retaliate, and still others are a means of expressing outrage. When there has been a period of intense political violence or conflict resulting in one side losing power or being defeated, terrorism blooms. *Lost-cause terrorism* refers to acts of political violence where members of a group have lost a battle and act out in a final display of defiance or rebellion.

One of the most significant acts of lost-cause terrorism in the history of the United States was the assassination of Abraham Lincoln. While a great deal is known about the assassination, considerable misinformation and myth surround the events of April 14, 1865. The traditional lore about Lincoln's assassination is that John Wilkes Booth shot the President at Ford's Theater in Washington, D.C., only days after General Robert E. Lee surrendered his Confederate Army, that Booth was either mentally ill or crazed to have performed such a deed, and that leaders of the Confederate government were not involved in the assassination.[2] For years, the life of John Wilkes Booth has been studied and analyzed. Some people have concluded that Booth was emotionally unbalanced, paranoid, and prone to psychosis.[3] However, the psychology of a political assassin like Booth cannot be understood merely by observing the enormity of the crime and concluding that anyone who would perpetrate such a crime must be insane. As a study of assassins and near-lethal attackers sponsored by the U.S. Secret Service has shown, the act of political assassination is nearly always the product of an understandable and discernable pattern of thinking and planning, and targeted violence is generally not the product of a deranged or severely mentally ill individual.[4]

The killing of Lincoln—committed at the end of a long and bloody Civil War—was not the act of a crazed killer or madman. Rather, the assassination was carefully planned, part of a larger conspiracy to destabilize the government of the United States, and motivated to achieve a political goal. When Lee surrendered his troops on April 9, 1865—five days before the assassination of Lincoln—many believed it marked the end of the Civil War. However, only a portion of the Confederate troops were under Lee's command, and neither Jefferson Davis, the President of the Confederacy, nor Booth believed that Lee's surrender meant the formal defeat of the Southern states.[5] Because Booth was a civilian, because his actions were politically motivated, and because the assassination occurred at a time when the Confederacy had essentially lost the war, the Lincoln assassination was an act of lost-cause terrorism. To fully appreciate Booth's motives and the origins of his plan, it is important to understand exactly how he came to be the first person ever to assassinate a U.S. president.

Booth was born into a family of famous actors. His father, Junius Booth, was a well-known actor with a reputation for erratic behavior; he married a woman in England and had a child. After five years of marriage, Junius Booth entered into an adulterous relationship with Mary Ann Holmes, who became pregnant. He moved his mistress to the United States and ended up having ten children with her, one of whom was John Wilkes Booth. Six of the children managed to survive into adulthood. However, Junius Booth never married Mary Ann Holmes; thus, all of the Booth children were born out of wedlock. Junius visited his wife in England on only a couple of occasions during the remainder of his life.[6]

Mary Ann Holmes, Booth's mother, was devoted to her children. The oldest of the Booth daughters was the only child who withdrew from the family's penchant for fame and exhibited a "neurotic moodiness" throughout much of her life.[7] All the other children had a talent for the arts; along with two of his older brothers, Booth followed in his father's footsteps and became an accomplished actor, while his youngest sister, Asia, became a writer. John Wilkes Booth and his sister Asia were extremely close and in a memoir she later wrote about her brother following his death, she described him as a boy who was well-liked by his friends, well-mannered, and passionate about life.[8] However, his sister also noted that her brother had a more difficult side to his personality. Even as a youngster, Booth harbored strong ideas about the proper role people of certain classes, gender, and race should have in society, and these ideas foreshadowed many of the political beliefs that ultimately influenced him as an adult.

When Booth was fifteen, his father died while his two older brothers were traveling around the country pursuing their acting careers. His sister wrote in her memoir that the young Booth was left to care for his mother and sisters and that he hated the notion that women in his family had to dine at the same table as white laborers working on the family farm.[9] It was clear even during his teenage years that Booth held the belief that members of different social classes should not mix. Other events from his younger years also proved to be critical in giving shape to the political and social beliefs that led Booth to view Lincoln's assassination as necessary. At the age of thirteen, he attended a private school in Maryland where the father of one of his classmates was murdered by runaway slaves resisting their return to slavery. This event had a lasting impression on Booth, who wrote years later about his support for the Southern states and his positive views on slavery. He said, "The South has a right according to the constitution to keep and hold slaves. And we have no right under that constitution to interfere with her or her slaves."[10] Booth also wrote that he did not view slavery as a sin, but rather as a "happiness" for slaves and a "social and political blessing" for white Americans.[11]

When Booth was twenty-one, he attended the public hanging of John Brown—the legendary abolitionist who was convicted of treason against the state of Virginia for trying to incite an uprising of slaves in 1859. Although Booth was said to have admired Brown's strength of character, it was clear that Booth harbored intense loyalty to the Confederate states and a hatred for abolitionists. After Brown's death, "to Booth and his cohorts, Lincoln would soon replace John Brown as the hated symbol of [the] abolition [of slavery]."[12] Booth viewed Lincoln as a backward and ill-mannered tyrant whose stance on slavery was viewed as an attack on the rights of Southern land owners to maintain slaves.

Because Booth was a noted actor and traveled around the United States extensively, he came into contact with a number of well-connected and politically powerful people. Even Lincoln himself attended some of Booth's performances and admired the actor for his talents. Nevertheless, Booth's sympathies for the Southern cause during the Civil War were well known, and convincing evidence has emerged in recent decades that he was an agent for the Confederacy. In October 1864, Booth spent ten days in Montreal, Canada, and had meetings with George N. Sanders and Patrick C. Martin, who were both well-known Confederate agents. Martin and Booth devised a plan to free Confederate prisoners being held by the North in order to bolster the Southern military forces and facilitate a Southern victory in the Civil War.[13] Their plan called for capturing President Lincoln, transporting him to the Confederate capitol in Richmond, Virginia, and demanding the release of Confederate prisoners in exchange for Lincoln's return.

Through Martin, Booth was introduced to Dr. Samuel Mudd—a politically connected physician in southern Maryland whose home was located along a planned escape route that Booth and his co-conspirators would use to transport Lincoln to Richmond. Mudd later became famous as the doctor who set Booth's broken leg during the assassin's escape. Mudd introduced Booth to John Surratt, Jr., whose mother, Mary Surratt, operated a boarding house in Washington, D.C., and a tavern located thirteen miles southeast of Washington in Surrattsville, Maryland. The Surratt Tavern was a meeting place for members of the Confederate underground and was located along a principal travel route from the nation's capitol into the Southern states.[14]

In a meeting between Booth, Surratt, Mudd, and Louis Weichmann (a close friend of John Surratt and a boarder at Mary Surratt's home) at the National Hotel, Booth is said to have informed the others of his plot to kidnap Lincoln. The exact nature of what was said during this meeting is not known, and attempts to reconstruct the conversations of the meeting have resulted in conflicting reports.[15] However, there is general consensus that Booth stated his plan to kidnap Lincoln and that Surratt agreed to help, thus becoming a co-conspirator.

Although Booth was a staunch supporter of the Confederacy and openly expressed his support for slavery, his mother and siblings supported the Union. Because he had promised his mother he would never enlist in the Confederate military and take up arms against the North, Booth was left to find other ways of supporting the Southern cause. As a result, he joined the Knights of the Golden Circle, a network of Confederate spies that relayed messages to Southern agents, smuggled supplies from Canada to the South through Northern states, and gave material support to the Confederacy.[16] The cover that Booth's acting career provided, as well as the strength of his beliefs, led to him becoming a respected and valuable agent for the Confederacy. As the plot to kidnap Lincoln developed, Booth sought the assistance of others who could be trusted. He recruited Michael O'Laughlin and Samuel B. Arnold, childhood friends who had both served in the Confederate military. Booth convinced the men that Lincoln could be captured and moved quickly to Richmond in order to negotiate the release of Confederate prisoners and that the plan would ultimately lead to a victory for the South in the Civil War. O'Laughlin and Arnold were convinced of the feasibility of the plan and agreed to help Booth.[17]

John Surratt helped Booth by obtaining a boat that could be used to transport Lincoln across the river into Virginia and by enlisting the assistance of two other individuals. George Atzerodt, a part-time ferryman who had assisted in the transport of Confederate spies, was approached because his knowledge of travel routes and waterways in the area would be useful when Lincoln was to be transported from Washington into Richmond. Lewis Powell (also called Lewis Paine), a former Confederate soldier known for his strength, was brought into the plan; he was extremely devoted to Booth's cause.[18]

By today's standards, where U.S. presidents are surrounded by Secret Service agents around the clock and tight security deters all but the most persistent of potential attackers, the thought of kidnapping the President and transporting him out of the nation's capital might seem preposterous. However, it is important to remember that in 1865 the President was a much more approachable and accessible target. The U.S. Secret Service did not yet exist as a federal agency, and responsibility for protecting Lincoln fell on a group of Union army officers; however, the protection for the President was not organized formally under any specific governmental or law enforcement agency. In addition, there was a general view that leaders in a democracy such as the United States should be accessible and connected to the people they represent. After all, prior to 1865 a U.S. president had never been assassinated.[19] Moreover, Lincoln openly shunned protection and would often ride his horse alone through the countryside; it is believed that on one occasion, while he was riding alone, someone took a shot at him.

Despite this close call, as well as numerous warnings from others that he should be more careful with respect to his safety, Lincoln was less than cautious. He believed that in an open democratic society the President is often a target. He once said, "I long ago made up my mind that if anybody wants to kill me, he will do it. There are a thousand ways to getting at a man if it is desired that he should be killed."[20] On one occasion, Booth and his co-conspirators learned that Lincoln would be traveling unaccompanied to a soldier's hospital located near the city limits of Washington, D.C. However, Lincoln changed his itinerary at the last moment, leaving Booth enraged that his plans for capturing the President had failed.[21]

Of course, the plot to kidnap Lincoln never materialized. Somewhere during the course of finalizing matters and enlisting the cooperation of conspirators in the plot, Booth changed his plan from one of abduction to assassination. In doing so, he created a situation that would later permit some of his co-conspirators, such as John Surratt, to claim they agreed to the kidnapping plot but never conspired to assist with a plot to assassinate the President. Also, the series of events contributing to Booth's change in plans provides an opportunity to examine the methodical planning and thinking of an assassin.

Although Lee had surrendered his troops on April 9, 1865, Booth and his cohorts continued with their plan to kidnap Lincoln in the slim hope that negotiating the release of Confederate prisoners would bolster the South's military ranks and there might be a reversal of fortune resulting in a victory for the Confederate states. On April 11, however, hundreds of citizens in the nation's capital—happy over the looming end of the long and bloody Civil War—congregated outside of the White House to hear Lincoln speak about rebuilding the torn nation. Among those in attendance was an angry and defiant Booth, who was with Lewis Powell. Booth bristled at Lincoln's talk of a united country without slavery. A few minutes into his speech, Lincoln spoke about the rights that should be bestowed upon the newly freed slaves and said that he believed the right to vote was among the rights that should be granted. Upon hearing this, Booth became enraged over the prospect of citizenship for the freed slaves and said of Lincoln, "That's the last speech he'll ever make."[22] Booth supposedly ordered Powell to shoot Lincoln on the spot, but when Powell refused, Booth left in disgust and said, "Now, by God, I'll put him through."[23] This crucial speech by Lincoln, and Booth's response to what the President had to say, appears to be a critical point in turning the assassin's thinking from orchestrating a kidnapping to planning a murder.

Three days later, on the evening of April 14, Booth went to Ford's theater in Washington where Lincoln was watching a presentation of the play "Our American Cousin." Booth took his horse to the rear of the theater, gave the reins to Edmund Spangler, an attendant at the theater who was also an old friend of the Booth family, and asked the man to watch his horse while he went inside the theater. Because Booth was a famous actor who had made professional appearances at Ford's in the past, Spangler must have thought nothing of seeing Booth at the theater that evening while the President was in attendance. Despite the fact that Spangler had no apparent connection to the assassination conspiracy, the fact that he held Booth's horse during the course of the assassination resulted in Spangler being prosecuted as an accomplice, and he was sentenced to six years in prison for his "role" in the assassination.

Upon entering Ford's theater, Booth walked down a flight of stairs, underneath the stage, back up a flight of stairs, and exited the theater through a side entrance. He walked down an alley, went into a saloon next to the theater, and ordered a drink. A short time later, he left the saloon and re-entered the theater through the front entrance. Once again, the fact that he was a recognized actor familiar with the layout of the theater served to help him gain entrance to Ford's and to move about easily. Booth walked up to the balcony level and went down a corridor to the outer door of a vestibule with an entrance to two boxes. There is some controversy about whether Booth made a visit to the theater earlier in the day to plan his attack because a hole had been drilled in the door to Lincoln's box. The fact that Booth used this hole to survey the seating layout in the box and to check Lincoln's location before entering suggests Booth knew the hole was there and made use of it right before the assassination.

Once inside the vestibule, Booth entered the President's box, took out a single-shot Derringer pistol, cocked the gun, and fired a lead sphere into the back of Lincoln's head from less than two feet away. Major Henry R. Rathbone, an officer in the Union army who, along with his fiancée, had accompanied the Lincolns to the play that evening, lunged at Booth immediately. The assassin wielded a sharp knife and injured Rathbone severely in the ensuing struggle. Booth then leapt from the box onto the stage. His boot got caught on the way down, and he landed awkwardly on the stage, breaking his leg. As he crossed the stage in front of a stunned crowd, Booth shouted, "Sic semper tyrannis!" ("Thus be it ever to tyrants!" the state motto of Virginia) and exited the theater.[24]

In the ensuing pursuit of Booth, which would take twelve days and end in Booth's death during a shoot-out with Union soldiers on the Virginia farm of Richard Garrett, a broader conspiracy to overthrow the U.S. government was discovered. The conspiracy that Booth organized included not only the murder of Lincoln, but also the assassination of Vice President Andrew Johnson and Secretary of State William H. Seward.[25] George Atzerodt had been chosen to assassinate the Vice President, and Lewis Powell had been appointed to assassinate Seward. These attacks were to be carried out on the same evening that Booth assassinated Lincoln. However, Atzerodt developed second thoughts and never attempted the attack on the Vice President. Powell, on the other hand, was successful at entering Seward's home and gravely wounded the Secretary of State. Both Atzerodt and Powell were captured during the subsequent pursuit of Booth and his conspirators; both were convicted and executed for their part in the conspiracy.

Edmund Spangler and Dr. Samuel Mudd were sentenced for their part in the conspiracy but were later pardoned by Andrew Johnson after serving nearly four years of their sentences. Although Spangler's pardon is generally viewed as appropriate, given the lack of clear evidence of his involvement in the conspiracy, Mudd's pardon has been one of the more controversial aspects of the Lincoln assassination. While Mudd's family was successful in getting a pardon issued after working diligently to clear his name, several scholars who have studied the Lincoln assassination provide convincing evidence that Mudd was deeply involved in the conspiracy.[26]

The fact that Booth's plot to kidnap Lincoln evolved into a successful assassination is notable in a number of important respects. First, that Booth was able to earn the trust and respect of Confederate agents to carry out such a daring mission as kidnapping the President of the United States points to the fact that he was anything but an emotionally unstable, mentally ill person. Rather, he was interpersonally skilled, passionate about his political beliefs, and rational in his thinking. He was able to plan and organize a broad conspiracy to destabilize the government of the United Sates in order to benefit the Confederacy. It is not likely that a mentally ill, or legally insane, individual would be capable of orchestrating the meeting of minds necessary for a criminal conspiracy, unless, of course, the other criminal minds were equally insane, which is extremely doubtful in this case, given the number of individuals involved. In addition, Booth's plans had the broader political goal of helping the Confederacy win the Civil War. Booth was also able to remain faithful to the promise he made to his mother not to take up formal arms as a soldier in the Confederate army.

Several key incidents were no doubt critical in shaping Booth's thinking. Given his strong support for the Confederacy, his racist beliefs, and his intense hatred of Lincoln, the surrender of Lee's troops at Appomattox and Lincoln's speech on April 11 in which he expressed his support for citizenship and voting rights for freed slaves pressed Booth to a point of desperation where assassination and disruption of the U.S. government seemed like the only hope for helping the Confederacy. These events, in addition to the lack of a formal protective service devoted to keeping the President safe from harm, created the perfect set of circumstances for the murder of Abraham Lincoln. America's first encounter with the assassination of a president was indeed an act of terrorism in support of a lost cause.

BEGINNING THE DYNAMITE ERA

THE HAYMARKET BOMBING

All sins cast long shadows.

—Irish Proverb[1]

THE LATTER HALF OF THE NINETEENTH CENTURY WAS A PERIOD OF SIGNIFicant technological and industrial innovation that brought two critical developments that would have a profound impact on the future of terrorist acts in the United States. Technological advances yielded new inventions and more efficient ways of mining raw materials and manufacturing goods. Dynamite and other explosive materials provided mining companies with a highly effective method for breaking through rock that allowed railroads to be laid in remote, mountainous regions and mining companies to access valuable resources underground. At the same time, industrial growth led to larger corporations with increasing payrolls and the need to manage large numbers of employees. These two trends ultimately converged in the labor movement that sought fair pay, safer working conditions, a reasonable work day, and other rights and privileges for the working class. Of course, managers and owners of large corporations sought to retain the ability to negotiate their own terms of employment without interference from government regulators or labor unions.

One example of the attraction to technology that developed among labor activists is found in the writings of Johann Most, a German-born militant activist who arrived in the United States in 1881 and spent the last twenty-five years of his life as "the most vilified social militant of his time."[2] Most was an ardent supporter of terrorism, and explosives in particular, as a means to overthrow capitalists and corporate owners, whom he perceived as having monopolistic control over the working class. In one of his many writings on the subject, Most commented that "the importance of modern explosives for social revolution need hardly be stressed nowadays. They are going to be the decisive factor in the next period of world history."[3] Most's prediction turned out to be true, as the era of dynamite as a weapon of terror in the United States began on May 4, 1886, when a bomb exploded at a labor protest in the area of Chicago, Illinois, known as Haymarket Square.

The events leading up to the Haymarket tragedy began a few days earlier on May 1, when a series of coordinated labor strikes and demonstrations took place throughout the United States.[4] Labor activists had been lobbying for an official eight-hour work day, and the purpose of the demonstration was to make organized labor's demands known to corporate owners. One of the demonstrations in Chicago turned violent on May 3, when unarmed, striking workers clashed with police officers outside the factory building of the McCormick Reaper Works.[5] Two strikers were killed, and several others were wounded; the confrontation triggered a massive backlash.

A prominent labor activist named August Spies had witnessed the confrontation. When he read in local newspapers the next day that six workers—an erroneous number—had died in the incident outside the McCormick factory, Spies was outraged.[6] He printed and distributed a flier that read:

REVENGE!
Workingmen, to Arms!!!

Your masters sent out their bloodhounds—the police—they killed six of your brothers at McCormicks this afternoon. They killed the poor wretches because they, like you, had the courage to disobey the supreme will of your bosses. They killed them because they dared ask for the shortening of the hours of toil. . . .

You have for years endured the most abject humiliation; you have for years suffered unmeasurable iniquities; you have worked yourself to death; . . .

If you are men, if you are the sons of your grand sires, who have shed their blood to free you, then you will rise in your might, . . .

And destroy the hideous monster that seeks to destroy you. To arms we call you, to arms.[7]

Spies had initially entitled the flier "Workingmen to Arms," but he was unaware that a printer added the word *Revenge* in order to create a more dramatic title. The flier, which was distributed around the Chicago area on the evening of May 3, came to be known as the Revenge Circular and would ultimately become a critical piece of evidence against Spies as an alleged terrorist conspirator.

On the evening of May 4, 1886, a large gathering of about 300 labor activists, workers, and supporters gathered at Haymarket Square in Chicago to hear speeches on the issue of police brutality. For over two hours, the gathering remained peaceful, and despite the content of the Revenge Circular, the purpose of the meeting was not to incite violence. In fact, Spies was the first to speak and said, "There seems to prevail the opinion in certain quarters ... that this meeting has been called for the purpose of inaugurating a riot, ... however, let me tell you at the beginning that this meeting has not been called for any such purpose."[8]

Among the speakers were other labor activists and leaders, including Albert Parsons and Samuel Fielden. As an apparent exercise in free speech, the Haymarket gathering was calm and uneventful until sometime after ten o'clock. Fielden was wrapping up his speech when a large number of police officers entered the square and ordered the crowd to disperse.

As police tried to break up the gathering, an unknown individual threw a bomb into a group of the officers. The explosion caused police to open fire, and some individuals in the crowd returned fire.[9] When the rioting was over, one police officer—Mathias J. Degan—lay dead. Degan died from a laceration to his thigh caused by a metal fragment from the bomb, and six other police officers died over the next few weeks from wounds they received.[10] Sixty other police officers were injured, but most had suffered injuries caused not by the bomb but by friendly fire from fellow police officers.[11] Some high-ranking police officials later noted that an order had been given for officers to stop firing because it was nighttime, and it had become apparent that members of the police force were firing indiscriminately, wounding each other. Still, the fact that the incident had been triggered by a bomb and led to the deaths of seven police officers led to wide public outrage and very little sympathy for the labor activists.

Within two days of the bombing, Chicago police officers arrested a number of prominent anarchist leaders, many of whom had spoken at the May 4 gathering at Haymarket Square. On May 27, a grand jury indicted ten individuals for the death of Officer Degan. Named in the indictment were Albert Parsons, August Spies, Michael Schwab, Samuel Fielden, George Engel, Adolph Fischer, Oscar Neebe, Louis Lingg, William Seliger, and Rudolph Schnaubelt.[12] All persons named in the indictment had been arrested, except for Parsons, who left Chicago after the bombing because of fear over political backlash. He had been one of the speakers at the gathering, but he later turned himself in on June 21 to face trial.

Seliger avoided prosecution by becoming a witness for the prosecution. Schnaubelt had been identified by witnesses as the individual who actually threw the bomb.[13] However, he left the country after the Haymarket bombing, ultimately settled in Argentina, where he raised a family, and never returned to the United States.[14] The remaining eight defendants were charged with conspiracy to commit murder and stood trial for the Haymarket bombing.

Although the nineteenth century had its share of dramatic and controversial courtroom battles—including the trial of conspirators in the Lincoln assassination and the trial of Charles Guiteau, who assassinated President James Garfield—the trial of the Haymarket conspirators remains one of the most celebrated in the history of Chicago, if not the United States. Given the amount of publicity surrounding the case, the lead attorney for the defendants asked that the trial be moved to a different court because the judge who had overseen the grand jury proceedings had demonstrated a bias against the defendants. The case was ultimately transferred to Cook County Circuit Court Judge Joseph E. Gary.[15] However, the move failed to bring about the outcome sought by the defendants. Over a three-week period, nearly one thousand citizens from the Chicago area were examined during jury selection procedures.[16] Judge Gary failed to excuse potential jurors who demonstrated a clear bias toward the defendants or who stated that they had already formed opinions about the highly publicized case. In fact, one man Judge Gary ultimately deemed fit to serve on the jury, despite objections by defense attorneys, was M. D. Flavin—a relative of one of the policemen who had died in the Haymarket riot![17] Another man who was ultimately permitted to sit on the jury was a friend of another officer killed in the incident.

With a jury clearly designed to view evidence in favor of the prosecution, it is not surprising that after a trial lasting nearly a month and which saw 227 witnesses testify (including fifty-four Chicago police officers), it took the jury less than three hours to deliberate and return a verdict of guilty against all eight defendants.[18] None of the evidence presented at trial proved a direct connection between the bombing and any of the defendants. The alleged bomber, Rudolph Schnaubelt, remained at large, and evidence suggesting he was the person who had thrown the bomb was weak. Yet the prosecution's case essentially asserted that even though none of the defendants could be connected directly with the Haymarket bomb, they were responsible for inciting the violence that erupted on the evening of May 4, 1886. The key evidence that allegedly pointed to a conspiracy to instigate violence was the Revenge Circular.

Seven of the eight Haymarket defendants were sentenced to hang, while Oscar Neebe was sentenced to fifteen years in prison because the evidence of his guilt was not as strong as the proof against the remaining defendants. Before the sentence of death could be carried out against the others, however, more controversy would soon arise. One of the Haymarket defendants, Louis Lingg, committed suicide in his cell by lighting a small dynamite cap that had been smuggled into his cell.[19] Lingg left a suicide note, placed the explosive device in his mouth, and blew off half of his face.

The aftermath of the verdict in the trial of the Haymarket bombing defendants also saw their appeal denied, although one judge had expressed misgivings about the evidence in the case. A plea was also made for clemency to Illinois Governor Richard J. Oglesby. Some observers of the case believe that Lingg's suicide may have had some impact on Oglesby because the governor subsequently commuted the sentence of Samuel Fielden and Michael Schwab to life in prison.

On November 11, 1887, after a year of appeals and pleas for clemency, the remaining four defendants in the Haymarket bombing case—August Spies, Albert Parsons, Adolph Fischer, and George Engel—were hanged. Yet the case did not fade away following their deaths. In 1892, John Peter Artgeld was elected the new governor of Illinois. Even five years after the Haymarket defendants were put to death, radical extremists in Chicago continued their activities and fueled a movement to have Artgeld grant a pardon to the three remaining defendants who were serving prison sentences for the bombing.

On June 26, 1893, Artgeld issued a pardon, and Fielden, Schwab, and Neebe were released. Among the reasons given for the controversial decision was the fact that Artgeld had grave misgivings about the evidence proving the three men to be guilty, that Judge Gray had been biased in many of his decisions, and that the jury had been unfair. The pardon was not well received, however, and it ultimately proved to be a fatal blow to Artgeld's political career. He lost his bid for re-election in 1896.

It has been said that the five defendants in the Haymarket bombing case who died as a result of their conviction at trial—by either their own hand or by hanging—were the "first revolutionary martyrs in the United States."[20] The Haymarket riot and bombing, as well as the trial that ensued, was a key moment in American history, ushering in a wave of terrorist violence by anarchists motivated to destroy the existing social order. Moreover, the event was of immense propaganda value to the labor movement. As one anarchist leader noted, "We have said a hundred times or more that when modern revolutionaries carry out actions, what is important is not solely these actions themselves but also the propagandistic effect they are able to achieve. Hence, we preach not only action in and for itself, but also action as propaganda."[21] Indeed, the unknown individual who threw the bomb in Haymarket Square on May 4, 1886, was making a statement against what the terrorist saw as unbearable government power and oppression. The fact that questions arose about the guilt of those activists who were arrested, convicted, and executed in the case just added fuel to the fires of the extremist cause.

Finally, the Haymarket incident not only began an era of anarchist terrorism in the United States, but also cast a long shadow into the future as issues in the case were resurrected in the Chicago area a little over eight decades later. To memorialize the deaths of the police officers who had died in the 1886 bombing, the city of Chicago erected a ten-foot statue of a police officer in Haymarket Square. On October 8, 1969, at the start of the notorious Days of Rage riots in Chicago spurred by members of the terrorist organization known as the Weather Underground, a bomb destroyed the statute of the police officer in a renewed symbol of violent opposition to government power. Indeed, the propaganda effects of the Haymarket bombing make it one of the most symbolic terrorist incidents in American history.

A FALSE SENSE OF COMMUNITY

THE ASSASSINATION OF WILLIAM MCKINLEY

America is the place where you cannot kill your government
by killing the men who conduct it.
—Woodrow Wilson[1]

THE ASSASSINATION OF A POLITICAL LEADER IS A FAVORED FORM OF VIOLENCE among terrorist groups because the death of a single individual can often bring about dramatic and profound changes in government. When the leader targeted for assassination is a U.S. president, or someone else who wields significant power, the political changes have not only national, but also world-wide implications. Therefore, it is not surprising that when an assassin is able to strike down a political leader, questions immediately arise as to the presence of a broader conspiracy. Questions about the presence or extent of a conspiracy persist in many assassination cases, including the killing of Abraham Lincoln and John F. Kennedy, as well as Egyptian President Anwar Sadat. On the other hand, inaccurate stereotypes of assassins seem to persist; they are often seen as quiet, inadequate loners who have difficulty relating to others and compensate for their needs for recognition or attention through the drama of a highly publicized execution of a political leader.

The motivations of political assassins have less to do with compensating for psychological inadequacies and more to do with a set of ideological principles and beliefs. In rare cases, terrorists and assassins lack clear ties to a group and appear to operate instead as rogue individuals who nevertheless espouse strong political ideas. These freelance terrorists have often been called "lone wolves" and are particularly dangerous because they plan attacks in isolation and do not disclose their intentions to anyone until they carry out their intended act. While there are several prominent examples of lone-wolf terrorists in recent history, one of the most infamous cases of such an assassin is Leon F. Czolgosz, who assassinated President William McKinley at the Pan American Exposition in Buffalo, New York on September 6, 1901.

McKinley was elected the twenty-fifth President of the United States in November 1896. He was a gracious and charming individual, as well as an experienced congressman, who was credited with pulling the country out of an economic depression with his conservative and firm policies.[2] During his first term as president, McKinley expanded the global presence of the United States, and his policies were seen as spurring an economic recovery in which "factories opened their gates, workers returned to the mills, and once more smoke poured cheerfully from the chimneys into sooty American skies."[3] As a result of the success he had during his first term as President, McKinley was re-elected in 1900 and made an appearance at the Pan American Exposition in Buffalo to help celebrate American prosperity.

The afternoon of Friday, September 6 was hot and humid. McKinley had arrived on the grounds of the Exposition at about 3:30 p.m. after he had toured power facilities in Niagara Falls.[4] Throughout his stay in the Buffalo area, and during public appearances such as the visit to Niagara Falls, McKinley was followed by Secret Service agents. However, the level of protection afforded the President was nowhere near what it is today. At the time of McKinley's presidency, the Secret Service was not formally charged with protecting the chief executive of the United States government. Prior to McKinley, two U.S. Presidents had been struck down by assassins' bullets—Lincoln in 1865 and James Garfield in 1881. Neither of these presidents were given Secret Service protection. The creation of a federal law enforcement agency to protect government officials had been a source of controversy throughout the nineteenth century.

Originally, the Secret Service was created as an arm of the Treasury Department to combat counterfeiters following the Civil War. In 1894, however, Secret Service agents were dispatched to the White House to protect Grover Cleveland, who had been the target of several threats by anarchists.[5] This was the first time the Secret Service provided protection to a president, despite the fact that it had no legal mandate to do so. When McKinley took office, Secret Service protection became more pronounced. In 1898, an internal investigation by the Secretary of the Treasury discovered that Secret Service agents were being used to protect the president and auditors felt that the practice was "a blatant misuse" of the agency's budget.[6] As a result, the agency's director, William P. Hazen, was demoted to a field operative, and protection was withdrawn because guarding of the President's home was viewed as something more appropriate for a monarchy than a democracy, where leaders should be more accessible.

When the Spanish-American war broke out, legal provisions were finally made for protection of the President, and the Secret Service was permitted by law to provide the kind of protection that Hazen had originally intended for the chief executive.[7] However, after the end of the war, the funding for protection of the President was no longer provided. Nevertheless, the Secret Service continued to provide protection because, like Grover Cleveland before him, McKinley had received a number of death threats from anarchists. These threats were considered credible because anarchist groups had been successful in assassinating several European rulers. Against this historical background, McKinley came to the 1901 Pan American Exposition with Secret Service protection.

The heat and humidity of the Buffalo afternoon had taken its toll on McKinley's wife, who decided to return to their residence for a nap while the President went to the grounds of the Exposition to greet the public. After a partial change of clothing at the Exposition, McKinley went to the Temple of Music with John G. Milburn, a prominent Buffalo attorney and president of the Exposition, and George Courtelyou, McKinley's personal secretary.[8] The Temple of Music was selected as the site where the President would receive members of the public. An aisle approximately twelve to fifteen feet wide was created, with a row of chairs on one side and a wooden frame on the other. The aisle was set at a right angle, with those greeting the President coming in from the east entrance of the building and moving through the aisle to the south doorway as an exit.[9] An American flag was draped across the wooden backdrop, and McKinley stood at the center of the angled aisle to greet members of the public.

McKinley's permanent bodyguard, Secret Service agent George Foster, normally stood at the President's left to observe individuals as they approached. However, on this occasion, Milburn was next to McKinley and introduced guests. Foster was not happy with the arrangement, but he did not intercede. Instead, he stood directly across from the President and next to Samuel Ireland, a Secret Service agent who watched each person come forward to greet McKinley. Another Secret Service agent, Albert Gallagher, was positioned several feet to the left of Ireland and also across from the President. Gallagher's responsibility was to keep the people moving away from McKinley as they finished greeting him.

The Grand Marshal of the Exposition, Louis Babcock, who had selected the Temple of Music for McKinley's reception and who had been responsible for arranging the site, ushered people through the door and kept up the pace of people coming through the reception line.[10] Given McKinley's popularity at the time, there was a large crowd of people vying for the chance to greet him. There was not much time to accommodate everyone because ten minutes had been agreed upon beforehand as the time allotted for McKinley to greet well-wishers.

The rapid flow of people through the line made it difficult for Ireland and Foster to watch for suspicious individuals. After a young girl greeted McKinley, a man with a dark complexion and mustache attracted Ireland's attention because the man seemed to spend too much time with McKinley.[11] As the two Secret Service agents placed their hands on the man's shoulder and moved him along, they unknowingly made room for McKinley's assassin.

At 4:07 p.m., twenty-eight-year-old Leon Czolgosz stepped forward with his right hand wrapped in a bandage to conceal a .32-caliber Iver Johnson revolver that he held in his hand. Just three days earlier, Czolgosz had purchased the weapon at a Buffalo hardware store for $4.50, along with .32-caliber Smith and Wesson cartridges.[12] Czolgosz's reason for selecting the Iver Johnson revolver would later become an important detail in understanding his thinking leading up to the assassination—carefully folded newspaper clippings that Czolgosz carried in his wallet revealed that the .32-caliber Iver Johnson was the same weapon used by anarchist Gaetano Bresci to shoot King Humbert I of Italy.[13]

When McKinley saw that the man before him had his right hand in a bandage, he went to shake the man's left hand. However, Czolgosz brushed past the President's gesture, brought his left hand over to steady his right hand, and, with both arms in front of him, fired two shots into the abdomen of McKinley. Ireland immediately lunged toward Czolgosz, and the next man in line to greet the President, James Parker, grabbed the assassin by the throat. Foster and a number of other individuals fell on Czolgosz, who lost his grip on the weapon and was pummeled and bloodied by those who restrained him. McKinley wavered and was guided to a chair by

Courtelyou, but not before he was able to tell the men delivering blows to his assailant to "Go easy on him, boys!"[14]

McKinley underwent emergency surgery to remove the bullets from his body and to repair the damage to his internal organs. Although surgeons were able to find a bullet that failed to pierce the President's breastbone, the other bullet was never recovered despite the use of innovative imaging techniques available at the time.[15] McKinley's status appeared to improve initially, and it was largely believed that he would recover. However, his condition worsened on the sixth day, and he died on September 14, 1901, eight days after he was shot.

The death of McKinley made Czolgosz the third man to have assassinated a U.S. President. (The other two were John Wilkes Booth, Lincoln's assassin, and Charles Guiteau, James Garfield's killer.) Even before McKinley died, however, investigators immediately turned their attention to finding out the motive for the shooting and whether others were involved in the planning of the assassination. Czolgosz was taken quickly to police headquarters in Buffalo, where he was questioned. He said very little but initially told the police that his name was Fred C. Nieman. When asked why he shot the President, Czolgosz merely replied, "I done my duty" but offered little else other than admitting that he was an anarchist. James Vallely, a New York City police detective working the Exposition who first took custody of Czolgosz and who conducted the first interrogation, was well aware that anarchism in the early 1900s was associated with political violence and terrorism.[16] He did not need to ask Czolgosz for more details, so he waited for the district attorney to continue questioning.

During his interrogation, Czolgosz was described as arrogant, calm, and haughty and did not appear to be the least bit nervous or unsettled about his predicament. One of the most surprising aspects of Czolgosz's case was the speed with which the criminal justice system dealt with his guilt and handed down punishment. Eight days after McKinley's death, an indictment was handed down, charging Czolgosz with first degree murder. The lawyers assigned to defend him were reluctant to undertake the task due, in part, to the fact that their client was hated, sullen, and uncooperative.[17] Over a period of three days, Czolgosz was examined by three medical examiners hired by the district attorney to determine the sanity of the defendant. Under prevailing law in New York State, where Czolgosz was to be tried, a determination had to be made whether as a result of mental disease or defect he was unable to know the nature and quality of his acts at the time of the shooting, or he did not know his actions were wrong.[18] The stenographer's notes of interviews with Czolgosz, who later admitted that Fred C. Neiman was an alias, indicated that he admitted: "I am an anarchist . . . I fully understood what I was doing when I shot the President. I realized that I was sacrificing my life. I am willing to take the consequences."[19]

With Czolgosz admitting he shot the President and communicating a full understanding of the nature and apparent wrongfulness of his actions, it is not surprising that his trial was quick and the outcome certain. On Monday, September 23, his trial began at 10:00 a.m. The prosecution presented a convincing case. Czolgosz did not testify in his own defense, and his attorneys did not call any witnesses. On September 24, at 4:30 p.m., the jury returned a verdict of guilty, and two days later, Czolgosz was sentenced to death. He was transferred to Auburn Prison in upstate New York, where he was executed in the electric chair on October 29, just over seven weeks after he had shot McKinley[20].

Like most assassins, Czologsz's early experiences in his life had a significant impact on his thinking and helped shape his political beliefs. Despite the fact that he said little about his motives, the fact that he admitted to being an anarchist and that shooting McKinley was his "duty" provided ample insight into his motives. Although none of the physicians who examined Czolgosz prior to his trial found any evidence of insanity, subsequent re-examination of the Czolgosz case by other psychiatrists has led to alternative conclusions that he had an "insane delusion" that McKinley was an "enemy of the working class"[21] or that he had schizophrenia.[22] As the political scientist James Clarke has argued, none of these explanations of Czolgosz's being insane or mentally ill is convincing because they fail to take into account the context of his behavior.

Although his parents were residents of Czechoslovakia at the time he was conceived, Czolgosz was born in the United States near the city of Detroit, Michigan.[23] He was the fourth of nine children born to his parents. His mother died following the birth of her last child from internal bleeding and inadequate medical care when Czolgosz was twelve years old. Just before her death, she was reported to have said, "My children, the time will come when you will have greater understanding and be more learned."[24] These words would later be used to try to understand why Czolgosz shot McKinley.

Czolgosz came from a hard-working family that struggled to make ends meet. Like most immigrant families of the late nineteenth century, the children took on extra jobs to supplement their father's limited income. When Czolgosz was fourteen, the Haymarket tragedy gained wide publicity. The men condemned for the Haymarket bombing had voiced support for anarchy and the overthrow of ruling capitalists. The deaths of the Haymarket defendants also made a strong impression on the young Emma Goldman, the noted anarchist author and lecturer who would become an important figure in Czolgosz's life.

While working at a factory in 1885, Czolgosz went on strike with a group of laborers who were protesting poor wages and working conditions. The strikers were all blacklisted and labeled as troublemakers. As a result, they had considerable difficulty obtaining work. Several months after the strike, a new foreman was hired at the factory where Czolgosz and his co-workers had been blacklisted. Although the new foreman had a list of names, he did not recognize any faces. Therefore, Czolgosz changed his name to "Fred C. Neiman," the name he originally gave when he was arrested after shooting McKinley.[25] He chose the name "Fred" because it was a nickname that members of his family used for him and "Nieman" was chosen as a last name because it meant "nobody." Rather than representing some complex psychological disturbance of identity, Czolgosz's use of the alias was merely derived from an attempt to keep working in a limited and difficult job market.

When Czolgosz expressed his anarchist beliefs to investigators immediately after the assassination of McKinley, a massive search for conspirators led police to anarchist groups around the country. The results of this investigation revealed interesting aspects of Czolgosz's life in the years leading up to the assassination. A major focus of the investigation was in the city of Chicago because of its reputation as a hub for radical activity.[26] Several anarchists were detained who knew Czolgosz because the assassin had attended several meetings and had attempted to become involved in anarchist activities. Among the noted anarchist leaders who knew Czolgosz were Abraham Isaak, who edited an anarchist newsletter, and Emma Goldman. Czolgosz had met with Goldman in mid-July 1901, before his trip to Buffalo, and had been drawn to anarchism in part because of a speech he heard Goldman deliver in Cleveland. At the time of the assassination, Goldman was in St. Louis delivering a lecture. She was arrested on suspicion of conspiracy, and attempts were made to physically coerce her into confessing to being part of a conspiracy, but she never did.[27] The official investigation concluded that there was no conspiracy and that Czolgosz had acted alone.

However, the investigation into Czolgosz's alleged ties to anarchist groups revealed that he was never fully accepted into the movement, and some anarchist leaders actually believed that he was a police or government spy. When police questioned him about Czolgosz, Isaak said that Czolgosz showed a very poor understanding of anarchist principles. For example, Czolgosz would refer to Isaak as "comrade" and on one occasion said that he wanted to come to "secret meetings," despite the fact that anarchist groups met openly and did not operate under cover of secrecy. A memo was circulated among anarchist leaders to the effect that Czolgosz might be a government spy trying to infiltrate their movement, and as a result he was shunned and kept at a distance.

Despite his stated commitment to anarchist principles, there is no evidence that Czolgosz was ever embraced or accepted within anarchist circles. Although he strongly supported organized labor movements, held anti-government beliefs, and felt big corporations and government took advantage of laborers—ideals that are common to anarchist groups—Czolgosz never became part of the anarchist "community of belief." Psychiatrist and terrorism expert Jerrold M. Post noted that a common pattern among terrorist groups is the presence of a community of belief that refers to "scattered groups or individuals that share common values and philosophies regarding a social problem but lack a coherent command structure."[28] These individuals and groups communicate through various channels, including newsletters and meetings, and share their common beliefs by endorsing various books or holding certain leaders in high esteem. Anarchists of the late nineteenth and early twentieth century had such a community of belief—they shunned a formal organizational or leadership hierarchy (because of their disdain for organized government).

However, Czolgosz had only peripheral involvement in anarchist groups. The fact that he was shunned and never fully embraced by anarchist leaders and group members made him a much more dangerous figure. The false sense of belonging to a community of anarchist belief that was apparent to the likes of Emma Goldman and Abraham Isaak led to Czolgosz's being shunned as a possible informant who might hinder or harm the movement. Czolgosz was left on his own to ruminate and plan the assassination of McKinley and never communicated his ideas or plans with anyone else who might support and assist him. The communication of plans among individual terrorists is a key opportunity for law enforcement to monitor and intercept information to prevent or thwart future attacks. When individuals such as Czolgosz act alone, the opportunity to evaluate potential threats is hindered.

Nevertheless, the case of Leon Czolgosz and the false sense of belonging he showed with the anarchist community teach an important lesson that can be used to prevent terrorism. Although Czolgosz was shunned because he was viewed as a possible informant, his actions were nevertheless harmful to the anarchist movement. Given that there was no evidence of conspiracy and the shooting of McKinley was not formally endorsed by specific anarchist leaders, the assassination harmed the movement. Many leaders and activists were arrested, threatened, and intimidated, the popularity of McKinley led to strong negative public opinion toward anarchism, and ultimately many anarchist leaders suffered significant hardship. For instance, although it took several years, Emma Goldman was ultimately deported from the United States despite the fact that she was born a U.S. citizen. In short, the actions of Czolgosz brought the significant power of government agencies and law enforcement upon anarchist groups and leaders that ultimately led to their demise.

The case of Czolgosz provides an example that law enforcement agencies can use in their continuous efforts to fight terrorism. Fringe and radical groups that espouse controversial ideologies, but that may be composed of members who prefer to promote political and social change through appropriate legal and political channels, can be approached by law enforcement to report suspicious individuals who appear to have a false sense of belonging to the group. If group members know that law enforcement searches, seizure of property, and arrests might ensue if a fringe activist commits an act of terrorism not sanctioned by the group but carried out in the name of their ideology, there may stronger motivation for members to cooperate with law enforcement in reporting suspicious individuals. Such conditions might simplify the task of identifying one of the most dangerous and difficult terrorists to stop: the free agent, or lone assassin.

STOP THE PRESSES

THE *LOS ANGELES TIMES*
BOMBING OF 1910

The American press is extraordinarily free and vigorous, as it should be.
It should be, not because it is free of inaccuracy, oversimplification
and bias, but because the alternative to that freedom
is worse than those failings.
—Judge Robert Bork[1]

TERRORISM HAS OFTEN BEEN VIEWED AS A FORM OF THEATER, IN WHICH THE political goals of a particular organization are publicized through dramatic acts of violence intended to profoundly influence governments or other political institutions.[2] The most infamous example of terrorist drama in recent history occurred during the 1972 Olympics in Munich, Germany. Members of Black September, a group supported by the Palestinian Liberation Organization (PLO), took Israeli athletes hostage.[3] Images of hooded terrorists waving weapons from the balcony of the athletes' dormitory were transmitted across the world and have become a trademark of modern international terrorism. The incident ended tragically with the deaths of all eleven athletes, five of the terrorists, and one police officer when a rescue effort by German authorities failed.

The use of politically motivated violence to influence an audience of observers creates an interesting relationship between terrorists and the media. In fact, many textbooks on terrorism devote entire sections or chapters to the role of the media both in understanding terrorism and developing effective counterterrorism efforts. In democracies, where freedom of the press is a principal value, terrorist organizations often find they can use television and newspapers to further their message. On the other hand, restricted societies such as military dictatorships, where media content is controlled and censored, often prevent terrorists from having outlets readily available for publicizing their message.

Overall, there tends to be a common view that terrorist organizations welcome media attention if it will further their cause. However, this notion proved to be untrue in a dramatic bombing that was perpetrated decades ago when terrorists made a large newspaper a target, rather than an ally, in an effort to silence ideas that were seen as harmful to their agenda.

In the fall of 1910, Los Angeles was in the middle of a strike by metal workers who were attempting to form a union. Harrison Gray Otis was owner and publisher of the *Los Angeles Times*. The newspaper was founded in 1881, and Otis bought a 25 percent interest in the paper after he moved to Los Angeles from Massachusetts. In 1886, Otis bought out his partners and became sole owner. He was a staunch Republican and conservative who held strong anti-union views. The *Los Angeles Times* often published editorials that were viewed as antagonistic to organized labor, so during the strike, these editorials were an attempt by Otis to sway public opinion against organized labor.

The newspaper was housed in a multi-story building that stood on the northeast corner of Broadway and 1st Street in Los Angeles. In the early morning hours of October 1, 1910, a bomb exploded in the building as employees were working to get the next issue completed. The blast knocked down the southern wall of the building, and the weight of the printing presses caused each floor to collapse onto the floors below—a domino-like effect similar to that observed in the collapse of the World Trade Center towers during the September 11 attacks, albeit on a much smaller scale.

Still, the bombing of the *Los Angeles Times* building was the most deadly and destructive terrorist attack of the era. The collapsing floors caused the building's heating system and gas mains to break and ignite. Many of the paper's employees were trapped inside the fiery rubble.[4] Twenty-one people died, a number of other people were seriously injured, and there was $500,000 in property damage.[5] Two other bombs were also discovered.[6] Police officers found one bomb at the home of Otis, but they were able to move it to a deserted area where it was detonated without causing any personal injury or property damage. Another bomb was found at the home of Felix J. Zeehandlaar, Secretary of the Merchants and Manufacturers' Association, who had expressed opposition to labor unions in the city.[7] Police officers were unable to detonate the bomb because of a weak battery.

Although the bombing of the *Los Angeles Times* building currently ranks as the fourth deadliest terrorist attack ever to have occurred on American soil, in 1910 it was considered to be one of the worst criminal acts in the nation's history and one that shocked the entire nation. Both the city of Los Angeles and Otis hired a private detective, William J. Burns, to investigate the explosion and identify the perpetrators. Otis was so outraged that he wrote a scathing editorial in his newspaper in which he said that those responsible for the bombing were "anarchist scum" and "cowardly murderers" who had the "innocent blood of . . . victims" on their hands.[8] He did not hide the fact that he believed leaders of the organized labor movement to be responsible for the bombing. In fact, there was an ongoing conflict between Otis and members of organized labor dating back nearly twenty years before the *Times* bombing. A group of typographers at the newspaper had gone on strike in an effort to form a labor union, but Otis was successful in breaking the labor stoppage and vowed to never again hire a union worker.[9]

In terrorism cases, a dynamic that often occurs is for sympathizers of the group suspected of perpetrating an attack to deflect criticism by accusing victims of staging the incident in order to evoke sympathy or further a political cause. A recent example of this phenomenon is when certain factions alleged that the September 11 attacks were actually perpetrated by the United States and Israel as a pretext to invading Arab countries. A similar allegation was made in the *Los Angeles Times* bombing when union extremists alleged that Otis actually plotted and carried out the destruction of his own building to justify more aggressive tactics against the labor organizers.[10] Less extreme union leaders offered their own theory that a broken natural gas line, rather than dynamite, sparked the blast. The investigation, of course, dispelled all of these erroneous notions and revealed that the explosion was an act of terrorism.

A grand jury was convened to investigate the bombing, and over two hundred witnesses were called, including several dozen individuals involved with labor unions. The inquiry led to the identification of three people—J. B. Bryce, M. A. Schmidt, and David Kaplan—who were suspected of purchasing the dynamite used in the attack from a San Francisco supplier.[11] All three men were also known to have been in Los Angeles after the bombing but soon disappeared. Bryce was later identified as James B. McNamara through a detailed confession that Burns obtained from a man named Ortie McManigal. McManigal admitted to being one of the men who helped J. B.

McNamara set the bomb. Both J. B. McNamara and McManigal were arrested in Detroit on April 12. The break in the criminal investigation that ultimately led Burns to McNamara was the unexploded bomb placed at the Zeehandlaar residence, since the dynamite was left intact and Burns was able to trace it to the San Francisco factory where McNamara had purchased the explosive material.

The bombing of the *Los Angeles Times* building was one of several terrorist attacks perpetrated throughout the United States by extremists associated with the International Association of Bridge and Structural Iron Workers (IABSIW).[12] According to information that Burns obtained during the course of his investigation, John J. McNamara, J. B. McNamara's brother, was the secretary of the IABSIW and had reportedly directed a bombing campaign from the organization's headquarters in Indianapolis, Indiana. At around six o'clock on the evening of April 22, 1911, Burns entered the offices of the association where a meeting of union officials was taking place.[13] With fifteen of his own investigators and several detectives from the Indianapolis Police Department, Burns executed a search warrant and entered McNamara's office over the protests of the organization's president.

A search of the IABSIW headquarters revealed a box containing 100 pounds of dynamite in the basement.[14] The building's custodian, Harry Graff, told Burns' investigators that he recalled J. J. McNamara asking if he could store some boxes in the basement because there was no room in the union offices upstairs. The box found by Burns contained letters and papers that implicated McNamara. At the time of the search of the association headquarters on April 22, Burns arrested John J. McNamara.

Immediately after the arrest, a nationwide drive was undertaken to collect money for the criminal defense of the McNamara brothers. Funds were sought primarily from workers across the nation and others sympathetic to the cause of organized labor.[15] The practice of rallying American laborers to provide financial support for the criminal defense of union officials and labor sympathizers who were on trial was a common occurrence in high-profile cases, such as the trial of the *Los Angeles Times* building bombers and the famous trial of Sacco and Vanzetti that occurred over a decade later.

Samuel Gompers, President of the American Federation of Labor, persuaded the noted criminal defense attorney Clarence Darrow to defend the McNamara brothers. The defense fund drive secured enough money for Darrow to be given a $50,000 retainer and an expense fund of $200,000, which were very handsome sums of money at the time[16]. While Darrow's decision to get involved in the case was consistent with his penchant for representing sympathizers of organized labor, the *Los Angeles Times* bombing case is one that would come to haunt Darrow for the rest of his life.

The McNamara brothers were each charged with different bombing incidents. J. B. McNamara was charged with being responsible for the bombing of the *Los Angeles Times* building, while J. J. McNamara was charged with bombing the Llewellyn Iron Works plant in Los Angeles the following December and for being the mastermind behind the coordinated bombing campaign that swept across the country during the fall of 1910.[17] Assisting Darrow in defending the McNamara brothers was LeCompte Davis, an experienced lawyer with a reputation for being clever and tough. Three other lawyers were chosen to assist Darrow primarily because of their ability to elicit local sympathy. Joseph Scott was a leading Roman Catholic attorney in Los Angeles and could appeal to jurors sympathizing with the McNamaras, who were Irish Catholics. Job Harriman was a former mayoral candidate in Los Angeles for the Socialist Party. Cyrus McNutt was an experienced labor attorney who was an expert on the laws of the state of Indiana, where the brothers had been arrested.

The prosecution was directed by John D. Fredericks, District Attorney of Los Angeles, who was assisted by three deputy prosecutors—Chief Deputy W. Joseph Ford, Oscar Lawler (a former U.S. Attorney who helped assemble the facts and evidence), and Earl Rogers, who had assisted with the indictments.[18] Jury selection began in October and became a slow and laborious process that dragged into a second month. On the morning of December 1st, 1911, after the presiding judge, Walter Bordell, called the proceedings to order, courtroom observers were shocked when defense co-counsel LeCompte Davis rose and announced, "Your Honor, . . . We have concluded to withdraw the plea of not guilty, and have the defendant enter in this case a plea of guilty."[19]

Although the trial of the McNamara brothers never finished with jury selection, it is still one of the most celebrated criminal cases in the history of the United States. Therefore, courtroom observers were shocked by the unexpected turn of events, and newspaper reporters rushed to announce the guilty plea. The admission of guilt in open court dispelled any myths that the explosion was either an accidental gas explosion or the work of the newspaper's owner, Otis himself. After Judge Bordell confirmed with each of the defendants that they wished to change their plea to guilty, Darrow made a brief statement: "They had it on us. The country had a complete case. There was no loophole."[20]

As a result of their guilty pleas, the McNamara brothers were granted some leniency by Judge Bordwell when sentencing took place. J. B. McNamara avoided the death penalty and was sentenced to life in prison for the bombing of the *Los Angeles Times* building. J. J. McNamara, who had been charged with organizing a bombing campaign but who had not been directly implicated in the *Times* bombing, was sentenced to fifteen years in prison. During the sentencing hearing, Fredericks read a statement by J. B. McNamara that outlined exactly how the *Times* bomb was set. McNamara said that at 5:45 p.m. on the evening of September 30, 1910, he placed a suitcase containing sixteen sticks of 80 percent dynamite along with a timer that was set to go off at 1:00 a.m.[21] McNamara also said that he did not intend to kill anyone, which could be inferred from the fact that he had set the bomb to go off in the early morning hours when the building was expected to be empty. However, the resulting loss of life made the *Los Angeles Times* bombing the deadliest terrorist attack in the United States at the time.

In the aftermath of the McNamara trial, there were a few controversial issues that emerged. Many individuals in the organized labor movement who had supported the McNamaras and contributed to their defense fund felt betrayed by the sudden change of plea. Throughout jury selection, Darrow had dragged out questioning of potential jurors and seemed to be uncomfortable in his role in the case. Speculation after the trial focused on the notion that as defense investigators uncovered evidence in the case, Darrow became more convinced of the guilt of the McNamara brothers and encouraged them to change their plea. However, the most controversial issue for Darrow, and one that would haunt him for years, involved a far more serious charge.

The lead investigator for the defense, Bert Franklin, was found to have approached two potential jurors in the case—Robert Bain and George Lockwood.[22] Bain was a veteran of the Civil War and worked as a carpenter. Franklin had reportedly paid a visit to the Bain home and told the veteran's wife that he would take care of an overdue payment that was outstanding on the couple's home if Bain would agree to vote for acquittal. Although Bain wanted his wife to report the bribery attempt, she refused because Franklin had apparently told her she would go to jail if she reported the conversation to anyone. In addition, Franklin was said to have offered

Lockwood, a former police officer and jail guard, a payment of cash if he voted to acquit the McNamara brothers. Lockwood reported the bribery attempt to Fredericks. When Franklin arranged for the payment to be made on a street corner in downtown Los Angeles, Fredericks had police officers waiting to arrest Franklin. Unfortunately, Darrow was crossing the street at the time and happened to be present when police officers arrested Franklin on charges of bribing the jury.[23]

Soon after the McNamara brothers changed their plea, Darrow was indicted on charges of jury tampering, and for the next couple of years, he would work to clear his name. Many of his friends shunned him, and the cost of defending himself against the charges nearly bankrupted him.[24] The Lockwood bribery case was the first to go to trial. With a closing argument that brought the presiding judge and many jurors to tears and which is considered to be one of the greatest in the history of American law, Darrow was able to win himself an acquittal.[25] The jury decided that someone other than Darrow must have provided the money to influence Lockwood's vote. In the second trial involving the attempted bribery of Bain, the jury could not reach a verdict, and the district attorney decided in December 1913 not to undertake a third trial. Darrow returned to his home in Chicago and would ultimately go on to redeem his legal career.

With the McNamara brothers' guilty plea, all serious doubts were erased as to the true cause of the *Los Angeles Times* building explosion. Moreover, the reading of J. B. McNamara's statement in open court laid aside any doubt about who was responsible for the act of terrorism. Even though Darrow was never found guilty of attempting to bribe jurors in the case, those who study the history of American labor continue to debate Darrow's true culpability. His experience in the trial of the *Los Angeles Times* bombing illustrates some of the profound risks that lawyers face when they represent suspected terrorists. The Sixth Amendment of the U.S. Constitution provides a guarantee that all defendants in criminal cases—including defendants charged with terrorism—will be represented by an attorney. Furthermore, lawyers are under an ethical obligation to provide zealous representation to their clients within the boundaries of the law. That is, lawyers cannot commit a crime (such as attempting to bribe jurors) or facilitate the commission of an illegal act in the course of providing a criminal defense.

The *Los Angeles Times* bombing case generated an important question that continues to be raised in modern terrorism cases: Do criminal defense lawyers expose themselves not only to the possibility of public scorn but also to the danger of criminal prosecution if they decide to provide legal representation to terrorist suspects? Of course, there appear to be legitimate reasons for the indictment of Darrow. However, his experience raises the specter that lawyers may be reluctant to defend terrorist suspects because of the inherent personal and professional risks. The case of the *Los Angeles Times* bombers highlights the need to maintain the integrity of the American criminal process when adjudicating terrorist suspects and to assure that justice is administered in a fair, just, and constitutionally sound manner.

AN ECLECTIC CRIMINAL

THE CASE OF ERICH MUENTER

To him that you tell your secret, you resign your liberty.
—Anonymous[1]

AT 11:23 P.M. ON FRIDAY, JULY 2, 1915, AS U.S. CAPITOL POLICE OFFICER FRANK Jones sat in his chair near the front entrance of the Capitol building, a loud explosion went off in the Senate reception room.[2] The blast caused significant damage to windows, chandeliers, and plaster in the ceiling, but fortunately no one was injured. Investigators soon discovered that the cause of the explosion was a bomb, consisting of several sticks of dynamite that had been placed in the room earlier that afternoon. The Senate had been out of session, and legislators were not scheduled to return for several months. Because the explosion occurred on a quiet evening when there were no major activities scheduled in the Capitol building, it seems reasonable to conclude that whoever was responsible for planting the bomb had intended to make a political statement and did not intend to kill a large number of people.

Shortly after the explosion, a letter appeared in a local Washington, D.C. newspaper in which the author ironically claimed to have bombed the Capitol building in an appeal for peace. The man was angry over American financiers providing monetary assistance to Great Britain during the initial phases of World War I.[3] Unknown to investigators, the person responsible for planting the bomb in the Capitol building on the afternoon of July 2 had rented a small bungalow in New York City two weeks before the bombing under the false name of Patton.[4] Using another false name of Hendricks, the man purchased 120 pounds of dynamite and set out to refine his bomb-making skills. After planting the bomb in the Senate reception room, he traveled back to New York City and appeared the next morning at the Glen Cove, Long Island home of renowned financier J. P. Morgan.

As Morgan and his wife were getting ready to sit down to breakfast with the British Ambassador and his wife, the doorbell rang. The Morgan's butler, Henry Physick, answered the door and was greeted by a well-dressed man in his forties who asked to see Morgan. The visitor handed the butler a business card from the Summer Society Directory with the name Thomas C. Lester.[5] When Physick asked the man to state the nature of his business, the man presenting himself as Lester said he would not discuss the matter with the butler but claimed to be a friend of Morgan.

Although the United States had not yet entered into World War I, Morgan provided financial support to Great Britain in the form of loans, and as a result, there was concern in the Morgan household that the financier would be the target of aggression from pacifists and others who opposed the war.[6] Physick was understandably suspicious of the man who refused to state the nature of his business with Morgan. Before the butler could stop the man, Lester took a .38-caliber pistol from his left pocket and a .32-caliber pistol from his right pocket, pushed them into Physick's body, and forced his way into the Morgan home.[7] Without panicking, the butler led the gun-wielding visitor into the library and went to get Morgan.

When Physick was out of the library, he shouted for the Morgans to go upstairs, but Lester had encountered Morgan's two children. Although the Morgans and the breakfast guests had made their way upstairs through a back staircase, they heard Physick shouting that the man was heading up the front staircase. Confronted with an armed man near their children, Mrs. Morgan leapt at Lester, but Morgan immediately pushed his wife aside and tackled the intruder. In the ensuing struggle, two shots were fired, and Morgan was hit in the groin. As he fell on the attacker, Morgan managed to get one of the guns out of the man's hand and pin his other arm. Meanwhile, Physick found a large chuck of coal and smashed it over Lester's head. As the man lay stunned, a number of servants kept him immobilized but noticed a stick of dynamite in his pocket. They placed it in a bucket of water and waited for police to arrive.[8]

Morgan's wounds were not life-threatening, and he made a full recovery. However, the intruder's identity and the motives behind his actions proved to be by far the most interesting aspects of the case.

At his arraignment in a Glen Cove courtroom, the intruder gave his name as Frank Holt. He claimed to be forty years old and said that he was born in Dallas, Texas, where he lived with his wife and two children. Holt said that he had no intention of harming Morgan and merely wanted to get the financier to stop supporting war efforts by giving loans to European allies of the United States.[9] Holt claimed that he planned on keeping Morgan and his family detained in a room of the house so he could influence the financier's work and stop the loans. Furthermore, Holt said that he had intended to use the dynamite as a barricade so that no one would attempt to shoot at him while holding the Morgan family hostage for fear of causing an explosion.

As investigators pressed further, however, they began to have difficulty tracing Holt's past. His wife stated that she had met him in 1908 while Holt was attending a college in Fort Worth, Texas. The couple had married in 1910.[10] Indeed, they had two children, and several of Holt's fellow students said they had known him since 1908 when he came to the United States from Mexico. However, Holt's wife and his acquaintances in Texas could provide no information about his life prior to 1908.

In fact, the real name of the man who had planted the bomb in the U.S. Senate reception room on July 2 and who traveled to Long Island and attacked financier J. P. Morgan on July 3 was not Patton, Hendricks, Lester, or Frank Holt. The man's real identity was Erich Muenter, a man who had earned a Ph.D. from Cornell University and who had taught at Harvard.[11] During his teaching years, Muenter had borrowed several books on insanity from Professor Hugo Munsterberg—a man some consider to be the father of modern forensic psychology. Munsterberg saw pictures of the man identified as Frank Holt and immediately recognized him as a former colleague from Harvard. In 1906, Muenter was indicted for killing his wife by poisoning her, and he fled the Boston area after her murder. He went to Mexico and surfaced two years later in Dallas, Texas as Frank Holt.

After Muenter's arrest, an alienist—the term for psychiatrist in the early twentieth century—was appointed to evaluate his sanity. Dr. Carlos F. MacDonald was asked to render an opinion about Muenter's motives for bombing the U.S. Capitol building, attacking Morgan, and planning to bomb ocean liners that carried cargo across the Atlantic Ocean.[12] In an interview with MacDonald, Muenter provided some insight into the political motives for his actions:

MacDonald: But we are not at war?

Muenter: You are wrong, we are at war. We are actually at war, we are killing thousands of people every day.

MacDonald: But we haven't declared war?

Muenter: Yes, we are doing it underhandedly.

MacDonald: You know that the Germans maintained a large army for many years and were accumulating munitions of war all the time?

Muenter: That is quite different.

MacDonald: Why didn't you go there to stop them?

Muenter: Germany is not America, my dear Sir. It is merely for her protection in Germany, wedged in there between the Russians and France, and all those countries. If she didn't have those things they would have jumped on her.

MacDonald: If she did have those things?

Muenter: Oh, you are quite right, it is the whole trend of the age that has developed since Napoleon.

MacDonald: Do you think that you, single-handed, could arrest the whole trend of the age?

Muenter: No, but Mr. Morgan could.[13]

Based on his examination, MacDonald concluded that Muenter was paranoid and prone to episodes of excitement and dangerous behavior because of his brooding over the war. Furthermore, MacDonald concluded that there were no co-conspirators who had helped Muenter and that the terrorist had acted alone, even though MacDonald appears to have based his opinions solely on a psychiatric examination of Muenter.

The case was not without additional controversy, however. A scientist at Georgetown University conducted an experiment in which he attempted to reproduce the bomb Muenter claimed to have used in the bombing of the U.S. Senate.[14] Muenter said that he had used several sticks of dynamite in which he dug out a hole and placed the heads of matches inside. He also put a corked bottle containing sulphuric acid above the matches and claimed that the acid seeped through the cork, ignited the matches, and set off the dynamite. Using Muenter's description as a guide, the scientist was unable to detonate the bomb but admitted that if Muenter had used a different kind of explosive match the device may have worked.

Although a substantial amount of information was learned about Muenter and his crimes in a relatively short period of time, the case came to a sudden close three days following his arrest. At about 10:30 on the evening of July 6, 1915, a jail guard who was watching over Muenter stepped away from his post and left the door to Muenter's cell ajar as the prisoner feigned sleep.[15] When the opportunity arose, Muenter left his cell, climbed to the top of the cell block and committed suicide by diving head first into the concrete floor. A full inquest into Muenter's death was made, and the official cause of his death was ruled a suicide.

Muenter's history revealed that he was a versatile criminal who had killed his wife and evaded capture for several years. He managed to reappear with a new identity, remarry, and start a family. However, his claims of pacifism and the desire for U.S. neutrality in World War I, along with his need to influence U.S. foreign policy and deter financial support for Britain's war efforts, prompted him to engage in a diverse array of terrorist attacks. His bombing of the U.S. Senate was the first known attack on American soil against a federal government target that was intended to influence U.S. foreign policy. Moreover, whether his attack on J. P. Morgan was an attempted assassination or, as Muenter later claimed, an attempt to hold the financier and his family hostage, the eclectic terrorist practiced or intended to carry out a full range of terrorist acts in the span of a few days—including bombing, kidnapping, a possible assassination, and plots to bomb transatlantic ocean liners. Despite having no apparent support from others, Muenter relied on his intelligence and resourcefulness to carry out a series of terrorist attacks. Whether because of his expressed desire to not injure anyone or mere luck, it is fortunate that no one was killed or seriously injured in any of Muenter's attacks.

There is some indication that Muenter was indeed a pacifist and may have committed suicide due to guilt he felt over his actions. Following his suicide, a note to his wife was found in his cell that read: "All please pardon me for all the heartaches I have brought you. Pray with me that the slaughter will stop. My heart breaks. Good-bye."[16]

A QUESTION OF INNOCENCE

THE SAN FRANCISCO
PREPAREDNESS DAY BOMBING

*If truth and justice were the rule, there would
be no need for mercy.*
—Mendele Mocher Sforim[1]

THE FAMOUS BRITISH JURIST SIR WILLIAM BLACKSTONE OBSERVED: "IT IS BETter that ten guilty persons escape than one innocent suffer."[2] This argument is frequently used in debates about the merits of protecting the due process rights of criminal defendants. The issue of guilt or innocence may seem to have little relevance when talking about terrorism, since political extremists often seek out, rather than avoid, blame for acts of violence they commit to further their cause. With the exception of some lone-wolf terrorists, like the Unabomber and the Olympic Park bomber, who both evaded capture for years and often perplexed investigators by keeping their motives elusive, most terrorists are not only willing to claim responsibility for their acts but make sure they draw attention to themselves. As a result, terrorists who are put on trial commonly raise the defense of "political necessity," whereby they claim their actions were justified in order to prevent some greater social harm from occurring. Although this defense is rarely successful, it illustrates how the trials of terrorist suspects are different from those of other criminals.

However, one infamous trial of an accused terrorist bomber involved the traditional defense of innocence. The defendant claimed that he did not commit the crime, and for three decades, his case was a long, hard-fought battle for truth and justice. By the time he was released from prison in 1939, Tom Mooney was arguably the "most famous convicted murderer in the world."[3] His case is one of several involving a terrorist bombing committed during the height of the labor movement of the early twentieth century. Yet his case is noteworthy for the complexity of the facts, the highly polarized opinions about Mooney's guilt, and the number of years he and his lawyers worked tirelessly to clear his name from what many believed to be a wrongful conviction.

Mooney was born in Chicago, Illinois, on December 8, 1882.[4] As the oldest son of Irish immigrant parents, his childhood was difficult because of financial hardships in the family and the death of his father when he was ten years old. After Mooney's father passed away, his mother moved the family to Massachusetts, where she found work in a factory. As the young man of the house, Mooney managed to bring some money into the household by selling newspapers and delivering lunches to laborers.[5] Although he managed to tend to his studies and work odd jobs, Mooney finally left school at the age of fourteen and took a job as a foundry apprentice.

Over the next several years, he worked hard and in 1902 became a member of the International Molder's Union—something that would remain important to him throughout his life.[6] Mooney was also careful with his money, and he managed to save enough to travel abroad. He had a curious nature and believed he needed more education to succeed in life. During tours of various European countries, Mooney immersed himself in the culture and history of each place he visited by going to historical landmarks, art galleries, and museums.[7] One day during a visit to a museum in Amsterdam, Mooney met another worker from the United States, and the two men began a discussion that soon turned to the topic of socialism. On his way back to the United States, Mooney began reading heavily about socialism from various books he had purchased in Europe. His interest would ultimately move him farther into the labor movement.

Upon his return to Massachusetts, Mooney began to move slowly toward the West Coast. He first settled in his native Chicago, where he tried to enroll at a university. However, his limited finances made it difficult for him to pursue formal academic study. At the age of twenty-five, he arrived in California, and three important events occurred that solidified his future role as a labor activist. He met his future wife Rena, who provided him with a stable attachment, he became an active member of the Socialist Party, and he found work.

Between 1907 and 1916, Mooney was an ardent and outspoken activist for workers' rights. In 1908, he worked on the U.S. presidential campaign of

Socialist Party Candidate Eugene V. Debs, and in subsequent years, he worked with radical associations and admitted to finding the work exhilarating. In his later years, he would admit to having engaged in acts of sabotage by dynamiting industrial installations.[8] His activities made him a target among industrial capitalists, and even leaders of local trade unions in the San Francisco area believed Mooney was a "dangerous troublemaker."[9] Whereas Mooney wanted to disrupt the capitalist economy and replace it with socialism, the trade union leaders were more conservative and wanted to preserve free-market capitalism. Therefore, an attempt was made to discredit Mooney; someone planted explosives in one of his suitcases, and police officers were notified.[10] He spent two years in prison and was released after his case was appealed. Given the fact that Mooney had many enemies among corporate leaders and organized labor, it is not surprising that he was immediately targeted as a suspect when the City of San Francisco became the site of one of the deadliest terrorist bombings in the history of the United States.

In 1916, a number of national and international conflicts had a direct influence on political tensions in the United States. Not only was there an ongoing labor dispute between labor and corporate owners, but Europe was fully engaged in World War I, and President Woodrow Wilson was working to keep the United States out of the conflict. Moreover, the infamous Easter Rising in Ireland began that same year and started the war for Irish independence. San Francisco had a large Irish population that was highly supportive of military action. As such, tensions were high between pacifists and supporters of the military when a parade was planned for July 22, 1916 to support military preparedness. The event came to be commonly known as the San Francisco Preparedness Day Parade.

The purpose of the parade was to "boost patriotism and compel leaders in Washington, D.C., to increase defense spending."[11] Although pacifists and many in the labor movement called for citizens of the San Francisco Bay Area to boycott the event, business leaders were more vocal, and the event was widely attended and came to be one of the largest in the city's history.[12] The large attendance also assured that a terrorist attack would claim a large number of victims.

Although the starting time for the parade was announced publicly to be 1:00 p.m. on July 22, the official start time was 1:30 so that police officers would have enough time to clear the streets of traffic.[13] A number of veterans' groups and business officials took part in the parade, including Sons of the American Revolution, a group of Spanish War veterans, and various politicians and public figures associated with the San Francisco business community. Along the path of the parade, sidewalks were crammed with people who came out to watch. At the corner of Steuart and Market Streets, a crowd had gathered in front of a saloon. In the midst of the excitement over the parade, only a few individuals noticed when a person left a suitcase on the sidewalk next to the outside wall of the saloon.[14] One witness who was standing near the entrance later described the person as "approximately five feet ten inches in height," weighing "a hundred and seventy pounds," wearing a "soft black hat turned down all around," with worn dark clothing and "very dark skin or complexion," who appeared to be either Mexican or Italian.[15]

Another individual who was coming out of the saloon also saw the man and cautioned him that the suitcase might get stolen if it was left near the saloon. The man who set the suitcase down said, "Don't touch that suitcase . . . I know what I am doing."[16] A few other eyewitnesses would later state that they saw a man set the suitcase down and several witnesses admitted to having seen the suitcase near the saloon without necessarily seeing who placed it there. For nearly thirty minutes, the suitcase sat unattended while people focused their attention on the parade.

At approximately 2:06, a large explosion erupted in front of the saloon where the suitcase had been placed. Two men who were standing near the suitcase died instantly in the blast. A woman and her seven-year-old daughter were standing near the saloon and were thrown to the sidewalk. A row of men sitting at the bar in the saloon were knocked to the floor, and windows in nearby buildings were smashed. A six-year-old boy standing near the site of the blast had the flesh seared from his legs, and people within a range of fifty feet suffered injuries in proportion to their proximity. In all, ten people were killed, and dozens of others were injured, including forty-four people who needed to be hospitalized for treatment of their injuries.[17] At the time, the 1916 Preparedness Day Parade bombing ranked as the deadliest bombing in the history of the United States. There was an immediate public outcry for police officers to find those individuals responsible.

The investigation began almost immediately, but several errors severely contaminated the crime scene and made it virtually impossible to assemble the necessary evidence to answer a number of important questions about the bombing. For instance, when the last bodies of the injured and dead were removed from the scene and transported to the hospital, a policeman went to a nearby fire station, got a hose that he attached to a hydrant, and washed the sidewalk of blood, body parts, and pieces of the bomb. As one researcher later noted, "this simple act would render it impossible ever to accurately reconstruct what happened on the corner of Steuart and Market Streets at 2:06 p.m. on the afternoon of July 22, 1916."[18]

If this lapse in judgment were not enough, other important evidence was corrupted that dampened hopes of identifying the nature of the explosive device. About an hour and a half after the explosion, District Attorney Charles M. Fickert, who was responsible for prosecuting those responsible for the crime, personally supervised the search for evidence. When someone identified a crack in the wall of the saloon as being the likely site where the explosive device had been placed, Fickert ordered a police officer to get some tools and remove bricks near the crack in a search for clues.[19] A sledgehammer was used to break out a number of bricks from the wall of the saloon and to chip out pieces of the sidewalk in a search for evidence where the bomb had detonated. A series of photographs were taken of the crack in the wall before, during, and after Fickert and the police began their search of the location of the bomb. These photographs would later demonstrate how damage to the scene caused by the investigators made it impossible to determine whether the bomb had been placed at the scene or dropped from a roof above the site as Fickert would later claim in his prosecution of the case.[20] At the time of trial, Fickert was unaware of the existence of the photographs that showed mild damage to the wall and saloon before the bomb site was contaminated.

Thomas Mooney later claimed that at the time of the bombing, he was standing with his wife and two of her relatives on the roof of the Eilers Music Company Building, which was over a mile from the explosion.[21] A photograph taken of the parade would later prove that Mooney was telling the truth and that not only was he not near the site of the explosion, but that he could not have gotten to the roof of the Eilers Building between the time that witnesses saw the suitcase placed in front of the saloon and the time that the photograph was taken. Nevertheless, Mooney's reputation as a labor agitator in the San Francisco community made him a primary suspect, and four days after the bombing, he was arrested, along with his wife and several other labor activists, including Israel Weinberg, Warren Billings, and Edward Nolan.

A $17,000 reward had been offered by various business and political leaders after several of Fickert's initial witnesses were unable to identify

Mooney or any of the other defendants as the person who placed the suitcase containing the bomb.[22] Billings was the first to be prosecuted. The prosecution argued that he was "a mere tool who did the bidding of Mooney" and was convicted and sentenced to life in prison.[23] Weinberg and Mooney's wife were both acquitted at trial, and the charges against Nolan were ultimately dismissed. Mooney fared the worst of the group. He was convicted and sentenced to hang for the murder of the victims of the bombing. However, on November 29, 1918, President Woodrow Wilson commuted the sentence to life in prison.[24] The commutation of Mooney's sentence was fortunate because, as subsequent events and newly discovered evidence would later show, Mooney was innocent of the charges.

The principal evidence against Mooney was the testimony of two witnesses—Frank Oxman and John McDonald. McDonald was an itinerant worker who had arrived at the corner of Steuart and Market Streets approximately ten minutes after the start of the parade. He claimed to be standing on Steuart Street and saw a man he later identified as Billings place a suitcase down near the saloon and walk away.[25] Oxman appeared as a witness after Billings had been convicted but before Mooney went on trial. He claimed to have been standing on the corner of Market and Steuart Streets near the site of the explosion and saw an automobile, driven by Weinberg and containing Mooney, Mooney's wife, Billings, and an unidentified man, pull up in front of the saloon.[26] Oxman testified that he saw Mooney holding a suitcase on the running board of the vehicle and when the vehicle stopped, Billings, Mooney, and the unidentified man got out of the vehicle. According to Oxman, it was Billings who placed the suitcase in front of the saloon.

Although this eyewitness testimony was considered highly incriminating and contributed to Mooney's conviction, a number of subsequent events eventually led to claims that District Attorney Fickert was attempting to frame Mooney for the Preparedness Day Parade bombing. Among the various exculpatory pieces of evidence in Mooney's favor was the fact that the crime scene had been severely contaminated after the bombing. It was impossible to reconstruct the bomb or to determine with any precision where the materials for the bomb were purchased. Furthermore, none of the eyewitnesses who saw the person plant the suitcase containing the bomb provided a description that even remotely fit Mooney's appearance. The photograph that later showed Mooney to be on a rooftop over a mile away at the time the two major prosecution witnesses claimed he was elsewhere also added serious doubt to his guilt.

As if these issues were not enough to raise reasonable doubt, there were other troubling circumstances that arose. Four years after Mooney's conviction, one of the prosecution's key witnesses—MacDonald—contacted one of Mooney's appellate lawyers and provided an affidavit in which he claimed that his trial testimony was perjured and that he was induced to provide the false testimony by District Attorney Fickert and his assistants. Furthermore, several aspects of Oxman's and MacDonald's testimony were contradictory and raised doubts about the accuracy of their recollections of the event. In fact, two men would later come forward and claim that Oxman was not even in San Francisco on the day of the bombing and could not have seen what he had claimed at trial.[27]

Despite the doubts raised about Mooney's guilt, he met with repeated failure in his efforts to appeal his case and either get a new trial or have his conviction overturned. Over twenty years after Mooney's conviction, the California Supreme Court continued to find no legal merit in Mooney's claims of perjured testimony or impropriety on the part of the district attorney's office. The court concluded that Mooney "has not established by substantial, credible evidence that his conviction was the result of perjury on the part of prosecution witnesses or that the prosecuting officers caused or suffered to be introduced at [Mooney's] trial any testimony which they know, or had reason to believe, was false, or that they were guilty of suppressing or preventing the introduction of any evidence which, had it been given, would have been favorable to the defense."[28]

Mooney continued to have his supporters among labor activists who worked tirelessly for his release. It took twenty-two years, but in 1939, Culbert Olson, the newly elected Democratic governor of California, took office and pardoned Mooney and ordered both Billings and Mooney released.[29] Billings was not officially pardoned until 1961. Because his death sentence had been commuted, Mooney was fortunate enough to live to see his freedom. However, he was fifty-three when he was released from prison and in failing health. He died at the age of fifty-six. Billings fared a bit better; he married and lived an unassuming life until his death in 1972.[30]

There were some individuals who remained firm in their belief that Mooney had a direct hand in the Preparedness Day Parade bombing. However, there were too many problems with the eyewitness testimony and a lack of hard physical evidence as to who had perpetrated the bombing.

The case is an important one in the history of terrorism in the United States because it marked an escalation in the severity of violence that had characterized the battle between labor and capital in the late nineteenth and early twentieth centuries. At the time, the Preparedness Day bombing was the deadliest terrorist attack that had yet been perpetrated on U.S. soil.

In addition, Mooney's plight raised concerns that swift use of the death penalty in terrorism cases might result in an innocent individual, who was accused and convicted of committing a terrorist act based on flimsy or questionable evidence, being wrongly executed. If Woodrow Wilson had failed to commute Mooney's sentence, the legacy of the case may have been not only a wrongful conviction, but a wrongful execution as well. If nothing else, the investigation of the Preparedness Day Parade bombing illustrates the importance of treating each site of a terrorist attack as not only a rescue operation for victims and survivors, but also a crime scene where evidence must be preserved so that the true culprits can be arrested and punished for their actions.

OUTRAGE
THE ANARCHIST BOMBINGS OF 1919

Revolution is the festival of the oppressed.
—Germaine Greer[1]

TERRORIST ACTS PROVOKE FEAR DUE, IN PART, TO THEIR INDISCRIMINATE NATURE. The fact that they occur with little apparent warning and target innocent civilians adds to the perception that terrorism is difficult to control. When several attacks are carefully planned and coordinated to occur simultaneously, the impact terrorists have on their audiences can be profound. For example, one reason the September 11 attacks were so dramatic was the fact that not one, but four airplanes were hijacked and used to create massive casualties and destruction. While these attacks were being carried out, most people could not help but wonder how many tragedies would ultimately occur on that fateful day.

One of the most dramatic cases of coordinated, simultaneous terrorist attacks in American history occurred on June 2, 1919. The attacks were carried out by a group of Italian anarchists whose primary goal was to overthrow the U.S. government and cripple corporations and other symbols of capitalism. The anarchist movement was prominent in a number of ethnic groups in the United States during the late nineteenth and early twentieth centuries. Some anarchists were committed to communist philosophies and shunned the notion of private ownership of property; others favored unions as a mechanism for confronting the abuse of laborers by corporations; other anarchists shunned communism and the labor movement in favor of encouraging autonomous individuals to remain free of formal organizations and rebel by violent means if necessary.[2] Many anarchists avoided identifying themselves with a specific movement and instead supported general anarchist goals and philosophies, including rejection of formalized government and the embracement of "propaganda by the deed"—a euphemism for terrorism—to draw attention to their cause.[3]

Although a number of anarchist terrorist attacks had occurred over the years, June 2, 1919 was noteworthy because targeted bombings were directed at specific government officials and several attacks were carried out simultaneously over a large geographic area. The resulting fear and outrage from these attacks prompted a large-scale government crackdown on anarchist activities that came to be known as the "Palmer raids," named after A. Mitchell Palmer, who was then U.S. Attorney General and one of the intended victims of the attacks.

At about 11:15 p.m. on June 2, Palmer was retiring to the upstairs of his home at 2132 R Street in Washington, D.C., when he heard a thump at his front door.[4] Immediately after the sound came a thunderous explosion that shook the house and shattered windows in the neighborhood. Palmer's home was in an exclusive section of the nation's capital. Secretary of the Navy Franklin Delano Roosevelt, the Norwegian foreign minister, Navy Admiral Theodore F. Jewell, and Virginia Senator Claude A. Swanson all lived nearby.[5] The front of Palmer's house was destroyed, and many of his neighbors were thrown from their beds.

Palmer had been the target of an attempted bombing just one month earlier on May 1, when thirty-six package bombs were sent through the mail to prominent judges, politicians, and businessmen around the country. Those package bombs were intercepted before any could be detonated, and no one was injured. The attack on Palmer's home, however, was not an isolated incident; there were several explosions—all within an hour or two of one another—that occurred in seven cities on that same evening.

Two explosions occurred in Boston, Massachusetts.[6] One of the bombings took place just before midnight and targeted Judge Albert F. Hayden, a municipal court judge who had issued a harsh sentence to several protesters arrested a month earlier. When handing down his sentence, Judge Hayden said, "If I could have my way I would send [people who do not believe in our Government] and their families back to the country from which they came."[7] The Hayden home was nearly destroyed by a pipe bomb made with shrapnel packed around dynamite. Malcolm Hayden, the judge's twenty-year-old son, was the only family member staying in the house that evening while the rest of the family was at their summer home. Malcolm was returning home for the evening and was only several hundred feet from the home when the explosion occurred. He saw a car speeding away from the scene just before the explosion. Several homes in the neighborhood were damaged, but there were no injuries.

The other explosion in Boston occurred at 12:02 a.m. at the home of Leland W. Powers, a representative in the Massachusetts state legislature.[8] The bomb was similar in design to the one that nearly destroyed Judge Hayden's home. The side of the Powers' home was blown off in the explosion. At the time, Powers was at home with his children, and two maids were also in the house. Powers's four-year-old daughter was cut by a piece of glass, but the injury was not serious. In his capacity as an elected official, Powers had introduced an anti-sedition bill to the Massachusetts legislature that had passed just five days before the bombing. The bill called for anyone advocating or inciting an assault on public officials, destruction of property, or overthrow of the state government by force or violence to be sentenced to three years in prison. Needless to say, the bill was not popular with anarchists who had an extensive network in Massachusetts.

Within twenty minutes of the Powers home being attacked, another bomb went off at the apartment of Harry Klotz in Paterson, New Jersey. The city of Paterson had been a noted hub for anarchist activities for decades. Klotz presided over a manufacturing company and was also a member of the executive board of the Paterson Manufacturer's Association.[9] He had been on record as having opposed measures seen as favorable to laborers, such as a limited work week, and was presumed to be the motive behind the bombing. Klotz and his family were not at home, and no one was injured in the blast.

A fifth bombing occurred shortly before 1:00 a.m. in New York City. The explosion damaged a townhouse located at 151 East 61st Street belonging to Judge Charles C. Nott, Jr., a municipal court judge.[10] Nott and his three daughters were away at the time, but his wife was asleep in the home, and she was thrown from her bed. There was also a caretaker who lived in the house with his family, and they were also thrown from their beds by the explosion. A night watchman who oversaw a number of private homes on the block was killed in the blast. Although police officials originally thought that Nott might have been confused with a federal judge by the name of Knox who presided over the trials of radicals in New York City, Nott had sentenced two Italian radicals to long prison sentences several years earlier after they had been convicted of conspiring to blow up St. Patrick's Cathedral.[11] As a member of the legal establishment seen as oppressive by radical groups—despite a reputation in the community as a fair and balanced jurist—Nott remained a target of anarchist groups.

In Philadelphia, Pennsylvania, a church rectory was bombed at around 11:15 p.m., and in Pittsburgh, Pennsylvania, two other bombs went off at the homes of a federal judge and an inspector with the U.S. Bureau of Immigration. Both the judge and immigration official had presided over cases involving foreign radicals. Another bomb went off at 11:30 p.m. in Cleveland, Ohio, at the home of the Mayor Harry L. Davis. Davis had been targeted because of his efforts to suppress demonstrations by radical groups a month earlier.[12] No one was injured in these three bombings, although the explosions caused considerable damage to the properties.

The nine explosions spanned seven U.S. cities, and all occurred within a couple of hours. The synchronized nature of the attacks and the fact that they targeted prominent government or business officials who were known for their efforts to curb the activities of violent radical groups raised suspicion that the bombings were part of a coordinated terrorist conspiracy. The fact that most occurred at the private homes of the victims provoked fear and outrage. After all, the terrorists had taken the time to find out where the victims lived and to set the bombs to go off at a time when members of the victims' families—including their children—were likely to be present. Attorney General Palmer vowed to find "the criminals who were behind that kind of outrage."[13]

But there was other evidence that would ultimately confirm that the explosions were the work of Italian anarchists. The most significant evidence pointing to a conspiracy was the fact that several copies of a printed flyer were found scattered at each of the nine bombing sites. Known as the Plain Words circular, the flyer outlined a number of grievances against capitalism, organized government, and corporate America:

Plain Words

The powers that be make no secret of their will to stop, here in America, the world-wide spread of revolution. The powers that must be reckon that they will have to accept the fight they have provoked. . . . We have ben dreaming of freedom, we have talked of liberty, we have aspired to a better world, and you jailed us, you clubbed us, you deported us, you murdered us whenever you could. . . . The jails, the dungeons you reared to bury all protesting voices, are now replenished with languishing consciencious workers, and never satisfied, you increase their number every day. . . . It is history of yesterday that your gunmen were shooting and murdering unarmed masses by the wholesale; it has been the history of every day in your regime; and now all prospects are even worse. Do not expect us to sit down and pray and cry. We accept your challenge and mean to stick to our war duties. . . . Do no say we are acting cowardly because we keep in hiding, do not say it is abominalbe; it is war, class war, and you were the first to wage it . . . We are not many, perhaps more than you dream of, though but are all determined to fight to the last, till a man remains buried in your bastiles, till a hostage of the working class is left to the tortures of your police system, and will never rest till your fall is complete, and the laboring masses have taken possession of all that rightly belongs to them. . . . There will have to be bloodshed . . . there will have to be murder: we will kill, because it is necessary; there will have to be destruction; we will destroy to rid the world of your tyrannical institutions. . . . What has been done by us so for is only a waning that there are friends of popular liberties still living. Only now we are getting into the fight; and you will have a change to see what liberty-loving people can do. . . . Besides, you will never get all of us . . . and we multiply nowadays. Just wait and resign to your fate, since privilege and riches have turned your heads. Long live social revolution! Down with tyranny.

THE ANARCHIST FIGHTERS. [14]

The grammatical errors and awkward nature of the wording indicated that whoever wrote the flyer probably used English as a second language. Also, the themes expressed in the flyer, as well as the "signature" at the bottom, revealed that an anarchist group was behind the bombings. However, the message in the Plain Words circular contained many of the themes expressed in communiqués and statements made by present-day terrorist groups such as al-Qaeda. That is, the terrorists conveyed a sense of being under attack by the "system" and organized government. Just as Osama bin Laden expressed his belief that Western society, and the United States in particular, has attacked Islam and the Arab world through its policies and support for Israel, the anarchists stated in the Plain Words flyer that their bombings were part of a class war in which the working class has been assaulted by "tyrannical institutions" such as organized government and corporations. The anarchists attempted to justify their violent actions as a form of self-defense against a larger evil, similar to the way al-Qaeda attempted to portray its actions on September 11 as a form of self-defense against the United States.

Another key piece of evidence that linked the bombings to one another was all the explosive devices being similar in design. They consisted of packed dynamite surrounded by metal shrapnel and were highly destructive. Although the Plain Words flyer provided conclusive evidence that the June 2 bombings were part of a conspiracy, the most useful evidence that held out hope for identifying the perpetrators was found at the bombing site of Palmer's home.

As investigators sifted through the debris, they found that the person carrying the bomb had been literally blown to bits as the bomb went off. Given that none of the other bombings resulted in the death of the person setting the bomb and they were carried out under cover of night to facilitate the perpetrator's escape, there is no evidence to suggest that the bombing of Palmer's home was an act of suicidal terrorism. Moreover, suicide terrorism was not known to be a form of attack used by anarchist bombers. Two theories were offered by investigators about what might have occurred. One theory suggested that in his haste to get away, the bomber tripped and set off the bomb accidentally, while the second theory suggested that the bomber erred in his calculations in setting the device and the bomb went off prematurely.[15]

The site of the Palmer bombing was gruesome indeed. One of the police officers leading the search for clues noted that it was not possible to walk around the bombing site without stepping on human tissue. Pieces of the bomber's body were found throughout the neighborhood; a portion of one leg landed on a car a block away, part of the spinal column landed inside the bedroom of a neighbor, and pieces of human tissue were hurled through windows across the street from Palmer's house.[16] In addition, pieces of the bomber's clothing were found, including a pair of brown socks, parts of a white shirt, a brown derby hat, and pieces of scalp that showed the man to have dark, curly hair. Two .32-caliber handguns and pieces of receipts from train tickets the bomber purchased were also found at the scene.

Investigators were able to come up with a fairly detailed description of the man:

The bomber was a tall, well-set-up young man, possibly Italian, with abundant curly black hair. At the time of the explosion he was wearing a derby hat, a black worsted suit with green stripes, and white shirt with stripes of different colors, a polka-dot bow tie, brown socks, and tan sandals.[17]

However, there were no fingerprints or dental records available so the police were unable to make an identification of the man. Nevertheless, police were able to reconstruct the man's means of travel from New York to Washington via Philadelphia by using the times of his trains. Despite the fact that they were even able to identify the purchase of a hat he made while transferring trains in Philadelphia, no formal identification was ever made.

Although the case of the Plain Words bombings was never officially solved, Palmer used the widespread outrage over the attacks to justify a number of actions intended to clamp down harshly on radical groups operating in the United States.[18] A series of raids that came to be known at the "Palmer raids" resulted in deportation proceedings against large numbers of immigrants believed to be anarchists or other radicals with anti-government views and a propensity for violence. An example of the extent to which federal law enforcement efforts went to target radicals was the case of Emma Goldman, the noted anarchist writer and lecturer who was cited by Bureau of Investigation Director J. Edgar Hoover as a "dangerous anarchist" posing a serious threat to the security of the United States.[19] In August 1919, Hoover was successful in having Goldman deported, even though she was born in the United States and was a legal citizen.

As for the bomber of the Palmer house who was never officially identified by law enforcement officers investigating the case, subsequent historical research revealed that he was a man named Carlo Valdinoci, a twenty-four-year-old Italian radical who had been wanted by federal authorities for a couple of years.[20] Valdinoci had a legendary status among radical groups because he had been implicated in a number of other violent incidents by radical groups but had managed to evade authorities. He had been indicted for publishing radical literature, and a deportation warrant had been issued for him two years before the Palmer bombing.[21] Despite his elusive nature and legendary status among fellow radicals, Valdinoci ended up being killed accidentally by a bomb of his own making.

The case of the anarchist bombings of June 2, 1919 is instructive in a number of respects. It illustrates how resourceful and effective terrorist groups can be when they have an organized, highly trained, and mobile network of operatives who are intent on coordinating an attack. Law enforcement officials often have extreme difficulty penetrating these groups with informants who can provide information on pending attacks. In addition, copies of the Plain Words leaflet that were scattered at each bombing site provided clear insight into the motives of the attackers, who saw themselves as waging a class war on institutions associated with the United States, including corporations and the courts, by attacking prominent individuals associated with those institutions. Perhaps most important was the fact that the highly coordinated nature of the attacks and the organized manner in which they were carried out made the psychological impact of the attacks all the more profound.

Finally, the government's response of clamping down on radical groups and deporting dangerous radicals—even if those individuals were not directly involved in acts of violence—was successful in reducing the threat to the United States. Over subsequent decades, anarchism became a less potent threat than it had been in the late nineteenth and early twentieth century. However, the anarchist movement would not go away quietly. A little over a year after the June 2 attacks, anarchists perpetrated one of the deadliest terrorist attacks ever to occur on American soil.

PROPAGANDA
BY THE DEED

THE WALL STREET BOMBING OF 1920

Lawlessness is lawlessness. Anarchy is anarchy is anarchy.
Neither race nor color nor frustration is an excuse
for either lawlessness or anarchy.
—Thurgood Marshall[1]

AT AROUND NOON ON AN OVERCAST THURSDAY, SEPTEMBER 16, 1920, A MAN drove a horse-drawn wooden cart up the northern section of Wall Street in the heart of the financial district in New York City. The cart was dilapidated and pulled by an old bay horse that had recently been fitted with a new set of shoes. Although automobiles were beginning to take over the city streets, horse-drawn carriages were still a common sight. So when the man parked the wagon on Wall Street, it attracted very little attention.

As the driver brought the carriage to a stop, he was near the corner of Broad and Wall Streets, where the U.S. Assay Office and a Subtreasury building stood next to each other on one side of the street and the J. P. Morgan Building—the main offices of the noted financier—stood prominently on the other.[2] Parked in the "symbolic center of American capitalism,"[3] the carriage concealed hundreds of pounds of metal weights, explosive material, and a timing device. The weights were the kind used in old-fashioned window sashes and were packed around the explosives to create massive amounts of shrapnel when the bomb exploded.

After leaving the wagon unattended, the driver disappeared into the crowd. Various witnesses gave conflicting descriptions of him. Some said he had a dark complexion and appeared to be Jewish or Italian.[4] Other witnesses later claimed to have seen two or three drivers near the wagon, but none of the descriptions proved to be particularly helpful.

At one minute past noon, the timing device inside the wagon triggered a huge explosion. The wagon was completely destroyed, and the only thing left of the horse were the hooves, which were thrown several yards away and landed near Trinity Church. The horseshoes were new and contained a series of markings that would later permit investigators to trace the shoes to a manufacturer in Buffalo, New York.[5] The explosion rocked buildings within a half-mile radius of the center of the blast at 23 Wall Street. Young Joseph P. Kennedy—the father of President John F. Kennedy and Senators Robert F. and Edward Kennedy—was working in the financial district at the time and was knocked to the ground by the blast; he was not seriously injured.[6]

A large ball of fire and a cloud of green gas hurled up in the air, blew out windows throughout the financial district, and ignited cloth awnings covering windows that were twelve stories above street level.[7] Active trading on the floor of the New York Stock Exchange was interrupted abruptly as glass shattered and sent people heading for the exits. The building sustaining most of the damage was the one housing the offices of J. P. Morgan & Company. There was "broken glass, knocked over desks, scattered papers, and the twisted remains of some steel-wire screens that the firm had providentially installed over its windows not long before, and that undoubtedly prevented far worse carnage than actually took place."[8] One Morgan employee was killed instantly, and another died the next day. Several pieces of shrapnel pitted the external marble facade of the Morgan building. For reasons that are not entirely clear, the pock marks were never repaired and remain a present-day reminder of the bombing.

The death toll from the explosion quickly climbed to over thirty individuals. Although various accounts of the 1920 Wall Street bombing provide differing numbers of people who were ultimately killed in the blast, the final death toll reached forty when Francis B. Stoba died in November—nearly two months after the explosion—from injuries sustained while walking in front of the Assay office. In addition to the dead, over two hundred other individuals were seriously injured and required hospitalization.[9]

Three of the Wall Street bombing victims could not be identified because their injuries were so severe. Some victims were decapitated, and others were so badly mangled that only pieces of them could be used for identification. The fact that some of the dead could not be identified prompted speculation that the driver of the wagon had been unable to flee before the timer set off the explosion. However, this theory was dispelled in favor of others that proved to be more credible.

An immediate investigation was launched that took local and federal law enforcement officers to places throughout the United States. Investigators from the New York City Police Department went to every manufacturer of window sash weights in the city to determine if someone had made a substantial purchase in the weeks leading up to the explosion.[10] The federal government took the lead in the investigation under the direction of William J. Flynn, who was the Director of the Bureau of Investigation[11]—the original name of the federal law enforcement agency that would later become known as the Federal Bureau of Investigation. After surveying the bombing site the day after the explosion, Flynn concluded that the act of terrorism must have been carried out by "Galleanists," or followers of Luigi Galleani, a major figure in the anarchist movement. Galleani was an advocate of "propaganda by the deed"—a descriptive phrase in the anarchist movement that meant acts of terrorism, and bombing in particular.[12] According to Flynn, Galleanists were suspected of having carried out the bombing in retaliation for the prosecution of Nicola Sacco and Bartolomeo Vanzetti, two anarchists implicated in a Massachusetts bank robbery who were believed to have been subjected to an unjust prosecution and trial.[13]

The theory that anarchists were responsible for the bombing got a boost when a leaflet was discovered in a mailbox a couple of blocks away from the site of the explosion. A letter carrier was emptying the mail when he found five copies of a leaflet that read:

REMEMBER
WE WILL NOT TOLERATE
ANY LONGER
FREE THE POLITICAL PRISONERS
OR IT WILL BE
SURE DEATH FOR ALL OF YOU
American Anarchist Fighters.[14]

Despite the lead, however, the investigation into the Wall Street bombing would end up becoming a mix of dead ends, missed opportunities, and painstaking police work that ultimately produced no resolution to the case.

Police officers visited a number of printing shops throughout the country to try to locate the exact place where the lettering for the leaflet had been purchased. However, the extensive leg work produced nothing. One promising lead was the horseshoes from the hooves of the horse. The hind shoes had the letters "JHU" and "NOA" inscribed on them about an inch apart and were believed to be the initials of the person who had recently placed the shoes on the horse.[15] After visiting nearly 5,000 stables along the eastern coast of the United States, investigators were able to trace the horseshoes to an Italian blacksmith in New York City who had shod the horse, but the finding did not provide any convincing leads to the identity of the person who paid the blacksmith or owned the horse.[16]

The large number of deaths and injuries, as well as the physical devastation at the bombing site, made the search for physical evidence extremely difficult. Nevertheless, there were enough fragments from the horse and wooden wagon to allow police to reconstruct the vehicle in which the bomb was transported. The metal pieces of shrapnel had been deliberately broken into pieces and police officers found five hundred pounds of them scattered over a several-block area.[17] Whoever had constructed the bomb had packed the heavy metal pieces around the explosive device in order to send hundreds of pieces of heavy shrapnel flying in all directions. The bodies of those who were killed had been shredded by the shrapnel, and many of the surviving victims were maimed or permanently disabled. If nothing else, the shrapnel pointed to the bomber's intent on causing as many deaths and injuries as possible.

Although only a few fragments of the explosive device were discovered, these pieces were enough to permit a bomb expert to assist police in reconstructing the device. In one of the earliest cases in the United States of forensic science being used to reconstruct an explosive device from fragments, several bomb experts were consulted to identify the substance that caused the explosion. An experimental physicist at Johns Hopkins University by the name of Robert W. Wood earned the nickname "the Sherlock Holmes of science" when he was able to duplicate the bombing device.[18] Another explosives expert, Dr. Walter T. Scheele, submitted a seventy-page report to Flynn in which he concluded that fifty pounds of blasting gelatin were used in the attack.[19]

Several key pieces of physical evidence—including the leaflet, horseshoes, wagon pieces, metal fragments, and eyewitness statements—provided investigators with valuable leads. However, the Wall Street bombing investigation also had more than its fair share of bizarre characters and false leads. One of the most unusual, if not colorful, characters to emerge in the case was Edwin Fisher, who had been a U.S. Open mixed doubles tennis champion several decades earlier. Fisher had a lengthy history of mental illness and had warned of a pending attack on Wall Street a couple of days before the explosion took place. He sent a postcard to the chief officer of the French High Commission, where Fisher had once worked, and another to an agency on Broadway.[20] The postcards were sent from a Toronto hotel where Fisher was staying just days before the blast. They carried the simple message: "Greetings. Get out of Wall Street as soon as the gong strikes at 3 o'clock, Wednesday, the fifteenth. Good luck. ED."[21]

Of course, Fisher's prophecies captured the interest of law enforcement officers, and he was questioned at great length. It soon became clear, however, that Fisher had no prior knowledge of the explosion, and his prediction had been similar to other bizarre statements he made over the years. Still, Fisher's warnings continued to prompt bizarre speculation. For instance, Dr. Walter F. Prince, a scientist at the American Institute for Scientific Research, commented publicly that Fisher may have received a "psychic tip" about the Wall Street bombing through some telepathic means.[22] In the end, Fisher's warnings provided no useful leads and were ultimately considered to be a bizarre coincidence.

A $100,000 reward was posted for any information leading to the arrest of the individuals responsible for the bombing.[23] The vast number of eyewitnesses and clues provided investigators with a number of leads that involved a nationwide investigation of radical groups consisting of anarchists, socialists, labor activists, and others with anti-American sentiments.

The first arrest in the case came a little over two weeks after the bombing, on October 3, when a twenty-three-year-old Russian immigrant by the name of Florean Zelenska was taken into custody in Pittsburgh, Pennsylvania.[24] Zelenska aroused the suspicions of passengers on a train when some of his statements led others to believe he might be carrying explosives. When police were summoned, Zelenska scuffled with officers and was briefly knocked unconscious. A search of his hotel room revealed that he had dynamite, percussion caps, and a fuse.[25] Although Zelenska originally told police he used the materials for mining, it was later discovered that he had never worked in a mine. Moreover, Zelenska was alleged to have boasted, "See what we did in Wall Street."[26]

Zelenska's arrest was initially viewed as a possible solution of the Wall Street crime.[27]

Although investigators later learned that Zelenska had been in New York City at the time of the bombing, Flynn ultimately eliminated the Russian immigrant as a suspect when the investigation revealed that Zelenska had no ties to radical groups and was nowhere near Wall Street when the bombing occurred.[28] Nevertheless, Flynn charged Zelenska under the federal Interstate Comment Act for carrying explosives on the train he took from Cincinnati to Pittsburgh.

The case of Florean Zelenska is but one example of a number of mistaken arrests, false leads, and investigative dead ends that characterized the investigation into the Wall Street bombing. For several years, the investigation pursued a number of avenues and suspects, but as time passed, the trail of clues ultimately went cold. The New York Police Department and federal investigators finally ended their investigation into the bombing in 1940 with no convictions and without a viable suspect ever identified. For the next seventy-five years—until the Oklahoma City bombing in 1995—the Wall Street bombing remained the deadliest terrorist attack on American soil and still ranks third behind the September 11 and Oklahoma City attacks.

Although the case remains officially unsolved, a number of theories have emerged over the years about who may have perpetrated the attack and why. One of the most intriguing and well-argued theories has been offered by the noted historian and expert on early twentieth-century anarchism, Paul Avrich. According to Avrich, a key event that occurred five days before the Wall Street bombing was the indictment of Sacco and Vanzetti on September 11, 1920.[29] Avrich claims that an associate of Sacco and Vanzetti, Mario Buda—who was also known by the name Mike Boda—assembled the powerful bomb and acquired the horse and wagon that was used in the Wall Street bombing.[30] Boda had a history of extensive involvement in anarchism and the radical labor movement and was experienced with explosives. Following the Wall Street explosion, Buda obtained an Italian passport, returned to his homeland, and never came back to the United States.[31] He evaded the attention of investigators by leaving the country. If Buda acted alone as a lone-wolf terrorist, there would have been no co-conspirators to provide investigators with clues about his involvement.

Buda's close friendship with Sacco and Vanzetti—and the view among many in the anarchist movement that Sacco and Vanzetti had been railroaded for their political views by an unfair justice system—are facts consistent with demands made by the American Anarchist Fighters in their leaflet found near the Wall Street bombing to "free the political prisoners." However, Avrich also admits that Buda's identity as the Wall Street bomber cannot be proved because "documentary evidence is lacking."[32] Still, Buda matches the description of several eyewitnesses who claimed to see the driver of the wagon. Furthermore, the theory that Buda was the perpetrator is one that has been accepted by many individuals who have studied the case.[33]

Although the Wall Street bombing remains somewhat of a mystery, there are other aspects of the case that are interesting. For one thing, the profound devastation the blast caused, including the large number of fatalities and injuries, signaled a turning point in anarchist violence. Many of the other bombings that had been carried out by anarchists to that point, including the simultaneous bombings of government targets in 1919, were fairly selective and appeared to target individuals or properties that were largely symbolic. The Wall Street bombing was indiscriminate and malicious in that a large number of innocent civilians were injured or killed, and those who perpetrated the bombing seemed to want a large number of civilian deaths.[34] As such, the bombing was a turning point of sorts that ushered in an era where mass destruction and devastation from a terrorist attack were possible.

Another interesting aspect of the case was the behavior of the stock market following the explosion. Like the September 11 attacks, the Wall Street bombing of 1920 occurred at a time when the Dow Jones Industrial Average was falling—it had been down 22 percent since the beginning of the year.[35] Following the bombing, the market continued to fall another 24 percent, before it began to recover slightly around Christmas and then hit a low point in August 1921.[36] From that point, the market grew expansively throughout the 1920s until the great crash of 1929. However, the positive lesson from the Wall Street bombing—and one that followed the September 11 attacks—is that the national outrage brought about by the devastating attack also brought national support for the financial markets that allowed them to recover and grow.

RUSH TO JUSTICE

THE CASE OF GIUSEPPE ZANGARA

Whatever disagreement there may be as to the scope of the phrase "due process of law" there can be no doubt it embraces the fundamental conception of a fair trial, with an opportunity to be heard.
                                                    —Oliver Wendell Holmes[1]

THERE IS NO ARGUING THAT THE DEATH PENALTY IS A HIGHLY CONTROVERSIAL form of punishment in the American criminal justice system. A theme that frequently arises in debates over the morality, effectiveness, and ethics of the death penalty is that the time between a capital defendant's conviction and execution is too long. Those who favor the death penalty often argue that justice is delayed for victims' families when a convicted person's appeals are permitted to drag on for years. Those who are opposed to the death penalty argue that keeping someone confined on death row for years constitutes cruel and unusual punishment and life without the possibility of parole is a better alternative.

The case of assassin Giuseppe Zangara is remarkable in one very interesting respect: merely *five weeks* passed between the time Zangara attempted to assassinate President-elect Franklin Delano Roosevelt on February 15, 1933 and the execution of Zangara on March 20, 1933 for the murder of Chicago Mayor Anton Cermak, who died as a result of the injuries he sustained in the assassination attempt.[2] In the short period of time it took to convict and execute the obscure assassin, several substantive and procedural legal issues involving his psychological functioning were raised, particularly questions about his sanity and motives.

In the early 1930s, the United States was in the midst of a severe economic depression and many Americans hung their hopes for recovery on Roosevelt, who was elected the thirty-second President of the United States. After returning from a cruise and shortly before his inauguration,

Roosevelt stopped briefly in Miami, Florida, to deliver a speech at a rally on February 15, 1933. The rally had been publicized in the newspapers, and a crowd of approximately 25,000 people gathered to hear the President-elect.[3]

After delivering a very brief, 145-word speech from the back of a Buick convertible, Roosevelt handed the microphone to Redmond Gautier, the Mayor of Miami. As he did so, Giuseppe Zangara, an Italian immigrant who was barely five-feet tall, pulled a five-shot .32-calibre revolver from his pocket and, while standing on a chair that was about twenty-five feet from the rear of Roosevelt's car, fired five shots at Roosevelt. Zangara would later write about his efforts to get a clear shot at Roosevelt:

> I tried to get close to him, but there were too many people around him. I wanted to get in front of him in order to get a good shot at him, but the people kept on pushing me back further all the time and I could not get to see him. . . . When I saw I could not get near him I decided to shoot him from a distance. While he was talking I could not get to see him because all of the people were crowded around him. He only spoke for about a minute from the car and sat down immediately after. When he did I only could see his head, although by that time I was standing on a park chair.[4]

The muzzle of Zangara's gun was so close to the cheek of Lillian Cross, a woman standing directly in front the assassin as he fired, that there were powder burns on her cheek. Zangara lost his balance while he was firing and missed his principal target. The President-elect was immediately surrounded by Secret Services agents and driven away from the scene unharmed.

However, each of Zangara's five shots found a victim. The wife of a utility company executive sitting near Roosevelt was hit in the abdomen; she was critically injured and was near death for several weeks, but survived. Another woman was hit in the hand; another bullet grazed her head and was later found in the collar of Chicago Mayor Anton Cermak with a piece of the woman's hat still attached to the bullet. A New York policeman who came to pay his respects to Roosevelt suffered a mild wound to his scalp; the bullet causing his wound then hit a twenty-two-year-old chauffeur in the head but caused no serious injury. A Secret Service agent, Robert Clark, was also injured in the back of his hand. Clark had been standing near the rear of Roosevelt's automobile and initially did not believe he had been injured in the assassination attempt. He reported no injury, but Roosevelt noticed that Clark had been wounded. Although there were questions about whether Clark was actually grazed by a bullet or had someone else's blood on his hand, he remains listed as a Secret Service agent who was wounded in the line of duty.[5]

The most serious injury was to Anton Cermak, who was standing near Roosevelt. Chicago's mayor had been hit by a bullet that entered his right side through the lower rib cage, caused his right lung to collapse, injured his diaphragm and liver, and lodged near the spinal column. Cermak's condition was first listed as serious, and there were initial doubts he would survive. His condition improved, and it appeared he might recover; on February 24, his physicians gave him an 80 percent chance of recovery. Despite the optimism, Anton Cermak died from his injuries on March 6, nineteen days after he was shot.

Immediately after the shooting, Zangara was tackled and restrained; his clothes were literally ripped from his body. He was taken to the Dade County Jail, and shortly after midnight he was questioned without an attorney present by Florida State Attorney Vernon Hawthorne, Dade County Sheriff Dan Hardie, the County Solicitor Charles Morehead, two Secret Service agents, and Roosevelt's private secretary Marvin McIntyre.[6] A stenographer was present to take down Zangara's statements word for word. Because of Zangara's broken English and heavy Italian accent, Hardie conducted the hour-long interview because he was touted as "something of a linguist" and he felt he could communicate with Zangara.[7]

A reading of the transcript later revealed, however, that Hardie merely spoke to Zangara in a form of broken English that was similar to the assassin's heavy accent and that he only used two foreign words during the course of the interview—and Spanish words at that. For example, one exchange where Hardie introduced the state attorney to Zangara went as follows:

Hardie:	Joe, I asked you questions. Before you tell me—see, if this man die—if somebody die you shoot, I hang you. That will be too bad for you. If you like me all right you tell me the truth.
Zangara:	I tell you the truth.
Hardie:	This big man is big lawyer—grande lawyer.

Zangara: I understand, speak in English.[8]

During the course of the interview, Hardie was able to obtain a full confession from Zangara.

Twelve hours after the shooting, Zangara was arraigned on four counts of attempted murder. Rumors circulated that a lynch party was assembling outside of the county jail to remove Zangara forcibly from the custody of law enforcement and distribute its own form of punishment. Consequently, the Honorable E. C. Collins, a Dade County judge assigned to the case, ordered extra security. Zangara was assigned two lawyers who were "leaders of the Miami legal community" and a third who was an Italian-American property lawyer who was fluent in Italian.[9] These lawyers immediately requested that Judge Collins appoint a sanity commission to evaluate Zangara's mental condition.

In a very unusual move, the judge asked Dr. Gerald Raap, president of the Dade County Medical Society and a physician tending to one of Zangara's victims (Anton Cermak), to select two psychiatrists to evaluate Zangara. Raap chose Drs. I. Henry Agos and T. Earl Moore. On the day they were appointed to evaluate Zangara, the two physicians rushed to the county jail and met with the defendant sometime before midnight on Friday, February 19. The next day, a Saturday, court reconvened, but Zangara's attorneys requested a delay before entering a plea so they could review the findings from the evaluation conducted by Agos and Moore.

With speed and efficiency that are rather unusual by today's standards, Agos and Moore delivered their report to the court on the morning following their late night examination. Barely eighty words in length, the full text of the report was as follows:

The examination of this individual reveals a perverse character, willfully wrong, remorseless and expressing contempt for the opinions of others. While his intelligence is not necessarily inferior, his distorted judgment and temperament is incapable of adjustment to the average social standards. He is inherently suspicious and anti-social. Such ill-balanced erratic types are classified as a psychopathic personality. From this class are recruited the criminals and 'cranks' whose pet schemes and morbid emotions run in conflict with the established order of society.[10]

When asked to render an expert opinion on whether or not Zangara was insane at the time of the shooting, neither of the psychiatrists chose to discuss this point because they believed they had not been asked to reach such a legal conclusion.

After further court proceedings on Saturday, in which the judge asked Zangara a number of questions and the defendant once again admitted his guilt, the judge adjudicated him guilty and sentenced Zangara to twenty years on each of the four attempted murder counts. The sentences were to run consecutively, meaning that Zangara would serve eighty years in prison.

Shortly after Anton Cermak died from his injuries on March 16, Zangara was re-arraigned—this time on charges of murder. He appeared to have been offered minimal legal assistance by his attorneys, who entered the report by Drs. Agos and Moore into evidence, presumably to demonstrate the difficulty they were having with their client, who seemed willing to admit his guilt to anyone who talked with him. However, the issues of whether Zangara was competent to stand trial (i.e. whether he had the capacity to readily assist his attorneys with his defense) or competent to enter a plea of guilty were never formally adjudicated.

Different judges had presided over Zangara's first arraignment and sentencing. When he was arraigned the second time on a charge of murder, Judge Uly O. Thompson presided and found Zangara guilty. Before sentencing the convicted assassin to death, Judge Thompson took the opportunity to make use of the media attention surrounding the case to make a strong statement in support of gun control. "It is my firm conviction," said Judge Thompson, "that the Congress of the United States should immediately pass legislation, or an act, for the confiscation of all firearms that may be carried and concealed about the person of anyone. It is a ridiculous state of society, in my opinion, that an assassin may be permitted to arm himself and go at liberty throughout the land killing whom he will kill."[11] Ironically, the judge never mentioned in his statement how to identify would-be assassins before they commit an act of political violence so their weapons could be confiscated.

Two short weeks after the death of Anton Cermak, and merely five weeks after his assassination attempt on Franklin D. Roosevelt, Giuseppe Zangara was executed in the electric chair at Raiford State Penitentiary in northern Florida. In the days leading up to his execution, he was asked whether he had any remorse for his actions. His only response was to state that he was sorry he had not killed Roosevelt; however, Zangara could not remember the name of the victim he had killed. On the day of his execution, Zangara went willingly and defiantly to his death, stating with a heavy Italian accent, "No, don't touch me. I go myself. I no 'fraid of 'lectric chair. I show you. I go sit down all by myself."[12] His last words were purported to be, "Viva Italia! Goodbye to all poor people everywhere! . . . Pusha da button! Go ahead, pusha da button!"[13]

The origins of Zangara's motive for assassination lie in many of his early experiences. His mother died when he was two years of age, and he carried a life-long resentment over the fact that his father took him out of school at the age of six and put him to work.[14] Throughout his life, Zangara had a hatred of capitalists and formal government because he thought they created the basic conditions that forced his father to remove him from school and put him to work. Zangara complained frequently of severe stomach problems, which remained a constant obsession throughout his life.

The brief psychiatric evaluation submitted by Agos and Moore remains the only known mental health evaluation that was ever performed on Zangara. It is cursory, extremely brief, and provides no meaningful insights into his motives or thinking surrounding his assassination attempt on Roosevelt. However, while awaiting his execution date at Raiford State Penitentiary, Zangara was permitted to write a detailed memoir of his life that was later translated from his native Italian and published in a book detailing his assassination attempt. This document provides the most insight into his motives and the origins of his ideas about assassination.

Aside from the resentments he carried from his early childhood experiences, Zangara wrote of his duties in the Italian military where he served in his late teens and early twenties. His dislike for military service was intense, and he frequently asked for a transfer. He was a captain's attendant and had to perform basic duties such as shining the officer's shoes, performing house work, and preparing meals. During this period of his life, Zangara's resentment grew over the fact that he found the officers to be sons of capitalists while the soldiers lowest in rank were like himself—from the families of common laborers.

In his memoir, he wrote:

I used to roam the streets of Rome hoping that I should see the King. I never saw the King, although I saw many superior officers. All the time I was a soldier I saw nothing but the sons of the

Capitalists as officers and the sons of the working people were the common soldiers. That was why I wanted to kill the head of such a government. Because I thought that this was the only way to help the poor working people.[15]

Several facts later emerged about Zangara's movements and motives leading up to his assassination attempt. Prior to focusing on President Elect Roosevelt, Zangara initially thought of assassinating the sitting President at the time, Herbert Hoover. According to the warden of Raiford State Penitentiary, Zangara had said he once traveled to Washington, D.C., and waited outside the White House to shoot Hoover; however, he abandoned his plans.[16] Zangara shifted his attention to Roosevelt when he learned that the President-elect was returning from a trip and would be making an appearance in the Miami area where Zangara had been staying.

Overall, Zangara's motive appears to have been an intense hatred of capitalists and government leaders. Although he shared many of the philosophies of anarchists, he did not appear to have any formal involvement in anarchist organizations. He was a resentful loner with no close ties or connections to other people. Political scientist James W. Clarke, who conducted an extensive study of American assassins and classified them according to their motivations and behavioral patterns, classified Zangara as a "nihilist" because he was able to reason and perceive things accurately but maintained a broad hatred of society.[17] According to Clarke, political assassins like Zangara feel alienated and do not fit in with mainstream society. Consequently, they view assassination of the political figure as a means of getting back at a target that symbolizes society in general. Although Clarke believes that nihilist assassins commit murder of political figures for personal reasons—to end one's life in a fit of rage—their motives are not political. However, Zangara's motives were political in a broad sense, inasmuch as Roosevelt represented a member of the ruling class that Zangara grew to hate during his early years.

The case of Giuseppe Zangara is noteworthy not only for the rapidity with which he was convicted, sentenced, and executed, but also for the superficial nature of the mental health examination that was undertaken of him. We learn very little about his reasons for wanting to assassinate Franklin D. Roosevelt from the only formal mental health examination known to have been conducted on him. The issues of Zangara's competence and sanity were never formally adjudicated. However, it seems reasonable to presume that he knew the nature and consequences of his actions and was therefore sane at the time he attempted to shoot Roosevelt. Moreover, the psychiatric examination of Zangara seemed to be in keeping with the rapid momentum that had gathered following his assassination attempt and the rapid justice that resulted in a quick pronouncement of guilt and a death sentence that sealed his fate. He was questioned directly about his involvement immediately following the shooting by a panel of law enforcement officers and individuals who had an interest in seeing Zangara admit his guilt. Of course, the case occurred long before Miranda warnings were part of the criminal justice process.

If we really want to understand the origins of Zangara's motives, the psychiatric evaluation and court transcripts offer very little insight. His personal memoirs, written while he was awaiting execution, provide one of the richest sources of information about the only person ever to have made an assassination attempt on a President-elect of the United States.

DOOMED FROM THE START

THE NAZI SABOTAGE PLOT OF 1942

He who does not prevent a crime when he can encourages it.

—Seneca[1]

IN RESPONSE TO THE TERRORIST ATTACKS OF SEPTEMBER 11, 2001, THE UNITED States took military action against the Taliban government in Afghanistan. A primary reason for the military response was the Taliban's providing sanctuary to al-Qaeda, the terrorist group responsible for the devastating attacks. The success of this military action has been measured, in part, by the number of al-Qaeda members who have been captured and placed at the U.S. military holding center for prisoners of war in Guantanamo Bay, Cuba. There have been lingering debates about how these prisoners should be adjudicated, and military tribunals are often mentioned as the most likely legal forum for dealing with these cases. Even Zacarias Moussaoui, the so-called twentieth hijacker, who was convicted of federal criminal charges stemming from his involvement in the planning of the attacks, was once mentioned as a possible candidate for trial by military tribunal. Adjudication by military tribunal was considered for Moussaoui because of concerns over the possibility that classified government documents might fall under disclosure laws in a regular criminal proceeding and be issued to Moussaoui, who was serving as his own legal counsel.

As seen in the case of the conspirators behind the assassination of Abraham Lincoln, military tribunals have been used before by the government of the United States to deal with acts of terrorism. However, one of the most unusual cases of terrorism in U.S. history that used a military tribunal demonstrated just how quickly and severely justice can be administered to terrorists who operate on American soil. The case is unusual not only for the boldness of the plan, but also for the inept—if not brazen—manner in which it was carried out.

Six months after the Japanese attack on Pearl Harbor, in the evening hours of June 13, 1942, a German U-boat named *Kreigsmarine* surfaced just off the coast of Long Island at Amagansett, New York.[2] A pair of German sailors paddled a rubber dingy from the submarine to the shore, nearly capsizing in the choppy surf. Also on the small raft were four men who disembarked from the dingy once it reached the beach.[3] The men unloaded four wooden boxes they had carried with them that contained explosives, blasting caps, timers, and other materials—including sulfuric acid, chlorate mixtures, and TNT—that could be used in carrying out acts of mass destruction.[4] The four men—George Dasch, Ernst Burger, Richard Quirin, and Heinrich Heinck—were dressed in German navy uniforms so that if they were captured they would be able to claim proper treatment as prisoners of war under the Geneva Convention. The team was led by Dasch, who had lived in the United States for several years, had once served in both the German and U.S. Army, and later returned to Germany.

Four days after Dasch and his co-conspirators landed, a second German U-boat arrived near Ponte Vedra, Florida, a small beach town located eleven miles south of Jacksonville. Once again, four Germans rowed a small rubber dingy to shore and disembarked with four wooden boxes containing TNT, blasting caps, detonators, timers, and other materials used in the construction of explosives. The four German men—Edward Kerling, Herbert Haupt, Werner Thiel, and Hermann Neubauer—also wore German navy uniforms, as Dasch's team had done, in order to claim prisoner of war status in case of capture.

These eight Nazi saboteurs were hand-picked by Walter Kappe, a leader in a pro-Nazi organization in the United States called the German-American Bund.[5] Kappe's task of identifying suitable candidates for undergoing terrorist training to further the German war effort had emerged as part of a plan Adolf Hitler hatched in December 1941 that called for terrorist missions to be carried out against the United States. Although the Nazis had been successful in training terrorists at a secret German army school, Hitler focused his sights on the United States once it entered World War II.

Many of the candidates Kappe chose were selected for a combination of reasons, including their familiarity with American culture, fluency in English, desire to commit sabotage in the United States, and devotion to the Nazi cause. Dasch had been selected to lead one of the terrorist groups because even though he had been born in Germany and had family there, he had lived in the United States for several years and spoke English extremely well. Burger was selected because he had emigrated to the United States and had become a citizen; he later returned to Germany and accepted the mission as a way of escaping from a concentration camp where he had been sent for criticizing Germany's occupation of Poland. Others in the group, including Quirin, Heinck, Neubauer, and Kerling, had left Germany and lived in the United States but remained openly loyal to Hitler and Nazi Germany. Haupt was the youngest of the group and, though born in Germany, was a U.S. citizen because his parents had become naturalized citizens.

Training of the men was conducted on a large farm near Brandenburg, Germany. Overall, the focus of the terrorist training was on conducting clandestine bombings and acts of sabotage within the United States. Specific targets included the Chesapeake and Ohio Railroads, Hell Gate Bridge in New York City, hydroelectric power plants in Niagara Falls, New York, various aluminum manufacturing plants in the United States, water and power supply systems for New York City, cryolite plants in Pennsylvania, and inland waterways near Cincinnati, Ohio, and St. Louis, Missouri.[6] In addition, the German terrorist plot was aimed at provoking fear and terror among the civilian population of the United States with the hope that the bombings would result in the U.S. government persecuting innocent German-Americans and lead to civilian revolt against the authority of the federal government.

In ways that strangely parallel the training of al-Qaeda terrorists, the German saboteurs underwent extensive training on the construction of explosives using common items. For example, one drawing that Burger made showed how a glass tube filled with dried peas and water could be sealed with two pieces of cork, each configured with a screw, and two pieces of wire to create a crude timing device.[7] The saboteurs were required to commit all of their lessons to memory to prevent anyone from discovering their plans and alerting police.

During two weeks of training, the men learned how to commit acts of sabotage. They learned to write with invisible ink so they could communicate with one another without detection, were given tours of aluminum and magnesium plants in Germany, and provided with detailed plans of manufacturing plants in the United States by technicians who had supervised construction of those plants. Upon completion of their training, the men were given a week of rest, during which they were allowed to visit with their families one last time before leaving on their secret mission.

Once they had completed their training, two teams were formed—one led by Dasch that was to land on Long Island and another led by Kerling that was to land in Florida. The two teams left from the coast of France in separate German U-boats; Kerling's team left first but landed later than Dasch's team because of the longer distance they had to travel to reach their destination. Little did Kerling's team realize, however, that when they had landed in Florida on June 17, the entire mission had been exposed by Dasch, who had landed with his team four days earlier.

As soon as Dasch's team landed on Long Island, they were confronted almost immediately by John Cullen, a young seaman with the U.S. Coast Guard who was stationed about a half mile from the site where the Nazi saboteurs landed. Cullen was making his night patrol, unarmed, when he came upon Dasch and the others. Although the Nazi saboteurs had been trained to kill anyone who might stand in their way, Dasch engaged in a dialogue with Cullen. Dasch gave Cullen a false name and told the seaman that his group was fishing for clams. When Cullen became suspicious and asked for their fishing permit, Dasch warned the nineteen-year-old seaman that if he wanted to see his family again, he should do exactly as instructed.[8]

From the $85,000 the group was given to support their mission—an amount equal to nearly $750,000 by today's standards—Dasch gave Cullen $280. All of the saboteurs had been given forged documents, including Social Security cards and Selective Service registration cards with false names.[9] After Cullen realized his only hope for escape was to take the money, he accepted it and went directly back to the Coast Guard station where he turned in the money and informed his superiors of what he had encountered. Meanwhile, the men accompanying Dasch confronted him with the fact that he said too much to Cullen and reminded him that their orders were to kill anyone who stood in their way.

Nevertheless, Dasch and his group managed to evade authorities, and took a train to New York City, where the four men separated into pairs, secured hotel rooms, and bought new clothes. The men took advantage of the huge amount of cash and freedom from Nazi surveillance by going on shopping sprees, going to nightclubs, and visiting prostitutes.[10]

Although Dasch was chosen as a leader of one of the two groups, he had no intention of seeing the plot through. Apparently unnoticed by those who trained him was the fact that he was neglectful of his lessons at the

German farm where they trained, and he had intended all along to turn himself in, along with his collaborators, to the Federal Bureau of Investigation.[11] He believed that by revealing the conspiracy to the U.S. authorities he would be hailed as a hero both in America and in Germany when the Nazis were defeated. To carry out his act of betrayal, and given the risk of possibly being killed by one of the other saboteurs if his intentions were known, Dasch felt he needed to obtain the support of at least one of his cohorts.

One morning before breakfast, Dasch decided to approach Burger. The two men were sharing a hotel room, and Dasch believed that he had picked up on a hint of disdain for the Nazis based on Burger's concentration camp experiences. Before the two men ate, Dasch opened the window and told Burger that "the two of them were going to have a talk; if they didn't agree with each other, only one of them would leave the room alive, for the other would go flying out the window."[12] When Dasch told Burger that he did not believe in the mission—under the codename Operation Pastorius—and wanted to contact the FBI, Burger stated that he was completely with Dasch, and the betrayal was set in motion.

Initially, Dasch contacted the local FBI office in New York City, introduced himself as Franz Daniel Pastorius, and told FBI Agent Dean McWhorter that he had information of the utmost importance that needed to be given directly to FBI director J. Edgar Hoover.[13] McWhorter suggested that Dasch come in for an interview, but Dasch (posing as Pastorius) stated that he would contact the FBI office in Washington himself. Dasch then traveled to Washington, D.C., where he sought a meeting with FBI officials.

Before leaving, Dasch divided the money the group had been provided with and left a note for Burger that he was going to "straighten everything out."[14] Upon his arrival in Washington, Dasch registered at the Mayflower Hotel and called the information service of the U.S. government to obtain the phone number of the Washington FBI office. The agent who took Dasch's call was Duane Traynor. When Dasch disclosed the fact that he was part of a group of Nazi saboteurs that recently arrived from Germany, Traynor knew that Dasch's story was legitimate because Cullen, the U.S. Coast Guard seaman, had reported his encounter with the saboteurs, and information about the incident had remained classified.

For the next several days, Dasch provided a detailed account of the sabotage plan to the FBI. His entire confession yielded 254 typewritten, single-spaced pages that outlined the terrorists' training, identities, and plans.[15] By the time Kerling's group landed in Florida, the entire plot had been exposed by Dasch, and federal agents quickly moved to arrest all seven of the remaining terrorists still at large.

Although all of the saboteurs were caught before they could carry out any act of violence, a few controversies began to emerge in the case. Despite the fact that the plot had been exposed by Dasch's coming forward and turning himself in along with the others, FBI Director J. Edgar Hoover mounted a public relations coup by making it appear FBI agents "had been waiting on the shore to scoop up the terrorists the moment they made landfall."[16] Therefore, the American public believed that the Nazi plot was thwarted by efficient law enforcement procedures rather than by a co-conspirator who decided to go to the authorities. Military officials were furious over Hoover's public claim. Some military officers were concerned that other saboteurs might still be at large and Hoover's public comments might force them into hiding. Nevertheless, once the plot was made public, large numbers of German nationals in the United States were detained and questioned as potential Nazi sympathizers.

Hitler was said to be furious when he learned that the saboteurs had been captured. He may well have been equally angered by the fact that there was no massive undermining of the U.S. government by the American public—as he had predicted—in the face of federal roundups of German-Americans once the plot was uncovered.

Another controversy emerged concerning how the terrorists were to be prosecuted. President Franklin Delano Roosevelt was clear from the beginning that he wanted swift and severe justice for all eight saboteurs. He initially told Francis Biddle, his attorney general, that he thought a military court martial was the preferred method because it would carry the death penalty, which Roosevelt said was "almost obligatory."[17]

On July 2, 1942—less than a month from the time the saboteurs landed in the United States—Roosevelt signed a presidential proclamation that appointed a military commission to prosecute the eight terrorists. Seven high-ranking generals were appointed to preside over the commission, hear evidence, and pronounce sentence; yet none of the officers had any formal legal training. Biddle was to prosecute the case, and the eight saboteurs were assigned two lawyers to represent them—Col. Cassius M. Dowell and Col. Kenneth Royall.

Consequently, one of the more controversial aspects of the case was the legal representation afforded the defendants. Although Dasch was provided with his own legal counsel, the remaining seven terrorists were all represented by the same two lawyers. Such an arrangement would draw immediate legal challenge today because the individual terrorists may have had legal defenses that conflicted with one another.[18] Given the fact that the U.S. was fully involved in World War II and public opinion called for conviction and execution of the saboteurs, granting them full protection under the laws of the U.S. Constitution did not appear to be a priority at the time.

Another controversy arising from the case was the issue of Dasch and the fact that he voluntarily went to the authorities to expose the plot. He was originally told by the FBI that if he pleaded guilty, he would be sentenced with the others to avoid being seen as the one who exposed the mission. Dasch later claimed that he was told he would receive a presidential pardon after six months.[19]

The trial of the eight Nazi saboteurs began on July 8, 1942 under very tight security and secrecy. Those who attended the proceedings were not to disclose anything about the trial to the media. Only general press releases were issued, and none of the attorneys were permitted to give anything other than general statements to the press.

Kenneth Royall, one of attorneys for seven of the saboteurs, later stated that it "was pretty apparent in the beginning that the commission was against us."[20] With the trial still in progress, the defense attorneys filed a motion to have the military commission declared a violation of the defendants' constitutional rights. Their argument was based on a landmark U.S. Supreme Court case from the post-Civil War era, *Ex Parte Milligan*,[21] that held a military trial of a civilian was unconstitutional. The basic argument advanced by legal counsel for the Nazi saboteurs was that the military commission set up by Roosevelt's proclamation was a violation of the defendants' rights as guaranteed under the U.S. Constitution. The lawyers felt that the terrorists should be tried in civil, rather than military, courts.

In a rare move, the Supreme Court agreed to hear the case of the seven accused spies (Dasch did not join in the case) because the questions raised by the defendants were core constitutional issues at a time of war that required legal interpretation. The Supreme Court's willingness to hear the case—particularly since the military commission was still hearing evidence—concerned Roosevelt, members of Congress, and the public because a ruling favorable to the saboteurs might delay or hinder justice.

The legal case associated with the prosecution of the Nazi saboteurs, *Ex Parte Quirin*,[22] was argued before the Supreme Court on July 29, 1942. Two days after hearing oral arguments, the Supreme Court ruled against the defendants and upheld both the legality of the military commission and the jurisdiction of the military court. Two days later, on August 1, the military commission completed the trial. On August 3, the commission submitted its findings to Roosevelt. Although the American public was informed that the President was studying the evidence, matters moved rapidly behind the scenes. A decision had been made that six of the saboteurs—Quirin, Heinck, Neubauer, Kerling, Haupt, and Theil—were to be put to death by electrocution. Because of their cooperation with authorities, the two remaining saboteurs escaped death; Berger was given a life sentence, and Dasch was sentenced to prison for thirty years. Roosevelt signed the order, but his decision was not released to the press until several minutes after the executions had been carried out. The six condemned saboteurs were electrocuted on August 8, 1942, less than two months after they first landed in the United States.

The secrecy surrounding the deaths of the prisoners has been a lingering source of controversy, particularly since their fate was not made public until their executions had been carried out. Although they were given an opportunity to have their appeal heard and decided by the Supreme Court before the end of their military trial, the court's official written decision was not issued until October 29, 1942—almost three months after the execution of the defendants. The opinion in *Quirin* is noteworthy not only because it was written after the defendants had been tried, sentenced, and executed, but also because it made clear distinctions between the military tribunal that had been ordered by Roosevelt in a time of war against Nazi saboteurs and the military tribunal that had been used in *Milligan* to prosecute an American civilian following the Civil War. The major difference between the two, according to the Supreme Court, was the fact that the constitutional tribunal in *Quirin* was used to prosecute members of an enemy army sent to carry out acts of sabotage in a time of war, whereas the unconstitutional tribunal in *Milligan* had been used to prosecute a civilian during a time of peace.

As for Dasch and Burger, they served six years of their prison sentences. On March 20, 1948, President Harry S. Truman commuted their sentences, and they were ordered to be released and deported to Germany. Berger managed to avoid publicity and died in anonymity.[23] Dasch tried to counter Germany's public view of him as a traitor, but he was unsuccessful; he died in 1991.[24]

As for the case of *Ex Parte Quirin*, it has become a major legal precedent that is cited today in arguments upholding the constitutionality of military tribunals as a mechanism for bringing terrorists and suspected terrorists to justice. Some people argue that keeping terrorist suspects in military holding centers or prosecuting suspected al-Qaeda sympathizers and co-conspirators by military tribunals violates rights guaranteed under the U.S. Constitution.[25] It is interesting, therefore, that the legal issues raised in the prosecution of eight Nazi terrorists who planned acts of terrorism on American soil during World War II are as relevant today as they were over half a century ago.

DRAWING ATTENTION
TO A CAUSE

THE ASSASSINATION ATTEMPT ON
HARRY S. TRUMAN

Patriotism is not short, frenzied outbursts of emotion,
but the tranquil and steady dedication of a lifetime.
—Adlai Stevenson[1]

THE STUDY OF PRESIDENTIAL ASSASSINATIONS PROVIDES A WEALTH OF INTER-
esting material on a form of political violence that can change the course of
world events. An exploration into the motives that precipitate an assassination attempt on a U.S. president can sometimes shed light on the political or
social forces that induce certain people to influence democracies.
Individuals who study human behavior and the workings of the human
mind are sometimes drawn to study the psychology of presidential assassins
because the killing of a world leader can have reverberations across most
regions of the world and over long periods of time. Therefore, prevention of
this extreme form of political killing is of paramount importance.

Since George Washington took office, there have been four presidents
killed by an assassin while in office: Abraham Lincoln, James A. Garfield,
William McKinley, and John F. Kennedy. In only two of these cases (the
Lincoln and McKinley assassinations) can it be safely concluded that the
assassin had clear political motives, while in the others the motives were
influenced by mental illness (the Garfield assassination) or unknown (the
Kennedy assassination). There have been six unsuccessful assassination
attempts on a sitting U.S. President (Andrew Jackson, Harry S. Truman,
Richard Nixon, Gerald R. Ford twice, and Ronald Reagan). Three presidential candidates have been targeted by assassins, with one being killed
(Robert F. Kennedy) and two who were wounded but survived (Theodore

Roosevelt and George Wallace). The case of Giuseppe Zangara's assassination attempt on Franklin D. Roosevelt was noted earlier to be the only attempt on a President-elect. There are no doubt other assassination plots that have been identified and thwarted by the U.S. Secret Service, but the details of some remain elusive given the secrecy that surrounds the protective mission of the law enforcement agency responsible for protecting the President.

In some cases—like the assassinations of the Kennedy brothers, Lincoln, and McKinley—there continues to be rampant debate about whether the assassin acted alone or was part of a broader conspiracy. In only one presidential assassination case, however, has a conspiracy ever been proven definitively. On November 1, 1950, two members of the Puerto Rican Nationalist Party—Oscar Collazo and Griselio Torresola—attempted to assassinate Harry S. Truman while the President was staying in Blair House in Washington, D.C., while the White House was being renovated.[2] In retrospect, the assassination attempt was very poorly planned and had almost no chance of success. Yet it is notable because it involved a conspiracy involving a small group motivated by strong nationalism and a desire to influence U.S. foreign policy.

The Puerto Rican Nationalist Party was headed by Pedro Albizu Campos, a Harvard-educated man who had bitter feelings about the racism he experienced while serving in the U.S. Army during World War I.[3] Campos was an ardent advocate of Puerto Rican independence, and he resented U.S. involvement in the affairs of the island. In the mid-1930s, Campos was imprisoned for his role in a series of violent riots and the assassination of a police chief in Puerto Rico.[4] He spent several years in prison before being released in 1943. Although a majority of Puerto Rican citizens rejected Campos's extremist views and advocacy of violence, many shared his hostile views of U.S. colonialism.[5] Still, the nationalist movement was never able to muster enough political support in Puerto Rican elections.

Born in Puerto Rico, Collazo came from a poor family and dropped out of school after the eighth grade. He became a strong supporter of Campos and the independence movement. Arriving in the United States as a young adult, Collazo found work in various menial jobs. Although he lived in New York City until his arrest, he returned to Puerto Rico periodically for visits.[6] Over the years, he gained a reputation as a good worker who was "well-liked by his employers and fellow employees."[7] A few years after his arrival in the United States, he met his wife, who was divorced and had two children of her own. Collazo's marriage was said to be close and loving; he raised his two step-daughters as if they were his own, and he was a devoted husband and father.[8]

Aside from his stable work and family life, Collazo remained active in the Puerto Rican Nationalist Party and knew Campos personally. Another active member of the party was a man by the name of Griselio Torresola. Like Collazo, Torresola came from an impoverished family and never finished formal schooling.[9] Unlike Collazo, however, Torresola did not have a stable work history, and he was not known as a family man. When he came to the United States in 1948, he left behind a wife and infant daughter. He married a well-educated and accomplished Puerto Rican woman in an informal ceremony in New York City, as he believed that he had divorced the wife he left behind.[10] Also unlike Collazo, who had no experience with weapons, Torresola was an experienced gunman who believed in violence as a way to move the Puerto Rican nationalist movement forward.

After Campos was released from prison, Collazo and Torresola became more galvanized in their revolutionary ideas. Campos was so taken by Torresola's enthusiasm that he chose his ardent follower to take charge of the movement if anything were to happen to him. In a note to Torresola, dated September 21, 1950, Campos wrote:

My Dear Griselio:
If by some circumstance it may become necessary that you assume leadership of the Movement in the United States, you will do it without any kind of qualms. We leave everything concerning this affair to your high patriotism and sound discretion.
     I embrace you
     Alibizu Campos[11]

This note, as well as another in which Campos urged Torresola to assume financial responsibility for the cause, would later be viewed by the U.S. Secret Service as evidence of a larger conspiracy, involving the leader of the Puerto Rican Nationalist Party, to assassinate President Truman.[12]

Throughout 1950, Torresola accumulated a cache of weapons that were used in an October 28 revolt intended to overthrow the Puerto Rican governor. When Torresola's sister was wounded and his brother sentenced to life in prison for the murder of a police officer during the revolt, Torresola fled to the United States and showed up at Collazo's home on October 29.

Through their discussions, they expressed frustration over the fact that their political activities had been unable to make any appreciable movement toward Puerto Rican independence. Collazo suggested that the two might do more by going to Washington, D.C., rather than their native Puerto Rico. He later explained the reasons for choosing to focus their efforts on American soil:

> I told [Torresola] that a better idea would be to come to Washington; as long as the American people didn't know what Puerto Rico was, or where Puerto Rico was, or which was the real Government of Puerto Rico, they would never care what was happening in Puerto Rico; that by coming to Washington and making some kind of demonstration in the capital of this nation, we would be in a better situation to make the American people understand the real situation in Puerto Rico; that Puerto Rico has no government; there is no Government of Puerto Rico[13].

Collazo and Torresola decided that if they assassinated President Truman, their act would draw worldwide attention to their cause, lead to political unrest in the United States, and advance the Puerto Rican nationalist movement.[14]

On Tuesday, October 31, 1950, Collazo and Torresola purchased new suits, bid farewell to their families, and boarded a train for Washington. Upon their arrival in the nation's capital, they went sightseeing, bought some postcards, and visited Blair House.[15] The selection of Blair House as a stop on their tour was not incidental. In 1948, a number of severe structural problems were discovered at the White House, and President Truman and his family were moved to Blair House so that repairs could be undertaken. Across the street from the White House on Pennsylvania Avenue, Blair House was a convenient move, but it afforded none of the protective features of the White House. Only a small, five-foot wide yard, low hedge, and shoulder-high iron fence separated the entrance to Blair House from the street.[16] As Collazo and Torresola studied the President's security, they were unaware that President Truman's bedroom window was unprotected and located directly above the main entrance to the building.[17]

On Monday, November 1, Collazo and Torresola were still unclear about their specific plans. In the morning, they took another trip to look over Blair House and made observations about the various locations of security officers and entrances to the building. Although neither man had any particular dislike for President Truman, they were intent on making a political statement that would let citizens of the United States know the strength and conviction of the Puerto Rican nationalist movement. "Our intentions were to make a demonstration on the steps of the Blair House," Collazo later said, and they were willing to die for their efforts.[18] Although it was unclear at this point what the nature of the demonstration would be, in retrospect, the actions of Collazo and Torresola ended up being a poorly planned, seemingly unsophisticated assassination attempt.

After the two men had lunch, they returned to their hotel to complete their plans. Collazo did not know how to use a semi-automatic pistol, so Torresola—who was an excellent shot and proficient with a weapon—instructed the novice on how to load and fire. They then took a taxi cab to Blair House and arrived at approximately 2:15 p.m.[19] President Truman, who was in his bedroom napping at the time, was scheduled to leave for an appearance in half an hour. Torresola and Collazo (who was not wearing his eyeglasses) approached Blair House from different directions. At the front of the building, Collazo walked up and tried to shoot security guard Donald Birdzell at point-blank range. However, the gun misfired, and only a sharp click was heard.[20] As Birdzell spun around, he saw Collazo pounding on the gun, which caused the weapon to fire; Birdzell was wounded in the right knee.

The commotion immediately drew the attention of U.S. Secret Service agent Floyd Boring and security officer Joseph Davidson, who were at a security booth at the east end of Blair House. Birdzell had limped out into the street, away from the entrance of Blair House in order to draw Collazo's fire, and began firing back at the would-be assassin. Davidson had now drawn his weapon and began firing at Collazo, who was sitting on the steps of Blair House firing back at the officers. As bullets whizzed past him and ricocheted off the iron fence, Collazo was able to reload his weapon and continue firing.[21] He was grazed on his nose and ear by bullets, and another ripped through his hat.

At just about the same time that Collazo began his attack at the front entrance, Torresola approached a back door to Blair House and surprised security officer Leslie Coffelt. As Torresola approached Coffelt in his booth, he shot the officer in the chest, abdomen, and legs. The mortally wounded officer fell back as security officer Joseph Downs stood in a doorway and drew his weapon. Torresola managed to shoot Downs three times and gained direct access to Blair House with an unimpeded path to Truman. Luckily, Coffelt was still conscious and managed to draw his weapon and shoot Torresola in the head, killing the would-be assassin.[22]

The entire gun battle took less than three minutes, and a total of thirty shots were fired. Coffelt was the only fatality among law enforcement officers. Torresola was killed, while Collazo survived his wounds and would later stand trial. Birdzell's wounds proved to be temporarily disabling, and Downs survived despite being critically injured. In the midst of the shooting, Truman had come to the window to see what was happening and was waved back by a Secret Service agent who feared there might be other conspirators. The President would later say to an aide that, "a President has to expect such things."[23]

At his trial, Collazo refused the advice of his attorney to plead insanity and testified in his own defense. In politically motivated crimes, where the guilt of the defendant is clearly based on evidence presented at trial, often the most obvious defense is insanity. This was true in the trials of Leon Czogolsz, Unabomber Ted Kaczynski, and Sirhan Sirhan (Robert F. Kennedy's assassin). However, most politically motivated terrorists refuse the insanity defense because they believe a psychiatric defense diminishes the validity of their political motives. Rather than be perceived as "crazy" or "mad," those who are truly dedicated and willing to die for their cause would rather face the death penalty than plead insanity. The strength of conviction that accused assassins have in their political beliefs creates a legal challenge that is difficult to surmount for the attorney whose job it is to defend a suspected terrorist facing the death penalty.

Because Coffelt died in the attack, Collazo was charged with homicide, as well as several counts of assault with the intent to kill. In 1951, he was convicted of all charges and sentenced to death. However, President Truman, who was the intended target, commuted Collazo's sentence to life. Whether Truman's act was one of compassion or intended to prevent the Puerto Rican nationalist from becoming a martyr for his cause, Collazo spend nearly thirty years in prison before his fate would take another lucky turn. On September 10, 1979, President Jimmy Carter commuted Collazo's sentence to time served and thus permitted the man who had conspired to assassinate a U.S. President released. Before returning to Puerto Rico, Collazo said in a public statement, "I intend to continue where I left off, to keep on fighting for Puerto Rico's independence until I die."[24]

Approximately two months after Collazo's return, nationalists attacked a U.S. Navy bus near the capital of San Juan, Puerto Rico, killing two sailors and injuring ten others.[25] Although Collazo played no direct role in the attack, the renewed attention his release gave to the nationalist movement cannot be discounted as a contributing factor, since the attack had been the first on the U.S. military in Puerto Rico in ten years.[26] Despite undying conviction to his cause, Collazo lived a relatively quiet life in Puerto Rico until his death in 1994.

The attack on Blair House was the first assassination attempt on a sitting U.S. President involving a proven conspiracy since the assassination of Abraham Lincoln. Yet the attack on Blair House is the only assassination attempt on a U.S. President that involved two gunmen.[27] Although Collazo's and Torresola's attack has been characterized as unsophisticated and disorganized, it is clear that their motives were political and they wanted their actions to direct the attention of the world, and the United States in particular, to the issue of Puerto Rican independence. Still, the fact that their actions were seen as haphazard and unsuccessful hindered, rather than helped, their cause. Because the actions of Collazo and Torresola were seen as unsophisticated, their cause was likewise not given the attention they sought. Perhaps the most surprising legacy of the case is the fact that a convicted, would-be presidential assassin was ultimately released from prison and allowed to return to his native land. If Collazo and Torresola had been successful in killing Truman, it is a certainty that the legal outcome could have been different—they would have either been executed or spent the rest of their lives in prison.

A SECOND WAVE OF
FOREIGN POLICY
PROTESTS

THE 1954 ATTACK ON
THE HOUSE OF REPRESENTATIVES

Ballots are the rightful and peaceful successors of bullets.
—Abraham Lincoln[1]

A NUMBER OF FACTORS DETERMINE THE SPECIFICS OF WHEN, WHERE, AND HOW a terrorist attack occurs. Among the more interesting variables that law enforcement and security forces use to increase vigilance and awareness of pending attacks are calendar dates that hold significance.

Another dramatic act of terrorism motivated by Puerto Rican independence was a shooting attack on the U.S. House of Representatives in 1954. The four individuals who carried out the attack—Lolita Lebron, Irving Flores Rodriguez, Rafael Cancel Miranda, and Andres Figueroa Cordero—chose March 1, 1954 as the date for their political statement. Although Lebron would claim after her arrest that the attack was to coincide with the beginning of an Inter-American conference in South America and was intended to embarrass the United States,[2] the date was important for another reason. On March 1, 1917, a law had been passed in the United States granting Puerto Ricans U.S. citizenship.[3] Like Collazo and Torresola, Lebron and her associates intended to draw the attention of the world to the Puerto Rican independence movement.

Born in Lares, Puerto Rico in 1919, Lebron was thirty-four years old when the attack was carried out.[4] Known as a shy child, Lebron later won a beauty pageant as a teenager. She had a daughter out of wedlock but later left her child with her mother when she decided to go to New York City in the 1940s in search of a better life.[5] It is both interesting and paradoxical that Lebron would look to the United States for prosperity—a nation she later sought to embarrass through an act of terrorism.

While living in the United States, Lebron went to school and worked as a seamstress. She married briefly and had another child—a son—whom she would send back to Puerto Rico to live with relatives. During her years in New York City, Lebron became a follower of Pedro Albizu Campos, the leader of the Puerto Rican Nationalist Party and the man who inspired Collazo and Torresola in their assassination attempt on Truman.[6] As she grew more radicalized in her political views over the years, Lebron became a logical choice to lead the group of individuals that attacked the House of Representatives.

In late February 1954, Lebron sent Miranda to Washington, D.C., to check out security precautions and survey the physical surroundings of the Capitol building. Miranda provided Lebron with information needed to plan out the attack. "I had all the secrets, all the plans . . . Me and me alone," she would later say.[7]

On the day of the attack, Lebron, Cordero, and Rodriguez traveled to Washington and met up with Miranda. After having lunch, they set out for the Capitol building, but got lost and had to ask for directions. When they finally arrived at the Capitol, they made their way to a gallery overlooking the floor where more than 240 Congressional representatives were actively debating an immigration bill.[8] Although a security officer had questioned Lebron and her associates before they entered the gallery, he merely asked if they had cameras because they were prohibited from use in the House of Representatives. The officer never checked the four visitors for weapons.

The legislative proceedings were suddenly interrupted by gunfire, as bullets hit marble columns and wooden tables. As the gunfire continued, Lebron shouted "Viva Puerto Rico Libre!"—meaning "Long live free Puerto Rico."[9] As she was yelling, the other attackers hung a Puerto Rican flag over the balcony and continued shooting. Members of the House began darting in different directions; some hid under their desks and others ran for the exits.

Representative James Van Zandt was a Navy veteran who had been in combat situations. He crawled along the floor into a coatroom and ran up the stairs to the gallery where one of the attackers had been wrestled to the ground. Van Zandt grabbed Miranda and managed to get his weapon away

targets on U.S. soil in order to affect specific U.S. foreign policies."[21] However, as the case of Erich Muenter's bombing of the U.S. Senate in 1915 shows, there was a prior act of terrorism against a U.S. government target on American soil that was intended to influence U.S. foreign policies at the time of World War I. Therefore, the Truman assassination attempt and House of Representatives shooting attack actually represent a second wave of terrorist attacks against government targets that were intended to influence U.S. foreign policy.

Even though the target chosen by Lebron and her associates was a legislative body of the U.S. government, the case demonstrates the central role Presidents have in dealing with terrorism both domestically and internationally. Specific executive decisions and policies can effectively ease tensions and bring about peaceful resolution to conflicts, or they can fan the flames that fuel terrorism, both from outside and within the United States. Even if President Carter's decision to grant clemency to Lebron and the others had some legitimate basis, it could well be perceived by many as harmful to counterterrorism efforts. If nothing else, the pardoning of Lebron and her compatriots afforded them the opportunity for a triumphant return to their native land where they could continue to support their original cause.

FIRST IN FLIGHT

AMERICA'S FIRST AIRLINE HIJACKING

Innovation violates tradition—attacks it in
public and steals from it in private.
—Mason Cooley[1]

THROUGHOUT THE COURSE OF HISTORY, TERRORISTS HAVE PROVEN THEMSELVES to be highly skilled at adapting to technological advances. International relations and political violence expert Bruce Hoffman has characterized the concept of terrorism as "the archetypal shark in the water. It must constantly move forward to survive and indeed to succeed."[2] One of the many ways terrorists change and adapt over time is to use—or misuse—new inventions or scientific discoveries to further their cause. The invention of dynamite gave anarchists a powerful weapon for wreaking havoc, and many terrorist attacks over the past century have involved the use of explosives. In the latter part of the twentieth century, the expansion of computers and the Internet provided terrorist organizations with a valuable tool for communicating throughout the world, spreading propaganda, and raising funds.

One of the most significant innovations during the middle of the twentieth century was the growth of commercial air travel. As with other advances, the growth of passenger air travel during the 1940s and 1950s brought about a new kind of criminal activity that spurred a new enterprise within the airline industry—security and safety. A number of air tragedies occurred during the period of rapid growth, including the first mid-air bombing of a U.S. passenger flight near Chesterton, Indiana, on October 10, 1933, and another highly publicized mid-air bombing on November 1, 1955.[3] These incidents had all the appearances of traditional crimes. Although the 1933 mid-air bombing was never officially solved, it is generally believed to have been committed as part of a criminal scheme, and the 1955 bombing was committed by a man who hid a bomb in the suitcase of his mother, who was on board the flight; he killed her so he could collect on a life insurance policy.

America's introduction to the use of commercial airplanes by international terrorists occurred on May 1, 1961, when an electrician from Miami by the name of Antuilio Ramirez Ortiz hijacked a National Airlines twin-engine airplane to Cuba.[4] The incident was the first U.S. hijacking. During a flight from Marathon, Florida, to Key West, Ortiz pulled out a pistol and knife and demanded that the plane be flown to Cuba. He was flying under the false name of "Elpir Cofresi," and he told the pilot that he had been offered $100,000 by a Dominican criminal to assassinate Cuban leader Fidel Castro.[5] Ortiz claimed to be sympathetic to the Castro regime and hijacked the plane so he could warn the Cuban leader of the plot.

At the time of the hijacking, the United States had no federal statute covering the specific crime of air piracy, so Ortiz was charged with assault and transporting a stolen aircraft across state lines.[6] His desire to travel to Cuba had apparently been developing for some time. During the Cuban revolution, Ortiz served as a gun runner for Castro and later came to the United States to seek work. When he experienced discrimination and had difficulty finding a job, he became despondent and sought advice from the Cuban consul. When Ortiz expressed his dissatisfaction with the United States and a desire to return to Cuba, the consul said half-jokingly, "Well, there are two things you can do: You can hijack a plane or you can hijack a boat."[7] Over the next few months, Ortiz ruminated over the conversation and subsequently hijacked the airplane. Whether the plot to assassinate Castro was genuine or merely a story Ortiz made up in order to gain favor with the Cuban government upon his arrival is not clear.

When the National Airlines flight arrived in Cuba, Castro returned the plane, crew, and passengers to the United States the same day. Ortiz, on the other hand, did not fare so well. For the next two years, he lived comfortably in Cuba until he decided to return to the United States.[8] His efforts to leave Cuba brought about a series of arrests. In 1963, he was held for over one month in a Cuban jail, and then in 1965, he was arrested again and charged with espionage, which resulted in a three-year prison sentence. Upon his release in 1968, Ortiz went to the Swiss Embassy in Cuba and made arrangements to leave the country via Mexico.[9] However, the Cuban government prevented him from leaving the country. In 1969, he married for a third time and found work as an electrician. His wife was able to leave Cuba in 1970, and she settled in the United States. In 1972, Ortiz tried to leave Cuba once again, this time on a small boat. He spent two days at sea but was found and handed over to the Cuban government; he spent another three years in prison for espionage. During his incarceration, Ortiz was subjected to "very rough treatment."[10] He later expressed profound regret for his actions and provided a warning to other Cuban exiles in the United States who are would-be hijackers that "It's a big mistake" to return to Cuba.[11]

After his release in 1975, Ortiz was finally permitted to leave Cuba. He flew to Kingston, Jamaica, and then spoke with a U.S. Embassy official there who allowed him to enter the United States.[12] The official notified the FBI, and when Ortiz arrived at Miami airport, he was arrested on November 21, 1975 for the hijacking he had committed fourteen years earlier. Ortiz spent only about four years in a U.S. prison for the hijacking, which seems surprising by today's standards. Not only was there no criminal statute for hijacking at the time Ortiz commandeered the flight in 1961, but what is even more surprising about the case is the complacency of the U.S. government toward the problem of airline hijacking that followed in the wake of the incident. Another airplane was forced to fly to Cuba a little over month after the Ortiz hijacking when Alfredo Oquendo demanded at gunpoint that an Eastern Airlines flight be diverted to Havana on July 24, 1961.[13]

President John F. Kennedy's administration was the first to confront formally the problem of airline hijacking in the United States. Although it supported a number of tough measures, such as a proposed sentence of life in prison for hijackers and the implementation of regulations calling for the bolting of cockpit doors and prohibitions against people carrying weapons on flights or threatening passengers or staff, there were still strong public opinions that the government was not doing enough to stop hijacking.[14] By today's standards, many of the regulations seem rather obvious, yet it is important to remember that during the early years of commercial airline travel, there were no uniform regulations or standards for screening passengers and their belongings. The original thinking was that airline safety was something that should be left to the individual airlines. It was generally believed that no one flying on an airline would deliberately place themselves in danger by overpowering the pilot and risking a crash. The failure to screen passengers seems absurd today, yet what is most surprising is that it took over a decade for formal airline safety regulations to catch up with the emerging threat of air piracy.

From 1961 to 1968, twenty-one airplanes were hijacked in the United States, and all but one of them were taken to Havana, Cuba.[15] According to historian Timothy Naftali, who consulted with the 9/11 Commission and prepared a detailed history of American terrorism during the last half of the twentieth century, the complacency toward airline hijacking resulted in routinized responses:

> Hijackings to Cuba were so frequent that U.S. pilots flying in the southern United States routinely carried maps of Havana's Jose Marti Airport. The Swiss embassy in Washington, D.C., which handled U.S. official messages to the Cuban government, had forms prepared for whenever Washington wished to formally request the return of a hijacked plane, its crew, and passengers. All the Swiss needed to do was to fill in the flight number and date the request.[16]

Although the rash of hijackings to Cuba was viewed as something of a travel inconvenience, 1968 is also generally viewed as marking the year in which international terrorism emerged as a global threat.[17] A number of hijackings by Palestinian terrorists resulted in the deaths of several passengers and prompted increased concerns about passenger safety. With the prominence of international hijacking emerging through a series of high-profile attacks on Israeli airlines in 1968 and 1969, the administration of President Richard M. Nixon was forced to confront airline hijacking more aggressively. On September 6, 1970, members of the Popular Front for the Liberation of Palestine (PFLP) hijacked four airplanes flying from Europe to New York.[18] Although not technically occurring on American soil, these hijackings were noteworthy because the hijackers made clear that they were targeting the United States because of its foreign policies.[19] A total of 306 individuals became hostages in this incident, and President Nixon had to assess the capabilities and readiness of the United States to deal with international terrorists.

The policy of the United States at the time was to negotiate with terrorists in order to ensure the safe return of hostages.[20] However, Nixon also encouraged a more active approach to dealing with the problem. He formally created a federal air marshal program and stated publicly that any countries where hijacked planes landed would be held accountable for protecting the lives of Americans and the property of U.S. companies.[21] Although Nixon is to be credited with making airline hijacking a prominent national security issue, it is surprising that it took nearly a decade after America's first hijacking and the administrations of three U.S. presidents before this form of international terrorism received the attention it deserved.

In the early 1970s, many issues became the focus of attention, including the Vietnam War, Watergate, and Nixon's resignation from the Presidency. With respect to terrorism in the United States, there were growing threats emerging from domestic groups like the Weather Underground and Puerto Rican nationalists who were continuing their efforts to bring about independence through a series of attacks in the United States. However, the problem of airline hijacking by international terrorists did not go away following the stricter policies instituted by the Nixon administration.

JUSTICE DELAYED

BOMBING OF THE SIXTEENTH STREET BAPTIST CHURCH

Opinions founded on prejudice are always sustained
with the greatest of violence.

—Francis Jeffrey[1]

ACTS OF RACIALLY MOTIVATED VIOLENCE ARE OFTEN CALLED HATE CRIMES, and in recent years there has been increased recognition that enhanced criminal penalties are needed for these kinds of offenses. Some racially motivated crimes are carried out by individuals or small groups who are so consumed with hatred that they target innocent victims for no other reason than the victims are members of a particular racial or ethnic group.

The United States has a long history of deep racial conflict, including a civil war fought over the issue of slavery, amendments to the U.S. Constitution following the Civil War that have been enforced inconsistently, and nearly a century of segregation laws that hindered progress for minorities. Despite several advances brought about by landmark court cases like *Brown v. Board of Education*[2] and the passage of sweeping legislation like the Civil Rights Act of 1964,[3] racial tensions continue in the United States.

There is perhaps no other racist movement or group in the United States that has been as closely associated with violence toward African Americans as the Ku Klux Klan (KKK). Originally formed in 1866 during the aftermath of the Civil War, the KKK was organized as a fraternal association by a group of citizens from the South hoping to advance their belief in the supremacy of the white race and the Protestant Christian faith.[4] Although not all members of the KKK can be considered political terrorists and not all factions in the organization have practiced political violence, the ideology of the group promotes violence against racial and religious minorities in the United States and has prompted numerous attacks—some

that are relatively unknown and others that have commanded wide attention.[5] Attacks carried out by members of the KKK have intimidated racial
minorities, influenced social attitudes, and asserted the doctrine of white
supremacy. As such, many of these attacks are rightfully considered acts of
terrorism.

Although there have been numerous racially motivated attacks
throughout the history of the United States, one of the most outrageous
took place on September 15, 1963 in Birmingham, Alabama. On that day—
a Sunday, no less—the 16th Street Baptist Church was bombed, claiming the
lives of four young African American girls. Indeed, the public tragedy
endured for decades as the perpetrators of the crime went unpunished. Yet,
the bombing occurred at the height of civil rights protests and activities in
the city of Birmingham and spurred passage of the federal Civil Rights Act
of 1964.[6]

Founded in 1873 on the west side of the city, the 16th Street Baptist
Church was an expansive brick structure nearly as old as the city of
Birmingham itself.[7] The church was situated on the corner of 6th Avenue
North and 16th Street, and while the front entrance faced 6th Avenue, the
site of worship was widely known for the main street that ran down its side
(i.e., 16th Street) rather than the one it faced.

In 1963, the 16th Street Baptist Church had a congregation of over four
hundred individuals, including many prominent black lawyers, teachers, and
dentists in Birmingham.[8] Because of its prominence, size, and strategic location near the downtown area, the church served as a central gathering spot
for civil rights rallies. The Reverend Martin Luther King, Jr. spoke from the
steps of the church in the spring of that year, calling for peaceful protests to
end racial inequality as the civil rights movement adopted its theme of "We
Shall Overcome."[9] In May, King and his associates arrived at an agreement
with city business leaders to desegregate lunch counters and restrooms in
Birmingham and to have more blacks hired as sales clerks.[10] The gains made
by King and other civil rights leaders led to considerable racial tension and
violence. A day after the agreement, a prominent black hotel near the 16th
Street Baptist Church was bombed, and the home of King's brother was also
targeted. The bombings triggered rioting by 2,500 black protesters. In
August, the home of a prominent black attorney was bombed. By the time
September came, racial tensions were running high, and groups of angry
whites, some of whom displayed Confederate flags, were protesting orders
to desegregate. The 16th Street Baptist Church bombing took place just fif-

teen days after a U.S. Federal Court had ordered Birmingham public schools to be integrated.[11]

On the morning of September 15, fourteen-year-old Addie Mae Collins walked to services at the 16th Street Baptist church with her two sisters.[12] After the three girls stopped briefly to play football in a nearby field, they arrived at the church before their weekly Sunday school class that began at 9:30 a.m. Also arriving at the church was fourteen-year-old Cynthia Wesley, who was dropped off by her father shortly before class was to begin. Cynthia's closest friend, fourteen-year-old Carole Richardson, who was also driven to the church by her father, was waiting at the church.[13] Eleven-year-old Denise McNair had originally planned to attend another church with her father, but because she was running late, she ended up at the 16th Street Baptist Church with her mother.[14]

Prior to the morning church service at 10:30 a.m., adults gathered on the main floor, while children and adolescents went down into the church basement for Sunday school class. Shortly after the lesson had ended, Cynthia and Carole asked for permission to go to the girl's restroom. Addie Mae was also in the restroom with her sister Sarah. When Denise McNair arrived at the church and went down to the basement, she also went to the restroom to freshen up. There she saw the three other girls getting ready before the church service.

Unknown to the girls, or anyone else attending the church service that morning, a box containing several thick sticks of dynamite had been placed underneath the concrete steps leading up to the side entrance of the building.[15] The box had been placed sometime the night before, but the greater challenge would soon become trying to identify the person responsible for placing it there.

As the congregation was waiting in the sanctuary for the service to begin, a loud explosion ripped through the church. The exact moment of the blast was ruled to be 10:22 a.m. when it caused a clock inside the church to stop running.[16] Because the bomb had been placed underneath the side entrance stairs, the part of the church that took the brunt of the blast was the brick wall separating the girl's bathroom from the outside. The explosion pulverized a huge section of the thirty-inch thick wall, as well as the window and heavy limestone window sills inside the bathroom[17].

Of the five girls in the bathroom at the time of the blast—Addie Mae Collins, her sister Sarah, Cynthia Wesley, Carole Robertson, and Denise McNair—only Sarah Collins survived. She had nearly two dozen pieces of glass embedded in her face and eyes and a deep cut on one of her legs. For several days, she did not know that her sister and the other girls had been killed. When Sarah was finally released from the hospital after two months, she was able to see only out of her left eye and was given a glass eye on the right side.[18]

The bombing was a profound tragedy that merely added fuel to the fires of racial conflict and tension in the city of Birmingham. In the immediate aftermath of the explosion, a crowd of angry African Americans gathered at the intersection of the church as police clad in riot helmets and armed with shotguns tried to keep the angry onlookers at bay.[19] Rioting broke out as some individuals threw rocks and bricks, while others overturned cars owned by white individuals and "several vacant houses and a small shop" were set on fire.[20] Meanwhile, a crowd of approximately 2,000 whites gathered the same afternoon to protest the proposed desegregation of a public high school in a Birmingham suburb.

The tense atmosphere in the South had been exacerbated by an order from the federal government to integrate public schools in the wake of the landmark U.S. Supreme Court decision in Brown v. Board of Education. The Federal Bureau of Investigation sent several agents to Birmingham to investigate the bombing in what was to become the "most intense probe since the search for gangland figure John Dillinger in the 1930s."[21] Despite several decent leads, including a description of a mysterious two-toned Chevrolet automobile with a whip antenna that was believed to have been parked near the church prior to the bombing, the investigation was hampered right from the beginning.

City officials organized a fund drive to raise money so a reward could be offered for information leading to the arrest of any individuals responsible for the many bombings that had plagued Birmingham during the year. A few pledges contained racially hostile comments or gestures, including Confederate money or fake bills as a means of taunting the reward committee. Despite the fact that nearly $80,000 was raised, the money went unclaimed because investigators were not able to bring the investigation to a successful close—at least not for decades.

From the beginning of their search for the bombers, FBI agents suspected three members of the Ku Klux Klan who had been on a list of suspects believed to have a connection to the racially motivated bombings in Birmingham. The prime suspects included a fifty-nine-year-old truck driver by the name of Robert E. Chambliss, a twenty-five-year-old man named

Thomas Blanton (who owned a vehicle like the one seen near the scene of the bombing), and forty-five-year-old Troy Ingram.[22]

Although investigators developed what they believed to be a sound case against the KKK members, FBI Director J. Edgar Hoover felt a conviction would be difficult to win, and in 1965 he blocked efforts to prosecute the suspects.[23] By 1968, federal investigators backed out of the investigation, and for a few more years, it appeared the case might never be solved.

In February 1971, the case received renewed interest when Alabama Attorney General Bill Baxley decided to reopen the investigation. One of Baxley's first acts as the newly elected Attorney General was to assemble a team of lawyers and investigators from his office to work on the case. He hired a former Montgomery, Alabama police detective by the name of Jack Shows whom Baxley told to make the church bombing case his "number one priority."[24] Although Baxley's staff had a number of suspects—including ex-KKK members and a racist attorney who was a vocal opponent of black civil rights and who espoused the belief that black citizens should be returned to Africa—none of the leads proved to be particularly helpful.[25]

As the investigation floundered for a few more years, Baxley felt if there was any hope of ever solving the 16th Street Baptist Church bombing case, he would need to have access to FBI files on the case. However, J. Edgar Hoover had a reputation as a fierce defender of FBI case files, and he held steadfast to a rigid policy that Bureau files were not to be shared with any other agencies. Of course, Hoover's policy existed before the U.S. government eased public access to government records through the Freedom of Information Act. The law permits citizens to gain access to previously secured government records as long as certain conditions are met to protect the privacy of innocent parties, national security interests, and other classified information.

When J. Edgar Hoover died on May 2, 1972, Baxley believed he might have greater success at gaining access to the FBI files, but he faced repeated problems. His pleas for a look at the FBI records were unsuccessful until 1975, when two fortuitous events occurred: Baxley had a chance encounter with a friend who happened to work in Washington for a major newspaper, and the Freedom of Information Act was passed. Baxley's friend contacted U.S. Attorney General Edward M. Levi and said he was prepared to write a story on how the FBI was hindering the Alabama Attorney General from pursuing the case.[26] With the threat of an unflattering story looming, Levi was able to have the files delivered to Baxley's office. Results from the records released proved to be mixed. While they provided a number of useful leads for Baxley, there were other materials in the files that were not included, which delayed justice in the case even further.

Over the next two years, Baxley's team focused their attention on Robert E. Chambliss, who was among the original suspects. A key witness against Chambliss was his niece, Elizabeth Cobbs, who had been visiting her aunt the day before the bombing and who had a conversation with her uncle that proved to be highly incriminating. Cobbs testified that Chambliss was very agitated and angry, swearing, using racial epithets, and boasting that he had "enough stuff put away to flatten half of Birmingham," meaning that he had explosives hidden that he planned on using.[27] Furthermore, Chambliss was said to have made a statement to his niece that after the following day—September 15 and the day on which the bombing had taken place—blacks "will beg us to let them segregate."[28]

While Cobbs' testimony proved to be the key piece of evidence against Chambliss, there was other incriminating evidence, including an eyewitness who claimed to have seen an individual matching Chambliss's description in a car near the church around the time of the bombing, and a police officer who claimed that during the course of a previous investigation, Chambliss had made comments about offering to provide dynamite to anyone who would be interested in blowing up blacks.

The case against Chambliss was largely circumstantial. But on November 18, 1977—a little over fourteen years after the bombing took place—a jury convicted Chambliss of the murder of Carol Denise McNair. Although Chambliss claimed at his sentencing that he played no role in the bombing of the 16th Street Baptist Church, he received a life sentence. He died in prison on October 29, 1985 without ever admitting his role in the crime.[29]

Baxley ran for governor of Alabama in 1978—the year after the first conviction in the case—but lost. He confided to friends that he believed the prosecution of the church bombing case, while publicly applauded by many, may have been viewed unfavorably by many white voters and thus hindered to his gubernatorial aspirations.[30]

The saga of the bombing case continued when the Jefferson County district attorney reopened the investigation. He found that not only had J. Edgar Hoover believed a conviction in the case would be difficult, but the former FBI Director had actually blocked evidence prosecutors could have used.[31] The exact reasons for Hoover's reluctance to pursue a prosecution in the case remains something of a mystery. However, it is interesting to note that several factors may have contributed to the unwillingness of Hoover to prosecute those responsible for the bombing.

Beginning in the 1950s, the FBI began a very secret and highly controversial program known as COINTELPRO—or, counterintelligence program. The purpose of COINTELPRO was "to disrupt, disorganize and neutralize" specific targets chosen by Hoover.[32] Many of the original targets were individuals suspected of having communist ties and many of the strategies used in COINTELPRO were highly controversial and illegal. For example, from the time Dwight Eisenhower was President through the administration of Lyndon Johnson, the FBI had the Internal Revenue Service supply tax information on over half a million people and several thousand organizations that were targeted for investigation.[33] During the civil rights era of the 1960s, Hoover suspected that communists had infiltrated the movement, and so the Reverend Martin Luther King, Jr. became one of the targets of the COINTELPRO investigations. Aside from the use of tax information as a means of harassing individuals and organizations, the COINTELPRO techniques also included illegal wiretaps, the collecting of intelligence on domestic targets, and other strategies that were carried out in a clandestine manner. When Hoover finally shut down the entire COINTELPRO project in April of 1971, public and government pressure was mounting to determine if laws had been broken during the series of counterintelligence programs. Hoover wrote to all his supervising agents that although the COINTELPRO investigations had been "successful over the years, it is felt that they should *now* be discontinued for security reasons because of their sensitivity."[34]

Since the KKK and many of its members had been targets of Hoover's investigations, it is likely that many of the questionable law enforcement techniques used during the COINTELPRO investigations were matters Hoover wanted to keep secret. This may have contributed to his reluctance to pursue prosecution of the 16th Street Baptist Church bombing case, since to do so might have risked bringing the FBI's investigative strategies under fire and would have made a successful prosecution difficult. Although these observations are speculative, it is clear that when COINTELPRO was shut down, Hoover passed away, and the Freedom of Information Act was passed, Baxley was able to get the files he needed to make his prosecution of Chambliss a success.

In 1988, federal and state prosecutors reopened the investigation and pursued charges against two other primary suspects in the bombing. A case comprised almost entirely of circumstantial evidence was mounted against two other individuals who had been identified as strong suspects back in 1963—Thomas Blanton and Bobby Frank Cherry. Prosecutors relied on the testimony of Cherry's granddaughter, who said she remembered her grandfather saying that he had "helped blow up a bunch of niggers back in Birmingham," and one of Cherry's ex-wives testified that he had boasted of being the individual who had the fuse on the bomb.[35] In addition, an interview conducted by FBI agents during the course of the investigation in the 1960s revealed that Cherry had been at a Birmingham store where the bomb had been assembled.

The prosecution of Cherry was hindered because the trial judge ruled that the ex-Klansman was not competent to stand trial. However, after a brief delay, during which Cherry's capacity to understand the charges against him and to assist in his defense was evaluated, the prosecution proceeded when Cherry's mental status cleared.[36] Despite the fact that attorneys for Blanton and Cherry argued that the government had relied on the testimony of unreliable witnesses whose memories were distorted after so many years, both men were convicted and sentenced to life in prison for the murders of Addie Mae Collins, Carole Robertson, Cynthia Wesley, and Denise McNair. Like Chambliss, Cherry denied any involvement in the bombing; he died on November 18, 2004.[37]

It took nearly forty years for the families of the four young girls killed in the bombing to see the case come to a conclusion and justice be served. The bombing of the 16th Street Baptist Church in Birmingham, Alabama was a major turning point in the civil rights movement and prompted a series of significant social changes, including passage of the landmark Civil Rights Act of 1964. In addition to the tragic deaths, the case is also surrounded by a highly controversial domestic intelligence program conducted by the FBI that may have prevented the church bombing case from being resolved expeditiously and that cast a dark shadow on the history of American counterterrorism efforts for many years.

AN UNSHAKEABLE OBSESSION

THE ASSASSINATION OF ROBERT F. KENNEDY

What passes in the mind of man is not scrutable by any human tribunal; it is only to be collected from his acts.
—Sir John Willes[1]

As one of the most politically tumultuous periods in U.S. history, the 1960s were marked by the assassination of two national leaders in 1968. On April 4, civil rights leader Martin Luther King, Jr. was killed by James Earl Ray in Memphis, Tennessee. Two months later, on June 5, U.S. Senator and Presidential candidate Robert F. Kennedy was assassinated by a Jordanian immigrant by the name of Sirhan Bishara Sirhan shortly after Kennedy won the California Presidential primary. King's assassin, who was motivated by racial hatred, ultimately pleaded guilty and was sentenced to ninety-nine years in prison. On the other hand, the trial of Sirhan Sirhan for the murder of Kennedy has been characterized as "the longest, most detailed defense of an assassin based on psychiatric evidence" and is a classic case in forensic psychology.[2]

Shortly after 1:00 a.m. on the morning of June 5, 1968, Kennedy delivered his victory speech at the Ambassador Hotel in Los Angeles. His last public comments ended with the famous line: "So, my thanks to all of you, and it's on to Chicago, and let's win there!"[3] As Kennedy made his way through the kitchen pantry of the hotel and shook hands with supporters, Sirhan burst through the crowd, yelled, "Kennedy, you son of a bitch," and fired eight shots from an Iver-Johnson revolver.[4] Two of the shots hit Kennedy near the right armpit, and another entered just behind his right ear and shattered into pieces, causing massive injuries to Kennedy's brain. Several of the remaining bullets injured bystanders.

Within seconds of the first few shots being fired, Sirhan was wrestled to the ground as he continued firing into the crowd and emptied his weapon. He was contained by a number of Kennedy's supporters, including professional football player Roosevelt Grier and author George Plimpton. Another of Kennedy's supporters, Olympic decathlon champion Rafer Johnson, was able to wrest the gun from the assassin's hand and kept the weapon in his jacket pocket until police arrived.[5]

The wound to Kennedy's head was the most serious; it caused considerable brain damage, and despite the efforts of surgeons who removed the bullet fragments, the Senator died twenty-five hours after being shot. Sirhan initially refused to tell police officers his name and frequently turned the tables on his interrogators by asking questions about irrelevant matters. Nevertheless, he was quickly identified through purchase records involving the Iver-Johnson revolver he used to shoot Kennedy. Police were led to Sirhan's residence, where they found a detailed notebook containing incriminating statements. One journal entry made by Sirhan on May 18, 1986 at 9:45 a.m. contained the following:

> My determination to eliminate R.F.K. is becoming more and more of an unshakable obsession... R.F.K. must die... R.F.K. must be killed... Robert F. Kennedy must be assassinated before 5 June 68.[6]

Although Sirhan would later claim that he had no clear recollection of shooting Kennedy, the primary motive for the assassination was ultimately believed to be Sirhan's rage over Kennedy's proposed sale of U.S. jet fighters to Israel. As a Palestinian-born immigrant from Jordan, Sirhan was outraged over Kennedy's expressed support for Israel.

During his childhood, Sirhan had several traumatic experiences as a result of both tragic accidents and political violence that occurred regularly in the Palestinian city of New Jerusalem, where he was born and raised. His parents were Jordanian Christians who belonged to the Eastern Orthodox church.[7] He was the fifth son born to his parents, and he had four younger siblings. His oldest brother was hit by a car and killed when Sirhan was two years old. When Sirhan was four, a dynamite-laden truck exploded near the home of the British High Commissioner for Palestine, who happened to live near the Sirhan family.[8] The blast shook the family home and caused young Sirhan to clutch himself and shake uncontrollably with fear for several hours. Shortly after this incident, Zionist military personnel set up a machine gun nest in the family bathroom. Sirhan cowered in the basement with his family and had to be reassured by his mother that "the fighting will stop in a day or two."[9] As violence continued, the Sirhans became Palestinian refugees and had to flee their home. After settling in a temple in the older section of Jerusalem, Sirhan's mother told him that he had "to be a man now," after he expressed his wish to return to their old house.[10] He had other traumatic experiences, such as finding a human hand floating in a bucket of water.

The family qualified for Palestinian refugee status, and they were all able to obtain U.S. visas in 1956. A year later they arrived in New York City and later settled in Pasadena, California. Sirhan's father was a domineering individual who was physically abusive to his son and unable to find steady work.[11] In 1957, he abandoned the family when Sirhan was thirteen and returned to Jordan, providing another emotional injury that Sirhan was forced to confront. Although his father returned to the United States in 1959 to work, he never contacted his family and ultimately returned to Jordan for good in 1966.

After his father abandoned the family, Sirhan was raised by his mother in the Los Angeles area. He attended John Muir High School in Pasadena, where he studied foreign languages and was a member of the California Cadet Corps—an ROTC-like military group for high school students.[12] Following graduation from high school, he attended community college but did not attend classes regularly and struggled to find an academic niche for himself. The emotional turmoil Sirhan experienced throughout his life continued when his sister died of leukemia in 1965. The death devastated Sirhan, and he dropped out of college soon thereafter. He held a variety of menial jobs and did not succeed at any. He developed an interest in exercising and caring for horses at a local racetrack, and his small stature made him a candidate to become a racing jockey. He received a jockey's license in 1966, but a series of accidental falls—one that was serious and two others that were minor—led Sirhan to give up riding as a career.

Many high-profile trials involving an isolated loner who commits a major act of violence with political motivations have dealt with questions about the perpetrator. Sirhan's case was similar to those of other well-known defendants where the political ideas of the defendant seem remotely connected to the crime because there is no conspiracy or involvement with a group that supported the assassin. At trial, Sirhan's lawyers raised a defense of diminished capacity and attempted to persuade jurors that he was "an immature, emotionally disturbed, and mentally ill youth."[13] While there was no dispute at trial that Sirhan had fired the fatal shot, the defense tried to portray the assassin's actions as unplanned, impulsive, and without premeditation. Because Sirhan had several war-related traumatic experiences during his childhood and claimed to have no specific recollection of the actual shooting, the defense argued that Sirhan lost touch with reality and was in a trance-like dissociative state when he shot the Senator.

The defense psychiatrists included Drs. Eric Marcus and Bernard Diamond, who examined Sirhan and concluded that he was suffering from paranoid schizophrenia and was in a dissociative state at the time of the assassination. Dissociative states are defined as disruptions in the normal processes of memory, consciousness, or identity that render a person capable of performing highly complex behaviors without necessarily being fully aware of one's surroundings. As a result, the person may have limited memory for details of an event or even complain of having "blacked out" during the incident. In the case of Sirhan's mental state at the time he shot Kennedy, defense experts testified that they did not believe Sirhan could formulate the capacity to appreciate the seriousness of his actions and to premeditate the murder because of his dissociative state.[14]

To rebut the defense experts, prosecutors presented testimony from Dr. Seymour Pollock, a highly respected and nationally renowned forensic psychiatrist. Pollock concluded that Sirhan's writings—particularly his repetitive statements to the effect that "R.F.K. must die"—merely served to increase the assassin's courage to commit the act of shooting Kennedy and clearly pointed to premeditation and planning.[15] While Pollock believed that Sirhan was paranoid, the prosecution expert did not find that the assassin's thinking rose to the level of a psychotic obsession or compulsion. Rather, Sirhan's strong identification with the Palestinian cause was felt by Pollock to be rational and understandable in light of Sirhan's background.

Among the more colorful, if not controversial, issues raised at Sirhan's trial involved the interpretation of psychological tests that were administered by Dr. Martin Schorr, a forensic psychologist hired by the defense. One of the tests given to Sirhan by Schorr was the well-known Rorschach, in which a series of inkblots are presented to a person and responses are scored and interpreted to render insights about the personality of the individual taking the test. According to some observers of the trial, Schorr seemed to value the Rorschach more than the other tests he administered and testified that it "is a most diagnostically revealing X-ray of the personality."[16]

Sirhan gave fifty-six responses to the ten inkblots—an extremely large number by most standards—and Schorr used the results to craft an intricate picture of Sirhan's psychological motives for killing Kennedy. The testimony about Sirhan's test results was laced with highly technical and detailed language about the Rorschach that "confused everyone in the courtroom."[17] Under cross-examination, Schorr was asked to read a portion of his report:

> By killing Kennedy, Sirhan kills his father, takes his father's place as the heir to the mother. The process of acting out this problem can only be achieved in a psychotic, insane state of mind. Essentially, the more he railed and stormed, the more the mother protected Sirhan from his father, and the more he withdrew into her protection. . . . The mother finally lets down the son. She, whom he loved, never kept her pledge and now his pain had to be repaid with pain. Since the unconscious always demands maximum penalties, the pain has to be death. Sirhan's prime problem becomes a conflict between instinctual demand for his father's death and the realization through his conscious that killing his father is not socially acceptable. . . . He finds a symbolic replica of his father in the form of Kennedy, kills him, and also removes the relationship that stands between him and his most precious possession—his mother's love.[18]

When the prosecutor asked Schorr on cross-examination who had written the passage, the psychologist responded that he had written it himself.

A problem soon emerged in the wake of Schorr's reading this section of his report, however. After Sirhan's mother heard the psychologist's proposed explanation of her son's actions, she demanded to see her son immediately so she could understand what it meant. Was it possible that she had some unconscious role in the assassination? The Oedipal themes in Schorr's report appeared to be confusing and unsettling to the assassin's mother. Furthermore, *The New York Times* identified a passage from *A Case Book of a Crime Psychiatrist* by the eminent forensic psychiatrist Dr. James A. Brussel, who gained notoriety for his accurate profile of New York City's "mad bomber."[19] The newspaper published the section from Dr. Schorr's report that had been read in court alongside a passage from Dr. Brussel's book, and the two were nearly identical. When he was later confronted on the witness stand with the similarity, Schorr admitted that he had used some of the language in Brussel's book. The revelation appeared to be a blow to the defense.

The prosecution called a rebuttal witness, clinical psychologist Dr. Leonard Olinger, to shed further doubt on the interpretation of Sirhan's psychological test results made by Schorr. Olinger gave a detailed account of purported errors in the scoring of the Rorschach and some of the other tests that seemed to lose jurors. Observers in the courtroom noted that much of the professional Rorschach jargon used by the expert witnesses seemed to result in jurors whose "faces ... ranged a gamut of expression from boredom to stupefaction."[20]

The jury rejected Sirhan's claim of diminished capacity, and the assassin was found guilty of murdering Kennedy. Although he was initially given the death penalty, Sirhan's sentence was commuted to life in 1972, when the death penalty was repealed in the State of California. Still, in all of the psychiatric and psychoanalytic jargon that was bandied about at Sirhan's trial, the political motives of his crime have often been cited as a footnote to the case. Several errors in handling evidence from the assassination and some inconsistencies in the testimony of witnesses have contributed to lingering doubts among some conspiracy theorists about whether Sirhan was even the actual assassin of Robert F. Kennedy. However, the fact that Sirhan was caught with a gun in his hand by several bystanders and continued to fire in Kennedy's direction as he was tackled leaves little doubt that he was Kennedy's assassin.

The widely held view of the motive behind the assassination of Robert F. Kennedy has been that Sirhan was enraged with the Senator for advocating the sale of fifty phantom fighter jets to Israel.[21] Certainly, Sirhan's experiences as a child are consistent with the classic histories of individuals who often gravitate to or become members of terrorist organizations. He was radicalized by the experience of being displaced from the family home by political violence and soldiers converting the family bathroom into a machine-gun nest. Although Sirhan was Christian and not Muslim, he identified strongly with the Palestinian cause, since he and his family became refugees and were forced to leave their country because of the violence. Therefore, it is not surprising that he became enraged at a politician who overtly supported the State of Israel.

Kennedy's statement that he favored the selling of jets to Israel was made during a speech at a Jewish temple in Portland, Oregon on May 26, 1968.[22] Furthermore, Kennedy's support for Israel was not aired publicly in the Los Angeles area where Sirhan lived until May 20. However, Sirhan's first journal entry in which he wrote that "R.F.K. must die!" was made on May 18.[23] Even though Sirhan testified in his own defense at trial and claimed that he was angry with Kennedy over the proposed sale of the fighter jets, there are lingering questions. Did Sirhan develop a fixation on Kennedy because of a declining psychological state that was merely fueled by the statement about support for Israel, or was his primary motive political? The fact remains that by killing Kennedy, Sirhan altered the course of the 1968 presidential election—a very volatile year in American history—and therefore altered the political future of the country.

Sirhan's trial is also a classic case study in forensic mental health because it illustrates how various experts, examining the same subject, can often arrive at widely divergent opinions. When looking at the testimony of forensic experts from the 1969 trial through the lens of present-day standards, many of the issues and methods that prevailed at the time seem controversial by today's standards. The Rorschach inkblot method remains a controversial psychological test, with many professional psychologists questioning its reliability and validity and others finding value in the test as a measure of personality and psychological functioning. The psychoanalytic themes used to explain Sirhan's actions—particularly the notion of an unresolved Oedipal conflict—would most likely not pass the legal standards of admissibility today because such theoretical principles are extremely difficult, if not impossible, to test and prove with a reasonable degree of scientific certainty. Furthermore, the attempts to provide psychoanalytic explanations for a political assassination merely added to the confusion that exists in a case where interesting questions remain that may never be answered to the satisfaction of everyone.

A YEAR OF LIVING DANGEROUSLY

THE BOMBING ATTACKS OF 1975

A crisis unmasks everyone.
—Mason Cooley[1]

THE 1970S WAS A DECADE OF CONSIDERABLE POLITICAL UNREST THAT WAS unique in many ways. Among the more prominent events during that time were massive protests against the Vietnam war: the shooting deaths of student protesters at Kent State University in 1970: the end of the Vietnam war: the Watergate scandal that ultimately led to the resignation of President Richard Nixon in 1974: America's bicentennial celebration in 1976: and the taking of American hostages in Iran in 1979. However, 1975 stands out as a year when terrorism in the United States was multi-faceted, which is a fitting description for the middle year of a politically tumultuous decade.

Two noteworthy events in that year were the assassination attempts made against U.S. President Gerald Ford in September. Both attempts were unsuccessful. They occurred fifteen days apart and involved the only female Presidential assassins in U.S. history. On September 5, Lynette "Squeaky" Fromme pulled a .45-caliber automatic pistol from underneath her clothing and attempted to fire at President Ford as he appeared in front of the state capitol building in Sacramento, California.[2] Fromme was a former member of mass-murderer Charles Manson's cult, and her apparent motive was to draw attention to efforts at having the convicted cult leader freed. She was convicted of the assassination attempt and sentenced to life in prison. Two weeks after Fromme's assassination attempt, Sarah Jane Moore fired a shot at President Ford on September 24 as he was visiting San Francisco.[3] Moore had a history of personal problems and attempted to assassinate Ford after her identity as an FBI informant against various radical groups had been discovered and she began to fear her life might be in danger. Although the two assassination attempts against Ford are noteworthy, neither were politically motivated and cannot rightfully be considered acts of terrorism. Nevertheless, they highlight the political volatility in 1975, which was a year punctuated by a number of high-profile bombings perpetrated by a number of different groups.

The year began with a deadly bombing that targeted a well-known spot in New York City's financial district. On January 24, a bomb went off at about 1:20 p.m. at the Fraunces Tavern, located at the corner of Pearl and Broad Streets.[4] With a historical legacy of being a popular luncheon restaurant among people working in the financial district, the tavern was crowded when the explosion occurred; four people were killed, and fifty-three others were injured.[5] In a nearby telephone booth, police found a message from a group called Fuerzas Armadas de Liberacion Nacional Puertorriqueña (Puerto Rican National Liberation Armed Forces, or F.A.L.N.). The message said, "You have unleashed a storm from which you comfortable Yankies (*sic*) cannot escape."[6] The apparent motive for the Fraunces Tavern attack was retaliation for a bombing in Puerto Rico that had killed two individuals at a meeting over independence. Members of F.A.L.N. believed the bombing had been ordered by the Central Intelligence Agency.

The F.A.L.N. was a terrorist organization formed by members left over from two weakened Puerto Rican nationalist groups that had carried out over a hundred bombings throughout the United States since at least the late 1960s and which were also believed to be behind the assassination attempt on President Truman in 1950 and the shooting attack on the U.S. House of Representatives in 1954.[7] Although motivated to attack the United States as a means of gaining independence for Puerto Rico, the terrorists had carried out relatively smaller attacks under different names. When the F.A.L.N. emerged in the 1970s, its members were using increasingly stronger explosives than its predecessors. Their bombs became more destructive as the group began using propane tanks to increase the power of the explosions. Members of F.A.L.N. used unassuming airline bags, canvas bags, or—in the case of the Fraunces Tavern bombing—attaché cases to transport their explosives.[8] The Fraunces Tavern bombing was one of the more visible examples of how F.A.L.N. bombs had become more powerful and deadly.

A few days after the Fraunces Tavern bombing, a bomb exploded in a bathroom at the U.S. State Department building in Washington, D.C., and another bombing was attempted at a government building in Oakland, California.[9] Both attacks took place on January 28 and were carried out by members of the Weather Underground, an extremist group formed by radical members of Students for a Democratic Society (SDS). The principal motive for the bombings was to protest against the industrial-military strength in the United States and its involvement in the Vietnam war. However, the Weather Underground was not finished in January. Before the end of 1975, the group would bomb the Banco de Ponce in New York City on June 16 to show its support for Puerto Rican independence and a copper company in Salt Lake City, Utah on October 10 to protest the ousting of President Allende of Chile, a socialist leader who opposed by the United States.[10]

The assassination attempts against President Ford in September garnered much of the media's attention during early fall. But concerns about terrorist violence returned to the forefront of the media in December when a large bomb exploded at about 6:30 p.m. near the TWA baggage claim terminal at LaGuardia Airport in New York City on December 29. Given that the explosion occurred just four days after Christmas, the terminal was crowded with travelers.[11] The bomb tore through the terminal, leaving broken water pipes, dangling electrical wires, and blown-out ceiling tiles. Although most passengers had just picked up their baggage at the terminal prior to the explosion, there were a number of airport employees, limousine drivers, and people waiting for rides who were standing nearby.[12] Eleven people were killed in the explosion, and seventy-four others were injured. Based on the number of casualties, the LaGuardia Airport bombing ranks as the fifth deadliest terrorist attack on American soil. If not for the fact that the bomb went off at a time when passengers had pretty much cleared out of the terminal, the number of deaths might have been much higher.

When investigators began surveying the scene, they were able to determine that the bomb had most likely been placed in a coin-operated locker that was next to one of the baggage carousels. Given the placement of the bomb, it blew the lockers apart and caused pieces of shrapnel to fly in all directions, causing the deaths of all victims and injuries to several others.[13]

No individual or group claimed responsibility for the bombing, which left investigators to pore through the bomb site for clues. A pair of anonymous calls were received shortly after the bombing that claimed other explosive devices had been placed in the airport. Officials had to shut down LaGuardia so that bomb-sniffing dogs could go through the airport. No other bombs were found, but not before a false alarm occurred when a dog focused on one locker in particular, which later turned out to have a package of hotdogs inside.[14]

Various theories emerged about groups that might have been responsible for the bombing at LaGuardia. Among the list of suspects was the F.A.L.N., which was responsible for the Fraunces Tavern bombing earlier in the year. Other groups suspected of the bombing included the Jewish Defense League and the Palestinian Liberation Organization (P.L.O.), yet the only thing that ever made any of these groups likely suspects was circumstantial evidence—these groups were known at the time to be involved in committing acts of terrorism, but there was no physical evidence linking them to the LaGuardia bombing.

One of the most promising leads came a year later in 1976 when a group of Croatian nationalists hijacked a commercial U.S. airliner and planted a bomb in a locker that killed a police officer. The similarities between the Croatian hijacking and the LaGuardia bombing in terms of how the explosives were planted made the Croatian group strong suspects. The Croatian hijackers never denied responsibility for planting the LaGuardia bomb even after they had been convicted and sentenced for the hijacking, and had no strong motive to deny their involvement. To this day, the LaGuardia bombing remains officially unsolved.

The terrorist bombings of 1975 are intriguing for a number of reasons. For one thing, they were carried out by various groups with different motives. The F.A.L.N. was motivated by Puerto Rican nationalism, the Weather Underground was motivated by violent opposition to U.S. foreign policies and industrial-military power, and the motivation for the LaGuardia bombing remains unknown. The 1975 terrorist bombings occurred in the middle of a four-year period that historian Phillip Jenkins described as constituting a "generalized American terrorist crisis" involving "the violent activities of Cuban, Puerto Rican, Jewish, Croatian, Armenian, Palestinian, and African-American extremists, together with far-leftists like the Symbionese Liberation Army."[15]

According to Jenkins, what is more intriguing about the terrorist attacks in America during the mid-1970s is the fact that there were more terrorist movements and more deadly attacks than had occurred in previous years. Yet each of the bombings in 1975—and indeed other attacks that had occurred both before and after that year—was viewed as a discrete criminal act that did not necessarily point to a broader terrorist network or threat that was looming within the United States. Jenkins suggests that the reason the terrorist attacks of the mid-1970s did not provoke a national panic was because a more prevalent concern in the American consciousness was illegal activities by police officers, intelligence agencies, and indeed the U.S. government. Among the various high-profile investigations attracting attention were Watergate, the House Select Committee on Assassinations inquiry into the killings of John F. Kennedy and Martin Luther King, Jr., and the Church and Rockefeller Commissions that investigated official wrongdoing.[16] Perhaps the public skepticism over the ability of law enforcement and government officials to provide honest answers to questions about why specific crimes were being committed—regardless of whether such skepticism was justified—may have prevented the 1975 bombings from taking on broader significance.

Although the terrorist attacks of 1975 have long been forgotten, and remain unknown to many, they are among the more lethal and deadly in American history. The first World Trade Center bombing in 1993 was a highly visible attack that ushered in a lethal foreign terrorist threat that ultimately led to the attacks of September 11, 2001. Yet the LaGuardia bombing claimed more lives that the first World Trade Center attack, and it has faded from public consciousness. If nothing else, 1975 represents a year laced with assassination attempts, bombing attacks, and other criminal acts that the American public seemed to view as discrete events rather than as a growing movement of political violence and terrorism motivated by both foreign and domestic concerns that would continue to make the United States a target in future attacks.

FAKE BOMBS

THE HIJACKING OF TWA FLIGHT 355

Oh what a tangled web we weave, when first we practice to deceive!
—Sir Walter Scott[1]

IN 1976, THE U.S. BICENTENNIAL CELEBRATION AND THE SUMMER OLYMPICS in Montreal, Canada were two highly publicized events that were likely targets for international terrorists, yet they both passed without major incidents. Shortly after the close of the 1976 Olympic Games, however, a major airline hijacking in the U.S. was carried out by a group of individuals trying to garner world-wide attention to the issue of Croatian independence. Croatia was controlled by the Serbian-dominated federation of communist Yugoslavia.[2] Although Croatia would ultimately gain its independence following the break-up of the Soviet Union and a Yugoslavian civil war in 1991, during the 1970s, a violent struggle was being waged by Croatian separatists against the Yugoslavian secret police.[3]

On the evening of September 10, 1976, TWA Flight 355 departed from LaGuardia airport in New York City with 86 passengers on board. The flight was scheduled to arrive in Chicago, Illinois, later that evening. However, James Roscoe, a telephone repairman from Long Island and a passenger on the flight, soon focused his attention on a man and woman who were sitting next to him and speaking somewhat nervously in a foreign language[4]. Shortly after the aircraft took off, the couple got up and went to one of the restrooms. Within minutes, the man and woman ran down the aisle of the airplane toward the cockpit with what appeared to be explosives strapped around their waists. At the same time, three other individuals emerged from among the passengers carrying packages that they claimed were bombs. The five individuals soon made their way to the front of the plane, and a short time later, the captain made an alarming announcement to the passengers:

Ah ... ladies and gentlemen ... this is the captain speaking ... I have something to report which is unique. Please don't be alarmed. This plane has been taken over by hijackers. Please don't be alarmed. We are now flying to Montreal as they have demanded. We will do exactly as they ask. Stay calm. I request—no, I insist that you keep in control. I assure you that your safety—the safety of us all is my first and primary concern, and that I will do everything to insure that goal. Just do what they say, and they assure me that no one will be hurt. Again, I insist that you stay calm and follow their orders.[5]

Although knowledge of the fate of the four hijacked airliners on September 11, 2001, would be enough to send airline passengers of today into a panic, the hijacking of TWA Flight 355 occurred in a different era. The hijackers of Flight 355 seemed to want the passengers to remain calm. As one of the hijackers walked down the aisle, he announced to the passengers, "We are going to pass out papers for you to read. Read them, please. You should not worry. We have no intention of killing anybody. All we want is for our declaration to be published in the American newspapers. We are not asking for difficult things. We want the world to recognize the injustices against our people—the people of Croatia."[6]

Despite assurances given by the hijackers that no one would be harmed, the passengers were understandably unnerved by the presence of five individuals who were displaying objects that appeared to be explosives. What none of the passengers knew at the time—but the hijackers clearly did—was that the objects were made out of clay and not capable of harming anyone. Still, the drama of the hijacking would take a deadly turn.

The couple sitting next to Roscoe at the beginning of the flight were Croatian national Zvonko Busic and his American-born wife Julienne. The idea to hijack a commercial airliner in the United States came to Zvonko Busic out of "sheer desperation" over the plight of Croatian dissidents who were working to gain independence from the Soviet-controlled bloc.[7] Among the major issues of concern to Busic and his dissident colleagues was the fact that Yugoslavian Secret Police were alleged to be assassinating Croatian dissidents throughout the world. Busic and his wife settled in the United States and had tried unsuccessfully to bring the Croatian demand for independence to the attention of the press and Western governments. A hijacking was seen as a means of bringing human rights abuses in Yugoslavia and the murder and imprisonment of political dissidents to the attention of the world.

Julienne Busic later claimed that her husband had previously participated in only peaceful political activities such as demonstrations and public education. The selection of a TWA airliner was merely by chance, but Busic made an important miscalculation when researching the airline and selecting a flight for hijacking. Although the plan called for the airliner to be flown across the Atlantic Ocean to Europe and Busic wanted an international flight, the New York-to-Chicago aircraft was not equipped for nonstop, trans-Atlantic travel.[8] As a result, the hijacking turned into a drawn-out fiasco that nevertheless brought the wide media attention Busic and his followers were seeking.

At the very last moment before launching the hijacking, Busic enlisted the help of three other individuals whom he believed to be trustworthy. Julienne Busic initially opposed the idea of a hijacking when her husband told her about it, but she agreed to participate. "I just didn't feel that it was an effective tool. I felt that it would alienate more people, but I couldn't think of a different or better option, either," she later said.[9]

The hijackers were able to make their way through airport security because they were carrying no bombs, just a metal pot and some clay that could be explained away as art supplies. However, the clay and pot were used to fashion crude models that resembled bombs and would later fool the passengers and crew of Flight 355.

Although Julienne Busic claimed that she and the other hijackers "were adamant about not having any weapons on the plane because we wanted to be sure nobody could possibly be hurt," the plot seemed to be a classic example of Murphy's law—if something can go wrong, it will, and things went tragically wrong.

The pilot diverted the flight's path and landed in Montreal, Canada, as the hijackers demanded. Once the plane was on the ground, Busic and the hijackers informed authorities that they had placed a bomb in a locker located across the street from Grand Central Station in New York City and another bomb "somewhere in the United States."[10] The paper the hijackers passed out was entitled *Declaration of the Headquarters of the Croatian National Liberations Forces*. Also placed in the locker were two copies of the *Declaration* that the hijackers demanded be published in several newspapers, including *The New York Times, Washington Post, Chicago Tribune, Los Angeles Times,* and the *International Herald Tribune*. Although the Busics had considered having the statement published legally through a paid advertisement, they did not have the $50,000 needed to do so and they also felt that if it was a paid advertisement, their message would lose its impact.[11] A highly publicized hijacking was just the thing the Busics felt they needed to bring attention to their political message. The hijackers warned that their bombs would be detonated if their demands were not met.

Armed with instructions from Busic about the locker in which the bomb was said to have been placed, New York City police officers were dispatched to the scene. Inside the locker, they found a sealed pressure cooker containing a bomb.[12] The police carefully took the bomb to a demolition area and attempted to detonate it using a remote control device. After about fifteen minutes, during which police tried to explode the bomb safely, explosives experts from the police department approached it "without wearing protective gear."[13] Brian J. Murray was one of the police officers who approached the bomb when it went off unexpectedly. Murray, a father of two young children, was killed in the blast, and three other officers were injured. The other bomb the hijackers claimed to have placed was never found.

After Flight 355 refueled in Montreal, Busic and his associates had the pilot fly to Gander, Newfoundland. Unaware that a New York City police officer had been killed by the real bomb planted in the locker, the hijackers were planning to fly the aircraft to Europe after refueling. When the plane landed in Gander, Busic agreed to release thirty-five hostages as a gesture of goodwill, with the stipulation that authorities agree to drop copies of their *Declaration* over New York, Chicago, and Montreal by helicopter.[14]

After the group of passengers was released, Busic ordered the pilot to fly to Europe so that additional leaflets could be distributed over London and Paris. However, the error Busic made in selecting TWA Flight 355 for international travel presented a problem:

> Since the hijacked plane, a Boeing 727, was used only on domestic flights, it was not equipped with navigational instruments for a cross-Atlantic flight. It also did not have the capacity to drop leaflets from the sky. A second TWA jet, a Boeing 707 with such equipment and capabilities, flew to Gander and escorted the plane to Europe.[15]

After another stop for refueling in Iceland, the hijackers flew to London, where they arranged for the Boeing 707 escort to drop leaflets over the city and then on to Paris where more leaflets were to be dropped. Although the hijackers had planned further travel for Flight 355, the incident came to an end when the plane landed at Charles de Gaulle airport in Paris.

Throughout the entire ordeal, FBI agents had been negotiating with the hijackers to arrange for the safe return of all passengers on board. The U.S. authorities had conceded to several of the demands made by the hijackers; their leaflets were distributed over major cities, and the *Declaration* was published in the various newspapers. However, French authorities were determined to keep the hijacked aircraft from taking off, and a critical point came when troops surrounded the plane and shot out the tires.[16]

For two days, negotiations between the French authorities and the hijackers continued. During this period, one of the hijackers got on the aircraft's loudspeaker system and delivered an ominous message that made passengers fear for their lives:

> My fellow passengers, my friends ... the negotiations have reached a critical point. They are not going well. We must now pray.... Pray for our captain, for our government, for the French, for the hijackers that they will be strong, and be able to reach an accord.... but we must each and every one of us come to terms with our God as best we know how. Make peace with our Lord. Ask Him for forgiveness for our sins.[17]

As the hijackers then led the passengers in the recitation of "The Lord's Prayer," the tension on the aircraft understandably reached panic levels. Indeed, the hijackers were becoming desperate themselves. They were unable to confirm if their demands for distribution and publication of the *Declaration* had been met. They also learned during the two-day standoff with French authorities that the New York City police officer had died from the bomb placed in the locker.

In the end, the hijackers surrendered peacefully, and all remaining hostages were released. However, in the final moments before release, another terror-filled episode for the passengers occurred. As the hijackers were trying to confirm if their demands had been met, they quickly herded everyone to the rear of the plane. A diabetic passenger collapsed and required medical attention from a physician on board.[18] After a few tense moments, one of the hijackers assured the passengers that the ordeal would soon be over and that they would be safe. The passengers were then told, "You are free to go now. You see, my friends, there are no bombs, they are not real. . . . Just clay, my friends, just clay."[19] In fact, none of the hijackers had any explosives or weapons; the plane had never been in any real danger of being destroyed—at least not from the hijackers' "bombs."

Zvonko and Julienne Busic, along with their three co-conspirators, were extradited back to the United States and charged with air piracy. Because the Busics were also responsible for planting the bomb in the locker that accidentally killed officer Murray, they were both convicted of homicide. Under the felony murder rule in prosecutions for certain violent crimes like airline hijacking, if someone dies in the course of the commission of the crime—even if there was no specific intent to kill someone—the perpetrators are still considered guilty of homicide. This rule, and the more severe criminal sentence that results, is intended to deter others who might consider engaging in highly risky behaviors during the commission of crimes. However, one of the questions raised in the aftermath of the hijacking was: If the hijackers had no intention of harming anyone as they stated, and had not used real explosives or any weapons during the hijacking, why did they plant a real bomb in the locker?

In an interview conducted years after the incident, Julienne Busic stated that real explosives were used in the locker across from Grand Central Station because the hijackers wanted to convince authorities that their fake weapons on the plane were real so their demands would be met.[20] Although the hijackers intended to prove their strength and determination to the authorities without necessarily harming anyone, the deception proved to be tragic, and the real explosive in the locker resulted in the death of a law enforcement officer.

The Busics both received mandatory life sentences. After spending approximately ten years in prison, Julienne Busic began corresponding with Kathleen Murray, the widow of the officer killed in the hijacking fiasco.[21] The two women shared stories about their families and exchanged photographs. Whether Julienne Busic was attempting to seek forgiveness from the slain officer's widow or merely explaining the political motives behind the incident, Murray found the correspondence cathartic, and a bond seemed to develop between the two women who had experienced the loss of their husbands, albeit in very different ways.[22]

In 1989, Julienne Busic was paroled and continued her correspondence with Murray. However, the unusual relationship turned sour when Busic was later hired by the Croatian embassy in Washington, D.C., to handle cultural and press matters when the nation finally gained its independence.[23] Murray was outraged that a convicted hijacker, whose politically motivated crime resulted in the death of her husband, was awarded a position of employment with status.

In the years following her release from prison, Julienne Busic has continued her efforts to win the freedom of her husband. She has used her contacts through the Croatian embassy to gather support for her husband and to perhaps win his parole. Her relationship with Kathleen Murray was also used in this regard when she asked the officer's widow to "intercede on her husband's behalf."[24] One can only wonder if one of Julienne Busic's motives in reaching out to Murray was to obtain a favorable ally in her fight to have her husband paroled.

Zvonko Busic also corresponded with Murray several years after the hijacking. In a rather awkward and ambivalent plea for forgiveness, Busic wrote to the officer's widow: "Forgive me, but I must tell you I never felt guilty for your husband's death, [but I] regretted it very much."[25] Julienne later expressed her profound "shock and sorrow" over the officer's death.[26] The Busics themselves had their share of difficulties following their conviction. They divorced in 1982 but remarried in 1988.[27] Although Julienne Busic remains on life-long parole, she was able to gain a respectable position working for the Croatian government. Zvonko Busic remains incarcerated in a U.S. federal penitentiary.

The U.S. government experienced internal conflicts of its own in the wake of the hijacking of TWA Flight 355. Although the case had very little impact on U.S. counterterrorism policies, the State Department was angry with the manner in which FBI agents had handled the case. After the incident had been resolved, the State Department sent two officials to FBI headquarters to "reprimand the bureau for 'violating' U.S. terrorism policy."[28] Of course, the policy to which the State Department officials were referring was the "no concessions" stance President Nixon had adopted in the early 1970s. Some officials in the U.S. government believed that the FBI's decision to distribute the hijackers' leaflet and to allow it to be published in various newspapers was in direct violation of this policy. However, a high-ranking FBI official refused to accept any criticism for how the incident had been handled, particularly since the hijacking came to a peaceful end with no deaths among the passengers or hijackers.

The hijacking of TWA Flight 355 is an example of nationalist-separatist terrorists who targeted a domestic U.S. flight in an effort to gain media attention for their cause. Although the hijackers were successful in obtaining several concessions from the FBI and indeed raised international awareness of their call for Croatian independence, their act had no appreciable effect in achieving what they sought to do. It took over a decade before the momentum for independence began, and Croatia was merely one of many smaller regions that gained independence in the wake of the collapse of the Soviet Union.

According to Julienne Busic, many people in Croatia believe that Zvonko Busic should be released from prison "on simple humanitarian grounds."[29] However, it is important to remember that it is not only an act of air piracy for which he was sentenced, but also the death of a law enforcement officer. Even though the hijacking may have been motivated by the revolutionary zeal of a young idealist and his wife, who may have never intended to harm anyone, events took a very tragic turn that resulted in permanent consequences for many who were involved.

SPILLOVER EFFECT

THE ASSASSINATION OF
ORLANDO LETELIER

In a war of ideas it is people who get killed.
—Stanislaw Lec[1]

IN THE FIELD OF TERRORISM STUDIES, VARIOUS TERMS FOR CLASSIFYING POLITI-
cally motivated violence have been used. Terrorist groups are sometimes
described as either left-wing or right-wing. Terrorist acts can be classified
according to the motivation behind them. There are different kinds of terrorism, and many textbooks draw a distinction between *international* and
domestic terrorism.

Domestic terrorism typically refers to violence that is confined to a particular country and involves issues that are related to the political processes
of that country. Therefore, domestic terrorist attacks involve targets that
symbolize something of importance to the domestic conflict and occur
within the borders of the country.[2] Examples of domestic terrorist groups
in the United States include supremacist groups, like the Ku Klux Klan, or
separatist militias that are hostile to the U.S. government. International terrorism, on the other hand, is global and involves violence that knows no
borders and involves targets that have broad significance. When most people
think of international terrorism, they often think of groups like al-Qaeda
that have a sweeping agenda for political change throughout the world.
While it is certainly true that international terrorism involves conflicts that
span international boundaries, another form of international terrorism is
known as the *spillover effect*.

Terrorism scholar Gus Martin, a professor at California State University
in Dominguez Hills, defines spillover effect as violent domestic conflicts in
a particular country that play out internationally.[3] In other words, violent
political struggles that occur in one country end up spilling over into coun-

tries that do not necessarily have a connection to those conflicts. For example, the Liberation Tigers of Tamil Elam (LTTE) are a violent terrorist group in Sri Lanka fighting for independence from the Sri Lankan government. The LTTE has been known to attack targets in India because the policies of the Indian government have been perceived by the group as sympathetic to the Sri Lankan government and therefore against the interests of the LTTE.

The United States has been the target of terrorist attacks by both domestic groups that are hostile to the government and international groups that view the U.S. as an enemy. However, one of the most dramatic assassinations ever to have occurred on American soil is a vivid example of the spillover effect. The crime has been called "the most brazen act of international terrorism ever committed in the capital of the United States" prior to the September 11, 2001 attack on the Pentagon.[4] Were it not real, the story might seem to any casual observer as something culled from the pages of a novel of international intrigue or the fictional screenplay of a movie. The tragedy, which played out on the streets of Washington, D.C., was motivated by the domestic conflicts of different political factions in the country of Chile, and appeared at first glance to have little direct relevance to U.S. interests.

On the morning of September 21, 1976, Michael and Ronni Moffitt drove to the home of Orlando Letelier, which was located on a quiet cul-de-sac in Bethesda, Maryland.[5] The Moffits were assistants to Letelier at a think tank based in Washington—the Institute for Policy Studies. Prior to working at the Institute, where he was known as "the most respected and effective spokesman in the international campaign to condemn and isolate" the Chilean dictatorship of Augusto Pinochet,[6] Letelier had served as the Chilean Ambassador to the United States from 1971 to 1973. His appointment had been made by Salvador Allende, who was the President of Chile from 1970 until 1973.

A brief history of Chilean politics and Allende's ascent to that country's highest political position is important for understanding how political conflicts and rivalries within Chile spilled over into a bloody assassination on the streets of the nation's capital. Allende founded the Socialist Party in Chile in 1933 and had made unsuccessful bids for the Chilean Presidency in 1952, 1958, and 1964.[7] Because of Allende's communist and socialist political leanings, the United States government opposed Allende in favor of his democratic-oriented opponents. The CIA secretly funded the political candidacies of Allende's opponents and credited covert funding operations as helping assure Allende's defeat in his previous bids for the Chilean presidency.[8]

However, the elections of September 4, 1970 brought different results. The Popular Unity Party, which was formed by the unification of working class individuals from the communist and socialist parties of Chile, ran Allende as its candidate, and he won. Despite his apparent victory, Allende's election provoked controversy and "a frantic, virtually minute-by-minute reaction with the Nixon administration."[9] Among the various efforts undertaken by the U.S. government to make sure Allende did not take office was an attempt to influence members of the Chilean Congress to ratify results of the election and block Allende from taking office. The CIA also provided support to a group that kidnapped and assassinated the commander of the Chilean Army under Allende.

In spite of these efforts, Allende became President of Chile and undertook the task of making appointments to various positions. Among the individuals close to him was Orlando Letelier, who became prominent in Chilean politics through his work in banking. A lawyer by training, with a specialty in economics, Letelier and his wife lived in Washington during the 1960s and became actively involved with Allende in his bid for the presidency of Chile. When Allende was finally elected in 1970, he chose Letelier as the Chilean Ambassador to the United States due, in part, to Letelier's experience and connections through his work in international banking. For nearly two years, Letelier resided at the Chilean Embassy located off Sheridan Circle on Massachusetts Avenue in Washington. Letelier met with President Richard Nixon and had regular dealings with members of the Nixon administration, including Secretary of State Henry Kissinger.

However, considerable political unrest continued in Chile during the Allende presidency, and in September 1973 a military coup led by General Augusto Pinochet resulted in the end of Allende's rule. On September 11— an infamous date in the annals of terrorism history—Allende died as he and some of his loyal soldiers were attacked by armed forces leading the coup.[10] Although conventional reports over the years held that Allende had been killed by Pinochet's forces, subsequent forensic testing conducted decades later concluded that Allende had shot himself as the military forces were surrounding his office.[11] Pinochet became the military dictator of Chile, and many officials and loyal followers of Allende's administration were executed. Letelier was in Chile at the time of the coup, but his life was spared.

Pinochet had him placed in a military concentration camp, where Letelier and others associated with Allende were subjected to harsh conditions.

After being confined for one year, during which time he was subjected to tortuous interrogation methods and threats of death, Letelier was released from prison by Pinochet, expelled from Chile, and had his citizenship revoked. The officer in charge of his release gave Letelier some final words, warning him that his troubles were not over. "Once you are outside [of Chile], remember … the arm of DINA [the Department of National Intelligence, or Chile's secret police] is long. General Pinochet will not and does not tolerate activities against his government."[12]

Shortly after his release, Letelier was offered a fellowship at the Institute for Policy Studies. The Institute was founded in 1962 by two former officials of the Kennedy administration as a think tank to develop critiques of and alternatives to U.S. foreign policies. Since its founding, the Institute "became the center for radical thought and civil rights activism in the mid-1960s" and had offices in both the nation's capital and the Netherlands.[13] At the Institute, Letelier worked with a married couple—Michael and Ronni Moffitt—who assisted him in his research. Michael Moffitt was an economist, and Ronni Moffitt, who had started out as a secretary at the Institute, became the Institute's fund-raising coordinator.[14]

The Institute's primary areas of study at the time of Letelier's involvement were both the causes of and solutions for disparities between wealthy and poor nations. From this base, Letelier was able to unify a strong international resistance movement against the Pinochet dictatorship. In 1976, for example, Letelier made several trips to the Netherlands, where there was a strong resistance movement and an active Chilean community of political exiles.[15] Letelier believed that the European country was ideal for initiating an international economic boycott against Chilean interests that would serve to topple Pinochet's military dictatorship.

Manuel Contreras, the Director of Chile's secret police force—the Department of National Intelligence (DINA)—was responsible for eliminating resistance to Pinochet both within Chile and abroad. Members of his police forces viewed socialism and communism as "a cancer on the body of Chile" and believed that the only means of preserving free markets and capitalism in the country was to uphold the Pinochet government and get rid of opposition through "bloody surgery" and "elimination"—phrases that referred to assassination and killing.[16]

As Letelier's international efforts to unify the resistance movement against Pinochet's government gained more attention and grew in strength, the Chilean exile became a target. His travels to Holland in 1976 highlighted his growing international influence. It is against this political and historical background that the Moffitts drove to Letelier's Bethesda, Maryland home on the morning of September 21, 1976 to pick up Letelier and head to work. At approximately 9:15 a.m., they all got into Letelier's Chevrolet Chevelle; Letelier got behind the wheel, Ronni Moffitt sat in the front passenger seat, and Michael Moffitt sat in the back seat.[17] None of them noticed a large gray vehicle that had been parked near Letelier's home and began following them as they headed for the Institute for Policy Studies.

A little over five minutes into the commute, Letelier's car turned onto Massachusetts Avenue and proceeded down Embassy Row in the nation's capital. After passing the Chilean embassy, where he had once served the Allende government, Letelier drove into Sheridan Circle. The man in the gray vehicle, who was still following a few cars back, took an instrument panel that was plugged into the cigarette lighter and pressed one button, then another.[18] The second button detonated a bomb that had been placed three days earlier on the chassis of Letelier's car, underneath the driver's seat.[19]

Michael Moffitt, who was sitting in the rear seat and who survived the explosion, later reported that he first heard a hissing sound, then a flash over the head of his wife in the front seat, followed by a deafening roar.[20] An attorney driving a car directly behind Letelier saw the Chevelle lift off of the ground and crash down in flames. Michael Moffitt fell out of the car and saw his wife stumbling to the curb. Thinking she was safely out of the vehicle, he went to the driver's side where he saw Letelier turned completely around and facing the back of the vehicle. Although Letelier attempted to say something, Moffitt noticed that the bottom half of Letelier's body had been blown off. The former Chilean ambassador was dead by the time he arrived at the hospital. When Moffitt ran back to check on his wife, he noticed she was bleeding profusely from her mouth. Her injuries proved to be grave, and she died while being treated in the emergency room.[21]

The brazen attack in the midst of morning rush hour had immediate reverberations. Moreover, the "terrorist attack took place fourteen city blocks from the White House; indeed, the blast could be heard at the State Department just a half-mile away."[22] Several prominent politicians who knew Letelier from their dealings with him when he was the Chilean

Ambassador were quick to condemn the assassination, and many quickly recognized that the Pinochet dictatorship was probably behind the act of terrorism. Letelier was eulogized in the halls of Congress by several congressman and senators, including Tom Harkin and Edward Kennedy.[23] Senator James Abourezk pointed out the significance of the assassination as a spillover act of terrorism that had international repercussions: "The tragedy goes beyond the cold-blooded murder of Orlando Letelier and Ronni Moffitt ... It means that the tyranny of the dictatorship has now been extended ... to the United States."[24]

Because the murders of Letelier and Ronni Moffitt occurred on American soil, the FBI took the lead in the investigation. With assistance from informants in the CIA, attention focused on the Chilean secret police (DINA) and Pinochet's regime. Furthermore, CIA reports revealed an extensive operation known by the codeword CONDOR—which was derived from the name of Chile's national bird—that was organized by Manuel Contreras. The first CONDOR meeting occurred when Contreras invited other directors of national intelligence agencies and secret police forces from several countries in South America to meet in October 1975.[25] Although the purpose of the meeting was secret and generally described as an opportunity to develop international cooperation throughout South America for improving the national security of the countries involved, CONDOR "became the most sinister state-sponsored terrorist network in the Western Hemisphere, if not the world."[26] Despite initially strong suspicions that the Chilean government had been involved in Letelier's assassination, Pinochet was nevertheless invited to meet with President Carter at the White House in September 1977—a year after Letelier's death.[27]

The Pinochet dictatorship had been supported by the United States because the military leader had ousted a communist government and was a champion of free market economics. His rule was seen as lending further hope to keeping communism at bay in South America and encouraging economic policies that were consistent with U.S. interests. Nevertheless, the FBI investigation focused on an anti-Castro community in Southern Florida, where individuals known to be involved in international terrorism were operating. After extensive legal maneuvering, evidence obtained in the course of the investigation led officials in the U.S. Justice Department to demand from the Chilean government the opportunity to question agents from Chile who may have come into contact with two individuals whose passport photos had been obtained. One of the pictures was of a man who had used the alias Juan Williams, yet whose real name was Michael Vernon Townley. It turned out that Townley was an American-born citizen who had grown up in Chile since the age of fourteen because his father had been selected to be the general manager of an automobile plant in Santiago.[28]

Townley had developed connections with Cuban exiles and had worked for a period of time as a CIA operative. Due to his extensive skill at speaking several languages, his American citizenship, and skill as a trained assassin and terrorist, Townley was chosen by Contreras to kill Letelier. He was able to enter the United States under an alias and was the person who planted the bomb under Letelier's car three days before the assassination and detonated it from the gray sedan. When officials in the U.S. Justice Department learned of Townley's identity, they demanded that he be turned over to American authorities. Although Pinochet reportedly claimed to have no knowledge of Townley's whereabouts while secretly hiding him, the Chilean government was finally forced to admit that Townley was a DINA agent, and he was turned over to U.S. officials.[29] Townley was subsequently tried and convicted for the assassination of Letelier.

However, when the case of Orlando Letelier's murder was solved, the complicity of the Chilean government "caused a major crisis in U.S.-Chilean relations, as well as a severe scandal in Chile."[30] A number of secret CIA documents concerning the Letelier assassination that were later released produced a variety of surprising revelations. Following the assassination, internal CIA documents questioned whether Pinochet would be able to survive as Chile's leader, which was no doubt a concern given the fact that he had been favored by U.S. presidents in the years following his overthrow of the Allende government. In addition, CIA documents showed that Townley had considered using nerve gas in the bomb he used to kill Letelier.[31] Although no nerve gas was subsequently used, the mere fact that consideration was given to using the substance raised questions about Townley's instructions and motives. Did his plan involve merely the assassination of Letelier, or did he give thought to staging a dramatic terrorist bombing, complete with nerve gas, to instill fear in Chilean exiles throughout the world who were considered enemies of the Pinochet regime? Also, was thought given to instilling fear in people offering support to exiles like Letelier? If so, then among those whom the bombing was intended to intimidate were Americans sympathetic to Letelier and others who opposed the Pinochet regime.

Despite a massive effort to cover up the involvement of the Chilean government in one of the most dramatic assassinations ever to have occurred in the United States, Pinochet would subsequently fail in his efforts to maintain power and control. He lost his power by 1990, and within a few years, efforts were undertaken to bring him to justice for numerous international human rights violations. Townley was formally arrested and convicted, as was Contreras who ended up completing a seven-year prison sentence in 2001 for his role in the assassination.[32] The U.S. Justice Department case on the Letelier assassination remains open with respect to the involvement of others, including Pinochet.[33]

On October 16, 1998, Pinochet was arrested as he was recuperating from back surgery in a hospital in England.[34] The warrant for his arrest was the culmination of nearly two decades of international effort to bring him to justice for his alleged role in the killing of his political enemies. A Spanish lawyer by the name of Juan Garces had spent years writing about Chilean political affairs in an attempt to expose atrocities allegedly committed by the Pinochet regime.[35] Garces brought an international criminal complaint against Pinochet, while the former dictator was outside Chile, and initiated the arrest. Although Pinochet was held for several months, his lawyers were successful in getting him released, and he returned to Chile. When he arrived in the spring of 2000, the attention surrounding his arrest in England prompted a number of Chileans to file judicial cases against him, and a special prosecutor was appointed. Pinochet had been granted immunity from prosecution for any past offenses as part of the political maneuvering that led to him stepping aside, but the special prosecutor recommended that the immunity be suspended.[36] The legal saga involving the prosecution of Pinochet has continued because his lawyers have argued that the former military dictator is mentally infirm due to dementia. Although it is well accepted that he had a direct hand in the assassination of Letelier, Pinochet may never face formal prosecution in a Chilean, American, or international court for the terrorist act. Manuel Contreras, his former director of DINA and coordinator of operation CONDOR, was arrested in January 2005 and sentenced to an additional prison term of twelve years for his role in the kidnapping and disappearance of another communist opponent of the Pinochet regime.[37]

The case of Orlando Letelier's assassination involved an act of state-sponsored terrorism that was supported by the Pinochet government. Yet the evidence ultimately pointing to Pinochet created a severe conflict for the United States government because the once-favored ruler was now being accused of supporting international terrorism that had suddenly hit home. This conflict is not unlike current issues that the United States faces in its foreign policies where it must maintain positive diplomatic relationships with countries like Saudi Arabia that have a questionable history of working to end international terrorism. Often, the position of ambivalence is uncomfortable when positive international relationships are necessary to further the battle against terrorism, yet foreign governments must be held accountable for failing to do more in their efforts to defeat terrorism. With so many of the September 11 hijackers coming from Saudi Arabia, the United States must re-examine its policies.

Letelier's assassination also illustrates how the domestic conflicts of a foreign country—in this case, Chile—spilled over into the streets of the United States. Not only did the guard's warning to Letelier upon his release from the concentration camp and his expulsion from Chile prove to be prophetic, the "bloody surgery" that eliminated political opponents of Pinochet and his regime claimed the life of Ronni Moffitt, an innocent American citizen who happened to be in the wrong place at the wrong time.

One of the most troublesome lessons of this case is the fact that a man who was lucky to have survived the violent overthrow of a government in which he worked was ultimately unable to express his ideas freely and to have an opportunity to persuade others that his ideas had merit. In the war of ideas about whether Allende's or Pinochet's policies were better for Chile, Orlando Letelier and Ronni Moffitt were two very tragic casualties.

BACKLASH

AN ALLEGED PLOT TO KIDNAP THE GOVERNOR OF MINNESOTA

There are, in every age, new errors to be rectified and
new prejudices to be opposed.
— Samuel Johnson[1]

A COMMON PHENOMENON THAT HAS OCCURRED IN THE WAKE OF SEVERAL large-scale terrorist attacks has been the targeting of innocent civilians who are members of the same ethnic or racial group as the suspected terrorists. After September 11, 2001, for example, there was a reported increase in the number of attacks on Muslims in the United States, in apparent retaliation against those who were suspected of carrying out the devastating acts.

In one widely reported case, an Indian immigrant who was a member of the Sikh religion was killed in front of an Arizona gas station because his manner of dress was believed to be similar to that of Arabs.[2] The killer was ultimately convicted after failing to convince a jury that he was insane at the time of the murder. This tragedy highlights the dangers of vigilantism and reactionary retribution that fails to recognize either the rule of law or proper political, military, and legal channels for dealing with terrorism. Stereotypes and prejudices are significant problems that underlie both the causes of and reactions to terrorism. In 2000, the Federal Bureau of Investigation reported that 28 crimes motivated by hate were committed against Arabs in the United States, and in 2001, the number increased dramatically to 481.[3]

Recent history provides a vivid example of how the backlash of prejudice and bias can create problems in dealing with terrorism effectively. On November 4, 1979, the U.S. Embassy in Tehran was overtaken by Iranian militants who had opposed the regime of Mohammed Rez Pahlavi, commonly known as the Shah of Iran.[4] There were nearly 70 Americans at the embassy taken hostage and held for 444 days during "the most profound crisis of the Carter presidency" and one of the most turbulent periods in the recent history of U.S. international affairs.[5] Although the Shah's regime collapsed and he left Iran on January 16, 1979, the Iranian militants overtook the embassy in November after the Shah was allowed to enter the United States for medical treatment.

The Iranian hostage crisis not only affected U.S. foreign relations but also increased tensions among American citizens and Iranians who were living in the United States at the time. The provocation of these tensions was due, in part, to Iranian students in the U.S. who demonstrated their support for the embassy takeover during protests in public arenas such as college campuses and city streets.[6] Some of these demonstrations were met with rock-throwing and ethnic slurs by small groups of angry Americans who took offense at the anti-American demonstrations by foreign students on American soil. At one point, President Carter ordered an administrative response by having the registration visas of Iranian students reviewed to determine if some should be deported.[7] Although a federal court order interrupted screening, the process continued and resulted in a finding that 11 percent of 53,000 Iranian students were not in compliance with federal immigration law. Only twenty students were ultimately deported, however, and another 823 agreed to leave the United States voluntarily.[8]

A number of Iranian students were found to be in compliance with U.S. immigration laws, and most were living here peacefully. However, many encountered problems of their own in the form of restricted access to funds for their education because of frozen Iranian assets, threats of violence, and persecution. For example, two Iranian students at Northeastern University were assaulted by members of the school's football team, and at a technical school in South Carolina, over one hundred Iranian students were suspended during an examination period before a state legal ruling held the action to be unconstitutional and the students were reinstated.[9] However, one of the most bizarre incidents of backlash against Iranian students during the 444-day hostage crisis occurred when four Iranian students and another student from the Sudan were arrested and charged with conspiring to kidnap Al Quie, the governor of Minnesota.

At the time of his election in 1978 to the Minnesota governorship, the Republican Quie had spent nearly a quarter century in public service as a state senator and U.S. congressman from Minnesota.[10] On November 9, 1979, Quie was holding a reception for foreign students at the governor's mansion in St. Paul. Police officers received a tip from an informant some-time prior to the reception that an attempt would be made to kidnap Quie, and a description was provided of the car that the suspects would be driving.[11] When a search was made near the governor's residence, officers found a car matching the description, and inside the vehicle, there were two shotguns and a handgun. Two individuals inside the vehicle at the time of the search were arrested, and three others who had apparently been brought to the reception in the car and had already made their way into the governor's mansion were also arrested. Four of the suspects were Iranian students from Mankato State University in Minnesota and identified as Hormoz Asadi, Hady Heidary, Feraidonoon Ghodoosi, and Mohammad Noori.[12] A fifth suspect, Antoun Stamboulish who was a twenty-five-year-old Sudanese student from the university, was also arrested.

Stamboulish and two of the Iranian students had been invited to attend Quie's reception and had entered the governor's mansion while the two other Iranian students waited in the car. When police officers found the weapons in the vehicle, all five were arrested and charged with conspiracy to commit kidnapping, conspiracy to commit assault, and possession of a pistol without a permit. What was highly unusual about the case, however, was the fact that the students who had been invited to attend the reception had entered the governor's mansion and left their weapons in the car. If they were intending to kidnap the governor, why did they leave the weapons in the vehicle? Furthermore, what possible motive could the students have for kidnapping the governor of Minnesota, and who was the person that had tipped police off to the alleged plot?

The day after his arrest, Stamboulish was released from police custody after an assistant county prosecutor ordered the Sudanese student to be freed. There was "no evidence whatsoever" to indicate that Stamboulish was involved in any plot to kidnap the governor.[13] Furthermore, an investigation into Stamboulish's status at Mankato State University revealed that he had been active on campus in trying to ease tensions between American and Iranian students. It appeared he was in the wrong place at the wrong time and had been arrested because of his association with the Iranian students.

However, Asadi, Heidary, Ghodoosi, and Noori also proclaimed their innocence. As for the weapons in their vehicle, the Iranian students were able to prove to police that they had used the guns earlier in the day during target practice at a firing range.[14] The explanation not only satisfied police but clarified why the weapons were left in the vehicle while the students attended the reception. In addition, the students had a legitimate reason for being at the governor's mansion, although the fact that they happened to have two rifles and a handgun in their possession is perhaps an indication of questionable judgment on their part. In light of the informant's warning, the suspicions of police officers seemed reasonable at the time, since the make of the vehicle and the presence of weapons in the vicinity of the governor's mansion raised questions about security. To add further confusion to the case, the individual who had informed police of the alleged plot refused to testify for reasons that are unclear from published reports on the incident.[15]

After four days of trying to sort out details of the alleged plot, police officers released the four Iranian students. County Attorney Tom Foley noted that although there had been sufficient evidence to arrest the students, the evidence did not support formal charges.[16] Interestingly, Foley noted in his statement about the decision to release the students that there had been "no pressure from the federal government."[17] This comment reflects how local law enforcement officers who dealt with cases involving Iranian students during the course of the hostage crisis in Iran during 1979 and 1980 had to deal with a novel issue that they had not confronted before: What impact would their local handling of suspects and criminal investigations have on international relations?

Without the testimony of the informant or corroborating evidence to support a case against the students, the investigation never led to formal charges or an indictment. Details of the case remain unclear, and the information upon which the police informant relied to support the allegation remains highly suspect. Although the investigation never produced any reliable evidence of a formal kidnapping plot, the incident is still included as a formal terrorist incident in at least one large database on world-wide terrorism. The National Memorial Institute for the Prevention of Terrorism maintains an extensive database on global terrorist incidents and organizations. The alleged plot against Governor Quie is listed as a kidnapping plot by an "other group," and the database includes the following description of the incident:

> Five persons were arrested in Minneapolis, Minnesota at the governor's mansion on charges of conspiring to kidnap Governor Al Quie. A reliable source said four were Iranian students and one was

Sudanese. Two shotguns and a handgun were taken from the car. Demonstrations were held during the day at the nearby University of Minnesota.[18]

What the incident report fails to include in its description is that the "source" was not reliable and the suspects were released four days later and never charged with a criminal offense. This example of how some incidents find their way into databases illustrates a persistent problem in researching terrorism. The secrecy that surrounds counterterrorism efforts—for reasons of national security or the integrity of law enforcement investigations— makes it difficult to rely on journalistic accounts of certain events. Firsthand reports and sources provide the most reliable information for the study of terrorism, but they are often inaccessible or elusive. As a result, terrorism researchers must often rely on sources who are removed from the event.

The alleged plot to kidnap Governor Quie by foreign students remains an interesting, if bizarre, footnote in the recent history of terrorism in the United States. Not only does the case raise the important question of data reliability in terrorism research, but it also demonstrates how highly volatile situations like the Iranian hostage crisis can lead to a rush to judgment in some criminal investigations. Local law enforcement agencies maintain a critical role in efforts to prevent terrorism, and valuable resources can be wasted if they are used to pursue false leads. When prejudice leads to back-lash against members of certain nationalist, ethnic, racial, or religious groups with no connection to terrorism, valuable law enforcement resources are wasted. Therefore, confronting the problem of prejudicial and stereotypic thinking is an important part of any counterterrorism measures.

GROUP REMNANTS

THE U.S. CAPITOL BOMBING OF 1983

Myths and legends die hard in America.
—Hunter S. Thompson[1]

THROUGHOUT ITS HISTORY, THE U.S. CAPITOL BUILDING HAS BEEN A FAVORITE target of those individuals who have political or personal grievances against the government. According to the U.S. Capitol Historical Society, Martin Van Buren wore pistols for protection when he presided over the Senate as Vice President in the 1800s.[2] Many infamous acts of terrorism at the Capitol include Erich Muenter's bombing of the Senate reception room in 1915 and the shooting attack on the House of Representatives by Puerto Rican nationalists in 1954.

During the Vietnam War, the Capitol building was targeted by members of the Weather Underground (also known as the Weathermen) on March 1, 1971, when a bomb exploded in a men's restroom near the Senate chambers. Although the Weathermen claimed responsibility for the explosion, which was carried out to voice opposition to the Vietnam War, no one was ever arrested in the case.[3] One notable attack on the Capitol illustrates how revolutionary movements that employ terrorism as a tactic often die hard. Unknown groups, who nevertheless claim responsibility for highly visible attacks, often emerge in a modified—and sometimes deadlier—form as the remnants of movements that authorities thought had been defeated.

On November 7, 1983, at approximately eleven o'clock in the morning, a bomb exploded outside the Senate chambers of the Capitol building.[4] The explosion tore a hole in the outside wall of the chambers, damaged a number of paintings in the hallway, and knocked a door from its hinges. At the time of the explosion, the building was nearly empty, so fortunately no one was injured in the blast.

A few minutes before the bomb went off, offices of the *Washington Post* received a telephone call from a member of a group calling itself the Armed Resistance Unit (ARU).[5] The caller warned that an explosion was about to occur in the Capitol building as a protest against U.S. military actions in Lebanon and Grenada. In addition, the group sent a communiqué to a Washington, D.C. radio station that stated:

> We purposely aimed our attack at the institutions of imperialist rule rather than at individual members of the ruling class and government. We did not choose to kill any of them this time. But their lives are not sacred.[6]

The ominous warning raised concern about how serious a threat the ARU posed to American citizens.

After the reign of violence carried out by the Weather Underground during the 1970s, some of its members would later boast that despite the numerous bombings it directed at corporate and military interests, not a single person died in any of their attacks. Although the argument has often been advanced by some terrorist organizations that their members should not be viewed as terrorists if only property is targeted, the bombing of property for political purposes is terrorism, according to most definitions.

The U.S. had already experienced a number of deadly terrorist attacks in Lebanon in 1983, including the April 18 bombing of the U.S. Embassy that claimed sixty lives and the October 23 bombing of the U.S. Marine barracks that claimed 241 lives. The U.S. invasion of the island of Grenada to rescue American citizens was believed to be the event that triggered the November 7 bombing.

The ARU was a group known by various other names, including the Revolutionary Fighting Group, the Red Guerilla Resistance Unit, the May 19 Communist Order, or the May 19 Communist Coalition. (The last two names were derived from the date on which black activist Malcolm X and Vietnamese communist leader Ho Chi Min were born).[7] The ARU was comprised of a small group of individuals from the Weather Underground and Black Liberation Army, two radical leftist organizations with their origins in the 1960s that had waned in prominence in the late 1970s.[8]

By 1976, most of the leadership and active cadre of the Weather Underground had been in hiding, and internal conflict and tension led to rival factions accusing one another of violating the primary goals of the organization, which was to fight American imperialism and the military-industrial domination. Within a few years, many Weathermen—including Bernardine Dohrn, Bill Ayers, Mark Rudd, and Cathy Wilkerson—turned themselves in to authorities and negotiated plea deals that allowed them to receive probation or brief jail sentences for the charges that had been filed against them years earlier.[9] Many of the Weather Underground who had been living underground later surfaced and faced "the difficult task of rebuilding old relationships, a sense of political purpose, and, for some, a sense of self."[10] Not all members of the Weather Underground surfaced or tried to lead legitimate lives, however; some remained committed to planning and carrying out acts of political violence.

The ARU committed a number of high-profile terrorist attacks. One of their more brazen acts was helping Black Liberation Army member Assata Shakur escape from a correctional facility in upstate New York on November 2, 1979.[11] Shakur had been convicted for her part in a 1973 shootout with law enforcement officers that resulted in the death of a policeman. In addition, the ARU carried out a number of armed robberies in order to fund their terrorist activities, the most famous of which was an October 20, 1981 armored car robbery in Nyack, New York that involved the shooting death of a Brinks security guard who was protecting $1.6 million inside the vehicle.[12] A number of ARU members were later arrested and convicted for their respective parts in the robbery.

Still, a number of Weathermen operating under the ARU name remained committed to violent revolution. Between 1983 and 1985, they committed at least eight known bombings localized around New York City and Washington, D.C. In the months leading up to the bombing at the U.S. Capitol building, the ARU was responsible for two bombings in Washington, one at the National War College at Fort McNair on April 26, 1983 and another at the Washington Navy Yard Computer Center on August 18 of the same year.[13] Bombs were also detonated in the New York City area at the FBI offices on Staten Island on January 28. Several other bombings occurred after the U.S. Capitol bombing on November 7, including an attack on the Washington Navy Yard Officers' Club on April 20, 1984, the Israeli Aircraft Industries building in New York on April 5, 1984, the South African consulate in New York on September 26, 1984, and the New York Patrolman's Benevolent Association on February 23, 1985.[14]

Among the series of bombings carried out by the ARU during this two-year period, the one at the U.S. Capitol was the most visible and highly publicized. But among the persistent questions raised in the aftermath of these attacks were: What was the ARU, who were its members, and what was it trying to accomplish?

The answers to these questions were soon found in June 1987 when a federal grand jury handed down a five-count indictment charging seven individuals with the eight bombings carried out by the ARU between 1983 and 1985.[15] Three of the individuals charged in the indictment—Laura Whitehorn, Linda Evans, and Marilyn Buck—were former members and supporters of the Weather Underground. Four other individuals named in the indictment—Susan Rosenberg, Timothy Blunk, Alan Berkman, and Elizabeth Duke—were listed as co-conspirators but not as primary defendants in the bombing of the U.S. Capitol building. In fact, these co-conspirators were serving various sentences for other offenses carried out by the ARU. For example, Rosenberg was already serving a sentence for her role in the Brinks armored vehicle robbery. Blunk and Berkman were also serving sentences for their roles in other offenses carried out on behalf of the ARU.

The indictment claimed that the defendants had conspired to "influence, change and protest policies and practices of the United States government concerning various international and domestic matters through the use of violent and illegal means."[16] Although Whitehorn, Evans, and Buck were operating under a new name—the ARU—their stated goals were essentially the same as those of the Weather Underground. A major goal of the ARU was to confront what the group perceived to be the militaristic and imperialist goals of the U.S. government.

In the interest of expediency and the certainty of obtaining a conviction, U.S. prosecutors agreed to a plea bargain for Whitehorn, Evans, and Buck in the U.S. Capitol bombing case. As for the other co-conspirators, the charges listed in the indictment were dismissed. Berkman, a physician, was already serving a ten-year prison sentence for possession of explosives, weapons, and false identification papers after he was arrested in 1985.[19] Moreover, Berkman was ill with Hodgkins disease and undergoing chemotherapy, so prosecutors agreed to dismiss the charges against him. Rosenberg and Blunk were serving a fifty-eight-year prison sentence for possession of explosives, and Rosenberg had been charged, but never tried, for her role in the Brinks armored car robbery. Nevertheless, prosecutors decided to dismiss the charges against the two for their respective roles in the U.S. Capitol bombing.

Whitehorn, Buck, and Evans all entered pleas of guilty to the 1983 U.S. Capitol bombing, as well as other offenses connected with their terrorism campaign. At their sentencing hearing, Federal District Judge Harold H. Green had harsh words for the defendants as he imposed a twenty-year prison term:

> You have committed acts of violence which are not excused by good purposes or political purposes.... The effects of these kinds of violence are just as devastating to the victims and to society at large as if they were motivated by greed.[20]

At the time of sentencing in 1990, the case seemed to have been resolved and might have served merely as an example from history of how remnant members from a disbanded terrorist organization reemerged in later years to carry out one last series of attacks in order to further their original goals. However, the case ignited once again in 2001, when President Clinton commuted the sentences of Linda Evans and Susan Rosenberg to time served and allowed them to be released from prison. The commutation of Rosenberg's sentence was perhaps the most controversial of all because the Brinks robbery had resulted in the death of a security guard. Whitehorn was released from prison after serving fourteen years of her sentence.

More controversy erupted when Rosenberg and Whitehorn were extended offers to teach or speak on college campuses. Rosenberg was extended an offer to teach a course at Hamilton College in upstate New York, but the offer was later rescinded after considerable outcry erupted over allowing a convicted terrorist to teach on a college campus. Similarly, Whitehorn was provided an opportunity to speak at Duke University, as well as other prestigious universities throughout the United States, on the issue of sexually transmitted diseases among prison inmates.[21] Even though the specific topics on which these convicted terrorists were to speak did not deal directly with their original goals and objectives, the fact that they were appearing on college campuses raised questions about the influence they might have on the current generation of college students.

The Weather Underground and its remnant factions like the ARU have their origins in the political unrest that was rampant on college campuses during the 1960s. However, the legacy of these groups endures and the political changes they sought to bring about remain contentious issues today, particularly in light of the division and conflict that exists over U.S.

military presence in Iraq and the manner in which the government is fighting the war on terrorism.

INFLUENCING AN ELECTION

AMERICA'S FIRST MODERN BIOTERRORIST ATTACK

There is a good deal too strange to be believed,
nothing is too strange to have happened.
—Thomas Hardy[1]

THERE IS NOTHING THAT EMBOLDENS TERRORISTS MORE AND REINFORCES THEIR use of violence as a means of bringing about political change than direct evidence that one of their attacks has influenced government policies. A series of bombings that were purportedly carried out by Islamic extremists tied to al-Qaeda in Madrid, Spain, had precisely the kind of impact that the terrorist group was looking to have. On March 11, 2004, just three days before general elections in which Spanish Prime Minister Jose Maria Aznar, a staunch ally of the United States in the war on terrorism, was expected to prevail, nearly 200 people were killed when a series of bombs exploded aboard a crowded commuter train. The bombings were carried out in retaliation for Spain's support of the U.S.-led invasion of Afghanistan and Iraq. In a rapid turn of events, the terrorists were rewarded when Aznar lost the election and the socialist candidate, Jose Louis Zapatero, was elected Spain's new Prime Minister. Immediately after being elected, Zapatero criticized the war in Iraq and pledged to bring Spanish troops home unless the United Nations took control of the military effort.

The fact that a terrorist attack successfully influenced a national election is amazing, but an attempt by terrorists to influence the outcome of an election had happened several years earlier in the United States. In what is generally believed to be the first major bioterrorist attack in the United States, members of a religious cult tried to influence a local election in the small town of The Dalles, Oregon in the fall of 1984. The first attack occurred on August 29, 1984, when members of the cult gave water that was contaminated with *salmonella typhimurium*, a common strain of salmonella bacteria that causes food poisoning, to two Wasco County commissioners who were visiting the cult's community on a routine fact-finding mission.[2] However, the main attack occurred in two waves from September 9 to 18 and from September 19 to October 10. A total of 751 people became ill when the salad bars of approximately ten restaurants were contaminated with *salmonella typhimurium*.[3] There were no fatalities associated with the contamination, but nearly a year passed before law enforcement officials learned that the mass food poisoning was not accidental and instead the result of an intentional terrorist attack.

The origins of this unique incident began in the 1960s when a charismatic and bright Indian guru by the name of Bhagwan Shree Rajneesh formed a cult. His followers came to be known as Rajneeshees. In the 1970s, the cult had attracted a large following of primarily upper-middle-class young adults from India, Europe, and the United States.[4] Many of the Bhagwan's teachings were controversial, such as his claim that there was no God and that casual nudity and sexual freedom were to be encouraged in society. As his worldwide reputation grew, the Bhagwan came to be known as the "Enlightened Master," and he was very successful at amassing considerable wealth through the contributions of his followers. In addition, the cult made money from the sale of books and tapes of the Bhagwan's teachings. Over the years, he was able to accumulate enough money to own ninety Rolls Royce automobiles.[5]

By 1980, controversy surrounding the Rajneeshee cult made it difficult for it to continue operations in India, so the Bhagwan sought a new location for his ashram—a secluded religious retreat for Hindu spiritual leaders. Ma Anand Sheela, one of his Indian followers who had attended college in the United States and whose real name was Sheela P. Silverman,[6] encouraged the Bhagwan to locate his new ashram in America, and under his direction, she was able to purchase a large piece of property in Oregon known as the Big Muddy Ranch.[7] The property was located in Jefferson and Wasco counties, which were adjacent to each other and located near the middle of the state. Wasco County, with a population of approximately 20,000 people, contained a majority of the ranch property. The small town of The Dalles, with a population of 10,000 people, was the seat of Wasco County government.[8]

Once the cult settled into its new location in 1981, it quickly expanded its presence within the community. The cult built a town for its residents on the ranch and officially incorporated as a municipality under the name Rajneeshpuram.[9] With its standing as a municipality, Rajneeshpuram was able to assemble its own police force called the "Peace Force." Law enforcement officers of Rajneeshpuram were able to get training from the state of Oregon and had access to computer databases maintained for law enforcement purposes.

Unlike most cults where a charismatic leader has influence over followers, the Rajneeshees had a unique form of self-governance. Despite the fact that the Bhagwan had authority over all cult operations, he did not have any direct involvement with his followers, and he was removed from the day-to-day operations of the cult. He would occasionally come out of seclusion to ride around Rajneeshpuram in one of his many Rolls Royces. Meanwhile, the person responsible for running all of the cult's operations was Sheela, who met daily with the Bhagwan to discuss all aspects of the businesses and operations that constituted the cult's activities.[10] Sheela had an authoritarian style of management, although she had a small group of assistants who were mostly female and whom she relied upon for input into decisions. However, she reported only to the Bhagwan, and since he was removed from direct contact with cult members, Sheela held considerable control over the cult. All members of the organizations had to accept her decisions, and if she encountered resistance or skepticism, she could expel members from Rajneeshpuram. Therefore, Sheela would have primary responsibility for problems the cult would encounter with local residents.

Although the Rajneeshees moved to Oregon to start over and establish good relationships with the surrounding community, the cult soon began to experience many of the same problems that had led to its move from India to the United States. Many people in the surrounding towns held Christian beliefs, and the religious teachings of the Rajneeshees clashed with these traditional values. However, the major source of conflict between the Rajneeshees and local residents was Oregon's strict laws placing limits on the amount of development allowed in rural areas. In an effort to circumvent these laws, the Rajneeshees manipulated the state's voter registration laws to take over the small town of Antelope, Oregon, near Rajneeshpuram.[11]

As the cult made further attempts to expand its control and development, tension with local residents only increased, and by 1984, the U.S. Attorney's office had undertaken an investigation into possible immigration violations by members of the cult, including the Bhagwan himself. Moreover, another investigation was undertaken to challenge the legality of Rajneeshpuram's incorporation as a municipality. The November elections of 1984 were approaching, and two of the three Wasco County commissioners were up for re-election. After consulting with the Bhagwan, Sheela formulated a plan to influence the outcome of the election, whereby two commissioners more sympathetic to the cult's interests would be elected. When the Rajneeshees were unsuccessful in getting enough signatures to have one of their candidates placed on the November ballot, an alternative plan was undertaken—one that was far more treacherous.

To make sure that the Wasco County election would result in defeat of the two commissioners who were seen as hostile to the goals of the cult, Sheela formulated a two-pronged attack. The first involved bringing in a large number of homeless people from around the United States to Rajneeshpuram in a "Share-a-Home" program. In exchange for housing, the homeless individuals were registered under Oregon's flexible voter registration laws and directed to vote for candidates in the local Wasco County election who were more favorable to the cult. Without one of their own candidates on the ballot, however, it was unclear if the cult had any candidates who were sympathetic to the Rajneeshees, raising doubts about the success of the voter-stacking plan.

The second prong of Sheela's plot to sway the election results involved making a large number of Wasco County voters ill so they would not be able to cast their ballot. According to one former cult member, Sheela had apparently discussed a plan with the Bhagwan to use bacterial or other biological agents to make people sick.[12] Approximately twelve individuals were involved in the attempt to develop and deploy a biological agent. The cult member primarily responsible for the program was Ma Anand Puja, whose real name was Dianne Y. Onang.[13] Puja was from the Philippines and joined the Rajneeshees in 1979. She was trained and educated as a registered nurse and ran the cult's health center. Despite the fact that Puja's position as Rajneeshpuram's leading medical authority seemed to be less dominant than other leadership positions within the cult, she wielded considerable influence and was feared by many cult members because of her tyrannical and intimidating behavior. As an example of her notorious ways, Puja was given the nickname "Dr. Mengeles," after the infamous Nazi physician known for his sadistic and inhumane experiments among inmates of concentration camps.

Although it remains unclear precisely when Puja developed her interest in biological agents, she had an intense interest in poisons and other lethal chemical and biological agents. In fact, she was suspected of having poisoned Sheela's first husband who was suffering from a potentially terminal illness. Since Puja and Sheela were extremely close and consulted regularly with the Bhagwan on administrative matters, it is not surprising that Puja became the lead person in developing a biological agent for use in Sheela's plan for influencing the local Wasco County elections.

Puja studied a number of toxic biological agents, including *salmonella typhimurium* (which causes salmonella food poisoning), *Giardia lamblia* (a microbe that causes giardiasis, a disorder characterized by severe diarrhea that is transmitted through infected rodents such as beavers), and the human immunodeficiency virus (HIV) that causes AIDS. She decided on salmonella for the attack because it was difficult to detect, easier to spread relative to the other agents she studied, and something she could obtain through licensed clinical laboratories. In Rajneeshpuram, Puja set up a clandestine laboratory where she was able to manufacture the salmonella strain. Her "germ warfare" laboratory, as it came to be known among leaders of the cult, could be dismantled quickly before law enforcement officers would be able to find it.

The first official use of salmonella by the Rajneeshees occurred on August 29, 1984, when the three sitting Wasco County commissioners came to Rajneeshpuram to collect information about the cult's operation to assist in their decision-making on matters before their board. Two of the commissioners who were seen as hostile to the cult, Judge William Hulse and Ray Matthew, were each given drinking water that was contaminated with salmonella. Each man became ill, and Judge Hulse's condition was serious enough to warrant hospitalization. There was another allegation that homeless individuals brought to Rajneeshpuram were given nonlethal toxins in order to control them and keep them placid; however, one homeless man was alleged to have died.

Sometime during the summer before the November elections, one cult member was given an eyedropper containing a brown liquid and told to place it on doorknobs and other places in Wasco County where citizens were likely to come in contact with the substance. Although it was believed that this liquid contained salmonella, this was not confirmed. Nevertheless, these activities clearly pointed to an increasing pattern of testing various methods for transmitting salmonella as preliminary stages for a larger attack.

In early September, the Rajneeshees began to pour vials of liquid containing salmonella into food products at various restaurants and supermarkets in the town of The Dalles. Over the next month, several establishments were the sites of deliberate contamination. The primary method for delivering the biological agent was to have a member of the cult conceal a plastic bag containing a light brown liquid with the salmonella agent and either pour the contents into the salad dressing or spread the liquid over the food at a salad bar. The Center for Disease Control ultimately established that 751 people became ill with salmonella food poisoning as a result of eating from the salad bars of ten local restaurants.

Although the Rajneeshees ultimately withdrew their candidate from the November ballot, and thus the salmonella poisoning did not have any apparent impact on the outcome of the election, the plot was successful in that such a large number of individuals became sick. The initial investigation into the contamination did not result in a common source for the salmonella contamination in the restaurants involved, such as a common food distributor, water source, or food supply. Moreover, neither restaurant employee error nor food handling were identified as contributing factors to the contamination.[14] Nearly a year would pass before the Rajneeshee cult was identified as being responsible for contaminating the food supplies in the restaurants, and the discovery occurred only after cult members were being investigated for other criminal activity.[15]

Despite the large membership of the Rajneeshee cult, only a small group of individuals had direct knowledge of the planning and implementation of the plot. This fact contributed to the relative success of the operation and also delayed the discovery of the source of the contamination as an intentional terrorist act. Much of the information came from detailed statements provided by David Berry Knapp, who was the mayor of Rajneeshpuram and a member of the cult's upper-level leadership.[16] Two other cult members provided detailed information about the plot that ultimately led to the arrest of a number of cult members for their participation.

Sheela ultimately faced a number of state and federal charges. She pleaded guilty in federal court to immigration fraud and setting up an illegal wiretapping system in Rajneeshpuram that allowed her to spy on cult members.[17] Her sentence was four and a half years on these charges; however, she also received a twenty-year sentence on state charges of attempted murder for her attempted poisoning of the Bhagwan's personal physician and another twenty-year sentence for setting fire to a county office. In addition, she was fined $400,000 and ordered to pay $70,000 in restitution for damage caused by the fire.

Puja was also sentenced to four and a half years in federal prison for the wiretapping charge and for her involvement in the salmonella outbreak. She was sentenced to twenty years in state prison for her involvement in the attempted murder of the Bhagwan's physician and the assault on county officials. Another cult member was sentenced to ten years for the attempted murder of the Baghwan's physician. Bhagwan Shree Rajneesh ultimately pleaded guilty to immigration fraud and agreed to pay a $400,000 fine. He left the United States and agreed not to re-enter the country without the permission of the U.S. Attorney General. For a period of time after leaving the United States, the Bhagwan had considerable difficulty finding a country that would accept him. Nevertheless, he was never prosecuted for any of the more serious crimes perpetrated by cult members, including the salmonella poisoning. He has since died.

One of the noteworthy features of the Rajneeshee case is how a small cadre of leaders in a large cult could devise, plan, and carry out an act of bioterrorism without other cult members informing the authorities or law enforcement officials. Cults, terrorist organizations, and other groups must rely on communication among members to develop plans and coordinate attacks. Therefore, terrorist communication is an area where law enforcement often focuses its counterterrorism efforts. If terrorist organizations have a weakness, it is in the realm of communication, because if statements, messages, or other forms of communication can be intercepted, then terrorist plots and attacks can be prevented.

Even large organizations and groups can be very effective at protecting themselves from intrusion by keeping the membership of planning committees to a minimum and confined only to the most trustworthy members. This is precisely what the Rajneeshee cult did and what contributed to the success of the contamination plot. Likewise, terrorist groups such as al-Qaeda communicate in ways that result in various cells being unaware of the plans of other cells. Sometimes, members of an individual cell are even unaware of the roles or responsibilities of other cell members.

Finally, it has been suggested that the true motive behind the Rajneeshee's plot is elusive. Bioterrorism expert Jessica Stern suggested that because the Rajneeshee's true motives are unclear, it is uncertain if the salmonella poisoning they carried out would fit most standard definitions of terrorism.[18] She has argued that if the cult merely wanted to make residents of The Dalles ill because of their adverse feelings toward the cult, and not to influence an audience, then the incident should not be recognized as an act of terrorism. However, it is important to note that the Rajneeshee plot occurred within the context of building political tensions between the cult and the residents of Wasco County. Moreover, subsequent interrogations of cult members who were close to the top leadership have revealed that the plot was intended to influence a local election, which is clearly a political motive. While individuals involved in the plot may have had other motives that were more personal (e.g., sadism, power), the primary motive was political, and the goal was to influence (and sicken) an audience. In every respect, the salmonella poisoning carried out by the cult members was a major bioterrorist attack that fortunately failed to achieve its ultimate goal and resulted in no fatalities.

A MEETING OF THE TERRORIST MINDS

THE CASE OF YU KIKUMURA

Consequences cannot alter statutes, but may help to fix their meaning.
—Benjamin N. Cardozo[1]

A BASIC PRINCIPLE OF AMERICAN LAW IS THAT PUNISHMENT SHOULD FIT THE crime, including the crime of terrorism. When a defendant is sentenced, the length of imprisonment or amount of money paid for a fine should be proportional to the wrongfulness of the person's actions. Although juries sometimes give input into sentencing recommendations—as when a jury in a capital case makes a recommendation for the death penalty or life without parole—it is judges who must ultimately hand down final punishment. However, judges are human, and they have personal nuances that affect the way they interpret the facts of a case, credibility of witnesses, and even the meaning of certain laws. As a result, there are often differences in the way individual judges hand out sentences in criminal cases. Two defendants who have committed the exact same crime under similar circumstances could be given sentences of different severity by judges who evaluate the case in different ways. Therefore, does punishment always fit the crime, or does it depend on the person passing judgment?

The Federal Sentencing Guidelines were developed by the United States Sentencing Commission and enacted to limit the amount of discretion federal judges had when imposing sentences in federal criminal cases.[2] The guidelines imposed a specific range of prison time that a judge could give a defendant for individual crimes, with the severity of sentences increasing proportionately with the severity of the crime. Although the guidelines were often criticized as limiting the degree of discretion a judge could have, they made the sentencing process uniform and predictable for all defendants and across the federal districts throughout the United States. Nevertheless, the Federal Sentencing Guidelines permitted judges to depart from the upper limits of a sentence and increase the severity of punishment if a case involved specific aggravating factors that warranted a harsher sentence. Some of the aggravating factors included possessing extremely large quantities of illegal drugs, a defendant's lying under oath at trial, or defrauding someone out of a very large sum of money.[3] There were also some mitigating factors that permitted judges to reduce a sentence, such as a defendant committing a crime under extreme emotional distress or cooperating with prosecutors in the prosecution of other defendants. But these limiting factors tended to have much less impact than the aggravating factors.

Although the Federal Sentencing Guidelines remained controversial in the decades following their enactment, they were applied regularly until 2004 when the U.S. Supreme Court issued its highly publicized ruling in *Blakely v. Washington*.[4] In *Blakely*, the defendant pleaded guilty to kidnapping his estranged wife, and the judge increased the sentence to seven and a half years from the four-year, five-month sentence prescribed under the Federal Sentencing Guidelines. The aggravating factor was the judge's finding that Blakely had been deliberately cruel in carrying out his crime. On appeal, the Supreme Court held that the judge's increase was improper because the aggravating factor had not been presented to a jury and found to be true beyond a reasonable doubt. The far-reaching implications of the *Blakely* ruling is that juries, and not judges, should make the determinations of fact that increase sentences for criminal defendants who are found guilty of federal crimes.[5] The *Blakely* ruling ultimately led to a pair of Supreme Court Cases in January 2005 that finally held the Federal Sentencing Guidelines to be unconstitutional. In *United States v. Booker* and *United States v. Fanfan*, the Supreme Court held that a defendant's Sixth Amendment right to a trial by jury required that the Federal Sentencing Guidelines merely advise judges and should not dictate mandatory sentences.[6]

The recent concern over the proper formula for fixing sentences in federal criminal cases brings to mind the case of a thwarted terrorist attack that was planned in the United States and resulted in a conviction and harsh sentence for the would-be bomber. A noteworthy feature of the case was the largest upward departure from the Federal Sentencing Guidelines, in terms of both percentage and absolute time, that ever occurred in the federal court system. In addition, the case involved a terrorist tied to a small but highly dangerous group with connections to other terrorist organizations and state-sponsors of global terrorism.

At around seven o'clock on the morning of April 12, 1988, New Jersey State Trooper Robert Cieplensky was patrolling one of the service stations on the New Jersey Turnpike.[7] The area was known to be the site of various assaults, robberies, and sex offenses that had occurred in recent years and where trafficking in illicit weapons and drugs was also known to have occurred. Cieplensky's attention was drawn to a disheveled man who began to act suspiciously after making eye contact with the police officer. The man was Yu Kikumura, who had entered the United States illegally using an altered passport issued under the alias of "Masatoshi Kishizono."

Cieplensky noticed that Kikumura began "milling around" and "walking in circles at a very slow pace" after heading toward a restaurant and that he changed his course back toward the parking area upon seeing the police officer.[8] According the Cieplensky, Kikumura did not fit the profile of a typical Monday morning traveler passing through the service area, who was described as:

> A gentleman going to work, dressed cleanly and/or neatly with a direct purpose in mind, stopping at the service area to use the rest room facilities or to get a cup of coffee or some breakfast or to use the telephone or to service his vehicle.[9]

Although Kikumura would later claim that the officer's attention and suspicions were improper and merely used as a pretext to search his vehicle, Cieplenski kept observing Kikumura's behavior. After walking around without clear purpose and glancing occasionally at the officer, Kikumura got into his car and left at high speed. At that moment, Cieplenski pulled Kikumura over for driving in an unsafe manner and asked for identification.

Kikumura produced an international driver's license, as well as temporary registration and insurance certificates for the car, all issued in the name of Masatoshi Kishizono. As Cieplenski was reviewing Kikumura's documents, he noticed a number of cardboard boxes in the rear seat of Kikumura's vehicle that contained gunpowder and metal shot. The amount of material in Kikumura's possession led Cieplenski to suspect the materials were not for personal use, so the officer conducted a more thorough search and found a number of cylindrical objects made out of fire extinguishers that appeared to be bombs. Kikumura was arrested and charged in a twelve-count federal indictment with interstate transport of explosives, intent to destroy property and harm people, unlawful possession of unregistered explosives, and violations of various immigration laws.[10]

A subsequent investigation of Kikumura's background and behavior since entering the United States revealed that he was a member of the Japanese Red Army (JRA). The JRA is a terrorist organization founded on a combination of leftist political philosophy and Japanese nationalism.[11] Like other left-wing terrorist groups, the JRA strongly opposes the control of economic resources by corporations. The origins of the group can be traced back to the 1950s during a period of increasing social unrest in Japan that was due, in large measure, to the economic pressures and cultural problems that emerged in the wake of Japan's defeat in World War II. During the 1960s, the wide protest movements on university campuses in the United States was mirrored by students in Japan who opposed the Vietnam War and U.S. military presence in Japan. The JRA emerged from a group of Japanese university students who committed their first terrorist act in 1970 by hijacking an airplane to North Korea.[12]

Throughout the 1970s, the JRA forged strong ties with other terrorist organizations, such as the Popular Front for the Liberation of Palestine, and attacked Israeli targets to show its commitment to fighting what it perceived to be imperialism and capitalism. Although the JRA was a relatively small terrorist organization, it had an international presence and members often operated as "mercenary terrorists" by making contacts with other radical groups and carrying out attacks on targets that were meaningful to these other groups.[13]

However, the JRA leadership in Japan was considered unstable, so one of its prominent leaders, Fusako Shigenobou, established a permanent JRA presence in the Middle East. The Federal Bureau of Investigation had a confidential informant placed inside a terrorist training camp located in the Bekaa Valley in Lebanon.[14] Although the terrorist camp was located in the Middle East and provided training to members of terrorist organizations devoted to attacking Israel, other terrorists from around the world also received training in the camp. Sometime in 1984, the terrorist organization that ran the camp developed a close working relationship with the JRA. The informant told the FBI that a small number of Asian individuals came to the camp and received training in bomb construction. Among the various procedures involved in the training were how to use ammonium nitrate to construct explosives, the manufacturing of detonators from various chemical compounds, and the use of flash bulbs as detonators for explo-sives.[15] Because the Asian men often wore masks during their stay at the camp, it was difficult for the informant to provide definitive identification.

In April 1985, three members of the JRA came to the camp for a week of training on the use of remote-control devices in the detonation of bombs. One of the men was Junzo Okudaira, who would later establish a permanent residence in the camp, along with several other JRA members. From the spring of 1985 into the spring of 1986, a number of JRA mem-bers made their way through the camp to receive training in terrorist tech-niques, including the art of constructing intricate bombs. One of the individuals who had a close connection with the training camp was Kikumura.

In May of 1986, Kikumura was arrested in the Netherlands for trying to smuggle "a cardboard orange-drink container filled with over two pounds of a high explosive."[16] As Kikumura was attempting to enter the country, authorities at the airport found a number of detonators hidden inside a radio, along with explosive material. According to investigators, the detona-tors were so well concealed, they appeared to be part of the radio.[17] Kikumura was highly skilled at not only building bombs but also conceal-ing his illegal activities from authorities. Although he was arrested and charged with possession of explosives, a technical violation of Dutch law prevented prosecutors from moving forward with the case, and Kikumura was released.

By the fall of 1986, Kikumura re-appeared at the Bekaa Valley terrorist training camp and boasted to the informant that he had been to several countries around the world. He was proficient in the use of hand weapons and had the working skills of a highly competent and dangerous terrorist. When Kikumura appeared in the camp, the JRA had a steady presence; its leader, Fusako Shigenobu, oversaw all higher level operations. During one of the JRA's many meetings at the camp, the FBI informant heard Shigenobu state that "the JRA's main enemy was the United States and that they wanted U.S. military bases out of Japan and opposed U.S. imperial-ism."[18] Shigenobu also told the informant that the JRA was planning a ter-rorist strike against the United States on its own soil. Furthermore, the FBI later learned that Shigenobu traveled to Libya in June 1987 after receiving an invitation; she never returned to the camp after her visit.

It is interesting to note that Shigenobu's travel to Libya occurred at a time when President Ronald Reagan had identified Libyan leader

Muammar Qaddafi as a state sponsor of terrorism and called Libya "a threat to the national security … of the United States."[19] On April 5, 1986, a discotheque in West Berlin, Germany, known to be frequented by members of the U.S. military, was bombed. A U.S. soldier and a Turkish woman were killed in the attack, and nearly 230 people, including fifty U.S. soldiers, were injured. The Reagan administration obtained strong evidence that Libyan-sponsored terrorists were responsible for the attack, so on April 14, the U.S. attacked several targets in Libya, including a family compound where Qaddafi and his family were sleeping.[20] Libya responded with a number of terrorist attacks directed at the United States. Shigenobu was angered by the U.S. attack on Libya and traveled there soon after. She was apparently set on using JRA resources and personnel to assist Libya in its international assault on the United States.

An understanding of the background of the JRA and the relationship of its leadership in the Middle East to Libya is important for having a full appreciation of how Kikumura ended up in the United States and comprehending his terrorist intentions. Two JRA terrorists—Kikumura and Okudaira—planned parallel terrorist attacks against U.S. military targets in response to the Libyan bombings. Okudaira became the prime suspect in a bombing in Naples, Italy, that occurred on April 14, 1988—two days after Kikumura's arrest at the New Jersey service area. Okudaira set off a car bomb outside a U.S. officer's club that killed five people and injured eighteen others.[21]

The FBI investigation into Kikumura's actions leading up to his arrest revealed that he began his planned attack on American soil around February 1988 when he obtained fraudulent passports in Europe and opened a Swiss bank account using an alias in order to fund his operation.[22] These actions implied that Kikumura had "organizational, technical, and financial support" in carrying out his plan.[23] In other words, Kikumura was supported by JRA money and technical know-how, with additional support from Libya and terrorist training operations in the Bekaa Valley.

Because Kikumura was fluent in English and had forged passports, he entered the United States on March 8, 1988 without incident. He began a lengthy series of activities that were intended to allow him to assemble his bombs and avoid arousing the suspicion of law enforcement.[24] He rented an apartment, purchased an unassuming vehicle, and drove nearly 7,000 miles around the United States in the span of one month to purchase the various materials he needed to build his explosive devices.[25] For example, during the last two weeks of March 1988, Kikumura visited such locations as New York City, Dimondale in Michigan, Chicago, Murfreesboro in Tennessee, and Lexington, Kentucky. His travel was "undertaken with the intent and purpose to facilitate the undetected gathering of the elements for, and manufacture of, powerful anti-personnel bombs."[26] He bought epoxy, wire, and contact cement in Lexington and switches and an electric circuit tester in West Virginia. In Pennsylvania, he bought flash bulbs to be used in a time-delay fuse. The lead shot he purchased was to be placed in the bombs and to serve as shrapnel that would shred flesh and wreak destruction, resulting in death or severe maiming to those near the blast.

Kikumura was represented by the two famed New York City attorneys, William Kunstler and Ronald Kuby, who would figure prominently in the defense of terrorist suspects in other cases, including the assassination of Meir Kahane and the first World Trade Center bombing case in 1993. Following Kikumura's arrest and indictment, his attorneys sought to have the physical evidence seized from his car suppressed by claiming that Cieplensky's traffic stop, search, and arrest violated Kikumura's Fourth Amendment rights. Even though Kikumura was not a U.S. citizen and had entered the country illegally, he was still entitled to the protection of rights granted under the U.S. Constitution. At his suppression hearing, Kikumura testified that the items seized by Cieplensky were in the trunk of his car and not visible as the police officer had claimed. Although Kikumura provided a vastly different account of how the search of his vehicle and subsequent arrest had occurred, the presiding U.S. District Court Judge, Alfred J. Lechner, Jr., did not lend any credibility to Kikumura's testimony and denied the motion to have the evidence suppressed.[27]

Kikumura was scheduled to go on trial in November 1988, but his attorneys agreed to a stipulated set of facts that were outlined in the government's indictment, presumably because the physical and circumstantial evidence against Kikumura was overwhelming. He therefore waived a jury trial.[28] His primary defense was the illegality of the search of his car, and his attorneys wanted to preserve the record for appeal to a higher court. The real surprise came, however, following Kikumura's conviction.

Judge Lechner found Kikumura guilty of transporting and receiving explosive materials through interstate commerce without a permit, transporting and receiving explosive materials with intent to damage personal property, possession of a firearm and ammunition by an illegal alien, unlawful possession of a firearm, and various violations of the immigration laws.

According to the Federal Sentencing Guidelines, Kikumura was initially facing a total of twenty-seven to thirty-three months in prison, fines ranging from $6,000 to $60,000 and a term of supervised release following completion of his sentence.[29] However, Judge Lechner found that the Sentencing Commission did not take into account Kikumura's terrorist motives and the fact that he intended to cause death or serious injury to other people. The judge departed from the Federal Sentencing Guidelines and increased Kikumura's sentence to 360 months in prison—a total of thirty years. Judge Lechner ordered that upon completion of his sentence, Kikumura be deported and not allowed to re-enter the United States.[30]

The severity of Judge Lechner's sentence was based on a number of aggravating factors. Kikumura's terrorist motives were noted by examining his training and connection to the Bekaa Valley training camp. In addition, Judge Lechner noted the parallels between Kikumura's plan and the successful bombing in Naples, Italy by his terrorist associate, Okudaira, just two days following Kikumura's arrest. Both Okudaira and Kikumura were JRA members, used altered passports to enter countries illegally, used rental cars and paid cash to avoid detection, built explosive devises with similar timing mechanisms, and coordinated their attacks to occur nearly simultaneously. When Kikumura was arrested, he had a map of New York City that marked the location of a Navy and Marine recruiting station.[31] When Kikumura was arrested, he was apparently headed to New York City to bomb the military recruiting stations on the same date that Okudaira bombed the U.S. Officer's club in Naples, Italy.

Furthermore, Kikumura's bombs were intricate and sophisticated. According to the FBI's investigation:

Kikumura had sawed the top off a fire extinguisher, hollowed out its contents, and filled the extinguisher with about three pounds of gunpowder, some wadding, about three pounds of lead shot, and a flashbulb connected to some wire running out of the top of the extinguisher. The bombs would detonate when an electric current passing down the wire caused the bulb to flash. The heat from the flash would then burn the gunpowder, producing a build-up of pressure in the extinguisher and resulting in an explosion that would spray lead shot and metal fragments from the fire extinguisher in all directions.[32]

From all of the evidence, Judge Lechner concluded that Kikumura was a terrorist, extremely dangerous, and intent on not only damaging property but killing people. In his sentencing opinion, the judge noted:

The need for self defense, to protect the public from additional crimes by the defendant, is compelling. Kikumura is dangerous. It is not only probable, it borders on certainty, that he will commit similar offenses in the future given the opportunity to do so. These offenses could not provide a more clear example of the need for specific deterrence with regard to an individual. . . . To permit Kikumura to mingle among the citizens of this or any other society before lengthy debilitation in the most secure prison facility is to invite not only him, but indeed others, to effect mind numbing calamity.[33]

Judge Lechner therefore used the aggravating factors of Kikumura's terrorist motives and his intent to harm others to increase the sentence dramatically.

Of course, Kikumura appealed his sentence, claiming among other things that Judge Lechner's departure was extreme and unwarranted under the Federal Sentencing Guidelines. The United States Court of Appeals for the Third Circuit agreed with Judge Lechner, finding that it was reasonable to infer Kikumura intended to kill people with his bombs, and a departure upward from the Federal Sentencing Guidelines was appropriate.[34] However, the appellate court found that the legal standard relied upon by Judge Lechner to support the aggravating factor of Kikumura's intent to kill—preponderance of the evidence—was erroneous and that the more appropriate standard should have been a higher test of clear and convincing proof. As a result, the court recommended Kikumura's sentence be 210 to 262 months[35]—the equivalent of about seventeen and a half to just under twenty-two years.

Kikumura's case was sent back to Judge Lechner for re-sentencing. When the convicted terrorist appeared on March 1, 1991, he was re-sentenced to 262 months in prison, a term of three years supervised release following his release from prison, and a $600 assessment for court costs.[36]

Although Kikumura appealed his sentence once again—this time on the grounds that he did not have legal counsel of his choice and that the proof in his case did not warrant such a severe sentence—the appellate court affirmed his sentence.

There were two interesting developments in the Kikumura case that occurred in the years following his sentencing. Both had no significant bearing on the outcome, but illustrate how some terrorism cases that make their way through the criminal justice system may be revisited from time to time. In February 1996, the FBI examiner who had conducted the analysis of Kikumura's bombs, J. Thomas Thurman, came under scrutiny when Frederick Whitehurst, a Special Supervisory agent for the FBI, made allegations of impropriety in FBI laboratory procedures.[37] Whitehurst alleged that Thurman testified falsely in Kikumura's case about specific tests that had been performed on evidence; violated FBI procedures by testifying outside his area of expertise; and misled the court by suggesting incorrectly that Kikumura intended to make a large bomb out of ammonium nitrate and other chemicals. However, a government investigation found that Thurman had done nothing wrong in Kikumura's case and did not provide testimony that was biased or speculative.

Also, nearly ten years after his conviction, Kikumura filed a civil suit against the warden of the federal penitentiary in Florence, Colorado, where he is serving out his sentence.[38] Kikumura claimed that his First and Fifth Amendment rights under the U.S. Constitution were violated when the warden prevented a minister from visiting Kikumura because the minister was Methodist and Kikumura had identified himself as a Buddhist. The proposed visit therefore failed to meet the Federal Bureau of Prison's standards for pastoral visits. On appeal, Kikumura had his one modest success within the U.S. legal system when the appellate court held that the trial judge had improperly dismissed Kikumura's claim and that he should be allowed to proceed forward with his allegation against the warden.

Despite these interesting sidebars in the Kikumura case, there are a number of important issues that were raised in the case. First, an alert New Jersey State Trooper identified Kikumura as a suspicious individual and arrested him lawfully. These actions thwarted a potentially deadly terrorist attack and saved innocent lives. Whether the officer was right or wrong in relying on a profile of a typical traveler at the service area to identify Kikumura as a suspicious individual, the fact that the arrest yielded a large number of potentially deadly bombs and a dangerous international terrorist is likely to be cited by those who support the use of some form of profiling to prevent terrorism. Second, the case exemplifies a common phrase often used in describing political conflicts, namely "The enemy of my enemy is my friend." The Japanese Red Army had long identified the United States as an enemy and trained with other terrorist groups in the Middle East as a way of showing solidarity and commitment to a common cause. When Libya and the United States engaged in a series of military confrontations in the 1980s, the Japanese Red Army took it as an opportunity to join forces and attack the enemy it shared with Libya. Kikumura's planned attack was a direct result of this conflict. Finally, the case illustrates the use of harsh criminal sentences for international terrorists as a means of preventing further attacks. Although it is doubtful that Judge Lechner's lengthy sentence would deter other terrorists who are bent on harming the United States, it served as a deterrent to Kikumura, who was prevented from being granted an early release so he might perpetrate other attacks.

FLASHPOINT

THE ASSASSINATION OF
RABBI MEIR KAHANE

Certain signs precede certain events.

—Cicero[1]

THE LESSONS OF HISTORY OFTEN TEACH US TO PAY ATTENTION NOT ONLY TO the causes of large-scale tragedies like 9/11 but causes of small-scale incidents that foreshadow dangerous trends in national and international political affairs. During the years bridging the end of the twentieth century through the beginning of the twenty-first century, the United States experienced the two deadliest terrorist attacks in its history—the Oklahoma City bombing in 1995 and the attacks of September 11, 2001. Much of the nation's preoccupation with terrorism during the 1980s was focused on events overseas, such as the Marine barracks bombing in Lebanon in 1983, the kidnapping of Westerners who were held hostage by foreign terrorist organizations, and the downing of Pan Am flight 103 over Lockerbie, Scotland in 1988. However, a significant assassination occurred on November 5, 1990 in New York City that clearly showed international political violence spurred by Middle Eastern conflicts was gaining firm roots on American soil.

The assassin's target was the highly controversial Jewish militant, Rabbi Meir Kahane. At the time, Kahane's murder appeared to be an isolated act of violence prompted by the anger of a devout Muslim over Kahane's fiery and provocative statements. However, any serious discussion of the events of September 11 and the emergence of international terrorism as a threat to the security of the United States recognizes the assassination as a harbinger of the terrorism that was yet to come.

Kahane was an Orthodox rabbi who founded the Jewish Defense League (JDL) in the late 1960s.[2] The JDL was based in New York City and fashioned as a vigilante group designed to protect Jewish residents in the United States from racially and ethnically motivated violence. Some experts who have studied Kahane's career as a right-wing radical have suggested he patterned the JDL after the radical Zionist group, the Stern Gang, which engaged in a number of terrorist acts during the 1940s to secure an independent Jewish state. Kahane endorsed the use of violence to protect Jewish interests, as is evident in one of his famous quotes: "Jews who defend other Jews with violence are right."[3] Moreover, Kahane advocated the removal of all Arab people from the biblically defined borders of Israel.

Within a couple of years of its founding, the JDL began a campaign of terrorist acts in the United States directed at the Soviet Union. During the early 1970s, the JDL was "the only group which deployed tactical violence on American soil in order to change the policy of a foreign entity."[4] Its goal was to change Soviet policies restricting the emigration of Soviet Jews to Israel. Although the JDL continued engaging in terrorist acts within the United States for several years, Kahane's involvement and influence diminished when he emigrated to Israel in 1971 and formed the Kach movement ("Kach" means "Thus" or "This is the way.")[5] He espoused strong commitment to the Jewish faith, but was an ultra Israeli nationalist who was anti-Arab and an advocate of violence. Although Kahane managed to get himself elected to the Israeli parliament in 1984, his Kach movement was banned because it was considered racist. Kahane was expelled from his seat in 1988. Around the time the Kach movement was banned in Israel, the head of the JDL was sentenced to ten years in a U.S. federal prison for his part in a series of bombings targeting Soviet interests in the United States during the mid-1980s.[6] For over two decades, Kahane had expanded his violent right-wing agenda in two stable democracies—the United States and Israel.

When he took the podium to speak at the Marriott Hotel in the heart of New York City on the evening of November 5, 1990, Kahane addressed topics about which he had long been preaching, including the immigration of Jews to Israel and the forcible removal of Arabs from the occupied territories. At the back of the lecture hall where Kahane spoke stood a thirty-five-year-old Egyptian-born man by the name of El Sayyid Nosair.[7] Accompanying Nosair to the speaking engagement was a friend by the name of Bilall Alkaisi who, like Nosair, was armed with a weapon. Both Nosair and Alkaisi and been following Kahane for over a year, often appearing at speaking engagements where the controversial rabbi presented his extremist views.[8] Their interest in Kahane was not so much the content of his speeches, but the tightness of the security surrounding the speaker; Nosair and Alkaisi were constantly surveying Kahane's protection and agreed they would kill the rabbi if the opportunity presented itself.

On the evening of November 5, after Alkaisi had gone to the men's room, Nosair saw an opening and approached Kahane as he was speaking with a group of people who had listened to his speech. With a coat draped over his arm, Nosair took a .357 Magnum from his waistband and waited for a man to finish videotaping Kahane so no permanent record would be made of what was about to take place.[9] Once the camera stopped recording, Nosair aimed his handgun from his hip and fired twice at Kahane. One of the shots hit Kahane in the chest, and the other hit him in the neck. The mortally wounded Rabbi fell to the floor as Nosair spun around quickly and forced his way out through the hysterical crowd.

As he lay on the ground, Kahane was unable to speak because blood from the wound to his neck had filled his mouth. While lying on the ground, he raised one finger in a Jewish tradition that signifies a silent rendering of a Hebrew prayer.[10] A short time after being rushed to New York City's Bellevue Hospital, Kahane was pronounced dead.

Meanwhile, Nosair had found his escape from the hotel to be less than swift and simple. In the midst of the chaos that erupted following the shooting, the assassin yelled, "It's Allah's will" as he ran toward the door.[11] Before he could get out of the meeting room, Nosair was grabbed by a seventy-year-old Jewish activist by the name of Irving Franklin. Nosair shot Franklin in the leg and continued out of the hotel. Nosair saw a taxi cab at the curb that he thought was being driven by another accomplice, an Egyptian-born immigrant by the name of Mahmoud Abouhalima.[12] Moments earlier, a security officer from the hotel had directed Abouhalima to move his cab from the front of the hotel, so Nosair was surprised when he entered the cab and found a stranger behind the wheel.

After Nosair ordered the drive to leave, the cab managed to make it to the next corner before a red light stopped the flow of traffic. A number of people from the Marriott hotel were now searching the street for Kahane's assassin. Nosair attempted to hide low in the back seat, but one of the individuals from the hotel spotted him and started banging on the cab. In the confusion, the frightened cab driver bolted from his vehicle, and Nosair jumped out of the opposite side. Carlos Acosta, a U.S. Postal Service police officer, happened to be standing in the entrance of a post office near where Nosair had emerged from the cab.

The officer noticed the commotion, initially thought he was witnessing a robbery, and took out his weapon. Nosair, on the other hand, mistook Acosta for a New York City police officer and realized that he would have to get by the uniformed officer if he was going to be successful in his escape. As Acosta confronted Nosair, the two men fired their weapons simultaneously.[13] Nosair managed to get off two shots; one hit Acosta in the chest, but the bulletproof vest the officer was wearing deflected the bullet into his shoulder, and the second luckily missed. Acosta got off just one shot that hit Nosair in the neck and ruptured the assassin's jugular vein.[14] Arriving shortly after Kahane, Nosair was taken to Bellevue Hospital and survived.

The initial reaction by New York City police officers investigating Kahane's murder was to view the incident as an isolated crime. Joseph R. Borrellit, the chief of detectives, told reporters that "What we have and all we know is that we have a lone gunman who committed a homicide in New York."[15] However, further investigation into the backgrounds of Nosair and his associates revealed that the assassination was anything but the work of a lone gunman. Evidence emerged that Kahane's murder was carried out by individuals who were part of a broader terrorist network.

Born in Egypt, Nosair entered the United States on July 14, 1981 and settled in Pittsburgh, Pennsylvania. He became a permanent resident on April 7, 1983, when he married a U.S. citizen who had converted to Islam.[16] In 1985, he moved to New York City after he had gotten into a conflict with a woman who was to perform housekeeping for Nosair's family. The woman accused Nosair of sexual assault, and a second woman also came forward with a similar claim. However, the charges against Nosair were dropped when the imam of his mosque intervened. Nosair became an American citizen under the name of El Sayyed Abdulazziz el Sayyed in September 1989.

During the time he spent in the New York City area, Nosair worked for the city as a maintenance worker in the Criminal Courts building in lower Manhattan.[17] To several of his neighbors, he appeared to be a responsible and quiet man with a devoted wife and three children. But Nosair also had a secret side to his life. A search of his possessions following his arrest revealed that he had three different driver's licenses, each with a different address. He became deeply involved with the Masjid al-Salam mosque in Jersey City, New Jersey, where Sheik Omar Ahmad Abdul Rahman preached. Rahman was a radical who preached the overthrow of secular

Arab governments and who had been imprisoned, but later acquitted of involvement in the assassination of Egyptian leader Anwar Sadat. One worshiper at the Masjid al-Salam mosque was an Egyptian-born man living in the United States who had once spent time in a federal prison for attempting to smuggle explosives, detonators, and a handgun to the Palestinian Liberation Organization.[18] Rahman, who was also known as the "blind sheik" because a childhood illness had robbed him of his eyesight, continued his fiery sermons over the years, and an informant for the FBI would later report that Nosair and Rahman had met together at a restaurant a few days before Kahane's murder.[19]

A year after the assassination, Nosair finally went on trial. He was represented by William Kunstler, an attorney known for his willingness to take on high-profile cases and who had represented other accused terrorists such as Yu Kikumura, the member of the Japanese Red Army who had been convicted for plotting to bomb military targets in the New York City area a few years earlier. Initially, Kunstler attempted to lay groundwork for an insanity plea, but Nosair would have none of it. He claimed not to have fired the gun that killed Kahane and alleged further that the controversial rabbi had been killed by one of his own followers.[20] As outrageous as Nosair's claim was, a number of factors ultimately led to his acquittal on the most serious charges he faced. His legal case was of considerable interest to Muslim extremists, and money for his criminal defense poured in from around the world; it is even alleged that Osama bin Laden contributed $20,000 to Nosair's defense fund.[21]

Because Kahane's body had been released for burial before an autopsy could be performed, Nosair's gun could not be linked to the crime. Furthermore, none of the eyewitnesses who fingered Nosair could say that they had seen him fire the gun. In what many observers call one of the greatest perversions of justice in the history of New York jurisprudence, Nosair was acquitted of Kahane's murder, and Kunstler was hoisted on the shoulders of Abouhalima—the man who was supposed to have driven Nosair's escape vehicle and who had not been charged—in a gesture of triumph.

However, Nosair was still convicted of shooting Franklin and Acosta during his escape and was sentenced to seven and a half to twenty-two and a half years in prison.[22] As for Nosair's accomplice, Alkaisi, he managed to evade capture and would later take part in the early planning stages of the first World Trade Center bombing in 1993. He was a trained explosives expert who had a falling out with other members of the World Trade Center plot and left the group.

One of the tragic legacies of Nosair's case lies in the missed opportunities to identify the broader threat Kahane's killer and his associates posed to the security of the United States. A few days after his arrest, FBI agents removed several boxes of documents and other materials from Nosair's home that provided evidence of other terrorist acts being planned, including the 1993 World Trade Center bombing. One of the major errors made in the case was in the handling of the numerous boxes of files and documents taken from Nosair's home. Included among the materials were diagrams, photos, military papers, and bomb-making manuals that could have provided law enforcement officers with evidence of the vast nature of the terrorist threat. Unfortunately, many of these materials were in Arabic, and for several years, they went untranslated until after the first attack on the World Trade Center in 1993.

Abouhalima would later be arrested as a co-conspirator in the bombing. One New York City police lieutenant, Eddie Norris, commented on the portentous nature of the Nosair case:

> Of course, like everyone else involved, I vastly underestimated the significance of Nosair. Nosair turned out to be the pioneer of a new kind of terrorism, the first to act out the malicious ideology of a rogue strain of Islam, that would eventually seek to eviscerate the American way of life. More than a symbol, he would prove to be, even as he sat behind bars, an instigator and source of inspiration for other like-minded militants. In fact, in any attempt to understand the events of September 11, 2001, it makes sense to begin with El Sayyid Nosair. That's where the law enforcement aspect of the September 11 story began, and where American law enforcement agencies first revealed themselves to be institutionally ill-equipped for the war this new enemy had brought to U.S. shores.[23]

After he was sent to prison, Nosair continued to receive a number of visitors who would later be convicted of the World Trade Center bombing, including Abouhalima and others. He remained convinced that he would be released from prison without having to serve out his entire sentence and even developed various plots to have his terrorist associates break him out of prison. One plot called for a dramatic storming of Attica prison, and in another plan, he suggested that three of his associates kidnap former President Richard Nixon and ex-Secretary of State Henry Kissinger in order to bargain for his release.[24] These far-flung aspirations contributed to the common, but dangerously erroneous, impression that Nosair and his associates were clumsy and unsophisticated. If anything, Nosair's diligence in trying to find a way to get himself out of prison merely illustrates the undying conviction he held to furthering his terrorist cause, and his case provides a vivid example of the undying commitment many terrorists have to attacking their enemies. With the benefit of hindsight, Kahane's assassination marked an important turn in the history of terrorism in the United States in that it brought the violence of the Middle Eastern conflict onto American soil.

INTERNATIONAL MANHUNT

THE CASE OF MIR AIMAL KASI[1]

*After all, the eleventh commandment (thou shalt not be found out) is
the only one that is virtually impossible to keep in these days.*
—Bertha Buxton[2]

IN THE YEARS FOLLOWING THE SEPTEMBER 11 ATTACKS, ONE OF THE LIN-
gering frustrations has been the fact that Osama bin Laden has evaded capture and remains the most wanted terrorist in the world. There has been
rampant speculation in the media and among various national security and
law enforcement experts about the general vicinity where bin Laden may
be hiding. If we are to understand the complex issues involved in conducting an international manhunt for terrorists, one significant case that has
often been overlooked is the search for Mir Aimal Kasi, the man who killed
two CIA employees and injured several others in a shooting spree near the
entrance to CIA headquarters on Route 123 in Fairfax County, Virginia in
January 1993.[3] The Pulitzer Prize-winning author Steve Coll, who has
conducted extensive research on counterterrorism issues, has noted that
"the first formal CIA plan to capture or kill Osama bin Laden began its life
as a blueprint to arrest Mir Amal [*sic*] Kasi."[4]

Born and raised in Pakistan, Kasi was the son of a wealthy business man.
His father owned a number of hotels and orchards near Quetta, Pakistan, in
the Baluchistan province that borders southern Afghanistan.[5] Kasi's mother,
who was his father's second wife, died when Kasi was nineteen. Like bin
Laden, Kasi came from a prosperous family and was afforded many privileges that were unavailable to those from lower socioeconomic classes. He
attended Baluchistan University and earned a master's degree in English literature in 1989.[6] In the same year Kasi earned his degree, his father died

unexpectedly from a heart attack. At the age of twenty-six, Kasi was unmarried, an orphan, and had no family grounding. Yet he had the financial means to travel. After spending a period of time in Germany, Kasi arrived in the United States in 1991. He took up residence in an apartment in Reston, Virginia that he shared with a friend named Zahed Mir.[7] Kasi found a job working as a driver for a local courier service. His intelligence and education afforded him skills to find a job that allowed him to become familiar with northern Virginia and the area surrounding CIA headquarters.

A number of factors contributed to Kasi's feeling estranged in America. During the two years between his arrival in the United States and his shooting attack, he spent many hours watching the news, which was dominated by reports on the Gulf War, the Israeli-Palestinian conflict, and turmoil in the Middle East.[8] Although it remains unclear when he became radicalized in his beliefs, he told his roommate Mir that he was considering "doing something big."[9] In a statement he later gave, Kasi admitted that he was angry over the fact that the U.S. had attacked Iraq, "upset with the CIA because of their involvement with Muslim countries," and "concerned with [the] killing of Pakistanians by U.S. components."[10] In January 1993, Kasi began to consider going on a shooting spree at either the Israeli Embassy in Washington, D.C., or CIA headquarters. He decided that CIA headquarters was a softer target "because CIA officials are not armed."[11]

A few days before the attack, Kasi went to a gun shop in northern Virginia and purchased an AK-47 assault rifle and 150 rounds of ammunition. Although he anticipated police would confront him during the shooting and he might be killed, Kasi purchased an airline ticket back to Pakistan in case he was lucky enough to escape.[12] On the morning of January 25, 1993, Kasi took his rifle, got into his car, and drove to the entrance of CIA headquarters on Route 123. With cars of federal employees lined up waiting to enter the headquarters, Kasi pulled his car into the left turn lane and stopped his vehicle. He opened his door and stepped out into the road carrying his AK-47. His first murder victim was a twenty-eight-year-old CIA agent in the clandestine service by the name of Frank Darling.[13] Kasi fired through the rear window of Darling's car as the agent's wife sat in the passenger seat. After the first shot, Kasi walked around the vehicle and shot Darling three more times. Kasi then began walking down a line of cars and fired at four other men in their automobiles. One of the men, Lansing Bennett, who died as a result of his wounds, was a sixty-six-year-old physician who analyzed the health of foreign leaders for the CIA. The three others, Nicholas Starr, Calvin Morgan, and Stephen Williams, were wounded in the attack but survived.[14]

Kasi later admitted that he made a conscious decision not to shoot women because to do so would have violated his religious beliefs. As for his male victims, Kasi was aiming for their chests. He fired off about ten rounds, looked around, and found "there wasn't anybody else left to shoot," so he got into his car and drove to a local park to hide.[15] When he thought it was safe, Kasi returned to his apartment, hid the rifle, drove to a hotel, flew to Pakistan the next day, and disappeared.

Meanwhile, law enforcement officials managed to piece together evidence identifying Kasi as the person responsible for the shooting attack. Two days later, Mir reported his roommate as a missing person to the police. On February 8, nearly two weeks after the attack, police officers came to Mir's apartment and conducted a search.[16] Among the pieces of evidence found were the AK-47 rifle, ammunition matching that used in the attack, and evidence that Kasi had purchased the weapon three days before the attack. An indictment was issued on February 16, charging Kasi with capital murder, malicious wounding, and five counts of using a firearm in the commission of a felony. Despite police officers having the identity of their suspect, Kasi remained an international fugitive whose exact whereabouts was unknown.

The CIA was able to track Kasi's general location to where Osama bin Laden is believed to be hiding—the rough terrain and lawless regions of the border between Afghanistan and Pakistan.[17] Although agents in the Counterterrorism Center at CIA headquarters asked agents in a Pakistan-based CIA substation to recruit local operatives who could help capture Kasi, several factors hindered their efforts. For instance, no one appeared willing to seek the multi-million-dollar reward money that was being offered to anyone who could deliver Kasi's exact whereabouts because under regional codes of conduct, "anyone exposed as Kasi's betrayer risked not only his own life but his family's as well."[18] People who are native to the region believe that to betray a fellow countryman to outsiders is an offense warranting death. Nevertheless, the Counterterrorism Center was able to form a team of Afghan tribal leaders to assist in the pursuit of Kasi by supplying the leaders with money, weapons, vehicles, communications equipment, and other materials to support their individual causes. The CIA also provided a locating device that could be used to signal if Kasi was captured so U.S. counterterrorism agents could move in to grab the fugitive.

In addition to the logistical problems of finding Kasi, there were a number of legal and foreign policy issues complicating the process of bringing the CIA shooting suspect to justice. One issue was whether U.S. law permitted Kasi to be abducted from a foreign country by U.S. agents and returned for criminal prosecution.[19] Another troubling matter was the tenuous, and sometimes conflicted, relationship between the CIA and the Pakistani intelligence service.[20] The strained relations made it difficult, if not impossible, for U.S. counterterrorism officials looking for Kasi to have access to information and local law enforcement resources in the regions of Pakistan where Kasi was believed to be hiding.

Like the search for bin Laden, the Kasi manhunt turned up very little in the way of successful leads. The fourth anniversary of the attack soon came and went with Kasi still at large and his whereabouts unknown. The failure to find Kasi raised questions about whether the United Stated could effectively track down international terrorists in parts of the world where international cooperation was limited, foreign relations were strained, and lawlessness was prevalent.

In May 1997, however, a major break came in the search. A man from the province of Baluchistan came to the U.S. consulate in Karachi, Pakistan, and told a clerk that he had information on the whereabouts of Kasi.[21] The man told a CIA agent at the consulate that Kasi was under the protection of a tribal leader in Baluchistan. Proof of the informant's credibility came when he was able to produce an application for a driver's license that had a picture of Kasi and a fingerprint that matched one on file with the CIA.[22] An elaborate plan was worked out involving cooperation between the CIA and FBI, who were able to solicit the cooperation of the tribal leader providing protection for Kasi. The plan called for the tribal leader to lure Kasi to a hotel during a purported business trip where FBI agents would be waiting to grab the fugitive.

At approximately 4:00 a.m. on the morning of June 15, 1997, the tribal leader knocked on Kasi's hotel door while FBI agents stood nearby. As Kasi came to answer the door, FBI agents broke in, subdued Kasi, and placed handcuffs and a gag on him.[23] An FBI agent immediately took the suspect's thumb print and used a magnifying glass to compare it right on the scene against Kasi's fingerprints that were on file. The agent found a clear match, revealing that the elusive Kasi had been captured.

With Kasi's arrest looming, CIA agents, as well as CIA Director George Tenet and National Coordinator for Counterterrorism Richard Clarke, hovered near a radio in the Counterterrorism Center back in the United States. The tension at CIA headquarters had risen steadily as Kasi evaded capture over the years. Clarke described the atmosphere as everyone listened for updates:

> The clock in the radio room rolled passed 4:00 a.m. Pakistani time. The radio remained silent. . . . With tension building in the crowded, overheated room, Tenet could not take it anymore: "Where the shit are they? Ask them where they are, it's 4:15 there." . . . The radio operator tried to hail the field team. Nothing. By 4:30 people were pacing in the corridor outside the radio room. Finally, the radio crackled, "Base, base, this is Red Rover. The package is aloft. Repeat, the package is aloft." Instantly champagne bottles appeared from under seats and were popped amid cheers and embraces.[24]

Many details of Kasi's capture, including the identity of the operatives and the locations to which he was taken following his arrest, remain vague due to national security concerns. However, it is known that immediately after his arrest, Kasi traveled by airplane for an hour, was transferred to a vehicle, driven forty minutes to a holding facility, and turned over to Pakistani authorities. The entire time he was in custody, FBI agents never left Kasi's side. Three days after his arrest, he was released from Pakistani custody to the FBI and flown to Fairfax County, Virginia, to face trial on the charges listed in his indictment. Counterterrorism Director Richard Clarke noted that a deliberate decision was made to have Kasi tried in the Virginia state courts, rather than the federal courts, because it was felt the prosecution would proceed more quickly.[0]

The search for Kasi took over four years and was given the highest priority by the U.S. government. The significance of his capture assured that all proper legal safeguards would be observed during his arrest, detention, and prosecution. He was read his rights against self-incrimination, and yet he waived those rights voluntarily and gave the FBI a complete confession of his culpability in the CIA shooting.[26] Despite confessing to the crime, Kasi entered a plea of not guilty and was tried before a jury in Fairfax County, Virginia, in November 1997. He was found guilty of all charges, and after the sentencing phase of his trial before the same jury that had determined his guilt, he was sentenced to death.

Kasi appealed his conviction first to the Virginia Supreme Court, where he cited ninety-two errors that he believed had been made during the conduct of his trial and sentencing.[27] The appellate court dismissed most of the claims because they were deemed to have no legal merit. However, among the issues the court was willing to consider was the legality of Kasi's arrest, detention, and confession. For instance, Kasi claimed that his confession was involuntary and that FBI agents had coerced him into incriminating himself. However, the Virginia Supreme Court noted, among other things, that Kasi had a good command of the English language—a fact consistent with his educational background—and understood his rights completely.

Another issue Kasi raised in his appeal claimed the Virginia courts had no jurisdiction over him because he was abducted illegally from his native country of Pakistan in violation of an extradition treaty between the United States and Pakistan and the Vienna Convention on relations between consulates of different countries. The court noted that even though Kasi was arrested by an FBI agent in Pakistan, U.S. law holds that constitutional guarantees, like the Fourth Amendment right against unlawful searches and seizures, do not apply to a criminal defendant who is not a U.S. citizen and in a foreign territory. Furthermore, the court did not find evidence of an extradition treaty that would have barred the FBI from arresting Kasi in Pakistan. Although Kasi raised several other issues in his appeal—including the fact that he did not have an impartial jury and could not receive a fair trial—all of his arguments were rejected, and his conviction and death sentence were upheld.

Unsatisfied with the result of his state court appeal, Kasi then filed a writ of habeas corpus in the U.S. District Court for the Eastern District of Virginia in which he raised many of the same claims he had raised in his appeal before the Virginia Supreme Court. However, the District Court denied his appeal, and in June 2002, the U.S. Court of Appeals for the 4th Circuit upheld the dismissal.[28] With few other legal options available, Kasi once again faced the death penalty.

As his pending execution approached, mounting concerns were raised by the U.S. government that Kasi's execution might trigger retaliatory terrorist attacks. A week before the scheduled execution, the U.S. State Department issued an advisory to that effect.[29] Kasi himself acknowledged the possibility of retaliation against the United States prior to his execution: "In Pakistan, a lot of people like me. So I believe there will be big chances for retaliation against Americans there."[30] Surprisingly, the man facing execution for a shooting attack that was motivated by anger toward the United States government added, "But personally, I don't encourage anyone to attack Americans."[31]

The U.S. Supreme Court refused to stay Kasi's execution, and the Virginia governor rejected Kasi's plea for clemency. On Thursday, November 14, 2004 at 9:07 a.m., Kasi was executed by lethal injection at the Greensville Correctional Center in Virginia.[32] His final words were reported to be, "There is no God but Allah."[33] Although he was convicted and sentenced to death within six months of his arrest, his execution did not occur until seven years after his conviction. As predicted by Richard Clarke, the Virginia courts moved rapidly to convict him, but the appellate process took time.

Kasi's case is considered a success in a number of respects. Although he remained an international fugitive for over four years, intelligence and law enforcement agents worked diligently to find him and bring him to justice. Despite the fact that his arrest, detention, and trial raised significant questions involving international law, treaties, extradition, and the constitutional rights of noncitizens in U.S. courts, Kasi's conviction and sentence were upheld. Although the international manhunt for Kasi might serve as a blueprint on the search for Osama bin Laden, the stakes are much higher in bin Laden's case. His status as an idealized, almost cult-like figure among Islamic extremists, his presumably vast financial and logistical resources, and his ardently devoted armed supporters who are willing to fight to the death to protect him, make the search for bin Laden all the more difficult. On the other hand, the massive destruction of the September 11 attacks, the fact that bin Laden is a major conspirator behind the largest mass murder in U.S. history, and the danger al-Qaeda continues to pose to the security of the United States make him the most wanted terrorist in the world. Indeed, the blueprint for action laid out in the Kasi case will need to be expanded and refined if there is to be any hope of bringing a successful end to the search for bin Laden, the most wanted international terrorist in history.

A NEEDLE IN A HAYSTACK

INVESTIGATING THE 1993 WORLD TRADE CENTER BOMBING

Remember we have only to be lucky once,
you will have to be lucky always.
—Provisional IRA[1]

A NEW ERA OF TERRORISM IN THE UNITED STATES BEGAN ON SEPTEMBER 1, 1992 when two men traveling from Pakistan arrived at Kennedy Airport. Although it would later be shown that the men were traveling together, they separated and attempted to pass through U.S. immigration using different stories and behaving in very different ways. One man was traveling under the name Khurram Khan and had a fake Swedish passport that he presented to the INS agent interviewing him.[2] When the agent held up the passport, she could clearly see that the man's photograph had been pasted over the picture of the passport's true owner. As the agent peeled off the picture, the man—whose real name was Ahmed Mohammad Ajaj—began shouting and acting in a belligerent manner.[3] He was taken into custody, where officials found a wealth of materials that were cause for alarm. Inside his baggage were books containing instructions for making large bombs, a videotape of a suicide bombing, handbooks on explosives, and various materials on demolition. For the next eight months, Ajaj remained jailed on immigration fraud charges, yet he stayed in contact with the other man with whom he had been traveling.

While Ajaj was creating his disturbance at the immigration counter at Kennedy Airport, the other man calmly approached another immigration officer and said his name was Ramzi Ahmed Yousef. He provided an identification card from an Islamic Center in Houston and provided an Iraqi passport issued under another name.[4] Yousef claimed that he had been perse-cuted in Iraq and was seeking asylum in the United States. Although the immigration officer interviewing Yousef suggested he be detained, her deci-sion was overruled by her superiors because there was no space left in the airport's detention center.[5] Yousef was released on his own recognizance and ordered to appear before an immigration judge in three months; he left the airport and proceeded to move about the United States.

Prior to coming to the United States, both Yousef and Ajaj had traveled extensively and had close ties with militant terrorists in Pakistan. Yousef had received training in the camps run by Osama bin Laden and had trained other terrorists himself in the Philippines. Ajaj once lived in Houston, Texas, but returned to Pakistan and is also believed to have trained in the terrorist camps near the Afghanistan-Pakistan border. Their mutual involvement with militant Islamic veterans of the war against the Soviet Union in Afghanistan during the 1980s led to Yousef and Ajaj meeting in the summer of 1992 at a terrorist training camp.[6] Although the specifics of what Yousef and Ajaj discussed during their early relationship are unknown, it is gener-ally believed that their meeting was the key moment when plans for the World Trade Center bombing in 1993 were developed.[7]

When Yousef was released on his own recognizance, he settled into an Arabic community in Brooklyn and received help from Mahmud Abouhalima—the same man who years earlier had been involved with, but never formally charged in, the assassination of radical Jewish leader Meir Kahane. Abouhalima helped Yousef get a chauffeur's license to be used for identification. Yousef also found a place to live. He was taken in by Mohammad Salameh, who was born on the West Bank and raised in Jordan before coming to the United States to find work.[8] Salameh had found menial jobs and ended up living in Jersey City. Since his tourist visa had expired, he was living as an illegal immigrant moving among various odd jobs when he met Yousef.[9]

With Ajaj in federal custody on immigration charges, Yousef oversaw the World Trade Center bombing himself, yet he remained in the back-ground and cleverly avoided drawing attention to himself. In addition to Salameh and Abouhalima, Yousef enlisted the services of several other indi-viduals, including Nidal Ayyad, Abdul Yasin, and Bilal Alkaisi.

Ayyad was perhaps the most successful of the group. Born in Kuwait, he came to the United States, where he earned a degree in chemical engineer-ing, found a good job at a New Jersey chemical company, got married, and was starting to raise a family.[10] Yasin and Alkaisi were Salameh's roommates, and Alkaisi had been among the supporters of Meir Kahane's assassin, El Sayyid Nosair, along with Abouhalima and Salameh.

How Yousef was able to induce individuals with such varying levels of education and success in American society to take part in the World Trade Center bombing remains something of a mystery. All of the conspirators came from Middle Eastern countries and shared a hatred of the United States. Much of their hatred was fueled by the fiery teachings of Sheik Omar Abdel Rahman, a well-known Islamic scholar who espoused strong hatred for Israel, the United States, and secular Arab governments.

In October 1992, Ayyad and Salameh opened several bank accounts, with some held jointly and others held with Alkaisi.[11] These bank accounts were used to finance a plot to bomb the World Trade Center—a symbol of American economic power, free trade, and capitalism. Although the exact source of the money that went into these accounts was difficult to trace, federal investigators were able to establish that Abouhalima had helped funnel money through various sources, including Muslim Brotherhood contacts in Germany, Iran, and various countries throughout the Middle East.[12] The money deposited into these accounts was withdrawn and given to Ayyad, who used his job at a chemical company to purchase various materials and supplies needed to build a powerful bomb.[13] In addition to chemicals, Ayyad arranged to buy from a welding company several hydrogen tanks that were used to increase the destructive force of the bomb.[14] Abouhalima was also able to obtain smokeless gunpowder.

Yousef and his co-conspirators used a storage locker that Salameh rented in Jersey City. Chemicals and other materials used in constructing the World Trade Center bomb were stored in the locker. Another key location used by the conspirators was an apartment in Jersey City shared by Salameh and Yousef that served as a base of operations where the chemicals for the bomb were mixed. The materials used to construct the bomb have not been described in most public accounts of the first World Trade Center attack in order to deter other terrorists who might copy the actions of Yousef and his co-conspirators. What is known, however, is that Yousef supervised construction of the bomb and followed guidelines outlined in the manuals Ajaj had with him when he was detained at Kennedy Airport.[15]

On February 23, 1993, Salameh rented a yellow Ryder truck in Jersey City and was required to do something that would later turn out to be a key factor that led to a successful arrest and prosecution: he had to pay a

$400 security deposit on the truck.[16] The truck was carefully selected so that it could hold up to 2,000 pounds of material without being conspicuous—"the perfect size for carrying a massive terrorist bomb to attack a target on American soil."[17]

Three days later, at about 4:00 a.m. on February 26, the yellow truck pulled out of the driveway of the Jersey City apartment and headed for New York City.[18] Yousef was riding in the passenger seat of the truck. Following close behind was Abouhalima in a dark blue Lincoln and other conspirators in a red Chevrolet. The caravan of vehicles stopped at a gas station where Abouhalima paid to have the truck and the Lincoln filled with gasoline. The full tank of gas assured a larger, fiery explosion when the bomb detonated.

By 8:00 a.m., the truck containing the bomb was in traffic and heading into New York City. Yousef directed the truck to a hotel in Manhattan where an old friend by the name of Eyad Ismoil was staying. Ismoil was a cab driver, and Yousef thought his friend would be more adept at navigating the busy New York City streets, so he asked Ismoil to drive the van.[19] Although Ismoil did not appear to have any idea what Yousef and the others had been planning, he was surprised when Yousef told him to drive to the southern end of Manhattan and enter an underground tunnel leading to the parking garage underneath the World Trade Center. Yousef told Ismoil to park on level B-2; they left the bomb-laden truck and departed the scene in the vehicles that had followed.

At approximately seventeen minutes past noon on February 26, 1993, the massive bomb exploded. It ripped the truck to shreds, tore a massive hole through five reinforced concrete floors above, blasted through a concrete wall separating an office and lunchroom from the parking garage, and sent massive clouds of thick, dark smoke up through the ventilation system of Tower One of the World Trade Center.[20] A pregnant woman working in the office next to the concrete wall on the same parking level as the truck was killed instantly; the blast caused massive internal injuries and seared the pattern of her sweater into her shoulder. Three men sitting in the lunchroom next to the office were also killed instantly. Another man, John DiGiovanni, who had parked his car just before the explosion, was thrown thirty feet and died of cardiac arrest induced by traumatic internal injuries.[21] Timothy Lang had also just parked his car—after DiGiovanni had cut in front of him—and was seriously injured, but survived.[22] In all, six people were killed in the World Trade Center bombing and more than

1,000 others were injured, with many working in the tower suffering from smoke inhalation. The first World Trade Center bombing had up to that time caused "more hospital casualties than any other event in domestic American history apart from the Civil War."[23]

At the moment of the explosion, Abouhalima was looking at the World Trade Center from a music store window several blocks away.[24] For several minutes, he watched nervously and wondered whether the bomb would detonate. The plan had called for enough explosives to be loaded into the Ryder truck that would cause one tower to topple into the other. As Abouhalima waited and watched, he grew more frustrated the longer the two towers continued to stand. He soon realized that the bomb had gone off, however, when he noticed several fire trucks and ambulances rushing by the music store and heading toward the World Trade Center.

Meanwhile, Yousef watched the Manhattan skyline from New Jersey and also experienced profound disappointment when the World Trade Center towers failed to topple into each other.[25] While rescue efforts were still happening, he returned to his apartment in Jersey City, collected his luggage, took a cab to Kennedy Airport—where he sought asylum status fraudulently just a few months before—and flew to Pakistan where he disappeared.

The next day, investigators made their way into the depths of the parking garage to observe the extent of the damage. They found a crater two-hundred-feet wide and several stories deep, raw sewage pumping into the hole, and twisted metal and debris scattered throughout the area.[26] Although the initial survey suggested a bomb, given the size of the crater and the nature of the damage, the immense range of debris, and the complications of having sewage dump into the crater created a huge barrier to investigators as they searched for physical evidence. Moreover, finding out the identities of the bombers was also likely to take months, if not years, because of logistical difficulties presented by the crime scene.

The case took a dramatic turn for the better when investigators found the proverbial "needle in the haystack" they needed to break the case.[27] An experienced explosives detective with the U.S. Department of Alcohol, Tobacco, and Firearms (ATF) named Joseph Hanlin, and a detective with the bomb squad of the New York City Police Department by the name of Donald Sadowy, were lowered into the bomb crater two days after the explosion.[28] They were wrapped in protective gear—including white jump suits, helmets, respirators, and gloves—and accompanied by a chemist, crime scene photographer, and sketch artist in order to sample and preserve evidence from the crime scene. Among the hazards that made the investigation dangerous was not only raw sewage, but also asbestos and dangerous chemicals that contaminated the scene.

Hanlin had more than two decades of investigative experience and was trained to identify debris from various types of bombs, including those that had been used throughout the Middle East. Since it had established that the explosion had been a bombing and was most likely a terrorist attack, investigators were selected to survey the site of the explosion based on their ability to identify clues among the debris. As Hanlin descended down into the pit of the crater, he saw several pieces of mangled vehicle parts, but one piece in particular caught his eye. Among the various pieces of metal were two parts of a gear assembly that were so badly twisted Hanlin concluded that they must have been right at the point of the blast and, quite possibly, from a vehicle containing the bomb.[29] The damage was so extensive that an obvious conclusion was a car or truck bomb had been used to transport the explosive material into the parking garage. Also near the gear assembly was another piece of twisted metal consisting of the differential housing from the same vehicle. When Hanlin and Sadowy examined the piece of evidence more closely, they found a series of dots and digits that turned out to be a vehicle identification number.[30] This number allowed investigators to trace the vehicle to a Ryder truck rental company in New Jersey.

One of the most astonishing points in the World Trade Center case came when investigators learned that the person renting the vehicle had been Mohammad Salameh and that he had reported the truck stolen. Of course, the claim was bogus and apparently an attempt either to provide the rental company with an explanation of why the truck could not be returned or to divert suspicion away from Salameh if investigators were ever able to trace the rented truck to him. In an act that would later be viewed by some as brazen and by others as inept, Salameh returned to the truck rental company and demanded his $400 deposit be returned. What Salameh did not know, however, was that a team of federal agents were waiting for him. They did not arrest Salameh immediately, but rather tried to get as much information as possible out of him. Ultimately, the investigators were able to piece together enough information to arrest most of the primary culprits in the World Trade Center bombing, including Abouhalima, Salameh, and Ayyad. Yousef, however, was nowhere to be found and would remain at large for the next two years.

Among the key questions in the investigation into the World Trade Center bombing was not only how the conspirators were able to carry out their plan, but also why the attack was carried out and, more important, whether there were other bombs to be detonated. Four days after the explosion, *The New York Times* received this letter, which provided a clue to the motive:

> The following letter from the LIBERATION ARMY regarding the operation conducted against the W.T.C.
>
> We, the fifth battalion in the LIBERATION ARMY, declare our responsibility for the explosion on the mentioned building. This action was done in response for the American political, economical, and military support to Israel the state of terrorism and to the rest of the dictator countries in the region.
>
> OUR DEMANDS ARE:
>
> 1—Stop all military, economical, and political aids to Israel.
>
> 2—All diplomatic relations with Israel must stop.
>
> 3—Not to interfere with any of the Middle East countries interior affairs.
>
> If our demands are not met, all of our functional groups in the army will continue to execute our missions against military and civilian targets in and out of the United States. This also will include some potential Nuclear targets. For your own information, our army has more than hundred and fifty suicidal soldiers ready to go ahead. The terrorism that Israel practices (Which is supported by America) must be faced with a similar one. The dictatorship and terrorism (also supported by America) that some countries are practicing against their own people must also be faced with terrorism.[31]

The letter clearly indicated that the bombing was politically motivated and threatened further terror attacks, including suicide bombings. When federal agents raided Ayyad's apartment following his arrest, they found deleted files on his computer containing "nearly identical drafts" of the letter sent to *The New York Times*.[32] Another letter found on Ayyad's computer that was about to be sent revealed that the World Trade Center bombing conspirators had failed to achieve their desired result of toppling the towers and wanted to continue their attacks:

We are, the Liberation fifth battalion, again ... Unfortunately, our calculations were not very accurate this time. However, we promise you that the next time it will be very precise and WTC will continue to be one of our targets.[33]

The trial of the World Trade Center bombing conspirators—absent Yousef—was a media circus, but the end result was that Salameh, Ayyad, and the others were convicted by a jury and each sentenced to 240 years in prison.[34] Those who were arrested for the bombing either denied their involvement, despite overwhelming evidence of their guilt, or attempted to portray themselves as passive victims of Yousef's manipulations.

Meanwhile, Yousef continued to pursue his global terrorism agenda. In late 1994, he formulated an elaborate plan to assassinate President Clinton and Pope John Paul II during their respective visits to the Philippines and had also developed a frightening plot to explode eleven airplanes simultaneously in mid-air over the Pacific Ocean.[35] Yousef had developed a highly volatile explosive material he was able to smuggle on board a jet liner in a test run that resulted in the death of a Japanese business man. Investigators later found that Yousef had obtained detailed plans of commercial aircraft and would have been capable of carrying out his attack. After a two-year manhunt, Yousef was finally captured in Pakistan in January 1995. Among the materials found in his possession was evidence that a collaborator in his plan to blow up commercial aircraft was Khalid Sheikh Mohammed—Yousef's uncle, a major al-Qaeda operative, and a major planner of the September 11 attacks.[36]

Although the 1993 bombing attack on the World Trade Center was not the success the terrorists had planned and the towers remained standing, the importance of the case for understanding the kind of terrorist threat that had made its way onto American soil cannot be overstated. For one thing, the case demonstrated a new terrorist challenge for the United States that involved individuals and groups with a global reach and funding from overseas who were determined to inflict mass casualties on American citizens.[37] The individuals involved in the first World Trade Center attack had been implicated in the assassination of Meir Kahane—an event that marked a new era of terrorist activity in the United States. Moreover, the benefit of hindsight highlights Yousef's connections to al-Qaeda operatives and training camps. The warnings in the letter on Ayyad's computer of future attacks on the World Trade Center foretold the catastrophic attacks of September 11 that occurred eight years later.

On the other hand, the first World Trade Center bombing also involved an impressive coordination of rescue and law enforcement efforts that minimized casualties and brought about quick arrests. Moreover, the prosecution of the conspirators, as well as the eventual prosecution and sentencing of Yousef, allowed federal investigators and prosecutors to assemble an extensive array of documents and materials that allowed a network of other conspirators to be identified. The subsequent prosecution of Sheik Omar Abdul Rahman and the identification of Khalid Sheikh Mohammed as a major terrorist operative were all important leads that emerged from the investigation of the 1993 World Trade Center bombing case.

Finally, the case underscored the need to increase public awareness of the terrorist threat that had emerged in the United States during the early 1990s. In this regard, it is worth noting Yousef's defiance and determination as he was being escorted to his first court appearance after being captured. While flying in a helicopter on the way to FBI headquarters at the southern end of Manhattan, past the World Trade Center towers along the New York City skyline, one of the federal agents accompanying Yousef said, "Look down there ... [t]hey're still standing."[38] With a quick response, Yousef said "They wouldn't be, if I had had enough money and explosives."[39] In fact, Yousef's words proved to be prophetic, since the attacks of September 11, 2001 later showed that more determined and better trained conspirators, with greater financial backing, would be successful in bringing down the World Trade Center towers.

OVERZEALOUSNESS

THE CASE OF THE SHEIK
AND HIS LAWYER

It's not the people in prison who worry me. It's the people who aren't.
— Arthur Gore[1]

ACCORDING TO *The Lawyer's Code of Professional Responsibility* ADOPTED BY the New York State Bar Association and which governs the practice of law in the state, lawyers have an ethical obligation "to represent the client zealously within the bounds of the law."[2] The types of activities in which lawyers engage during the course of their representation of clients depend on the specific needs of a case, but public trial advocacy, offering legal advice, and protecting the rights of the accused are among the most common things lawyers do on behalf of their clients. Moreover, lawyers take on many roles including counselor, advisor, and intermediary in situations that have some bearing on a case. They not only provide representation at trial and court proceedings, but also keep their clients abreast of political and other social events. Of course, a lawyer's ethical code also requires that zealous representation remain within the boundaries of what is permitted by law. When lawyers believe they are being asked to commit or facilitate a crime during the course of representing a client, their ethical obligations demand that they refrain from any illegal conduct.

In highly complicated criminal cases, lawyers sometimes find it difficult to balance conflicting ethical duties. One high-profile terrorism case that arose in the aftermath of the 1993 World Trade Center bombing literally put the conduct of a convicted terrorist's lawyer on trial. The result was a contentious case that raised profound questions about the risks criminal defense lawyers face when they agree to represent accused terrorists.

After the FBI arrested Mohammed Salameh, Mahmoud Abouhalima, Ahmad Ajaj, and Nidal Ayyad for their role in the first World Trade Center bombing, the investigation led federal agents to a Brooklyn mosque where Sheikh Omar Abdel Rahman was a central figure in the global jihad movement.[3] Rahman—often referred to as "the blind sheikh"—was born in 1938 in a small village in Egypt and became a renowned Islamic scholar who studied at the prestigious Al Azar University in Cairo.[4] Although unable to see since childhood, Rahman is believed to have memorized the Koran and became a formidable scholar who has been highly critical of the Egyptian government for many years. He spent time in prison for remarks made following the death of Egyptian President Nasser, whom Rahman criticized as an infidel. Rahman also served as a spiritual guide to the Egyptian Islamic Jihad, a group behind the 1981 assassination of Egyptian President Anwar Sadat.

After traveling to Pakistan in 1988 to meet with Afghan mujaheddeen fighting against the Soviet Union and Abdullah Azzam—an early collaborator with Osama bin Laden during the formative years of al-Qaeda—Rahman returned to Egypt. He was soon arrested and tried for his role in spurring anti-Christian riots.[5] Rahman was able to escape to the Sudan where he applied for, and received, a U.S. passport, despite his name appearing on a list of suspected terrorists who were barred from entering the United States. In July 1990, Rahman settled in New York City and became the spiritual leader of a Brooklyn mosque that was eventually be tied to the World Trade Center bombing.

Using the vast liberties and freedoms afforded him in the Untied States, Rahman made numerous speeches and wrote extensively. He often cited radical messages of the Egyptian writer Sayyid Qutb, who had been highly critical of the United States and who was executed by the Egyptian government because his radical teachings called for overthrowing the secular Egyptian government. Rahman accused the United States of being "the oppressor of Muslims worldwide" and instructed followers of the Islamic faith that it was their duty to attack such enemies of God.[6]

Although Rahman was not arrested in the immediate aftermath of the 1993 World Trade Center bombing, an FBI informant named Emad Salem provided startling new information that ultimately led to the sheikh's arrest. Salem had been an officer in the Egyptian army and was recruited by the FBI to infiltrate the Brooklyn mosque and a group of individuals in the Jersey City Arab community who had come under suspicion in the wake of the assassination of Meir Kahane in 1990.[7] During the course of his work as an FBI informant, Salem secretly recorded conversations he had with several individuals who sought spiritual guidance from the sheikh. These conversations uncovered an elaborate plan to bomb a number of New York City landmarks, including the Lincoln Tunnel, Holland Tunnel, George Washington Bridge, and New York City "Diamond District," where a carefully placed bomb was intended to kill several members of the Jewish community.[8]

In August 1993—just six months after the World Trade Center bombing and weeks before jury selection began for the trial of those arrested for the bombing—Rahman and over a dozen other individuals were arrested and indicted for the plot to blow up the sites in New York City. If successful, the plot would have paralyzed the city by effectively destroying major pathways in and out of Manhattan. Furthermore, Rahman was accused in the indictment of "leading a 'war on urban terrorism'" that included not only the plot on New York City bridges and tunnels, but also the World Trade Center bombing and the Kahane assassination.[9]

The wheels of justice moved slowly but deliberately, and Rahman was ultimately convicted of the charges against him and sentenced to life in prison. At the time of his federal trial in the U.S. District Court for the Southern District of New York on charges of terrorism, Rahman was represented by a court-appointed attorney by the name of Lynne Stewart. Following Rahman's conviction and sentencing in 1995 and subsequent denial of his appeals, Stewart continued to represent the sheikh as his attorney. She said the primary purpose of her ongoing representation was to improve the conditions of Rahman's prison confinement because of hardships he might face due to his blindness and diabetes.[10] Moreover, Stewart pursued the possibility of convincing officials of the U.S. government that Rahman should be returned to Egypt.[11] Whether Stewart's purported claim of advocating for the sheikh's return to his home country constituted a sound purpose is open to question, since Rahman had apparently fled Egypt because his radical teachings had led to prosecution in the country of his birth. Whatever legal purpose Stewart's activities served, her zealous representation would soon be interpreted by the U.S. government as constituting the aiding and abetting of terrorist activities.

Even after his conviction and incarceration in the federal prison system, Rahman continued to urge his followers to wage a global jihad against the United States in an effort to win his release.[12] Officials from the Department of Justice uncovered evidence that several terrorist organizations—including the Islamic Group, al-Qaeda, Egyptian Islamic Jihad, and

Abu Sayyaf—had threatened and carried out a series of terrorist acts aimed at securing Rahman's release from prison. For example, several assassins attacked a group of foreign tourists visiting an archaeological site in Luxor, Egypt, resulting in the deaths of fifty-eight Western tourists and four Egyptians.[13] Leaflets calling for Rahman's release were scattered at the site of the attack; one was even placed in the slit-open torso of a victim. This high-profile attack, as well as others, demonstrated how Rahman's global influence continued even as he remained physically secured in a fortified federal prison in the United States.

As a result of emerging evidence that Rahman was continuing to send messages around the world to his followers, the U.S. government began to place greater restrictions on him. His access to mail, telephone calls, visitors, and media outlets such as newspapers and television was monitored and restricted.[14] Moreover, Stewart was denied access to her client for a period of time. In 2000, she was allowed to resume contact with Rahman as long as she adhered to a series of restrictions the government placed upon her. These restrictions, called "special administrative measures" (SAMs), are invoked in cases where "there is a substantial risk that a prisoner's communications or contacts with persons could result in death or serious bodily injury to persons, or substantial damage to property that would entail the risk of death or serious bodily injury to persons."[15]

The SAMs required that Stewart limit the scope of her contact with Rahman only to those activities that were within the boundaries of legal representation and that she specifically refrain from permitting Rahman to have contact with any individuals outside the prison, except for his wife. Furthermore, Stewart was not to allow Rahman any contact with the media. If she was to continue serving as his lawyer, she would need to abide by the SAMs. With no other options available, she agreed to abide by the stipulations.

Although Stewart had represented other unpopular clients, her willingness to take on challenging cases was in keeping with the duty of all lawyers to devote a portion of their professional time and skills to making sure that all individuals have access to the legal system, particularly those who encounter economic or social barriers to adequate legal representation.[16] While Stewart agreed to the SAMs when she resumed her contacts with Rahman in prison, she was unaware that Attorney General John Ashcroft had secretly amended regulations governing the SAMs.[17] On October 31, 2001, Ashcroft approved changes which permitted the Federal Bureau of

Prisons to videotape and audiotape communications between attorneys and their clients who were being held by federal authorities. When Stewart began meeting with Rahman, she was unaware that her conversations were being monitored by the government.[18]

There are many relationships in our society—including husband-wife, priest-penitent, therapist-patient, and attorney-client—where the privacy of communications is considered to be of paramount importance. Under most circumstances, what a client says to his or her attorney is considered privileged and cannot be disclosed to others. A high value is placed on this privilege because it is generally believed that attorneys can best represent their clients and protect their rights only when there is some assurance that the client can be completely honest with his or her attorney. Nevertheless, the revisions to the SAMs that Ashcroft made had no exceptions for the attorney-client privilege because of significant national security interests in deterring future acts of terrorism.[19] Given Rahman's global influence and the important role he played in the first World Trade Center bombing, as well as the subsequent plot to attack New York City landmarks, he was a logical target for the government to monitor his communications with any-one—including his attorney—who might connect him to his followers. Moreover, the SAMs did not require that a search warrant be obtained before the communications between attorney and client were monitored, and neither party had to be given notice that the monitoring was taking place.

During the course of Stewart's contact with Rahman, the U.S. government uncovered two specific instances where it was believed she had violated the restrictions imposed upon her. On one occasion, Stewart allegedly made a public statement in which she conveyed a message from Rahman that he was withdrawing his support for a cease-fire in the terrorist violence that had occurred in the wake of the Luxor massacre.[20] In addition, the government claimed that Stewart had helped Mohammed Yousry, who was serving the role of interpreter for Rahman, and a law clerk by the name of Ahmed Abdel Sattar to compose messages from Rahman that were intended for his followers.[21] Although it was never established that Stewart actually understood Arabic or knew the content of the messages, it was alleged that she created distractions by making noise so that Rahman could converse with others in the interview room.

Initially, the federal government charged Stewart under a federal law making it a crime to provide material support and assistance to terrorist organizations, regardless of whether the person intended for the support to further terrorism or not. However, the judge in Stewart's case held that such a prosecution was unconstitutional because the government's legal theory was too vague and did not provide Stewart with sufficient notice that her release of the statement was sufficient to constitute material support for a terrorist organization.[22] In response to the judge's legal ruling, the prosecutors revised their charges against Stewart and charged her under a different section of federal law that requires specific intent, in that the person knows his or her actions constitute material support to terrorists. The judge accepted the government's revised charge, and the question for jurors in Stewart's case was whether she knew she was providing resources to terrorists that would be used to carry out a specific act of violence.[23]

A key point of clarification the jury needed to make was what material support, if any, Stewart had given to terrorists. She had not provided money, weapons, or other resources that are commonly viewed as constituting support for terrorism. According to the government, however, what Stewart made available to terrorists was Rahman himself. By issuing a public statement to the press from the convicted conspirator, and allowing him to communicate with an interpreter who could send his message to others, Stewart was making a key spiritual advisor and guide available to his followers.

Although Stewart later agreed that she had violated the restrictions, she argued that the ethical obligations imposed upon her as a lawyer demanded she zealously represent her client. Moreover, she claimed that she never received notice that her activities could be considered violations of federal law. In her defense, she argued that the secret revisions Ashcroft instituted and the secret monitoring of her interactions with Rahman, violated her due process rights. Whether making public statements on behalf of Rahman was addressing political and social factors related to his case or facilitating terrorism became the key issue to be decided by the jury.

Testifying for nine days in her own defense, Stewart told the jury that she was zealously representing her client and that it was not her intent to further the goals of the Islamic Group, a group counted among Rahman's many followers.[24] For an additional six days, U.S. Attorney Andrew Dember cross-examined Stewart about her claims and attempted to demonstrate that she was, in fact, trying to support the terrorist aims of Rahman and his followers. Dember made an issue over the fact that Stewart had continued to represent Rahman even after the sheik's appeals had been exhausted.[25]

The prosecutor was able to get Stewart to admit under cross-examination that she never filed a formal law suit addressing the prison conditions under which Rahman was living. This point was raised to cast doubt on the purpose of Stewart's legal representation of Rahman after his appeals were exhausted, since she asserted that one of her goals was to improve the conditions of his confinement. Although Stewart's attorney was able to get Stewart to testify that she did not personally support Islamic fundamentalism and that she supported the right of both Israel and Palestine to exist, in the end, the jury was not convinced.[26]

After hearing all the evidence, the jury deliberated thirteen days before finding her guilty of five counts of defrauding the U.S. government, conspiracy, and providing material support to terrorists.[27] The conviction carries a potential sentence of up to thirty years in prison; however sentencing has been delayed as Stewart appeals her conviction in the controversial case.

The case of Sheik Omar Abdel Rahman and his attorney illustrates a number of important yet controversial aspects of the legal strategies used to combat terrorism. An important illustrative feature is the fact that even after individuals have been convicted, sentenced, and imprisoned for their role in committing acts of terrorism, they can still wield considerable influence over their followers throughout the world. The measures taken by the government to restrict a convicted terrorist's contact with the world outside of prison, and to closely monitor communications between prisoners and their attorneys, are necessary in order to eliminate a critical source of political, philosophical, inspirational, and religious support that terrorist leaders provide to their followers.

In addition, the case provides a fascinating example of the controversies that exist when trying to differentiate between legitimate protection of constitutional rights and illegal activities that place innocent people at risk. The First Amendment of the Constitution guarantees individuals the right to freedom of expression and association, and the Sixth Amendment provides for the right to effective legal counsel in criminal cases. While Stewart's actions on behalf of Rahman confront the boundaries of these important constitutional rights, the jury decided that at a particular point, the right to expression and the ethical duties of an attorney end when they result in material support to terrorists that furthers their aims.

In some respects, the case of Lynne Stewart may represent an aberration. Although she agreed to the stipulations placed on her activities when she resumed her contact with Rahman, she admittedly violated those stipulations and opened herself to criminal prosecution. A jury found her actions were illegal, and thus the case may be instructive to other lawyers who agree to represent accused terrorists who have followers around the globe. With the prospect that many detainees in the war on terrorism may soon have their day in court, criminal defense lawyers will be needed to defend them. However, the Stewart conviction sends a warning to those who decide to venture into this treacherous area: legal representation ends when material support to terrorists begins. It remains to be determined how many competent attorneys will be willing to risk their professional livelihood and liberty to take on these difficult and demanding cases.

THOU SHALT KILL

THE PARADOX OF RELIGIOUSLY
MOTIVATED ASSASSINATION

O mortal men, be wary how ye judge.

—Dante[1]

OVER THE COURSE OF HISTORY, THERE HAVE BEEN NUMEROUS ACTS OF VIO-lence—including war, genocide, and assassination—that have been committed to further a religious cause. Indeed, religion has been used both to motivate and justify extreme acts of violence, including terrorism.[2] Because the taking of a human life is considered morally wrong under most religious teachings, it is curious that mainstream religions like Christianity, Judaism, and Islam have all been used at one time or another to condone violence.

Religious prohibitions against killing are frequently cited in the debate over abortion in the United States. Moreover, abortion has become such a contentious issue that it provokes very strong and sometimes violent confrontations between pro-life and pro-choice groups. Because acts such as the bombing of abortion clinics and the intimidation of women seeking abortions are intended to influence and change only those legal policies that relate to the termination of pregnancies, abortion-related violence is generally viewed as a form of "single-issue terrorism."[3]

One of the most extreme forms of violence perpetrated by a very small number of abortion opponents is targeting for assassination those physicians who perform abortions. In 1998, Dr. Barnett A. Slepian was shot to death while standing in the kitchen of his home in Amherst, New York. His assailant, James Kopp, was active in the pro-life movement and had taken part in a number of demonstrations. During the 1990s, seven physicians providing abortion services in the United States and Canada were killed by assassins.[4] One of the most visible of these killings occurred on July 29,

1994, when Paul Hill, a former Presbyterian minister, shot and killed Dr. John B. Britton and James H. Barrett, the physician's escort.

Britton was not a stranger to the abortion controversy. The sixty-nine year-old physician lived near Jacksonville, Florida, but made weekly flights to Pensacola to perform abortions. Because he had been the target of harassment and threats, Britton regularly wore a bulletproof vest when traveling, and he also used the services of an escort for protection. Barrett, a seventy-four year-old retired Air Force lieutenant, volunteered to drive Britton to the clinic.

In the early morning hours of July 29, after his flight arrived in Pensacola, Britton was escorted by Barrett and Barrett's wife, June, to the clinic where the physician regularly performed abortions. Hill walked toward the men with a twelve-gauge shotgun he had purchased a few days before the attack. The first shot hit Barrett in the head and killed him. Hill then pointed his weapon at Britton's head and fired; the shot killed the physician and injured Mrs. Barrett, who had been hiding on the floor of the pickup truck used to bring Britton to the clinic.

In a statement made after the attack, Hill stated that he suspected Britton wore a bulletproof vest and therefore aimed at the physician's head.[5] Given the efficiency with which Hill carried out the assassination and the fact that he aimed his weapon to achieve lethal results, there is little doubt that his actions were carefully planned and intentional. In light of Hill's religious training, and the prohibitions against killing that are found in Christian teachings, the question arose as to why Hill would commit murder in order to further the anti-abortion movement.

The origins of Hill's ideas about the moral justifications for assassinating abortion providers can be traced, in part, to March 10, 1993, when Michael Griffin shot and killed Dr. David Gunn near another abortion clinic in Pensacola, Florida. While Hill had long been an opponent of abortion and advocated violence against those who provided abortion services, it was Griffin's killing of Gunn that thrust Hill into the national spotlight and sparked a series of related attacks. Shortly after Gunn's murder, Hill appeared on a national television program and defended the use of violence to protect unborn children.[6] Hill outlined his thinking in greater detail when he wrote a paper entitled "Should We Defend Born and Unborn Children with Force?"

Hill made a clear distinction between "what is just and what is legal."[7] According to Hill's reasoning, man-made laws of societies might legalize certain acts such as abortion, but those same acts are not necessarily just under the law of God. Basing the foundations of his argument in Christian doctrine, Hill drew an analogy between slavery and abortion by noting that while slavery was at one time legal, it was not just, according the law of God. In the same way, Hill characterized abortion as a legal act that is nevertheless unjust. In addition, he argued that abortion is the taking of an innocent life and that those who follow God's law must defend those who cannot defend themselves. Hill posed the following question: "May we use force to protect unborn children from imminent death even if the government forbids us to do so?"[8] Using a number of biblical passages and scriptures, Hill stated that men must obey the law of God, rather than man-made laws, in order to protect innocent people from imminent death. He also escalated his argument by calling for a "defensive war" against civil leaders in the United States, since those leaders were not performing the duty Hill felt they are bound to carry out, namely protecting innocent lives.

Considering the fact that Hill wrote his lengthy paper in July 1993—two years before he killed Britton—it is clear that he had established in his mind that the killing of abortion doctors was morally right, just, and consistent with his own interpretation of religious doctrine. Because Hill viewed leaders in the United States as ineffective in protecting innocent babies, he argued that action must be taken against civil government to achieve the necessary goal of preventing abortions from occurring. He cited the U.S. Constitution to support his argument by noting that the First Amendment protects the right of abortion protesters to proclaim the "truth" about abortion and the Second Amendment protects the right of citizens to bear arms and maintain "a well-regulated militia."

As such, Hill argued for armed and aggressive disobedience against a civil government that viewed abortion as a legal act. Furthermore, he viewed the actions of Griffin as a prelude to broader violent action by noting that "just individual action often immediately precedes a just war."[9] Hill later said the Griffins' actions were an inspiration that led him to kill Britton. He found not only tacit approval for killing abortion doctors in religious doctrine but also a calling to active duty in a paramilitary war when Griffin killed Gunn—the first murder of an abortion provider in the United States.[10]

Critics of Hill's ideology have claimed that it is based on an extreme interpretation of Christian doctrine known as *dominion theology* and far-right, anti-government thinking that is often associated with the militia movement.[11] From both a psychological and legal perspective, however, it is interesting to note some of the erroneous interpretations that are made in Hill's rationale. For instance, his reliance on the First and Second Amendments of the Constitution in trying to support a defensive war against civil leaders, and his failure to recognize the rule of law lead him to argue for armed and violent revolt against the government, yet neither of these Amendments provides unrestricted rights to citizens. Speech that incites people to commit illegal action or to attempt violent overthrow of the government is not protected under the First Amendment; nor has a well-regulated militia ever been considered necessary if citizens decide to overthrow the government of the United States. In addition, there is an inherent confirmatory bias in Hill's use of religious doctrine to support his views.[12] He provides numerous biblical passages and scriptures to support his belief that assassination of abortion providers is just, despite equally compelling religious prohibitions against killing.

At the time he shot Britton, Hill painted automobiles as an independent contractor. Despite the fact that he had attended a religious seminary in Mississippi and had been ordained as a minister in the Presbyterian Church, he had difficulties finding a niche for himself. After three failed attempts at leading parishes, he joined the Orthodox Presbyterian Church but later renounced that denomination.[13] Despite his detailed written justification for killing abortion doctors, his writing must be interpreted in light of the fact that he did not find an audience for his views within the mainstream Presbyterian Church.

In the end, Hill was convicted of the murder of Barrett and Britton and was sentenced to death. His conviction and pending execution merely served to further polarize both sides of the abortion debate. One religious leader who later became a spiritual advisor to Hill on death row said that Hill had done a "good thing" by shooting an abortion doctor and saving the lives of numerous unborn children.[14] Those in the abortion rights movement, on the other hand, applauded his conviction, but feared his actions would prompt others to use lethal violence in furtherance of the pro-life cause.

On September 3, 2003, amid death threats to prison officials and protests, Paul Hill was executed by lethal injection at Florida State Prison. To the end, he was unremorseful and felt the murder of Britton was justified. Although he stated that he did not necessarily choose to die, he offered the following statement: "I'm willing and I feel very honored that they are most likely going to kill me for what I did."[15] In the weeks leading up to Hill's scheduled execution, there were renewed debates and protests about two highly controversial issues—capital punishment and abortion. Some abortion rights activists feared that the execution of Hill, who was seen as a hero to some anti-abortion protesters, would trigger new attacks on clinics and providers of abortion services. Letters containing death threats were received by prison officials and the attorney general in Florida, presumably from individuals who supported Hill and his ideas.

While it remains unclear if the execution of Hill will be used to justify future attacks on abortion providers, his case illustrates an important phenomenon that occurs in many cases of prolonged political or social conflict. The *contagion effect* refers to a process whereby a single violent act can provoke other individuals to commit similar acts of violence, resulting in the spread of violence. Paul Hill was clear in his public statements that he found inspiration in David Gunn, who had also murdered an abortion provider. Likewise, Hill has become an inspiration to others who share his belief in the moral rightness of assassinating abortion doctors. Many of his supporters felt a deep fury over the fact that he was convicted and sentenced to death. One person sympathetic to Hill believed he raised the standard for the anti-abortion movement in terms of how their battle must be waged. According to one report, a man supporting Hill said, "Some day, I hope I will have the courage to be as much of a man as he was."[16]

Religiously motivated violence is particularly dangerous and difficult to prevent because religious doctrine and scripture can be easily interpreted to provide justification. Furthermore, religiously motivated terrorists view the word of God as having greater authority and legitimacy than civil law created by people and imposed by state and federal governments. Moreover, when a person justifies an act of violence based on religious teachings, there is a risk of the contagion effect, where like-minded individuals who might not otherwise become violent, suddenly pose a threat because they find strength in the actions of someone who inspires them. The fear, of course, is that David Gunn and Paul Hill may have become an inspiration for an unknown number of individuals who share their views of justice.

REVERBERATIONS

THE POLITICAL CONTEXT OF A NEW YORK CITY HOMICIDE

An eye for an eye makes the whole world blind.
—Mahatma Gandhi[1]

AT APPROXIMATELY 10:30 ON THE MORNING OF MARCH 1, 1994, A VAN CONtaining fifteen Jewish students from a rabbinical seminary was traveling out of Manhattan on the southbound ramp of the Brooklyn Bridge.[2] The students were returning from a prayer vigil for one of their spiritual leaders when a car driven by twenty-eight-year-old Lebanese national Rashid Baz pulled up along side the van. Earlier that morning, Baz had driven into Manhattan to drop his aunt off at an appointment and dozed briefly in his car before heading back to Brooklyn.[3] Driving alone, Baz took a Cobray machine gun and initially fired toward the rear windows of the students' vehicle.[4] As he continued to pursue the van, Baz sprayed the driver's side with bullets and continued firing until the weapon jammed. He then took a 9mm semi-automatic pistol and began a third round of shooting until that weapon jammed as well.[5] Although Baz had a twelve-gauge shotgun, he did not use it in the attack.

When the shooting ended, two students were injured with gunshot wounds to the back of their heads. One of the students, sixteen-year-old Aaron Halberstam, died four days later, and the other, Nachum Sasonkin, survived but sustained grave injuries. Two other students were also wounded.[6]

After the shooting, Baz drove his vehicle to an automobile repair shop where its shattered windshield was repaired and evidence from the shooting was taken from the car. The owner of the vehicle, Bassam Reyati, who owned the livery car service where Baz worked, was later arrested and charged with hindering prosecution after he assisted in removing the car's broken windshield and leaving the vehicle on the street near his office. Reyati would later plead guilty in exchange for a sentence of five years on probation and a $1,000 fine.[7] The owner of the auto repair shop, Hilal Abd al-Aziz Muhammad, was also charged with hindering prosecution. He provided Baz with assistance by concealing the weapons used in the shooting, helping to remove the windshield, and throwing out shell casings from inside the car. Like Reyati, Muhammad was convicted and sentenced to five years on probation.

Police officers investigating the shooting attack were able to trace the vehicle back to Baz. Upon his arrest, he confessed but claimed that the incident was prompted by a confrontation in traffic.[8] When reports of Baz's admission were made public, the incident was initially portrayed as an example of road rage. However, a number of questions about Baz's motives and background arose: How was he able to assemble the arsenal of weapons he had in his possession and was he connected with any terrorist organizations or groups?

An important feature of the attack was its timing. Just four days before Baz opened fire on the van of students, a highly publicized act of terrorism had occurred nearly half a world away that would have a profound impact on Jewish-Arab relationships. On February 25, a Brooklyn-born physician living in Israel by the name of Baruch Goldstein entered the Ibrahimi Mosque at the Tomb of the Patriarchs in the West Bank town of Hebron.[9] Goldstein was dressed in army fatigues and carrying an assault rifle when he entered the Muslim holy place and opened fire on worshipers assembled for prayers. Although the crowd subdued Goldstein and bludgeoned him to death, he massacred thirty Muslim worshipers—mostly fathers and their sons—and injured nearly a hundred others.[10]

Goldstein's attack occurred during the Muslim holy month of Ramadan and provoked rioting among Muslim worshipers at the Al-Aqsa Mosque in Jerusalem.[11] There were calls for retaliation against Israel and Jewish people by a number of groups and organizations throughout the world. In Beirut, Lebanon, supporters of Hezbollah demonstrated and called for "Death to America" and "Death to Israel."[12] A state radio broadcast in Iran called for jihad against the Jewish people. Various extremist groups such as the Muslim Brotherhood in Egypt, Hamas, and Gama'a al-Islamiya announced that violent reprisals would soon be launched against Israel and Western interests.

The global reverberations of Goldstein's massacre created a volatile political climate. However, the question remained whether Baz was motivated by these calls for revenge or whether his attack was driven by something other than the Ibrahimi Mosque massacre. The initial investigation into Baz's background yielded very few clues. He was described as someone with a mixed or atypical religious background that was not consistent with someone who was an extremist. Baz was born in Lebanon to a Druze father and Palestinian mother. The Druze faith is considered an offshoot of formal Islam and has several mystical beliefs such as reincarnation and transmigration of souls.[13] Baz was not considered to be particularly religious by those who knew him well. He came to the United States in 1984 to escape violence in his native Lebanon. Although he entered the country on a student visa, he showed minimal effort in obtaining a degree, taking only single courses a semester at Rockland Community College and leaving school after the summer of 1985.[14] Over the next several years, he held odd jobs as a driver and married an American woman; he later separated from her.

In addition to his lack of academic success and marginal employment, Baz was also seen as an individual who carried grudges, harbored a strong interest in guns, and had a propensity for unpredictable behavior. Two years before the shooting, Baz drove a car he borrowed into the rear end of another vehicle on a busy Brooklyn expressway. When he emerged from his vehicle, he immediately shouted to the other driver, "I am a Muslim" and acted in a "menacing" fashion.[15] The incident ended peacefully; yet Baz's initial display of anger dissuaded the other driver from pursuing formal charges.

Following Baz's arrest, police officers portrayed him as someone who fit the standard profile of an angry, socially isolated individual with a strong interest in weapons and a reputation for unpredictable behavior. One officer suggested that Baz was like the fictional character Travis Bickle, portrayed by actor Robert DeNiro in the movie *Taxi Driver*. The officer believed that Baz was an estranged immigrant in an impersonal city walking around with an arsenal of weapons and "seemed to have things building up."[16] Another officer had the following to say about Baz: "For the moment, it seems he was riding around with a chip on his shoulder and a lot of guns, waiting to have the chip knocked off."[17] However, when Baz's case went to trial, a different picture emerged that shed light on his motive for the shooting and cast serious doubt on the theory that he was an angry, unpredictable loner.

At trial, Baz raised a defense of insanity and claimed he suffered from a mental disorder that prevented him from understanding or appreciating the wrongfulness of his actions. To prove insanity in New York State—where the shooting had occurred and Baz was put on trial—a criminal defendant must demonstrate that, as a result of a mental disease or defect, he or she was either unable to understand the nature or consequences of a criminal act (in this case murder) or did not know that his or her actions were wrong. Baz was evaluated by two mental health professionals, who testified that he suffered from posttraumatic stress disorder as a result of his exposure to war-related violence in his native Lebanon. The experts testified that Baz experienced a flashback during the shooting and believed he was back in his homeland of Lebanon at the time of the attack.[18] A psychologist for the prosecution, Dr. Terrence Keane, who is a nationally renowned expert on posttraumatic stress disorder, testified that Baz had a mild to moderate form of the disorder but did not suffer from flashbacks. Keane testified further that the severity of Baz's condition was not such that it should excuse him from criminal responsibility.

More important, one of Baz's own defense experts, psychiatrist Douglas Anderson, testified that Baz had a strong reaction to the Goldstein massacre in Hebron just a few days before the shooting of the Jewish students on the Brooklyn Bridge. In an exchange with the prosecutor, when asked about Baz's reaction to the Hebron incident and its impact on Baz's state of mind at the time, Dr. Anderson admitted "It had an enormous impact."[19] Dr. Anderson added that Baz "was enraged. He was absolutely furious. He was … I think Hebron put him from condition yellow to condition red."[20] In a videotape of his confession, Baz admitted he was angry over the incident and endorsed revenge but denied that he would necessarily act himself. Still, Baz convinced his own expert that he considered himself an Arab soldier and the weapons he carried with him revealed his desire to be ready for combat.[21]

The insanity defense mounted on Baz's behalf failed to convince the jury that he was not criminally responsible for his actions. He was convicted and sentenced to 141 years in prison for the murder of Aaron Halberstam and the attempted murder of several others. Evidence raised at his trial illustrates the importance of political context in understanding Baz's motive. Ten days after the attack, one terrorist organization, Hamas, released a statement in which it praised his actions:

Only Islam is the legitimate and exclusive representation of our people and its predicament; and the living proof of this is namely the holy warrior and Lebanese immigrant Rashid al-Baz, the son of Islam who took action against the souls of the evil dregs of the Jews in Brooklyn in America. His deed proclaims that you [i.e., the Jews] do not have the ability to tear Palestine away from our hearts, may a curse be on your heads.[22]

Despite the volatile context in which the Brooklyn Bridge shooting attack occurred, the case continues to be viewed by some individuals as either an isolated attack or an incident of road rage.[23] In subsequent years, the family of Aaron Halberstam fought to have the case re-examined by federal authorities and to be re-classified as an act of terrorism. The American Jewish Committee sponsored an independent review and assessment of the incident, which concluded that the attack was an act of terrorism.[24]

Although the Brooklyn Bridge shooting attack on March 1, 1994 is mentioned sporadically in various discussions on the recent history of terrorism in the United States, it is an important example of terrorist violence on American soil that occurred shortly after a tragic massacre—that was also an act of terrorism—yet occurred half a world away. The incident also demonstrates the difficulty in parsing out political motivations in an act that to most appearances seems like another random criminal act. The challenge of identifying the political motives of lone gunmen whose violence seems to be random is a problem that characterizes many shooting attacks that might be more accurately classified as acts of terrorism.

CONSPIRACY THEORIES

THE OKLAHOMA CITY BOMBING

If no one else is arrested or convicted, then the revolution can continue.
—Timothy J. McVeigh[1]

A MONTH AFTER HIS TWENTIETH BIRTHDAY, TIMOTHY MCVEIGH ANNOUNCED to his father that he was joining the U.S. Army.[2] By all appearances, the decision seemed to be the right one for the young man from Western New York. Following his graduation from high school, McVeigh worked at various menial jobs and took computer programming courses at a local business school, but nothing appeared to capture his interest. Although he was bright and did well on a math aptitude exam, McVeigh did not see the benefit of devoting himself to a course of academic study that would necessarily lead to a diploma. Instead, he preferred to keep to himself and remained committed to a survivalist lifestyle.[3] While growing up, he was captivated by movies like *The Omega Man* and *Red Dawn* that portrayed people dealing with cataclysmic events.[4] In keeping with his survivalist views, McVeigh was an avid reader of gun magazines. One magazine in particular would expose McVeigh to a book that would have a profound impact on the direction his life would ultimately take.

From an advertisement in *Soldier of Fortune* magazine, McVeigh bought a book entitled *The Turner Diaries* written by William L. Pierce, a former official in the American Nazi Party, who wrote the book under the pseudonym Andrew Macdonald.[5] The novel tells of a fictional gun enthusiast who constructs a powerful truck bomb that destroys the FBI building in Washington, D.C. in response to stricter firearms laws and expansive powers of the federal government. McVeigh was deeply influenced by the book, finding its right-wing, anti-government views to be consistent with his own. He would give the book to friends and later sold copies out of his car.[6]

In the Army, McVeigh seemed to find a comfortable home. He excelled in the use of weaponry, and the physical rigors of basic training catered to his strong survivalist interests. Overall, he would later view his first two years in the Army as "the finest period of his life."[7]

Aside from the fact that McVeigh's early experiences in the military seemed to agree with him, another important aspect about his time in the Army was the friendships he developed. Some of McVeigh's fellow soldiers viewed him as odd and were put off by his far-right political views; on at least a couple of occasions, he was cautioned to take a low profile with his efforts to expose others to *The Turner Diaries* because of its racist and provocative content.[8] Yet one fellow solder named Terry Lynn Nichols, who was older than McVeigh, shared many of the same political views. The two men formed what turned out to be a friendship that would last the duration of McVeigh's life. Another fellow soldier with whom McVeigh enjoyed target practice was Michael Fortier; the two also formed a lasting friendship.

In early 1991, McVeigh and the soldiers in his unit were deployed to Saudi Arabia to prepare for the Gulf War precipitated by Saddam Hussein's invasion of Kuwait. As a skilled gunner on a Bradley tank, McVeigh was involved in direct combat. The brief war was a resounding success for both the United States and Timothy McVeigh. Upon completion of his combat duties, McVeigh made a triumphant return to the United States, and his military skills had earned him the recognition of his superior officers and a coveted invitation to tryout for U.S. Army Special Forces training at Fort Bragg in North Carolina.[9] However, the positive momentum in McVeigh's life stalled when he failed to complete the Special Forces training. By the end of 1991, he left the Army disillusioned and more resentful of the U.S. government.

After returning home to Western New York, McVeigh returned to working at menial jobs. He supervised security guards at the Buffalo Zoo and also worked part-time at a gun supply store[10]. His anger and resentment toward the U.S. government led him to write letters to his congressman and local newspapers. In a letter published on February 11, 1992, McVeigh's right-wing views on crime control, racism, and taxes came through clearly:

More taxes are always the answer to government mismanagement. They mess up, we suffer. Taxes are reaching cataclysmic levels, with no slowdown in sight. . . . Politicians are out of control. . . . Maybe we have to combine ideologies to achieve the perfect utopian government. Remember, government-sponsored health care was a communist idea. Should only the rich be allowed to live longer? Does that say that because a person is poor he is a lesser human being and doesn't deserve to live as long, because he doesn't wear a tie to work?

What is it going to take to open the eyes of our elected officials?

America is in serious decline.

We have no proverbial tea to dump. Should we instead sink a ship full of Japanese imports?

Is a civil war imminent?

Do we have to shed blood to reform the current system?

I hope it doesn't come to that, but it might.[11]

In retrospect, McVeigh's ominous words about bloodshed as a means of reforming the government provided a clue to the depths of his rage.

A key incident that may have been the final straw in sending McVeigh on his course occurred on April 19, 1993, when federal agents surrounded the Branch Davidian compound near Waco, Texas. The Bureau of Alcohol, Tobacco, and Firearms (ATF) had undertaken a lengthy investigation and filed a number of weapons and drug charges against the compound's leader, David Koresh.[12] When Koresh and his followers failed to respond to demands by ATF and FBI agents to surrender after several days of negotiations, an assault was launched in which CS gas, Bradley assault vehicles, and armed federal agents attacked the compound. In the ensuing attack, seventy-four people—including several women and children—died in the fiery explosion from gunshots, severe burns, and smoke inhalation.[13] The tragedy was widely viewed as a failure of federal law enforcement in bringing the situation to a peaceful end, and the government's response was roundly criticized.

To right-wing paramilitary groups and others who were hostile to the U.S. government, the incident was particularly egregious because the power of federal law enforcement had been used to attack and kill American citizens. Among the outraged was Timothy McVeigh, who had visited the site during the siege and was interviewed and photographed by a team of reporters from a college newspaper.[14] An important detail of the Waco incident that McVeigh believed to be true was that the order to use force against the Branch Davidian compound originated in the law enforcement offices of the Oklahoma City federal building.[15]

Whether McVeigh was correct, the fact that he believed this to be so became an important point in the prosecution of the Oklahoma City bombing. Research has shown that "terrorists are rarely mindless or indiscriminate in their attacks" and select their targets for a particular purpose.[16] Some targets are selected for symbolic purposes, others for strategic reasons, and others for retribution. In the case of McVeigh's selection of the Oklahoma City federal building, the general view was that the building housed the agencies directly responsible for the Waco assault and its destruction by McVeigh was an act of revenge.

The significance of the Waco siege in pushing McVeigh toward violence was also noted in the fact that he chose April 19, 1995—the two-year anniversary of the Waco tragedy—to carry out what would up to that point be the deadliest terrorist attack on American soil. Shortly after 7:00 on the morning of April 19, McVeigh pulled out of the parking lot of the Imperial Motel in Kingman, Oklahoma.[17] He was driving a Ryder truck loaded with a 4,800-pound bomb made from a mixture of ammonium nitrate and fuel oil.[18] With the help of his army buddy Terry Nicols, McVeigh spent several months preparing the powerful bomb by using a fake name to purchase large quantities of ammonium nitrate and various other materials used to construct the explosive devise, including detonation cord, diesel fuel, and racing fuel.[19] The bomb had been patterned after a recipe outlined in *The Turner Diaries*, the right-wing, anti-government propaganda book McVeigh found to be so inspiring.

On his drive to Oklahoma City, McVeigh was careful not to draw attention to himself. He observed the speed limit and avoided committing any traffic infractions that might cause him to be stopped by law enforcement. Moreover, he arrived at the Alfred P. Murrah Federal Building after the morning rush hour so offices were busy and the body count higher. The date chosen for the attack was not only the second anniversary of the Waco siege, but also the 220-year anniversary of the Battle of Lexington and Concord that began the Revolutionary War. McVeigh's attire provided additional insight into his motive and mind set when he parked the bomb-laden truck on the northern side of the Murrah Federal Building:

As a token of his defiance, McVeigh was wearing his favorite Patriot T-shirt—the one with a drawing of Abraham Lincoln and the phrase SIC SEMPER TYRANIS—"Thus ever to tyrants"—... shouted by John Wilkes Booth after he shot Lincoln.... On the back of the shirt was the jolting image of a tree with droplets of red blood dripping off the branches, and superimposed on the tree, McVeigh's favored quote from Thomas Jefferson: THE TREE OF LIBERTY MUST BE REFRESHED FROM TIME TO TIME WITH THE BLOOD OF PATRIOTS AND TYRANTS.[20]

Before reaching his target, McVeigh pulled over to insert earplugs and light a five-minute fuse on the bomb. He then proceeded to the federal building, where he left the truck parked just underneath the windows of a daycare center located on the second floor and used by employees in the building.

McVeigh made his way to an escape vehicle parked a couple of blocks from the Murrah Building. At 9:02 a.m., the bomb went off, destroying the north facade of the structure, blowing out windows in hundreds of buildings in downtown Oklahoma, and lifting McVeigh himself nearly an inch off the ground.[21] The first wave from the explosion sent a wall of hot gases traveling at 7,000 miles an hour with the equivalent force of several tons.[22] Less than a second later, a second forceful wave caused by a vacuum from the hot gas lifted the federal building up, caused concrete slabs and metal beams to fracture, and all nine floors on the northern end of the building to collapse. The explosion killed 168 people, 163 of whom were in the Alfred P. Murrah Building at the time of the blast; four who were in the parking lot or one of the buildings directly across the street from the federal building; and a nurse who died while rushing to the scene to help victims.[23]

As rescue workers and first responders scrambled to locate survivors amid the wreckage and tend to the wounded, McVeigh traveled north away from Oklahoma City. In the days leading up to the bombing, he had contacted various individuals who were right-wing sympathizers he had met during the course of his travels. Despite all the care he had observed in constructing a powerful bomb and avoiding detection by law enforcement officers, McVeigh made a critical oversight that is surprising, given its simplicity yet high visibility. When he was about sixty miles north of Oklahoma City on Interstate 35, McVeigh was pulled over by an Oklahoma state trooper because of a missing license plate.[24] Under any other circumstance, the traffic stop would have been routine. A month earlier, however, an Oklahoma state trooper had been involved in a shooting with a motorist who pulled out a gun during a traffic stop; the incident had placed troopers on alert.[25] So when McVeigh told the officer he had a gun as he was bringing out his wallet, the trooper pulled his own gun and told McVeigh to turn and face the vehicle. After searching McVeigh's vehicle, the trooper took McVeigh into custody for driving without a license plate.

While McVeigh remained locked up in the Noble County Jail for two days, the police remained unaware that they had captured the primary suspect in the Oklahoma City bombing. For those two days, federal agents followed hundreds of leads that took them all over the United States. One lead in particular would ultimately lead investigators to McVeigh. Like the first World Trade Center bombing in 1993, investigators were able to locate a piece of metal from the truck used to transport the bomb. The rear axle of the Ryder truck was located in the rubble of the bombing site and contained an identification number used to trace the vehicle to a truck rental agency in Junction City, Kansas.[26] The truck had been rented to a man named "Robert Kling," and federal agents used a sketch artist to develop drawings of two men—John Doe #1 (Robert Kling) and John Doe #2 (an unknown individual)—who were believed to be the individuals who rented the truck. Using old-fashioned police work, investigators went door-to-door in the Junction City area in search of someone who might be able to identify either of the individuals. The manager of a local motel recognized John Doe #1, who investigators believed to be Robert Kling, but whom she knew by another name—Timothy McVeigh.[27] A computer check led federal investigators to the Noble County Jail where McVeigh was due to be released.

The day after the bombing, federal agents identified John Doe #1 as Timothy McVeigh and soon had enough information to indict Terry Nichols for helping McVeigh construct the bomb. McVeigh's other friend from the military, Michael Fortier, initially acted incredulous that his friend was implicated in the Oklahoma City bombing and was indignant when prosecutors threatened to charge him in the case as well. After a period of sparring with prosecutors, Fortier broke down and agreed to a plea bargain that saved him from the death penalty and provided a reduced prison sentence of twelve years in exchange for his testimony against his Army buddies.[28] The plea deal also provided Fortier's wife with immunity from prosecution, since she had laminated the fake driver's license that McVeigh used under the name Robert Kling to rent the Ryder truck used.[29] Fortier admitted to having helped McVeigh and Nichols transport stolen firearms and was also charged with lying to federal agents when they questioned him about McVeigh two days after the Oklahoma City bombing. Fortier helped McVeigh to scope out the Alfred P. Murrah Building and later claimed that he and McVeigh were unaware that a daycare center was located in the building. Also among the admissions made by Fortier was the fact that he had failed to notify authorities of the plot.[30]

The case against McVeigh was strong. With physical evidence obtained from the bombing site and eyewitness testimony linking him to the Ryder truck, as well as the testimony of Fortier and records of purchases that McVeigh and Nichols made for fuel, ammonium nitrate, and storage lockers, the result of the case was pretty much assured. After deliberating nearly twenty-four hours over a period of four days, the jury returned a verdict of guilty on June 2, 1997 on all eleven counts against McVeigh, including conspiracy and use of a weapon of mass destruction, destruction of government property with explosives, and eight counts of first-degree murder (for each of the federal law enforcement officials killed in the blast).[31] Nichols was convicted a little over six months later on December 23, 1997 by another federal jury of conspiracy in the bombing and eight counts of involuntary manslaughter.[32] He avoided conviction on the more serious counts of conspiracy to use a weapon of mass destruction and first-degree murder.

A number of factors were raised at McVeigh's sentencing. The number of fatalities (including the deaths of nineteen children in the daycare center), the devastation caused by the explosion, and the blatant symbolic attack on the U.S. government gave prosecutors a number of aggravating factors that called for the death penalty. For McVeigh's defense team, the fact that he had served his country with distinction in the Gulf War and had no prior history of major criminal behavior were mitigating factors weighing in favor of a sentence of life without the possibility of parole. In the end, McVeigh received a sentence of death for his role in the Oklahoma City bombing. Nichols was apologetic and sought leniency from the judge who passed sentence; the jury had apparently believed his claim that he never intended for anyone to be killed. He received a sentence of life without the possibility of parole.

Despite the appearance of a successful investigation and prosecution of the perpetrators of the Oklahoma City bombing, the case was not without deep controversy and lingering concerns about whether a conspiracy went well beyond McVeigh, Nichols, and Fortier. One unresolved issue was the identity of John Doe #2, who eyewitnesses said had accompanied McVeigh when he rented the Ryder truck. Furthermore, a piece of physical evidence at the bombing site raised suspicion that someone may have accompanied McVeigh when he parked the truck in front of the Murrah Federal Building: a severed leg could not be connected to any of the victims.

Stephen Jones, McVeigh's attorney who wrote a detailed account of his defense of the accused Oklahoma City bomber, noted that the government's initial indictment in the case was made against not only Timothy McVeigh and Terry Nichols, but also "others unknown."[33] The leg found at the bombing site turned out to belong to a woman who had died in the blast, but she had inadvertently been buried with a leg that did not belong to her. The difficulty in establishing the identity of the person to whom the extra leg belonged created speculation that one of the bombers died in the blast.

A theory that has persisted in the wake of the Oklahoma City bombing is that even if McVeigh and Nichols carried out their respective roles, they must have had some help. During the course of his defense of McVeigh, Jones traveled to London to obtain opinions from terrorism experts in the United Kingdom who had experience with bombs made from ammonium nitrate used in IRA attacks. According to Jones, a British army officer voiced skepticism that McVeigh and Nichols would have been able to carry out a massive attack alone:

I'm just telling you that no one else has ever been able to do it that way. Since we've been keeping records, and that goes way back before 1968, there's been no major incident of terrorism anywhere in the world, where anything like this number of people were killed and injured, that was the work of only two men. . . . Terrorism requires infrastructure, supplies, financing, safehouses, a getaway plan, lookouts, engineers, and leadership.

So if [McVeigh and Nichols] are guilty, they and no others, one has to ask oneself: What did [they] know that the PLO, ... Black September, and ... the IRA, and every other terrorist organization in the world that uses ammonium nitrate bombs, didn't know.[34]

When forming theories about vast conspiracies, it is always easy to ask rhetorical questions and assert that things are not always what they seem, even when proof is lacking. However, the theory that McVeigh and Nichols may have had help in their planning of the Oklahoma City bombing has some evidence to back up the claim. During his investigation, Jones learned of a former terrorist named Edwin Angeles who had co-founded and commanded an al-Qaeda-linked terrorist group in the Philippines known as the Abu Sayyaf Group.[35] In 1996, Angeles was arrested and decided to become a government informant. During the course of preparations for McVeigh's defense, Angeles claimed to have direct knowledge of a meeting between Terry Nichols and Ramsi Yousef—the mastermind behind the first World Trade Center attack in 1993—in which they were alleged to have discussed bomb construction.[36] Federal agents confirmed during the course of their investigation that Nichols had traveled to the Philippines at least five times between August of 1990 and January of 1995 when he was searching for, and ultimately met, his mail order bride and brought her back to the United States.[37]

In the very early phases of the investigation into the Oklahoma City bombing, there was speculation by some terrorism experts that the bombing was the work of Middle Eastern terrorists. Although the guilt of Timothy McVeigh and Terry Nichols has been established, the fact that they might have had ties to Ramsi Yousef and Middle Eastern terrorists was a theory that could have been used to mitigate their level of culpability. If they were able to provide evidence of others who might have been involved, then their lawyers would have leverage to bargain an arrangement that would save them from the death penalty.

Jones fought to have a deposition taken from Angeles and have it introduced at McVeigh's trial, but he discovered that the Philippine government had released the terrorist-turned-informer due to a lack of evidence.[38] Angered over the lack of support he received and the fact that he felt U.S. officials were placing a damper on his investigations in the Philippines into a possible Middle Eastern connection to the Oklahoma City bombing, Jones wrote:

> the most galling part of all, to me, was that the people who *ought* to have been proving, who had the power to intimidate and interrogate witnesses, some of whom were within their grasp and custody—I'm talking about our own Federal Bureau of Investigation, not to mention the so-called intelligence gathering agencies of our national government—just weren't interested. Instead of browbeat-

ing the minister in Manila to shut down our investigation, why weren't *they* grilling Edwin Angeles?[39]

In the end, the theory that Nichols and McVeigh had direct support from Middle Eastern terrorists or domestic terrorist groups was never proven in a court of law.

The final chapter of the Oklahoma City bombing was also not without controversy. Although McVeigh received the death penalty, his appeal raised a number of allegations, including problems with the handling of evidence from the Oklahoma City bombing by the FBI lab. Another issue McVeigh raised on appeal was the effectiveness of his legal representation. However, once he raised this claim, it opened the door for his attorney to respond and in doing so left no doubt about his role in the Oklahoma City bombing.[40] After a brief stay of execution, McVeigh decided to drop his appeal. He was executed at the federal penitentiary in Terre Haute, Indiana on June 11, 2001.[41]

The bombing of the Alfred P. Murrah Federal Building in Oklahoma City on April 19, 1995 is eclipsed only by the attacks of September 11, 2001 on the list of deadliest terrorist attacks on American soil. Like many profound events in history—including the assassinations of John F. Kennedy and Martin Luther King, Jr. or the attacks of September 11—the Oklahoma City bombing remains shrouded in claims of a broader conspiracy, the extent of which may never be fully known. But one interesting aspect of the conspiracy theory is the fact that seemingly divergent terrorist groups, such as those from the Middle East and right-wing domestic terrorists in the United States, share a common goal, namely destruction of the U.S. government. As a result, the global terrorist network is composed of organizations that share similar goals. This fact raises the possibility that groups will form strange alliances, increasing the challenge to law enforcement officers who are investigating terrorists attacks and intelligence and security agencies charged with preventing those attacks. If so, then McVeigh's statement to his attorney that "If no one else is arrested or convicted then the revolution can continue," may represent an ominous prediction of continued terrorist threats in the United States in the foreseeable future.

COMPULSORY NONSUIT?

THE CASE OF THE UNABOMBER

*Bad men, like good men, are entitled to be tried and
sentenced in accordance with law.*
—Hugo L. Black[1]

ON MAY 26, 1978, A PACKAGE WAS FOUND IN A PARKING LOT AT
Northwestern University in Chicago, Illinois, addressed to E. J. Smith, a
professor of rocket science at Rensselaer Polytechnic Institute in Troy, New
York. The return address indicated that the package had been sent by
Buckley Crist, a professor of computer science at Northwestern. Mary
Gutierrez, the woman who discovered the package, saw that it had sufficient
postage, so she tried to put it in a mailbox. When she was unable to fit the
package into the slot, she called Professor Crist, who sent a courier to pick
up the package. Upon seeing his name on the return address and knowing
that he had not sent the package, Crist called campus security and reported
the suspicious nature of the package.[2] When a public safety officer opened
the package, it exploded but caused only minor injuries.

This attack was the first of sixteen bombings eventually attributed to a
suspect known as the Unabomber, who managed to elude law enforcement
officers for nearly two decades. The bombing suspect was given the unusual name because most of his victims were connected in some way with universities or the airline industry. The second bombing attributed to the
Unabomber occurred on May 9, 1979, when a bomb placed inside a cigar
box was left on a table inside the Technical Building on the Northwestern
University campus in Evanston, Illinois. A student by the name of John
Harris opened the box, causing an explosion that inflicted cuts and burns
on him, but none of his injuries were serious.

Six months later, on November 15, a parcel bomb was routed to a Washington, D.C. post office and placed on an American Airlines flight from Chicago to the nation's capital. The bomb was rigged with a barometric device capable of measuring the airplane's altitude; it triggered an explosion when the airplane reached a height of 34,500 feet.[3] Although there was no major structural damage to the airplane, the pilots had to make an emergency landing at Dulles Airport in Virginia after smoke filled the cabin. Several passengers were treated for smoke inhalation.

The first victim of the Unabomber to incur serious injury was Percy Wood, President of United Airlines. On June 10, 1980, Wood received a copy of the book *Ice Brothers* at his home in Lake Forest, Illinois. He suffered serious facial and leg injuries when a bomb hidden in the pages of the book exploded. Among the remnants of the bomb were pieces of metal with the letters "FC" etched into the surface. These letters became an important clue used in the subsequent investigation to tie all of the Unabomber attacks to one another. The letters stood for "Freedom Club," a phrase referenced in communications the Unabomber subsequently had with law enforcement officers. Although "FC" was initially believed to be an important clue, it later turned out to be a meaningless phrase used by the Unabomber merely to confuse police.

From 1980 to 1985, the Unabomber was responsible for several other bombings targeting university campuses across the United States. A couple of the attacks resulted in no injuries because the bombs were defused before they detonated. However, in ensuing attacks, the injuries to victims grew in severity, reflecting the Unabomber's effectiveness at building destructive and lethal bombs. The first fatality attributed to the Unabomber occurred on December 11, 1985, when Hugh Scrutton, the owner of a computer store in Sacramento, California, found a package in the parking lot outside his store. When he attempted to move the package, it exploded, sending shrapnel into Scrutton's chest and puncturing his heart. Two other fatalities were subsequently attributed to the Unabomber. On December 10, 1994, advertising executive Thomas Mosser was killed when a package bomb sent to his home in North Caldwell, New Jersey exploded. Just over four months later, on April 24, 1995, another letter bomb killed California Forestry Association President Gilbert Murray in Sacramento, California.

The criminal investigation surrounding the Unabomber case was spearheaded by the FBI. Despite efforts to provide a criminal profile that would assist investigators in the apprehension of the suspect, the real break in the case came when a man named David Kaczynski contacted the FBI to express his belief that his brother might be the infamous Unabomber. In June 1995, the *Washington Post* and *The New York Times* shared the cost of publishing *Industrial Society and Its Future* by "FC," the moniker used by the Unabomber.[4] The two newspapers agreed to publish the 35,000-word manifesto because of concerns over public safety after the Unabomber threatened to blow up a commercial airliner flying out of Los Angeles if the document was not published.

David Kaczynski identified specific phraseology and wording in the manifesto similar to those he had seen in his brother's works. One of the sentences in the Unabomber manifesto that caught David Kaczynski's attention was the following: "But it is obvious that modern leftist philosophers are not simply *cool-headed logicians* systematically analyzing the foundation of knowledge."[5] "Cool-headed logicians" was a phrase David Kaczynski quickly recognized as one his brother used often during their philosophical discussions over the years. Also, the Unabomber manifesto contained a unique variation of a common phrase. At one point in the document, "FC" wrote "you can't eat your cake and have it too" instead of the more commonly used "you can't have your cake and eat it too."[6] Kaczynski's technically correct phrasing of the adage was in keeping with the exacting grammar and diction of the Unabomber manifesto, and also consistent with statements David Kaczynski had observed in his brother's previous writings. In addition, David Kaczynski saw parallels between trips his brother had taken and the locations of various mailings and bombing attacks that had been attributed to the Unabomber.

As a result of these tips, the FBI began an intensive investigation into Theodore J. Kaczynski who lived in a ten-foot by twelve-foot cabin in rural Montana. For nearly twenty-five years, Kaczynski lived in the cabin, situated on a 1.4-acre plot of land. He later estimated that he was able to live on as little as $400 a year by growing his own vegetables and foregoing the amenities of modern living, such as electricity and running water.[7]

On April 3, 1996, federal agents arrested Kaczynski. A search of his cabin revealed personal writings, a partially assembled bomb, and other materials that provided strong evidence that he was indeed the Unabomber. When Kaczynski was arrested, investigators found a wealth of evidence that provided detailed insight into his thinking and planning of the various bombing attacks ultimately attributed to the Unabomber. Kaczynski kept a detailed journal in which he outlined his various experiments on constructing more lethal bombs. Some of his early journal entries revealed he was disappointed that his early bombs had not resulted in the death of victims. For example, in a journal entry related to his first bombing attack, Kaczynski stated: "I hoped that a student ... would pick [the package bomb] up and would either be a good citizen and take the package to the post office ... or would open the package himself and blow his hands off, or get killed. ... I wish I had some assurance that I succeeded in killing or maiming someone."[8]

With respect to the second Unabomber attack involving the package bomb that injured Northwestern University student John Harris, Kaczynski wrote:

> I had hoped that the victim would be blinded or have his hands blown off or be otherwise maimed. ... At least I put him in the hospital, which is better than nothing. But not enough to satisfy me. Well, live and learn. No more match-head bombs. I wish I knew how to get hold of some dynamite.[9]

In several other journal entries, Kaczynski detailed the progression in his bomb-making techniques that ultimately led to more deadly devices. Over the years, his bombs became more powerful, and he ultimately achieved his intent to construct a package bomb that would kill. The first fatality attributed to one of his bombs occurred nearly seven years after his first attack, and two of the three fatalities attributed to him occurred nearly ten years later and within the eighteen-month period preceding his arrest.

One of the most fascinating aspects of the Unabomber case was the fact that Kaczynski was able to avoid detection and carried on his campaign of violence for nearly two decades. He was a terrorist of superb intellect who used his capabilities not only to perfect his bomb-making but also to develop methods for foiling the efforts of law enforcement to catch him. For example, Kaczynski had several pairs of aviator sunglasses he used as part of a disguise when mailing his package bombs. He also made a pair of double-soled tennis shoes that created the impression that the size of his footprints were different from his actual shoe size.[10] One of his journal entries revealed how he took human hair from the bathroom in a bus station and placed it between two pieces of electrical tape used in one of his package bombs; in this way, he would mislead forensic scientists attempting to use DNA evidence to link a particular individual to the bomb. It is easily arguable that if it were not for his brother's coming forward, Kaczynski's serial bombing campaign might have continued to this day.

A federal grand jury in Sacramento, California handed down an indictment on Kaczynski on June 18, 1996. The charge listed ten counts of criminal conduct in connection with three Unabomber attacks in California and another in Connecticut. Of course, Kaczynski felt betrayed by his brother and cut off what limited ties he had left with his family. In a public interview the following September, members of Kaczynski's family stated they had received letters from him in which he stated that he no longer wanted to have any contact with them even if his mother died; "there is nothing that could ever be important enough so that you would have to get in touch with me," he wrote to his brother.[11]

On October 2, 1996, Kaczynski was indicted by a federal grand jury in Newark, New Jersey for the 1994 mail bombing attack on Thomas Mosser—the only bombing for which the Unabomber ever publicly claimed responsibility. However, he was prosecuted in U.S. District Court in Sacramento where Judge Garland Burrell presided. In November 1996, the judge set a trial date for November 12, 1997. During the months leading up to the trial, Kaczynski's lawyers and federal prosecutors filed several motions in which they debated a number of legal issues pertaining to the admissibility of evidence seized from Kaczynski's cabin, including his personal journals and bomb-making materials.

A feature of the Unabomber case that ultimately distinguished it from many others involving terrorist suspects was the fact that major psychiatric issues were raised in pretrial proceedings. Based on extensive incriminating evidence the government had against Kaczynski, the only viable defense appeared to be insanity. However, Kaczynski was adamantly opposed to raising such a defense and expressed his position strongly and directly to his attorneys.

As part of their preparation for trial, Kaczynski's attorneys had their client evaluated by two forensic psychiatrists and two forensic psychologists. Kaczynski was resistant to being evaluated by mental health professionals and reportedly did not cooperate fully with the experts hired by his own attorneys. The lawyers told their client that they were seeking the evaluations only to keep legal options and strategies open. Kaczynski agreed to the evaluations only for that limited purpose, but remained firm in his wish not to raise an insanity defense. In a letter he later wrote to Judge Burrell,

Kaczynski expressed the sense of betrayal he felt when he learned that his attorneys were persisting in their plan to raise an insanity defense:

> When I unexpectedly learned in your courtroom that my attorneys had broken the promises ... made to me, I was shocked and horrified. The people who I thought were my friends had betrayed me. They had calculatedly deceived me in order to get me to reveal my private thoughts, and then without warning they made accessible to the public the cold and heartless assessments of their experts.[12]

One of the defense psychiatrists, Dr. Raquel Gur, was of the opinion that Kaczynski met the diagnostic criteria for paranoid schizophrenia, and neuropsychological testing by Dr. Ruben Gur was "not inconsistent" with this finding.[13] Three other defense experts were also of the opinion that Kaczynski suffered from paranoid schizophrenia. One of the reasons given by at least two of the experts to support their diagnosis was the fact that he was unwilling to submit to a psychiatric evaluation!

The prosecution retained two well-known forensic psychiatrists to evaluate Kaczynski, Drs. Phillip Resnick and Park Elliot Dietz. Given Kaczynski's refusal to submit to examinations by experts hired by his own attorneys, it is not surprising that Resnick and Dietz never had the opportunity to meet personally with Kaczynski.

A critical forensic psychiatrist issue that came to the forefront of the Unabomber case was Kaczynski's competence to stand trial. This issue arose shortly before testimony was about to begin in the case. After jury selection was completed in December of 1997, Kaczynski filed a motion to dismiss his attorneys and to be allowed to represent himself, due to the increasing tension and strain in the relationships he had with his lawyers over their insistence on the insanity defense. On January 7, 1998, Judge Burrell ruled that Kaczynski could not change his attorneys so late in the proceedings. The following day, the judge appeared to be leaning in the direction of permitting Kaczynski to defend himself if the defendant could prove himself competent. Whether the judge actually meant competent to stand trial or competent to serve as his own attorney was not clear. However, U.S. Marshals charged with securing court proceedings for the Unabomber trial noticed red marks on the defendant's neck and learned after an investigation that the previous evening, Kaczynski had tried to commit suicide in his cell by attempting to hang himself with his underwear.[14]

In the wake of Kaczynski's unsuccessful attempt to take his own life, Judge Burrell assigned a forensic psychiatrist, Dr. Sally Johnson, to conduct an evaluation of Kaczynski's competence to stand trial. The legal standard for competence to stand trial is outlined in the U.S. Supreme Court case of *Dusky v. United States.*[15] According to the test for competency set forth in *Dusky*, a criminal defendant is deemed to be not competent to stand trial if, as a result of a mental disorder, the person lacks the capacity to understand the legal proceedings in which he or she is involved or is unable to assist with his or her defense. For five days, Johnson conducted her evaluation of Kaczynski. In a nearly fifty-page report that was unsealed and made public in September of 1998, Dr. Johnson outlined her findings.[16]

She made a provisional diagnosis of schizophrenia, paranoid type, as well as a premorbid paranoid personality disorder with avoidant and antisocial features. Dr. Johnson's diagnosis has often been cited as evidence that Kaczynski may have had a viable defense of insanity because her tentative diagnosis of paranoid schizophrenia appeared to concur with the diagnosis offered by defense experts. However, a careful reading of Dr. Johnson's report reveals that her diagnosis was provisional, meaning that she was tentative in her conclusions because of "the limited duration of the diagnostic evaluation period and the fact that it would be useful to thoroughly review behavior and clinical symptomatology around those periods in Mr. Kaczynski's life that are closely associated with the criminal behavior" for which he was indicted."[17]

With respect to the issue of competence to stand trial, Dr. Johnson concluded that Kaczynski was of superior intelligence (his Full Scale IQ was 136 on formal testing), had the ability to read and interpret complex writing, and was "able to track the rather complicated discussion regarding legal issues in an area where the law was unclear."[18] Dr. Johnson concluded that Kaczynski was competent to stand trial "despite the diagnoses that have been rendered" and "is able to understand the nature and consequences of the proceedings against [him], and is able to assist his attorneys in his defense."[19]

However, Dr. Johnson also noted that Kaczynski might present challenges for his attorneys during the trial and might even have some difficulties if he was not represented by legal counsel and chose to act as his own attorney instead. More specifically, Dr. Johnson felt that Kaczynski was prone to focus on details and to be "reluctant to separate out useful detail from unnecessary detail."[20] She also felt that even if Kaczynski was to be provided with new lawyers, there was a strong likelihood that the conflicts he had with his current attorneys would continue with the new lawyers.

After Dr. Johnson submitted her report, Judge Burrell ruled that Kaczynski was competent to stand trial, a finding with which both the defense attorneys and the prosecutors agreed. However, the judge rejected Kaczynski's request to serve as his own attorney, saying that the request was not timely. The same day that Judge Burrell issued his ruling denying Kaczynski's request to represent himself, a plea bargain arrangement was reached in which Kaczynski agreed to plead guilty to thirteen counts in the indictment in exchange for a sentence of life without the possibility of parole. By agreeing to the plea arrangement, Kaczynski avoided the death penalty but agreed to give up his right to any appeal of his conviction.

On May 4, 1998, Kaczynski was sentenced to four consecutive life sentences. At his sentencing hearing, where victims and their families made emotional pleas for a harsh sentence, Kaczynski made a statement in which he argued that prosecutors distorted his motives and beliefs. The issue of Kaczynski's competence to stand trial raised a number of questions that continue to be debated to this day. The following issues do not appear to be disputed: 1) Kaczynski was deemed to be competent to stand trial on the basis of Dr. Johnson's evaluation and Judge Burrell's interpretation of the findings from that evaluation; and 2) Kaczynski had a right guaranteed under the Sixth Amendment of the U.S. Constitution to legal representation of his own choosing. In light of the U.S. Supreme Court ruling in the case of *Godinez v. Moran* (1993),[21] in which the standard for competence to stand trial is the same as the standard for competence to plead guilty or represent oneself in court, why was Kaczynski denied his request to exercise his constitutional right and serve as his own legal counsel?

This specific question has been debated extensively in the aftermath of the Unabomber case. One argument has been that Kaczynski was denied his Sixth Amendment right to a trial and to serve as his own attorney as a result of Judge Burrell's ruling that Kaczynski could not represent himself, even after Dr. Johnson's report was filed and the defendant had proven his competence as the judge requested.[22] Furthermore, even though Kaczynski had virtually no viable legal defense other than insanity, and any other legal strategy would most likely have ended with a conviction and death sentence, the decision to reject the insanity defense was solely Kaczynski's. In light of his agreement to forego his right to appeal his conviction as part of his plea arrangement, the issue of whether Kaczynski was denied his constitutional right to represent himself may never be addressed by an appellate court.

The evidence against Kaczynski was never laid out in a trial, and the facts pertaining to his planning and motives were never aired publicly in a legal arena. One could speculate that Kaczynski could have attempted to raise a defense based on the notion that his attacks were politically necessary to prevent technology from destroying civilization, but the likelihood that a court would permit such a defense to be raised is extremely remote. Furthermore, the likelihood that such a defense would convince a jury to acquit Kaczynski was extremely slim. Consequently, allowing Kaczynski to proceed to trial without raising a defense of insanity would have resulted in certain conviction and death. Although prosecutors were invested in securing a conviction of Kaczynski as the Unabomber attacks, a public trial might have been very useful to ongoing counterterrorism efforts by creating a public record of the various strategies and techniques Kaczynski used to avoid capture and further his terrorist agenda. Still, there is a wealth of material that remains available for study.

The psychiatric issues of competence to stand trial and insanity, as well as the absence of a public trial where prosecutors could offer proof as to Kaczynski's terrorist motives, obscure the fact that the Unabomber's motives were a complex blend of personal rage, political activism around a singular issue (i.e., technological advances in society), and a desire for revenge. The clearest evidence of Kaczynski's motives come from his own journal when he wrote the following on April 6, 1971, seven years before the start of his bombing campaign:

My motive for doing what I am going to do is simply personal revenge. I do not expect to accomplish anything by it. Of course, if my crime (and my reasons for committing it) gets any public attention, it may help to stimulate public interest in the technology question and thereby improve the changes for stopping technology before it is too late. . . . Of course, I would like to get revenge on the whole scientific and bureaucratic establishment, not to mention communists and others who threaten freedom, but, that being impossible, I have to content myself with just a little revenge.[23]

Aside from the psychiatric issue of Kaczynski's competence, the Unabomber case ultimately became a criminal equivalent of what is known in civil litigation as a *compulsory nonsuit,* which means that plaintiffs have their claims dismissed against their wishes without ever having an opportunity to prove their case in court. Kaczynski was ultimately forced to plead guilty and forego a trial only because he detested the thought of having his sanity questioned more than the thought of facing an almost certain death sentence. Although the U.S. Supreme Court has held that defendants found to be competent to stand trial are also competent to represent themselves in court, such was not the way the law of criminal competencies operated in what is perhaps the most celebrated "non-trial" of a terrorist in U.S. legal history.

As for Kaczynski, he made the following statement in the wake of his compulsory nonsuit: "Recent events constitute a major defeat for me. But the end is not yet. More will be heard from me in the future."[24] Although Kaczynski remains incarcerated in a high-security federal prison that also houses Ramsi Yousef, the purported mastermind behind the first World Trade Center bombing, the risk that Kaczynski still poses is that his manifesto and proficiency in evading law enforcement while carrying out a series of bombings may serve as a blueprint for like-minded terrorists in the future.

REGIONAL MANHUNT

THE CASE OF ERIC RUDOLPH

*The policeman on the street is the single most powerful person in the
entire American system of criminal justice.*
—Johnnie L. Cochran, Jr.[1]

THE OLYMPIC GAMES DRAW ATHLETES AND SPECTATORS FROM ALL OVER THE
world. They are meant to serve as a peaceful celebration of individual and
team excellence in sports of all kinds. Given their high visibility—with television, newspaper, and magazine reporters covering all aspects of the
games—it comes as no surprise that the Olympics are an ideal target for
terrorists. One of the most sensational terrorist attacks in history occurred
at the 1972 Olympics when Israeli athletes were taken hostage by members
of the PLO-backed group, Black September. When Atlanta, Georgia
became the site of the 1996 summer Olympics, elaborate security precautions were developed well in advance. Not only did the Olympics constitute an attractive international stage for terrorists, but the United States had
experienced its deadliest terrorist attack up to that time just a year earlier
when the Oklahoma City bombing claimed 168 lives.

In the early morning hours of July 27, 1996, tens of thousands of individuals were celebrating at an outdoor concert at Centennial Olympic Park
in downtown Atlanta.[2] The park was an expansive area allowing athletes,
spectators, and visitors to the Olympics to dine and socialize. Despite the
friendly ambiance, the largest security force in the history of the Olympics
was on hand, and four surveillance cameras provided additional protection
at Centennial Park. A rock concert had been scheduled as part of the
Olympic celebration on the evening of July 26. Shortly after midnight, Tom
Davis, an officer with the Georgia Bureau of Investigation assigned to security detail for the Olympics, was making his rounds near a lighting tower.

Davis was approached by a former police officer and private security guard, Richard Jewell, who was also working at the Olympics.

Jewell told Davis that a group of intoxicated young men were near a sound tower. They were throwing beer cans, and Jewell asked Davis how the situation should be handled. When the two men approached the tower, the group of men dispersed, but Jewell noticed a green, military-style backpack located under a bench.[3] At first, Davis said that he and Jewell should try to locate the owner of the backpack, and if they were unable to do so, then it would be considered suspicious. Just before 1:00 a.m., Davis and Jewell had not been able to find anyone claiming ownership of the backpack, so two agents from the bomb assessment unit were called. As they opened the flap and peered in, they saw wires and a pipe. At that point, the agents decided the bomb disposal unit should be called. However, Davis was confronted with another problem—should the area be evacuated or could the backpack be disposed of without causing alarm or panic?

Since Davis wanted to discuss the difficult situation with his supervisor, a decision was made to begin clearing people from the location of the suspicious backpack. Jewell took the initiative of moving individuals away from the tower. At 12:58 a.m., just before the backpack was inspected, an Atlanta 911 dispatcher received a call warning of an extremely dangerous situation.[4] A man warned the dispatcher, "There is a bomb in Centennial Park.... You have thirty minutes." A series of errors in communication between the 911 operator and the Atlanta Police Department's Command Center, however—including problems with identifying the address of Centennial Plaza—prevented anyone at the Olympics from receiving word of the bomb threat.

At 1:18 a.m., an explosion ripped through Olympic Park plaza. Davis was about twenty steps from the backpack when it blew up. A flash of heat and deafening sound knocked him to the ground. The bomb inside the backpack consisted of three galvanized metal pipes filled with explosive powder and masonry nails.[5] A timing mechanism powered by a twelve-volt lantern battery was used to set off the device. In addition, a one-eighth-inch thick steel plate was placed inside the backpack to direct the blast and nails in the direction of the crowd.

Alice Hawthorne, who was attending the concert with her daughter, Fallon Stubbs, was killed and a Turkish cameraman covering the aftermath of the explosion died of a heart attack.[6] Stubbs, who survived the attack, saw her mother lying on the ground but was unable to respond because of her own injuries.

Within hours of the bombing, the investigation was derailed by a series of problems that ultimately led to the case dragging on for years before it was resolved. The first of the problems was an erroneous criminal profile that led FBI agents to focus their suspicion on Richard Jewell, the man who had heroically notified police of the suspicious backpack and whose actions were believed to have prevented numerous deaths. Soon after the bombing, FBI profilers formulated an assessment of the unknown bombing suspect based on a combination of details that were known from the telephone warning and various psychological characteristics ascribed to individuals who perpetrated bombings of this type. The initial profile suggested that the bomber was a white American male who had an indistinguishable accent and who liked to operate "on the fringes of law enforcement who would plant a bomb so he could come to the rescue."[7] Jewell had been a security guard at a small liberal arts college in northern Georgia, and the president of the college informed the FBI of his concerns that Jewell might have been involved in the bombing, because he had been involved in "improper conduct" in the past.[8] A former neighbor of Jewell reported to the FBI that sometime in the mid-1990s, Jewell was observed to be acting nervously following an explosion in the woods near a house he was renting. In addition, Jewell had reportedly made statements to other employees at the Olympics that he wanted to be in the middle of anything that occurred and that he would be "famous."[9] These aspects of Jewell's background, along with the fact that he had been instrumental in finding the backpack and helped secure the area, led FBI profilers to suspect that he was involved.

The process of criminal profiling is intended to assist investigators in directing investigations by identifying possible psychological characteristics of unknown individuals who have perpetrated a crime. A profile is then used to narrow leads and assist investigators when they question suspects. In the case of the Olympic bombing, profiling led investigators to suspect Jewell, and he was placed under intense scrutiny. His television interviews as the hero who identified the backpack, the combing of his personal history for unusual behaviors, his interest in law enforcement, and statements he made to others about his aspirations seemed to fit the identified profile like a glove. As a result, he was interrogated extensively, and investigators searched his home and personal belongings for clues to confirm their suspicions that he had something to do with the bombing.

In the media, Jewell soon went from being a hero to the prime suspect. Despite the circumstantial evidence that raised suspicions about him, he managed to make a critical decision that would save him from arrest and wrongful conviction. He contacted a lawyer who helped mount a counter-attack in the media that ultimately convinced investigators of Jewell's innocence. Jewell's attorney began to question the motives of federal investigators and even reported that Jewell had taken and passed a lie detector test "with flying colors."[10] Although results from polygraph examinations are often not admissible as evidence in court and are of questionable reliability, the effect for Jewell in the media was successfully to raise doubt about the criminal investigation. In the end, Jewell's name would be officially cleared after an eighty-eight-day nightmare for him, and he later sought monetary damages from various media outlets for having been wrongly identified as the person responsible for the Olympic Park bombing.[11]

Over the next six months, the investigation stagnated, and there were no useful leads. A task force was assembled, which was given the codename CENTBOMB Task Force and consisted of various federal agents from the FBI and Bureau of Tobacco, Firearms and Explosives (ATF), as well as agents from the Georgia Bureau of Investigation.[12] With new agents involved, another attempt was made to formulate a profile of the unknown bomber. This time, FBI agents sought the services of the nationally known forensic psychiatrist, Park Elliott Dietz. As an expert who had assisted federal agents in scores of other cases, and who had developed an accurate profile in another bombing case that led to an arrest, Dietz seemed to be the best choice. Relying on a number of puzzling clues, such as the 911 call warning of the bomb and the military-style backpack used to conceal the explosive device, Dietz suggested that the bomber's intended targets were law enforcement officers responding to the bomb threat and that the perpetrator was a lone individual with military training, anti-government attitudes, and ties to right-wing militia groups.[13]

Although the revised profile offered new ideas for pursuing leads, the investigation languished until January 16, 1997, when a bomb exploded outside a professional building in suburban Atlanta that also housed a family planning clinic.[14] About forty-five minutes after the first bomb went off, and just as police officers and other rescue personnel arrived at the scene, a second bomb went off in a trash bin located in the parking lot. Seven people were injured, but there were no fatalities. A witness was able to provide a description of a man with a duffle bag and military tools who was near the building prior to the bombing.

Over a month later, on February 21, 1997, another bombing took place outside a gay and lesbian bar in Atlanta. This time, police officers were able to locate and study a second bomb placed near the scene before detonating it safely in a controlled setting.[15] No one was injured, but the clues to this bombing afforded investigators an opportunity to identify the materials used to build the bombs and ultimately to link them with the bombing on January 16 and the Olympic Park explosion. Several features of the cases were consistent with the profile developed by Dietz. The bomber's use of military-style backpacks, his detailed knowledge of how to construct a lethal pipe bomb, and the use of two different explosive devices set to go off at different times with the second intended to injure rescue personnel indicated that the bomber had military training and was targeting law enforcement officers, like Dietz predicted. However, the choice of targets, including a family planning clinic, gay and lesbian bar, and the Olympic games, raised questions about the bomber's motives.

Within days of the February 21 bombing, various media outlets began receiving anonymous letters providing detailed clues about the composition of each bomb that only the bomber would know, thus proving that the letters were from the serial bomber. They provided the first glimpse of his terrorist motives. The author of the letters claimed that the two recent bombings had been carried out by the "Army of God" and explained why the particular targets were selected:

THE ABORTION WAS THE TARGET OF THE FIRST DEVICE [at the family planning clinic]. THE MURDER OF 3.5 MILLION CHILDREN EVERY YEAR WILL NOT BE 'TOLERATED'. THOSE WHO PARTICIPATE IN <u>ANYWAY</u> IN THE MURDER OF CHILDREN MAY BE TARGETED FOR ATTACK. THE ATTACK THEREFORE SERVES AS A WARNING: <u>ANYONE</u> IN OR AROUND FACILITIES THAT MURDER CHILDREN MAY BECOME VICTIMS OF RETRIBUTION. THE NEXT FACILITY TARGETED <u>MAY NOT BE EMPTY</u>. . . .

THE SECOND DEVICE WAS AIMED AT AGENT OF THE SO-CALLED FEDERAL GOVERNMENT ...

THE ATTACK IN MIDTOWN [at the bar] WAS AIMED AT THE SODOMITE BAR (THE OTHERSIDE). WE WILL TARGET SODOMITES, THERE ORGANIZATIONS, AND ALL THOSE WHO PUSH THERE AGENDA.[16]

These letters provided additional confirmation of theories outlined in the revised profile that the unknown bombing suspect had strong anti-government attitudes and prominent religious beliefs that are associated with some Christian-based militia groups.

A major break in the investigation came when a fourth bombing tied to the still unknown bomber took place outside an abortion clinic in Birmingham, Alabama, nearly a year later on January 29, 1998.[17] In this case, an off-duty police officer guarding the clinic because of recurrent threats was killed, and a nurse reporting for work was seriously injured. The blast was so powerful that it shattered windows a block away. Unlike earlier cases where devices either never went off or failed to injure or kill a police officer, the bomber detonated the bomb from nearby using a remote-control device.

Wearing jeans, a long coat, and a brown wig, the bomber did not realize that someone saw him leaving the scene of the Birmingham bombing. A medical student living in a dormitory on the edge of a nearby park who was doing laundry when the blast occurred went outside to see what was happening. The student's attention was immediately drawn to an odd occurrence—while several people were either walking or running toward the site of the explosion, a white male wearing a baseball cap and carrying a backpack was walking casually *away* from the scene.[18] In this key moment, the student was not satisfied with merely making a mental note of the suspicious individual. He decided to follow the man, who proved to be elusive. Although the medical student lost sight of the suspicious man after nearly a half hour, he was able to enlist the help of another bystander who found the fleeing individual and observed him getting into his vehicle—a gray Toyota pickup truck with the North Carolina plate number KND1117.[19] This clue would ultimately lead investigators to identify Eric Rudolph as the man responsible not only for the Birmingham abortion clinic bombing but also the three Atlanta area bombings, including the Olympic Park bombing.

Rudolph seemed to fit the most recent profile of Olympic Park bombing suspect extremely well. He was a survivalist who was able to live in the wilderness for long periods of time.[20] He had been in the Army and received training in demolitions and explosives. However, he smoked marijuana heavily and voiced strong anti-government attitudes while enlisted. After failing to qualify to join the Army Rangers Special Forces unit, Rudolph became more of a discipline problem and often threw equipment, showed disrespect to others, and defied authority.[21] As his disciplinary problems in the military escalated, he was counseled repeatedly and ultimately left the Army after serving a little over a year. Rudolph and his family had ties to a militant, racist, and anti-Semitic organization known as the Christian Identity movement.[22] Rudolph frequently espoused several of the ideas associated with this movement, including attacking homosexuals, holding militant views against abortion, and harboring anti-government attitudes. In short, Rudolph appeared to fit Dietz's profile in nearly every way.

Rudolph's skill at surviving in the wilderness would prove to be the one factor that presented federal and state law enforcement officers with their greatest challenge in bringing the case to a close. Knowing that Rudolph was their prime suspect and knowing where he lived did not permit a quick arrest; for the next five years, Rudolph remained at large. When he learned through media outlets that he was being sought for questioning, he fled his trailer in January 1998 and began hiding in the forests of western North Carolina. Reports occasionally surfaced that Rudolph had been spotted buying supplies in nearby stores or foraging for food. Authorities also suspected, but could never prove conclusively, that some individuals in the rural region sympathetic to his anti-government views provided him with assistance.

During the five years he was able to elude capture, Rudolph was placed on the FBI's Most Wanted list and was later described by U.S. Attorney General John Ashcroft as "the most notorious American fugitive."[23] Rudolph's ultimate capture, however, is a classic example of the principle that one of the most effective tools for preventing and combating terrorism is the police officer on patrol or security guard on duty.

In the early morning hours of May 31, 2003, a police officer in Murphy, North Carolina was performing his weekend patrol. As a rookie officer, he was eager to perform his duties well, and during a check of businesses in the downtown area, he would routinely turn off the headlights to his patrol car in order to avoid detection as he patrolled through alleys. On that morning in May, his tactic paid off profoundly when he was able to observe an individual squatting in the middle of the road with something in his hand. The man ran down an alley when he saw the police car and hid behind some crates. When the officer shielded himself behind the open door of his patrol car, pulled out his weapon, and called for the man to come out with his hands up, the individual surrendered and was arrested. It took time to make a correct identification, but the man the officer arrested was Eric Rudolph, who had been searching for food in trash bins.

With the capture of the elusive Olympic Park bomber, the focus turned quickly to proving that Rudolph had committed the four bombings he was suspected of having carried out. Prosecutors were initially set on seeking the death penalty. In early 2005, nearly two years after his arrest, however, Rudolph agreed to plead guilty in exchange for a sentence of life in prison without the possibility of parole.[24] Although victims and their family members were disappointed, Rudolph did not receive the death penalty. Prosecutors stated that one of the main reasons for agreeing to the plea arrangement was the fact that Rudolph had ultimately disclosed to investigators the location of approximately 250 pounds of explosives he had hidden in the western North Carolina wilderness.[25] If the case had gone to trial, the location of the explosives might not have been identified by Rudolph, and the outcome of a trial was uncertain.

The case of the bombing at the Atlanta Olympics and the three related bombings carried out by Eric Rudolph underscores a number of important aspects of terrorism on American soil. There remains a current threat from domestic right-wing extremists who espouse strong anti-government, racist, anti-Semitic, and anti-abortion views, who believe terrorist violence is the way to bring about social and political change. Furthermore, the case illustrates significant problems authorities encounter in identifying and investigating terrorist threats, particularly when a lone individual operates clandestinely and possesses specialized skills—in this case the ability to survive in the wilderness for years—that create a more potent threat. Finally, the case illustrates that alert and resourceful police officers are one of the most effective tools in the arsenal against terrorism.

A FINGER ON THE TRIGGER

AMERICA'S FIRST SUICIDE TERRORIST BOMBERS

A good scare is worth more to a man than good advice.
—Edgar Watson Howe[1]

USE OF THE PHRASE "SUICIDE BOMBERS" TO DESCRIBE INDIVIDUALS WHO knowingly kill themselves and simultaneously cause the deaths of innocent people is a source of debate and controversy. Suicide has traditionally been defined as the intentional killing of one's self. However, suicide terrorists do not seek their own deaths as a primary goal, but are instead willing to die in the course of killing other people. Often the most effective suicide terrorist method is the detonation of a bomb in a crowded public place—such as a restaurant, shopping mall, or bus. Suicide terrorists are extremely effective and flexible weapons because they are difficult to spot, bring human judgment and intelligence to the detonation process, and are more difficult to prevent than bombs controlled by timing devices. A human weapons system "can effect last-minute changes based on the ease of approach, paucity or density of people, and the security measures [that can be seen]."[2]

In recent years, suicide terrorists have proven to be highly proficient at not only provoking fear but getting to highly protected targets. Israel has been the target of a number of high-profile bombings carried out by suicide bombers with powerful explosives strapped to their waists.[3] Many of these so-called belt bombs are packed with nails and other materials that produce shrapnel. The Liberation Tigers of Tamil Elam on the island of Sri Lanka is a terrorist organization that has developed some of the most proficient suicide bombers in the world. Many of their attacks defy the stereotype of a suicide bomber because many have been carried out by women, with the most infamous one being the 1991 assassination of Indian prime minister Rajiv Gandhi.[4]

The use of suicide bombers by terrorist groups is favored for many reasons. Suicide bombs are inexpensive and can be built using materials found in pharmacies or hardware stores. Furthermore, there appears to be no shortage of individuals who are willing to become martyrs for their cause. According to terrorism expert Bruce Hoffman, "suicide terrorism has become a mass movement," and "it is not as hard to make a suicide bomber as many people have wanted to believe."[5]

Although suicide terrorism has been much more prevalent in other parts of the world—in countries like Israel, Sri Lanka, and regions in the Middle East—the terrorist attacks of September 11 prompted concern that suicide bombers would be the next serious threat to the national security of the United States. Given the expansive size of the United States compared to other countries where suicide terrorism has been more prevalent, terrorist groups might be inclined to target densely populated areas. Any suicide attacks—regardless of where they occur—would likely trigger fear throughout the country and make Americans feel less safe in public places. A mistaken notion about suicide attacks in the United States is that we have not been targeted by this lethal form of terrorism prior to September 11, 2001. However, four years before those attacks, two suicide bombers were captured in a dramatic police raid that prevented what would have certainly been a deadly attack on American soil. The bombers—who were caught literally with their fingers on the trigger—were ready to blow themselves up in a crowded subway station in New York City and would have killed an untold number of people and injured countless others.

At approximately 10:45 on the evening of July 30, 1997, an Egyptian immigrant by the name of Abdel Rahman Mosabbah left the squalid apartment he was sharing with three other individuals at 248 Fourth Avenue in Brooklyn.[6] Two of his roommates were Palestinians named Gazi Ibrahim Abu Mezer and Lafi Khalil; the other roommate was a fellow Egyptian by the name of Mohammed Chindluri. Just two weeks earlier, on July 14, Mosabbah had fulfilled a dream by entering the United States as a legal alien with a green card and aspirations of economic success. He was planning to bring his family from Egypt once he established himself and saved enough money. He found the dingy apartment by word of mouth but considered it to be a far cry from his expectation of living a prosperous life in the United States. Furthermore, Mosabbah's life quickly became a nightmare on the evening of July 30 when Abu Mezer and Khalil shared their plans to blow themselves up in the crowded New York City subway system early the next morning.

Earlier that afternoon, two Palestinian suicide bombers had blown themselves up in the crowded, open-air Mahane Yehuda food market located in the center of Jerusalem.[7] The bombers used a combination of high explosives and shrapnel-producing metal to create devices intended to maximize fatalities and create carnage among those who managed to survive the attack. Furthermore, the two bombers coordinated the detonation of their respective devices. They entered the market together, each wearing a business suit that had been made for the occasion. Underneath their jackets, they each had two twenty-pound satchels filled with a highly volatile compound known as a "bathtub explosive" consisting of triacetone triperoxide—a combination of common drugstore products that can be mixed easily in a bathroom sink or tub.[8] As the two men stood approximately twenty-five yards apart, the first detonated his bomb and killed both himself and anyone standing near him. Numerous people were knocked to the ground, and several were critically injured. About three minutes later, as police and rescue workers were tending to the injured, the second suicide bomber detonated his device and killed or injured several others. The staggered timing of the suicide bombings is a favored technique intended not only to injure more people, including police officers and rescue workers tending to victims, but also to create fear of additional bombings, thus increasing panic and hampering aid to the injured. Shrapnel used in the belt bombs is also frequently soaked in rat poison to increase the rate of infection in the wounds of the survivors and to inhibit blood-clotting, thus increasing the likelihood that those who are injured will bleed to death.[9]

In all, seventeen people (including children) were killed, and 168 others were critically injured. The double suicide bombing rates as one of the deadliest in the history of the Israeli-Palestinian conflict. Moreover, the suicide attack spurred Abu Mezer and Khalil to try a similar attack inside the United States the very next day.

Mosabbah had been sharing the small apartment temporarily with the three other Middle Eastern travelers until he could secure employment and bring his family to the United States. Two of his roommates, Abu Mezer and Khalil, were Palestinian-born immigrants who had entered the country illegally. On the day of the Mahane Yehuda market bombing in Jerusalem, Abu Mezer approached Mosabbah and asked if he had heard about the attack and said he had something to show the Egyptian. Although Mosabbah expected Abu Mezer to show him another piece of literature with inflammatory speech that was hostile to Israel or the United States, Abu Mezer produced a satchel containing pipes.[10] The pipes were each covered with hundreds of five-inch nails held together with electrical tape. Also connected to the pipe bombs were red and blue wires attached to two industrial-size batteries.

Although Mosabbah was initially confused about what he was seeing, his confusion quickly turned to fear when he realized that Abu Mezer was showing him pipe bombs. With a fixed gaze and determination, Abu Mezer then said to his roommate, "Did you see what happened in Jerusalem? ... Well, tomorrow it will happen here."[11] He then took a pinch of gunpowder that had been used to make the bombs and added, "This is how the Jews will burn."[12]

It is unclear why Abu Mezer decided to tell his roommate what he intended to do, but he apparently felt quite confident his plan would be successful. He even told Mosabbah that it did not matter if the authorities were notified because the bombs were set to explode. Abu Mezer said that he would detonate the pipe bombs if anyone tried to stop him. What is clear, however, is that Mosabbah's fear was overwhelming, yet he made a decision that would ultimately prevent the devastating suicide attack from occurring in the crowded subways of New York City.

Without raising suspicion, Mosabbah left the apartment as quickly as he could, by telling his roommates that he was going out for a while. The combination of his fear and lack of familiarity with the American legal system created a sense of both urgency and confusion. His experiences in Egypt, where people would sometimes disappear into police custody and later return with stories of being tortured, made him wary of approaching the police. Nevertheless, he decided to notify the authorities of the bombing plot and called the operator at a telephone booth a block away from his apartment.[13] When his heavy accent made it difficult for the operator to understand him, Mosabbah hung up and continued walking until he found two Long Island Rail Road police officers outside a train station. When he told the officers of what he had been shown, they did not know initially if Mosabbah's story was valid or the ranting of a confused person. Two features of Mosabbah's presentation throughout the ensuing evening that would press the investigation further were his extreme fear and his persistence.

Over the next several hours, a variety of law enforcement agencies were notified, and Mosabbah was subjected to intense questioning. Police officers asked him detailed questions about the location of the apartment, the layout of the rooms, and the number of people in the apartment. When one officer drove by the address Mosabbah had given, some details matched the Egyptian's description of the neighborhood, but the entrance to the apartment was hidden behind a building facade, and police officers were uncertain if Mosabbah was telling the truth or merely setting them up for an ambush.

Police decided to raid the apartment with a team of specially trained officers. Mosabbah was brought along to show them the way to the entrance. The tension was heightened by the fact that Abu Mezer had threatened to detonate the bombs if anyone tried to stop him. Police officers were well aware of the fact that if the plot was indeed a suicide attack, the individuals planning the attack would give little thought to blowing themselves up, along with any police officers who happened to intervene.

Dozens of officers cordoned off several blocks around the Brooklyn apartment, and an entry team of six officers entered the apartment shortly before 5:00 a.m., accompanied by Mosabbah, who showed them exactly where the apartment was located. Since Mosabbah had the key to the apartment, the officers were able to enter quietly and unnoticed. Once inside, they made their way to the closed door of the bedroom where Abu Mezer and Khalil were still awake and talking to each other. As Chindluri slept on a cot in the outside room, the police used a battering shield to break through the door to the room where Abu Mezer and Khalil were lying down. With their weapons drawn, officers yelled for the men to stay down and attempted to secure the room. Abu Mezer fought back and a struggle ensued. Within seconds, both Abu Mezer and Khalil were shot several times. Police officers found the satchel containing the pipe bombs, but noticed that one of several switches had been turned on.[14]

Over the next several hours, a bomb disposal unit was summoned, and police officers questioned Abu Mezer as he awaited surgery at a hospital about how the bombs should be defused. When asked if he had planned on blowing himself up, Abu Mezer merely replied, "Poof" and admitted he was associated with the terrorist group Hamas and wanted to explode his bombs on a train that would kill as many Jews as possible.[15] He had selected a specific subway train to blow up at 8:00 a.m. on the morning of July 31 because he believed the train would have several Jewish passengers. If Abu

Mezer was being truthful—and there is no reason to doubt his sincerity—police officers prevented a devastating suicide attack only a few hours before it was scheduled to occur.

Although Abu Mezer gave vague responses about how the bombs could be defused, he told police to cut the wires. Given his determination to kill police if he was caught there, the bomb disposal unit was understandably reluctant to follow the captured suicide bomber's advice. Nevertheless, the bombs were successfully defused, and both Abu Mezer and Khalil survived the wounds they received during the police raid. When the New York Police Department and federal agents later detonated the bombs in a controlled setting, they were "shocked by the ferocious force of the devices."[16] The bombs would certainly have resulted in the death of dozens, if not hundreds, of people and injured many more. With the entire police operation deemed a success, questions arose about the motives of these two would-be suicide terrorists and who, if anyone, supported their operation.

The Office of the Inspector General in the U.S. Department of Justice conducted an extensive investigation into how Abu Mezer and Khalil were able to enter the United States illegally, remain undetected, and assemble the components of their bombs.[17] In 1993, Abu Mezer obtained a student visa through the Canadian embassy in Israel, which allowed him to remain in Canada as long as he was enrolled as a student. Although he had been detained twice by Israeli authorities for security offenses, Canadian officials did not check his criminal background. When he arrived in Toronto in September 1993, he applied immediately for a visa to enter the United States. His request was denied, so he then filed for political refugee status in Canada, which permitted him to remain in the country until a decision was made on his application.[18] While his request for asylum was pending, Abu Mezer was charged with two crimes. In 1994, he was arrested for using a stolen credit card, and in 1995, he received a conditional discharge and one-year probation for a minor assault charge.[19] There is no documentation that Abu Mezer ever enrolled as a student at a Canadian university.

In June 1996, Abu Mezer was apprehended twice for trying to enter the United States illegally. He attempted to cross the U.S.-Canadian border while jogging casually through a park, but U.S. Border Patrol officers caught him each time and sent him back to Canada. But in January 1997, he was caught trying to enter the United States illegally a third time, and Canadian officials did not accept Abu Mezer back into their country.[20] Official deportation proceedings were therefore started against him, but he stated that he intended to file an application for political asylum in the United States and was released from custody on a $5,000 bond. After retaining a lawyer, Abu Mezer filed his application for political asylum and in it claimed that he had been persecuted unfairly by Israeli authorities "because they wrongly suspected that he was a member of Hamas."[21] The Office of the Inspector General later determined that both the U.S. government's INS attorney and judge "skimmed Mezer's application at the hearing and ... did not notice the reference to Hamas in the application."[22] In between court hearings, Abu Mezer had informed his attorney that he had returned to Canada because he feared his refugee status there would interfere with his application in the United States. The judge presiding over his case ruled Abu Mezer was to be deported, but granted a sixty-day period during which Abu Mezer would be allowed to depart from the United States before the deportation order was finalized. It was during this sixty-day period that he was arrested for the suicide bombing plot in Brooklyn.

The circumstances surrounding Khalil's entrance into the United States were less convoluted than those of Abu Mezer, but no less suspicious or illegal. In November 1996, he went to the U.S. Consulate in Jerusalem, Israel and requested a C-1 transit visa permitting him to enter the United States and remain for up to twenty-nine days while traveling to another country. He claimed that he was traveling to Ecuador to visit an uncle and needed to have his trip routed through the United States.[23] When he requested the transit visa, the officer in the Consulate never investigated Khalil's claims, did not require that he produce an airline ticket showing he planned to travel to Ecuador, and failed to demonstrate whether Khalil had enough money to fund his trip. In December, Khalil flew from Jordan to the Netherlands and then connected to a flight to New York City. When he arrived in the United States, an immigration officer mistakenly thought his passport was a B-2 visitor's visa and stamped the passport with the incorrect status. The error meant that instead of twenty-nine days, Khalil would be able to remain in the United States for up to six months. There is no indication that he ever left the United States once he entered, even after the six-month visa expired. He was arrested over a month after his erroneously issued visa had expired.[24]

Following their arrest, Abu Mezer and Khalil were charged with conspiring and threatening to use a weapon of mass destruction and conspiracy to use a firearm—in this case, the pipe bombs—in a crime of violence.[25] At trial, Abu Mezer testified in his own defense, but he did not help his case.

He admitted coming to the United States to punish Americans for supporting Israel and said that he had written a letter to the FBI in which he
threatened to commit bombings as a message to the United States that it
should stop its support for Israel. In addition, he admitted traveling to
North Carolina in the months leading up to the planned attack in order to
look for work. While in North Carolina, Abu Mezer purchased materials
that he would ultimately use to construct his bombs—gunpowder, pipes,
caps, wires, switches, and batteries.[26] He testified further that he packed
nails around the pipe bombs in order to inflict as much damage as possible
and that his intended targets were Jewish people living in the United States.

Although Abu Mezer's self-incriminating testimony supported the
prosecution's case against him, he claimed that Khalil was never told about
the purchase of the bomb-making materials and that he was acting alone in
the plot. Khalil's attorney filed a letter with the court in which Khalil "cat-
egorically denie[d] any involvement in any bombing or other terrorist conspiracy" and expressed regret about any indirect involvement that may have
been perceived.[27] Abu Mezer was convicted of conspiring and threatening
to use a weapon of mass destruction and using a firearm during the course
of a violent crime and sentenced to two concurrent terms of life in prison.
He appealed his conviction on various grounds, including, among other
claims, that his sentence violated the double jeopardy clause of the U.S.
Constitution and that the questioning by police immediately after his arrest
violated his *Miranda* rights.[28] His appeal was unsuccessful, and he is serving
out his life sentences in a maximum-security federal prison.

Khalil faired better at trial; he was acquitted of the most serious charges
but convicted of possessing a fraudulent alien registration card.[29] Although
the offense was relatively minor and called for a prison sentence of zero to
six months, the trial judge was "convinced that Khalil was well aware that
Abu Mezer was assembling bombs ... [but] there was insufficient evidence
either that Khalil had possessed that knowledge before assisting in the relevant purchases or that he participated in any other way."[30] Considering the
extent of Khalil's involvement and the seriousness of the plot, it is surprising
that he was sentenced to only three years in prison. After serving his time,
he was deported to the Palestinian Authority, and his current whereabouts
are unknown.[31]

Several of the New York City police officers who conducted the successful raid were given medals and commendations for their bravery. The
Egyptian informant, Abdel Rahman Mosabbah, who made the critical

move of disclosing the plot, made out the best of anyone in the case. Not only did he provide information that led police to the bombers, he provided key testimony at the trial of Abu Mezer and Khalil. As a result, Mosabbah got to live out a variation of the dream of prosperity that he had when he came to the United States. He received millions of dollars in reward money from the Rewards for Justice Program established through the U.S. State Department to reward individuals who help prevent acts of international terrorism.[32] However, Mosabbah's good fortune was tempered by risk as well. His family was allowed to come to the United States to live with him, but they remain in the federal witness protection program under an assumed identity with persistent fears that terrorists or their sympathizers will seek retribution on him for thwarting their efforts.

The case of Abu Mezer and Khalil is particularly important in the study of terrorist acts committed in the United States and, more generally, in the study of suicide terrorism. Abu Mezer and Khalil are unusual cases of would-be suicide bombers who were thwarted in their efforts and survived so they could be interviewed and questioned about their motives, planning, and training. Following the successful police raid, Abu Mezer remained unapologetic for his actions and remained intent on killing as many people as he could in the United States. His motives were clearly aligned with Palestinian terrorist groups like Hamas that direct their anger at the United States for supporting Israel. Given his persistent desire to commit acts of terrorism, it is clear that a life sentence provides assurance that Abu Mezer will not be able to carry out further attacks.

Khalil's plight is a bit more puzzling. Although he claimed to have no involvement in the attacks and Abu Mezer's testimony supported this claim, it is quite possible that, together, Khalil's denial and Abu Mezer's absolution were an attempt to allow one would-be suicide bomber to be set free so he might one day carry out another attack. Of course, it is possible that Khalil was not directly involved but was merely manipulated by Abu Mezer. However, his culpability was strongly questioned by police, prosecutors, and the trial judge. Even if one is to believe that Khalil was a passive associate, the fact that he was with Abu Mezer when the bombs were discovered and struggled with police officers during the raid provides convincing evidence that he was a willing participant in the plan to detonate the bombs.

The case also provides a vivid illustration of the principle in terrorism prevention that the major weakness terrorists and their associates have is their communications. To plan and coordinate attacks, terrorists must identify co-conspirators, finance operations, communicate about targets, and work with supporters. All of these procedures require that terrorists communicate with one another, and a key to preventing terrorist attacks is intercepting these communications before an attack occurs. Unfortunately, law enforcement officers are not always in a position to intercept information, which often means that informants must be used to provide critical information. In this case, Mosabbah proved to be the key to preventing a tragedy in New York City. Furthermore, his brave actions prove that not all immigrants to the United States are terrorists or terrorist sympathizers. Most immigrants come to the United States to improve their lives and, in some cases, are important allies in efforts to combat terrorism.

Finally, the case provides yet another example of missed opportunities to identify individuals who enter the United States illegally with the intent to commit acts of terrorism. Abu Mezer was scheduled to be deported after trying to enter the country illegally on three separate occasions, yet he was released on bond and permitted to slip quietly away so he could plan a major terrorist attack. A more careful reading of the documents in his case would have raised strong suspicions about his ties to Hamas and might have led to a more rapid deportation process. Furthermore, a few simple administrative requirements would have prevented Khalil from entering the United States illegally. If he had been required to produce evidence of having the funds to support his trip to Ecuador, present a valid airline ticket, and prove he had an uncle in Ecuador, he might have been deterred from entering the country as he did. Certainly, the erroneous stamping of his visa was an unfortunate mistake that made it easier for him to remain in the country illegally.

As it stands, the case of Abu Mezer and Khalil represents the first known instance of suicide attackers planning an attack on American soil. The success of the police raid in thwarting the attack was remarkable in that no one was injured. However, as the events of September 11 have shown, the United States could not escape a dramatic terrorist attack. Furthermore, suicide bombers remain a persistent concern, and anything we can learn from the success of the case of Abu Mezer and Khalil will help us confront this threat in the future.

OUT OF THE BLUE

SHOOTING ATTACK AT THE EMPIRE STATE BUILDING

Every murderer is probably somebody's old friend.
—Agatha Christie[1]

IT IS OFTEN DIFFICULT TO DETERMINE WHETHER AN ACT OF VIOLENCE IS TRULY terrorism, based primarily on the motives of the perpetrator. One case of mass murder that illustrates this difficulty occurred on Sunday, February 24, 1997. Shortly after 5:00 p.m. on the observation deck of the Empire State Building, sixty-nine-year-old Ali Abu Kamal fired a .380-caliber Beretta handgun into a crowd of tourists.[2] A Swedish woman browsing in the gift shop, two Canadian college students taking photographs, and a Long Island couple leading their five children toward the exit were among the more than one hundred visitors to the famous site that day.[3] When the shots were fired, some people ran immediately for the exit, while others initially froze, believing the sound to be balloons popping.

Christopher Burmeister, a twenty-seven-year-old musician from Denmark, was killed instantly, and six other people were injured.[4] One of the most seriously wounded was twenty-seven-year-old Matthew Gross, a musician who played in a band with Burmeister. Gross was shot in the head and underwent extensive surgery and rehabilitation following the shooting.[5] The other shooting victims suffered serious injuries, but survived. Several bystanders were treated for emotional trauma.

When Kamal finished shooting into the crowd, he turned his gun on himself and fired a bullet into his head. He died several hours later at Bellevue Hospital.[6]

Kamal's suicide complicated the investigation. Nevertheless, police officers found a number of documents in his shirt pocket that provided insight into his thinking and led them to a number of people who could help retrace his steps in the days and weeks leading up to the shooting. One of the documents was an Israeli identification card given to Arabs who live in the Gaza strip.[7] Also found in his possession was a receipt for the .380-caliber Beretta handgun he purchased at a gun store in Florida a month before the shooting.

Another document found on Kamal's body was a two-page, handwritten document entitled "Charter of Honour." Two copies were found in a pouch he was carrying around his neck—one written in English and the other in Arabic.[8] The charter read:

Charter of Honour

Out of revenge for prestige, patriotism and retarding tyranny and suppresion, I consider those mentioned below as my bitter enemies and they must be annihilated & exterminated—

1. *The First Enemy.* Americans—Britons—French (though the French now seem friendly after Chirak's visit to Palestine) and the Zionists. These 3 Big Powers are the first enemy to the Palestinians ever since their three-partite Declaration in the early fifties, and they are responsible for turning our people, the Palestinians, homeless. The Zionists are the paw that carried out this savage aggression. My restless aspiration is to murder as many of them as possible, and I have decided to strike at their own den in New York, and at the very Empire State Building in particular. The Zionists have usurped my father's land at 'Abbassiya near Lydda Airport and which is now worth ten million US dollars at least.

2. *The Second Enemy.* A gang of rogues who attacked me on Saturday 26/6/1993 at my office in Gaza (Davaj), because I didn't agree to their command asking me to help them cheat in the final examination (Tawjihi). They were seven, and I have so far identified two of them. . . . If I could identify the others, ready to pay a reward for knowing them, I will kill all of them in revenge for this brutal attack, if I had the chance after the first strike.

3. *The Third One.* A ranking officer in the Egyptian Police Force, who had insulted and beaten me savagely for some passport formalities when I was in Cairo in the early eighties and without any justification. I didn't know his name, but I located his residence ... and he must be killed with his brother who helped him.

4. *The Fourth Target.* Three students ... all of Gaza, because they had beaten and blackmailed my son ... [one of the students] usurped $250 from my son and brutally beat him when he was sick. Their first two ... must be killed.

It is to be made clear that any act of provocation or offence against me or any attempt to impede my course of action shall be vigourously [*sic*] combatted whatever the consequences may be. It is to be placed on record that I must have carried out the first action a long time ago, but I was tied up all through this period with family obligations, observing certain commitments, at first towards my late parents, brothers and only sister, and later toward my children in an endeavor to help them lead a better life and with dignity. Now the American people must understand this message which runs deep in the blood of every real Palestinian.

I have written this Charter while I am in full senses and consciousness, aiming at informing all who may read it with the pros & cons and facts of the matter that led to this course of events, reiterating that we will never yield to any oppression or humiliation.

Either a life of Dignitiy & Glory or utter death.

Gaza, 1st January, 1996 (this is the original date of meditation).

Ali Hassan Ali Abu Kamal
(Jaffe)—Gaza in Palestine.[9]

Kamal's identification card, receipt for the gun he purchased, and charter provided the necessary leads for police to learn more about his background and to trace his movements leading up to the attack. Although an initial assessment led the police to believe that Kamal was a "deranged individual,"[10] an analysis of his life and motives lead to the conclusion that his attack was premeditated, clearly thought out, and spurred by a combination of both personal and political motives.

Born in a small coastal town in Palestine on September 19, 1927, Kamal and his family were displaced by the Arab-Israeli war in 1948 and settled in the Gaza Strip.[11] Although he was known to be conservative, he was not particularly religious. He worked for several years with the United Nations Relief and Works Agency performing relief work. Through this position, he was able to become fluent in English. Kamal was a high school and university English teacher in Gaza and over the years was able to save a fairly substantial amount of money.

Although Kamal earned about $3,000 per month, he was thrifty and invested his money wisely. By the time five of his six children had grown into adulthood, Kamal had managed to save $500,000 in various bank accounts.[12] He appeared to have no strong political connections and chose not to become involved with conflicts between the Palestine Liberation Organization (PLO) and Israel.

After teaching fifty years, Kamal took his savings and traveled to the United States, where he wanted to invest his money. He planned to form a company with some friends and to bring his family over to settle into a new life.[13] However, he lost all his money in a strange investment scheme that is not clearly understood; family members believed the loss caused Kamal to become emotionally unstable.

With respect to Kamal's specific movements in the months leading up to the Empire State Building attack, the record shows that he entered the United States legally by obtaining a travel visa. Entering the country on Christmas Eve 1996, he went to the Saudi Mission office at the United Nations to locate a friend, Taysir H. Badanoro, a friend from high school whom Kamal had not seen in over thirty years.[14] Badanoro worked at the Mission office and was surprised to see his friend after so many years. Nevertheless, Badanoro shared an apartment with his nephew and allowed Kamal to stay with them while his old friend looked for a job.

For the next two months, Kamal remained calm but secretive as he quietly kept the rage he felt toward his political enemies to himself while planning his attack. On January 11, 1997, he traveled to Florida, presumably to visit another old friend. Kamal checked into a low-cost motel where guests often paid in cash and rented by the week. While at the motel, Kamal told the owners that he was visiting friends, but he was vague about how long he would be staying. Although he paid his bill weekly, the owners noted that Kamal acted strangely during his stay. Although he was polite, he often stayed in his room or went for a walk, but on occasion would either lie on his bed naked or stand in the open door of his room while nude, facing a highly visible area of the motel. On one occasion, the owner told Kamal that he should close the door to his room. On another occasion Kamal reportedly propositioned a maid.[15]

Two weeks into his Florida trip, Kamal went to the Oaks Trading Post, a gun store down the highway from the motel, and purchased a .380-caliber Beretta, semi-automatic handgun. On the first of February, he left Florida and returned to New York City; only this time, he traveled by bus because he was now carrying the handgun.[16] Upon his return, Kamal stayed with Badanoro and his nephew but never told them about the gun. He continued to call his family several times a week. Badanoro and his nephew saw none of the rage Kamal later revealed in his *Charter of Honour*, seeing him instead as "an over-aged version of the classic immigrant, eager to make enough money to move his family to America."[17] The only noticeable evidence of Kamal's preoccupation with money during his stay in New York City was the fact that he spent quite a bit of money—sometimes $40 or $100 at a time—on lottery tickets, hoping to strike it rich.

The day before the fatal attack, Kamal made a visit to the observation deck of the Empire State Building. He said nothing to Badanoro, other than he wanted to see the tourist attraction. It remains unknown if Kamal's visit to the site was for planning purposes or if he intended to shoot someone but either lost his nerve or found the conditions unacceptable.

The morning of the attack, Kamal "gave his friend a calculator as a gift and left, saying he was going to buy some luggage, betraying not a trace of his murderous plans."[18] He went to the observation deck and this time opened fire.

The case of Ali Abu Kamal is interesting in a number of respects, primarily because the motives for his attack were prompted by a combined need to seek personal revenge and to make a political statement. Although hindsight is always clear, there is a risk of inaccurately claiming that certain behaviors or actions could have predicted his behavior. Yet there was very little indication that Kamal was making plans for a terrorist attack. He was aimless in his travel in the United States, he appeared to have no direction or purpose, and he distanced himself from his family. In addition, he suffered a significant loss of money, which undoubtedly diminished his feelings of accomplishment and status.

However, Kamal did not let others know about his financial problems, and his aimless travel and distancing himself from his family, while unusual, could be viewed as the behavior of a man who recently retired and was looking to start a new life in the United States. But lingering questions remain unanswered. For example, why did he not come to the United States sooner if he was looking to start over? Most of his children were grown, and Kamal appeared to be retiring from teaching. If he was interested in starting a new life, why had he not done so while his children were still young?

Also, what was the nature of his financial loss? It was never clear how he lost his money, and he never told his family. If he had let them know of his financial situation, might they have been able to help him? Of course, one could speculate that because he took his own life, Kamal was depressed and unable to see through his hopelessness and pessimism that his family could be a source of support. There is no evidence that he sought mental health treatment for depression, and any comments on his psychological state are speculative.

The best evidence for Kamal's true motive is in his Charter of Honour. Three of Kamal's four enemies or targets were individuals who had injured or attacked him or his family at some point during his life. These personal attacks occurred years ago, and the fact that he was specifying them in his charter, yet had apparently never let on to others that he harbored such strong rage and hatred, suggests that Kamal spent years ruminating about these events and waited for the opportunity to seek revenge. The precipitating factors of his attack are similar to those found in many cases of mass homicide. Kamal experienced a recent loss of status and esteem, withdrew from his family, traveled with no clearly identifiable plans, and engaged in a specific pattern of planning that included the purchase of a weapon. His principal motive of revenge against those who had wronged him could be viewed as personal, not political. Therefore, was his attack really an act of terrorism?

There are two interesting features to Kamal's thinking and behavior that suggest his attack was indeed a terrorist act. One important facet of his thinking was the order in which he listed his enemies in the charter; he listed the United States, Great Britain, France, and Israel (as seen in his expressed anger at "Zionists" who took over his native Palestine and "usurped" his father's land) before he listed the three enemies who had attacked him personally. Moreover, Kamal's selection of the Empire State Building is telling because he wanted to strike at a symbol of Western culture. As such, there was clearly a political motive involved in his act. Moreover, he targeted not the individuals who had personally injured or slighted him, but a cultural and government symbol.

Another important feature of his planning was his Charter of Honour. He took the time to write his thoughts out not only in English, but also Arabic, and he took the document with him where it was certain others would find it. One can only conclude from these actions that Kamal knew his actions would be publicized and that his charter would be publicized. Therefore, his stated political views were sure to garner attention.

Kamal's mass shooting was a terrorist attack because he had political motives, he sought to influence an audience by writing out his charter and assuring that it would be found and publicized, and he targeted innocent civilians in a highly visible location. Despite the terrorist nature of his actions, there remains the issue of his apparent lack of connection to any specific political or terrorist organization. In many ways, Kamal is similar to the lone-wolf terrorists who have a political purposes that is consistent with the aims of organized terrorist groups, but who operate either outside or on the fringes of such groups. Examples of this kind of terrorist discussed previously include Leon Czolgosz and Ted Kaczynski.

Of course, the personal injuries and attacks that Kamal suffered throughout his life cannot be discounted. They no doubt played a role in intensifying his anger and perhaps provided justification in his mind for the violence he unleashed. His case reveals that the right combination of desire for personal revenge, fueled by a number of injuries or attacks, and political hatred can provide a lethal mix that ultimately leads to a terrorist attack by a single person with no clear connection to any organization or group.

LEADERLESS RESISTANCE

THE ARSON FIRES OF VAIL SKI RESORT

Every man with an idea has at least two or three followers.
—Brooks Atkinson[1]

CERTAIN SOCIAL ISSUES, LIKE ABORTION, ANIMAL RIGHTS, OR ENVIRONMENTAL protection, are often found at the center of heated political disputes. Many legitimate groups with moderate views have used appropriate legal channels to advance their causes, such as lobbying legislators or filing amicus curiae (i.e., friend-of-the-court) briefs in crucial court cases. Some groups focusing on single issues, however, are radicalized and either endorse or carry out militant activities. The concept of "single-issue terrorism" is defined as "extremist militancy on the part of groups or individuals protesting a perceived grievance or wrong usually attributed to governmental action or inaction."[2]

Within the field of terrorism studies, single issue political violence is a unique problem. Unlike legitimate or moderate political groups and organizations favoring appropriate channels for dispute, single-issue terrorist groups embrace violence. Unlike terrorist groups with broader perspectives, however, single-issue terrorist groups are often "sub-revolutionary" in that they seek to change or influence policies or laws pertaining to one specific issue.[3]

Traditional terrorist organizations like the Irish Republican Army or the Liberation Tigers of Tamil Elam have a hierarchical structure where a senior leader or group of leaders oversee other individuals responsible for raising money or managing operations. These individuals in turn supervise operatives who carry out acts of terrorism. A problem that terrorist organizations with a traditional organizational structure face is susceptibility to informers and undercover agents who infiltrate the group and provide information to law enforcement officers.[4]

Single-issue terrorist movements, on the other hand, often adopt an organizational structure that is leaderless.[5] In a 1983 essay, white supremacist and anti-government advocate Louis Beam endorsed leaderless resistance as an appropriate method for fighting the U.S. government. He encouraged "like-minded individuals to form independence cells that ... commit acts of sabotage or terrorism without coordination from above ... while minimizing communication with other cells."[6] According to Beam, leaderless resistance:

> is based upon the cell organization but does not have any central control or direction.... Cells operate independently of each other.... All persons involved have the same general outlook, are acquainted with the same philosophy, and generally react to given situations in similar ways.... All members of phantom cells will tend to react to objective events in the same way, usually through tactics of resistance and sabotage.[7]

In recent decades, single-issue terrorist movements have rallied around issues like animal rights, environmental protection, and abortion. The leaderless resistance model has been adopted by several groups associated with these issues, like the Animal Liberation Front (ALF), the Earth Liberation Front (ELF), and various pro-life groups that have been responsible for targeted violence against family planning clinics and physicians performing abortions.[8] These groups often engage in acts of sabotage or vandalism. For example, animal rights terrorist groups have destroyed animal research laboratories, and environmental terrorist groups have targeted businesses believed to be destroying the environment. Although some single-issue terrorist groups pride themselves on the fact that they do not cause injury to any person and often state in their communications that they target only property, their acts result in major financial losses. As in other cases of politically motivated violence, spokespersons for these single-issue movements frequently espouse the view that the actions of these extremist groups should not be construed as terrorism. By any reasonable definition of the concept, however, these acts of sabotage are terrorism.

The most infamous and, in terms of economic loss, the costliest act of sabotage in U.S. history occurred in the early morning hours of October

19, 1998.[9] As some hunters were camping in the forest atop the mountain at Vail Ski Resort in Colorado, several fires were set deliberately within minutes of one another. One destroyed the Two Elk Restaurant, located near the top of the mountain and which contained more than a million dollars worth of rare Native American artifacts and memorabilia.[10] Another fire destroyed the building housing the Vail ski patrol. Three chairlifts were set on fire, including the housing for one of the most widely used lifts in Vail which serves as a major connection to various parts of the resort. A snack bar was also destroyed, as well as few outlying buildings. In all, there were seven major fires causing an estimated $12 million in damage.[11]

Firefighters were hampered by the sheer magnitude of the fires. Because they burned on top of the mountain, it was difficult to get equipment to where it was needed. Heat and smoke generated by the fires made the entire mountain appear as though it were on fire. Investigators were kept at bay until the fires burned themselves out or were extinguished. Nevertheless, evidence recovered at the scene, including a fuel container in the woods, revealed that the fires were set deliberately. The speed with which the fires spread, and the fact that seven were ignited in near succession pointed to an act of deliberate sabotage.

A number of theories were initially offered about who might have been responsible for the fires. The incident had occurred just as Vail Resorts was breaking ground on a controversial expansion. Vail had expanded over the years and became a winter haven for wealthy ski vacationers from all over the world, and the area had lost a large measure of its small-town charm. Local residents held differing opinions about whether the expansion had been positive, because it resulted in economic growth, or negative, because it also resulted in increased traffic, greed, and commercial interests that had destroyed Vail's traditional ambiance.[12] Some individuals speculated that a disgruntled employee or local person with a grudge against the ski resort might have been responsible.

However, the true motive behind the fires was sparked by an important court ruling issued just days before the arson attacks. Vail Resorts, the corporation managing Vail and several other ski resorts in Colorado, had been planning a large expansion that came to be known as Category III.[13] The Category III expansion was to break ground within a mile of an area known as the Gilman tract of Battle Mountain. This area was believed by some individuals to be a natural habitat of the lynx, a feline animal with a diminishing population on the verge of being listed on the U.S. Fish and

Wildlife Service's list of threatened or endangered species.[14] If any lynx were observed near the proposed expansion site, Vail Resorts would likely be unable to embark on its project. Despite claims that a lynx had been sighted near Vail, the presence of the animal could not be confirmed. Nevertheless, legal action was filed against Vail Resorts by a coalition of environmental protection groups—including the Colorado Environmental Coalition, Rocky Mountain chapter of the Sierra Club, Southern Rockies Ecosystem Project, Colorado Wildlife Federation, and Ancient Forest Rescue—to stop the expansion and protect the lynx's natural habitat.[15] Although litigation spanned over two years, the final legal battle was an appeal to Federal District Court Judge Edward Nottingham right before Vail Resorts was set to begin construction on the expansion. Judge Nottingham denied all appeals by the environmental groups and cleared the way for expansion. The fires were set on the evening before construction was to begin.

Two days after the Vail ski resort fires, a Portland, Oregon environmental activist by the name of Craig Rosebraugh received an anonymous e-mail that clarified the motive for the Vail fires and the group responsible for the acts of terrorism.[16] Rosebraugh was no stranger to controversy. He worked for a Portland-area organization known as the Liberation Collective that worked on various animal rights and environmental causes. He had received prior anonymous announcements and claims from a group called the Earth Liberation Front (ELF) concerning other acts of environmental terrorism. As an activist and protester, Rosebraugh's work had brought him to the attention of federal law enforcement agents. The Liberation Collective offices, as well as Rosebraugh's home, would later become the target of federal search warrants. Rosebraugh was issued several grand jury subpoenas demanding that he provide testimony about the source of the communiqués he received.[17] Nevertheless, he maintained an antagonistic relationship with the FBI, and the slogan "The FBI are the real terrorists" is said to have been displayed on the walls of the Liberation Collective offices.[18]

Rosebraugh claimed that on October 21, 1998, just two days after the Vail fires, he received the following anonymous email communication from ELF:

On behalf of the lynx, five buildings and four ski lifts at Vail were reduced to ashes on the night of Sunday, October 18th. Vail, Inc. is already the largest ski operation in North America and now wants to expand even further. The 12 miles of roads and 885 acres of clearcuts will ruin the last, best lynx habitat in the state. Putting profits ahead of Colorado's wildlife will not be tolerated. This action is just a warning. We will be back if this greedy corporation continues to trespass into wild and unroaded areas. For your safety and convenience, we strongly advise skiers to choose other destinations until Vail cancels its inexcusable plans for expansion.

Earth Liberation Front (ELF)[19]

More than a warning, the Vail fires represent the costliest act of environmental terrorism in U.S. history, and the perpetrators have never been identified. Not a single individual has been arrested, indicted, or prosecuted for the fires. Because they are believed to have been carried out by members of ELF in response to Vail's proposed expansion, yet the case remains unsolved, the fires show how dangerous and elusive certain terrorist organizations are, particularly when they engage in leaderless forms of resistance.

The ELF is "an international underground movement consisting of autonomous groups of people who carry out direct action according to the ELF guidelines."[20] According to these guidelines, the use of small cells consisting of anywhere from one to several people without a central command structure, keeps members relatively anonymous, and one cell does not know the members or plans of another cell. In this way, informers and undercover law enforcement agents have a difficult time infiltrating cells. Members of ELF believe this method of operation "helps keep activists out of jail and free to continue conducting actions."[21]

Anonymous cell organization also makes it easier for ELF members to communicate their motives publicly without attributing responsibility to a specific individual. Over the past several years, ELF has claimed responsibility for a number of attacks on businesses. These attacks have resulted in extensive economic losses, including damage to two U.S. Department of Agriculture buildings in Olympia, Washington in 1998; fires at the Boise, Idaho, offices of Cascade Office Products in 1999; and destruction of several sport utility vehicles at an Erie, Pennsylvania auto dealership in 2003.[22] Many of these attacks remain unsolved, despite the fact that ELF has publicly claimed responsibility.

Rosebraugh, who received the ELF communication regarding the Vail arson attacks, came under intense scrutiny by the FBI because he was seen as a "spokesperson" for ELF, and his role raised suspicions that he may know those people responsible for the attacks.[23] Rosebraugh has never been proven to be a member of ELF and has not been indicted for any ELF-related attacks, although he supports the organization and its goals. In fact, his antagonistic relationship with the FBI is chronicled in his published memoirs. He wrote that "ecoterrorism to me mean[s] some form of terror that is caused to the natural environment" and "there [is] a clear difference between terrorism, which aims to injure or kill people, and the actions of ELF, which are committed to protecting life."[24]

It is common in the field of terrorism studies to find individuals who engage in politically motivated violence—or those who do not necessarily engage in any form of violence but actively or passively support those who do—to reject the terrorism label. Even though the actions of some single-issue terrorism groups like ELF have never been associated with the death of another person, their actions are properly characterized as terrorism. The FBI defines terrorism as "the unlawful use of force or violence against persons or property to intimidate or coerce a government, the civilian population, or any segment thereof, in furtherance of political or social objectives."[25] Federal law enforcement considers acts of arson that have political motives, such as the fires at Vail Ski Resort, to be terrorism, even though the perpetrators and their supporters do not.

Groups like ELF are extremely difficult to investigate and disrupt because of their leaderless form of resistance. Their guidelines offer a blueprint for staging acts of sabotage and resistance, including inflicting economic damage to businesses or corporations they believe profit from exploiting the environment. These groups also strive to educate the public, presumably through visible attacks followed by tightly worded communications that outline their motives.[26] Despite the apparent endorsement of active resistance, ELF is careful to provide the following disclaimer to its website:

> The information contained within [the ELF] website and the domain names ... is NOT intended to encourage anyone to do anything illegal.... [The ELF] website and the domain names ... provide all information for education and research purposes only.[27]

It tests the boundaries of reason to believe that information provided by ELF does not encourage anyone to do anything illegal when the group endorses the infliction of economic damage on those who are believed to be destroying or exploiting the environment. The example of ELF and its arson attack on the Vail Ski Resort demonstrates how the line between free political speech and active endorsement of terrorist violence can be blurred beyond the point of distinction. Despite the denials of some, leaderless resistance in single-issue terrorist groups like ELF represents a particularly difficult and challenging threat to property and the economic interests of those who have the misfortune of drawing the attention of these groups.

Traditional law enforcement methods, like the issuing of search warrants and subpoenas are unlikely to be effective and may actually cause some individuals with tenuous ties to the group to become radicalized and militant.[28] Likewise, informants and undercover agents are likely to find it difficult, if not impossible, to infiltrate these groups, given their diffuse structure and lack of hierarchical leadership. Among the more hopeful prospects for dealing with single-issue terrorism and leaderless resistance movements is to monitor websites and other public materials closely to make sure they do not encourage criminal activities, induce violence, or promote sedition. In addition, moderate groups that embrace the rule of law and reject terrorism should be rewarded by being brought into the legitimate political process. In this way, policies and legal reforms can be formulated through proper channels and then publicized to gain wide support for making political changes through appropriate methods rather than violence.

OPPORTUNITIES LOST AND FOUND

THE ATTEMPTED MILLENNIAL BOMBING

Lack of recent information ... is responsible for more mistakes of judgment than erroneous reasoning.
—Matthew Arnold[1]

DURING THE LATTER PART OF THE 1990S, RISING CONCERNS EMERGED THAT terrorist groups would carry out spectacular acts of terrorism. Many of these concerns increased when several attacks were made against American interests by the terrorist group al-Qaeda, including the bombing of the *U.S.S. Cole* in Yemen and the near-simultaneous truck bombings of the U.S. Embassies in Nairobi, Kenya, and Tanzania. Many people feared that the new millennium would usher in attacks on American soil.

At about 4:00 p.m. on December 14, 1999, a green sedan joined other cars for the last ride of the day on the ferry traveling from Victoria, British Columbia to Port Angeles, Washington.[2] Gary Roberts, an immigration inspector for the United States, asked the driver of the sedan to produce his passport and driver's license and inquired where the man was heading. Traveling alone, the man said he was going to Seattle for a two-day business trip.

Given that U. S. Customs officials are more likely to pull over a lone driver, and that the man was coming from Montreal but was taking an unusual route into the United States considering his place of residence, Roberts decided to scrutinize the vehicle more carefully and examined the driver's documents. The name on the man's license, Benni Noris, was run through a computer, but Roberts found nothing unusual except for a note indicating a prior check had been run on Noris at the Los Angeles

International Airport in February that same year. When Roberts questioned Noris about his plans for returning to Canada, Noris produced a return ticket for the ferry and said he was going to fly back to Montreal. With suspicions still aroused, Roberts ordered Noris to open the truck of his vehicle where a suitcase, satchel, and backpack were found. A quick search of the suitcase revealed only clothing, and Noris was allowed to continue his trip on the ferry.[3]

Later, when the ship docked at Port Angeles, Washington, Noris was the last car in line. Doris Dean, a U.S. Customs inspector, asked Noris about his destination. He told her he was headed to Seattle. But as she questioned him further, Dean noticed Noris was "acting hinky," so she had him fill out a customs form in order to stall for time.[4] Dean's colleagues had completed their inspections for the day and were waiting for her to finish with the suspicious traveler. Dean asked Noris to open his trunk, but this time the search did not stop merely with the visible contents. Suspecting she had a drug dealer at her gate, Dean tipped off her colleagues that the driver might be a smuggler, and another customs inspector opened the spare tire compartment.

Inside the trunk there was no spare tire; instead there were bags filled with white powder, some black boxes, pill bottles, and jars containing a brown liquid. By this time, Noris was being held by a third customs inspector, but he escaped and ran when the contents of the trunk were discovered. After a brief chase on foot, Noris was found hiding under a nearby parked car but tried to flee again. He ran into traffic, bounced off a moving car, and was grabbed by two of the customs inspectors after he was unable to carjack a vehicle that had stopped at a light. He was brought back to the scene and held in the back of a patrol car.

The customs inspectors still believed they had captured a drug dealer, but Noris, of course, knew otherwise. When he saw the inspectors pick up and shake one of the jars containing the brown liquid, Noris got on the floor of the patrol car to shield himself from what he thought would be an explosion. Days later, customs inspectors learned that the strange liquid was a powerful and highly volatile substance in the same family of explosives as nitroglycerin; a wrong move could have resulted in all of them being blown to bits.

Although law enforcement officials soon learned that their last inspection of the day uncovered components of a highly powerful explosive device, the mystery was only beginning. Who was Benni Noris? Why was he bringing explosives into the United States? What was he intending to do, and what was his target? Were others involved? For whom, if anyone, did Noris work?

As one might expect, the name Benni Noris was fake. The man who tried to smuggle 130 pounds of explosive material into the United States was an Algerian native by the name of Ahmed Ressam. Born in 1967, he was the oldest child in a family where the Islamic faith was considered important but not an obligation. Ressam's father was a devout Muslim who attended regular religious services, but he did not require his five sons to follow his example.[5] During Ressam's childhood, the country of Algeria reflected a blend of traditional Muslim culture and European influences brought about by over a century of French imperial rule.

As a child, Ahmed Ressam played soccer, fished, and did many of the things that most carefree youth did while growing up. He did well in school, and his father had hopes that his oldest son would qualify for a free college education if he passed the difficult qualifying examination. During adolescence, however, Ressam began to experience severe stomach pains, and as they worsened, he began to have difficulty sleeping. At the age of sixteen, he was sent to Paris, France to be examined by physicians to determine the cause of his pains. After a series of tests, Ressam's family learned that he had a stomach ulcer. He had surgery and recuperated in Paris by himself.[6]

Civil unrest unfolded in Algeria during the late 1980s and early 1990s when Muslim fighters returned from the war in Afghanistan. Following his recovery from surgery, Ressam went from France back to his native Algeria and encountered this unrest. He also experienced personal difficulties. For example, he took the qualifying examinations for entrance into the university, but failed, and he was unable to find decent work. Moreover, Ressam continued to lead a lifestyle similar to that of a European youth rather one guided by Muslim tradition. He dressed in Western clothing, dated girls, drank alcohol, smoked hashish, and went to nightclubs. With few prospects for success and with the violence in Algeria escalating, Ressam decided to travel to Canada where he might find a job and start a new life. However, he apparently thought it would be more difficult for him to secure entrance into Canada by traveling directly from Algeria, and decided upon a brief stay in France. So in September 1992, Ressam packed his bags, obtained a thirty-day travel visa, and headed for France with a forged passport to find a new life for himself.

For the next year, Ressam worked at menial jobs on the French island of Corsica. Since his travel visa had expired, he became an illegal immigrant and was arrested in November 1993. Facing deportation to Algeria, he was released from custody to await trial. Once again, he assumed a false identity and then traveled to Canada. While going through immigration, his phony passport was discovered, and Ressam was jailed. Despite the fact that he was facing deportation, Ressam benefited from the liberal immigration laws of Canada. He invented a story of having faced unjust persecution and torture and applied for political asylum. While awaiting a court date, Ressam was able to qualify for welfare support from the Canadian government, obtain the services of an immigration attorney, and settle into life as a Canadian.[7]

Ressam missed his initial court date but faced no legal sanctions. He was given another court date so his case for political asylum could be heard. In the meantime, he returned to the nightclub scene, hooked up with other Algerian immigrants such as himself, and collected welfare payments of $550 per month. In addition, Ressam began to supplement his government-subsidized income with proceeds from petty crimes. He was arrested for shoplifting, fined, and ordered to leave Canada within six weeks. When he failed to show up for his subsequent court date, immigration officials simply did not follow up on his case. He continued to engage in shoplifting and petty theft. He soon met up with Fateh Kamel, a mujaheddeen from the wars in Afghanistan and Bosnia who made a living forging documents.[8]

Ressam's life of crime led to another arrest in October 1996, this time for stealing $300 from a hotel guest. Even though he had two convictions for theft and was an illegal immigrant, he was merely fined by the sentencing judge, placed on probation for two years, and released.

As Ressam continued to collect welfare payments, pass his time playing soccer with a group of young men from Algeria, and lead a life with no clear direction, a man named Abderraouf Hannachi eased his way into Ressam's group of friends. In his forties, Hannachi was seen by the younger men as a "jolly uncle" who spoke of his hatred of Western culture, particularly the United States.[9] He spoke of how greed, immoral dress codes, and entertainment in the West were corrupting the world and needed to be stopped. Hannachi's message found sympathetic ears among Ressam and his friends, who (ironically) decried the corruption of Western culture while capitalizing on its liberal immigration laws and continuing to collect payments from its welfare system.

Hannachi said he learned to fire weapons, assemble explosives, and fight in hand-to-hand combat in one of Osama bin Laden's training camps in Afghanistan. Hannachi appeared at mosques and was known in the Arab community of Montreal, Canada as a man worthy of respect. Ressam, Fateh Kamel, and other friends began long discussions about waging holy war against the corrupt Western world. However, they were unaware that Hannachi had been the target of an investigation by the Canadian Security Intelligence Service (CSIS).[10]

The CSIS had been informed by a man named Jean-Louis Bruguiere. Bruguiere was France's top terrorism expert who had been tracking Algerian extremists for nearly two decades. He had secured a wealth of information on potential terrorists. Fateh Kamel, Ressam's close friend, was implicated with other known Algerian extremists. Bruguiere told Canadian authorities that he believed Kamel had formed his own terrorism cell in Montreal. Ressam came under surveillance by Canadian authorities who began secretly taping conversations involving Ressam, Kamel, and their associates.

Despite this intense scrutiny, authorities did not know that Hannachi was a top recruiter for Abu Zubaydah—the military head of Osama bin Laden's al-Qaeda network and the person responsible for bringing recruits from around the world to train in Afghanistan's terrorist training camps. There are four levels of recruits in the al-Qaeda network.[11] The highest consists of "professionals," who are the most dedicated and given the task of conducting spectacular terrorist attacks. The second consists of "trained amateurs" who are given open-ended instructions to complete an unspecified act of terror; amateurs are given a lump sum of money to begin their operations and must support themselves with ongoing criminal activities. "Local walk-ins," the third level of recruits, are independent groups of Islamic radicals who have their own plans for terror, but who are looking to al-Qaeda for financial support. Finally, "like-minded guerillas and terrorists" are groups that have received some form of training in Afghanistan's camps, and that are guided by bin Laden's vision but have their own agenda.

At the urging of Hannachi, Ressam entered the ranks of trained amateurs in al-Qaeda. In March 1998, Ressam left Canada and traveled to Afghanistan to receive his training in the al-Qaeda camps. However, he needed a new identity—one that would allow him to travel readily around the world and avoid scrutiny by immigration officials like those who had targeted him when he first entered Canada. Before leaving for the training camps, Ressam stole a blank certificate of baptism from a local Catholic church in Montreal. He took the name of a Catholic priest who had been at the parish in 1970 and forged the priest's signature on the stolen certificate. Using the name Benni Antoine Noris, Ressam used the phony birth certificate and a current photograph of himself to obtain a Canadian passport.[12] He was ready to travel around the world as a "Canadian citizen."

On March 16, 1998, while intelligence officials were still listening to his conversations, Ressam bid a tearful farewell to his friends and left for Afghanistan. As Benni Noris, Ressam was able to obtain an airline ticket from Toronto to Frankfurt, Germany.[13] After meeting with members of the al-Qaeda network, he flew to Pakistan and met with Abu Zubaydah. Ressam stayed in an al-Qaeda safe house for several weeks, studied the Quran, and prayed. He was given a letter of introduction by Zubaydah and driven across the Pakistan-Afghanistan border to the Khalden training camp.

For the next several months, Ressam received basic training in hand-to-hand combat, the use of weapons (including knives, firearms, and grenade launchers), and explosives. He also received strength and endurance training. During Ressam's time at the camp, the bombing of the U. S. embassies in Kenya and Tanzania occurred, prompting President Clinton to order missiles fired on the al-Qaeda camps in Afghanistan. Most of the missiles missed their targets, and Ressam was not hurt in the retaliatory bombing.[14] After completing his training, Ressam was sent to another terrorist training site in Darunta, where he received additional training in the construction of bombs. He kept a notebook filled with diagrams and instructions for constructing explosives.

In January 1999, Ressam completed his terrorist training. He was given $12,000 and a specific assignment: find a safe house in Canada, secure a passport and weapons, construct a bomb, and detonate it somewhere inside the United States. After shaving his beard and changing his wardrobe to Western clothing, he traveled to Seoul, South Korea, and then to Los Angeles, where he waited at the airport (LAX) for his flight into Canada. While at a U. S. immigration station, Ressam was stopped and asked for his passport. Inside his bag were the notebook containing his bomb recipes, a shampoo bottle containing glycol, and an aspirin bottle filled with hexamine tablets; the glycol and hexamine were key ingredients for constructing a bomb.[15] When his alias Benni Noris was checked, no alerts arose, and he was allowed to pass. Unfortunately, the U. S. Immigration Service was unaware that Ressam, traveling as Benni Noris, had been photographed by Canadian investigators as he was leaving for the al-Qaeda training camps in March of the previous year. During his stopover in Los Angeles, Ressam took in sights of Western culture and decided the airport (LAX) would make a perfect target for his assigned mission.

Upon his return to Canada, Ressam's friends saw a change in him. He appeared confident and more like a soldier than the petty thief he had been before his trip to Afghanistan. Other members of his cell were unsuccessful in their efforts to join him because they were stopped by immigration authorities and could not enter Canada. Ressam's forged identity and passport afforded him the opportunity to travel internationally with ease. Based on the efforts of Jean-Louis Bruguiere, Ressam's friend Kamel had been arrested and extradited to France on charges of assisting terrorists. However, Ressam was able to avoid capture due mainly to his new identity.

Ressam was able to encourage other Algerian friends to assist him with his plans. While some wanted to bomb a Jewish suburb of Montreal, Ressam pressed forward with the mission he was given upon leaving the al-Qaeda training camps. He set his sights on LAX and gave a deadline for the attack: the end of 1999 and the beginning of the new millennium.

In August 1999, he purchased an array of electronic equipment, including wire, circuit boards, capacitors, integrated circuits, solder and a soldering iron, and various other materials he charged to a new credit card he was able to obtain under the name of Benni Noris.[16] He also purchased two electronic alarm watches—one for each bomb he planned to detonate. One was to explode and kill a number of people at LAX; the second was to detonate moments later and kill rescue personnel and law enforcement officers responding to the scene.

By this time, Ressam had moved into a new apartment in Montreal, but he made frequent visits to his old apartment where many of his Algerian friends still lived. Unbeknownst to the group, the apartment had remained under surveillance by Royal Canadian Mounted Police. On the morning of October 4, 1999, while Ressam was spending the night with his friends, police approached the apartment at 6:15 a.m. to make an arrest.[17] The raid Jean-Louis Bruguiere had long been wanting was finally carried out and, coincidentally, Ressam was spending the night. However, the police went to the front door and waited to be buzzed in to the apartment. When Ressam heard the bell, he rushed from the apartment out an unguarded back door, into an alley, and disappeared. Inside the apartment, police found a number of stolen passports and a knapsack belonging to Ressam containing an address book with telephone numbers for an agricultural supply store and other contacts that were meaningless at the time. Bruguiere was sent a copy of the book, but Ressam was nowhere to be found.

In spite of his brush with capture, Ressam was undeterred. He continued working on his bombs and sought to assemble a new terrorist cell that would assist him in carrying out his mission. He located three untrained Algerians who were willing to help.[18] Abdelmajid Dahoumane was a friend of Ressam living in Montreal who would assist in constructing the bomb. A second man, Mokhtar Haouari, was a thief specializing in credit cards who provided needed cash. A third man, Abdelghani Meskini, was a con man living in Brooklyn, New York who was to help deliver the bombs once Ressam made his way into the United States.

Ressam informed al-Qaeda leaders of his plans and sought to obtain the blessing of Osama bin Laden. He told his contacts in Afghanistan that he wanted to return to Algeria following the LAX bombings and was told he would be provided with money and the necessary documents once his mission was completed.

In November 1999, Ressam and Dahoumane flew to Vancouver, British Columbia and registered at a small motel where they rented a two-room cottage located on the back of the property. However, the behavior of the two men attracted attention. "The motel's housekeeper found it odd that the men rarely wanted their cottage cleaned. When she knocked, they insisted she just leave the clean linens and stay out of the back bedroom. They also left the windows open, unusual when temperatures dipped into the [thirties] at night. Sometimes, she smelled a noxious odor wafting from the room, sort of a sickening, overpowering cologne."[19]

Inside the cottage, Ressam and Dahoumane were making a highly unstable explosive. Many of the chemicals they were using had to be combined under very specific conditions, and a slight jolt could have detonated the mixture. Both men used throat lozenges to cope with pain caused by the noxious fumes. At one point, a corrosive spray from the mixture burned holes through Ressam's pants. Nevertheless, the two men were diligent in their efforts and, by December 14, they had completed their task. Ressam departed for the United States to meet up with Meskini and deliver the bombs at LAX before the new millennium.

Ressam was caught by the observant customs inspector as he tried to cross into the United States. After an intensive investigation by federal law enforcement officials that uncovered Benni Noris's true identity, as well as his links to the al-Qaeda terrorist network, Ahmed Ressam was sent to the federal courthouse in Los Angeles, California. Following a three-week trial, he was convicted of nine federal charges, including conspiracy to commit an act of international terrorism.[20] Maybe because Ressam faced a sentence of fifty-seven to a hundred and thirty years in federal prison, his terrorist training that had taught him how to avoid relinquishing information on the al-Qaeda network began to falter. After his conviction, he became more cooperative and reached an agreement whereby his minimum sentence was reduced to twenty-seven years in exchange for his willingness to testify truthfully against his associates and to reveal all he knows about al-Qaeda tactics, plots, and training procedures.[21]

The case of Ahmed Ressam was a success by law enforcement because he was arrested before he could carry out his plan, successfully prosecuted, and turned into an informant who assisted law enforcement officials in their efforts to combat international terrorism. However, the case is also one in which there were numerous failures and missed opportunities, particularly since Ressam went as far as he did with his plan. If he had slipped by the U. S. Customs checkpoint, crossed the border without scrutiny, or done something to divert attention away from himself (like travel with a group), he most likely would have succeeded in carrying out a major terrorist attack within the United States.

There were numerous instances where he should have been apprehended sooner. Canadian immigration authorities knew he was an illegal alien and Ressam had been slated for deportation more than once. He failed to appear for a couple of court appearances, yet no further attempts were made to locate him and hold him accountable for his violation of immigration laws. Furthermore, he had been arrested for petty criminal activity and never spent any appreciable amount of time in jail.

Other factors that prevented Ressam from being caught sooner were the lack of coordination between law enforcement agencies from various countries and the lack of responsiveness to requests made by French authorities to detain Ressam and his cohorts. For example, the French counterterrorism expert, Jean-Louis Bruguiere, had made repeated requests to have Ressam arrested and detained. In addition, immigration and customs agencies in the United States were unaware that Ressam was under investigation by Canadian authorities and had been photographed leaving for the al-Qaeda camps. If they had known this information when Ressam traveled through LAX on his return trip from Afghanistan, he might have been detained before he was able to begin planning his attack. Greater international coordination and cooperation could have led to Ressam's capture much sooner.

The behavior of Ressam and Dahoumane during their stay at the motel outside of Vancouver while they were constructing the bombs was also a key factor that could have led to an arrest. Their strange behavior—including the noxious odors emanating from their room and the fact that they would not let motel staff into one of their bedrooms—was noted by the motel housekeeper and should have tipped off someone that illegal activities were being carried out on the motel's premises. A call to law enforcement officials might also have led to the arrest and capture of Ressam. Of course, when Canadian officials raided Ressam's former apartment in Montreal where many of his friends were staying, an opportunity was missed to capture the al-Qaeda operative. If the rear door to the apartment had been guarded, Ressam could have been captured well before he began assembling his bomb.

The case of Ahmed Ressam is instructive in several respects. It reinforces the notion that an alert law enforcement officer who takes his or her job seriously and views strange situations or behaviors with skepticism might be in the best position to prevent a major terrorist attack. Also, the case teaches a valuable lesson about the psychological profiling of individuals who are suspected of engaging in criminal or terrorist activities. The most notable things that could have been used to target Ressam as a possible terrorist were not his ethnicity, nationality, dress, appearance, or religious beliefs. Rather, it was his *behavior* that should have given him away and ultimately led to his capture sooner. That is, he engaged in criminal activities (petty theft and forgery), violated Canadian immigration laws, traveled openly to a country to engage in terrorist training, made telephone calls to known al-Qaeda operatives, mixed noxious chemicals that created suspicion among employees at a motel where he was working on his bomb, and attempted to travel into the United States by a route (Vancouver-to-Seattle) that was extremely unusual for someone who resided where he did (Montreal).

It is clear that the cooperation of law enforcement agencies (both foreign and domestic) is critical for identifying terrorist suspects and preventing terrorist attacks. Other key factors include developing secure methods for identifying people accurately, preventing identity theft, and sharing information about terrorist suspects among various organizations. However, this case also teaches us that some of the most useful techniques and methods for preventing terrorist attacks are simple ones: an alert local law enforcement official or security guard, a vigilant employee or supervisor, or someone who sees something out of the ordinary and reports it to the proper authorities.

CONNECTING THE DOTS

SEPTEMBER 11, 2001

We would like to live as we once lived, but history will not permit it.
—John F. Kennedy[1]

SOME TERRORIST ATTACKS IN AMERICAN HISTORY, WHILE PROVOKING OUT-rage at the time they were committed, have faded into obscurity. Even when the scope of study expands beyond terrorism to other significant events, only a few incidents seem to linger in the public's consciousness. The bombing of Pearl Harbor, the assassinations of John F. Kennedy and Martin Luther King, Jr., and the Oklahoma City bombing have left an indelible mark. Among terrorist attacks, the events of September 11, 2001 are like no others. As the deadliest, most dramatic, and most carefully planned act of terrorism ever to have occurred on American soil, September 11 (or 9/11) is rightfully considered to be a turning point not only in U.S., but also world history.

The events of that fateful day have been told and retold, but they are worth reviewing briefly. Twenty-six al-Qaeda-supported terrorists attempt-ed to enter the United States at various times and through various means, beginning more than two years before the September 11 attacks.[2] Five of these terrorist conspirators were denied entrance into the United States because they were known to have connections to terrorist organizations or appeared to have insufficient resources or a clear purpose for their trip into the United States.[3] Twenty-one of the al-Qaeda terrorists were able to gain entrance into the country, and some were able to travel in and out of the United States several times in the months leading up to 9/11. For one rea-son or another, two of the terrorists did not participate in the attacks.

On the morning of September 11, 2001, nineteen hijackers—separated into three teams of five and one team of four—boarded four different domestic airline flights. At 7:50 a.m., American Airlines Flight 11 took off from Logan Airport in Boston en route to Los Angeles.[4] The five hijackers on board were able to take control of the airplane within twenty minutes after takeoff. At 9:16 a.m., Flight 11 crashed into the North Tower of the World Trade Center; the airplane was being flown by the al-Qaeda cell leader whose face became a trademark for the 9/11 attacks: Mohamed Atta. At 8:14 a.m., United Airlines Flight 175 departed Logan Airport in Boston, also headed for Los Angeles. Another team of five hijackers was on board. A little over a half-hour after takeoff, the hijackers were able to take control of the airplane. Flown by Marwan al Shehhi, Flight 175 flew into the South Tower of the World Trade Center at 9:03 a.m.[5]

When the first airplane hit the World Trade Center, many observers believed a catastrophic accident had occurred. However, the second plane pointed to a coordinated terrorist attack. Indeed, the scope of the plot was much larger. At 8:20 a.m., American Airlines Flight 77 took off from Dulles Airport in Washington, DC.[6] Within a half-hour following takeoff, the airplane was taken over by a team of five al-Qaeda hijackers. The airplane, being flown by Hani Hanjour—a citizen of Saudi Arabia who was in the United States on a student visa and who had come under suspicion by the FBI as a potential hijacker[7]—crashed into the Pentagon at 9:37 a.m.

Finally, United Airlines Flight 93 took off from Newark Airport at 8:42 a.m. en route to San Francisco.[8] Unlike the other hijacked flights, however, only four al-Qaeda hijackers were on board. Although they were able to take control of the airplane, the passengers—who had been in touch with people on the ground and had learned of the scope of the 9/11 attacks—fought to take back control of the airplane. At 10:03 a.m., Flight 93 crashed into a remote field in Shanksville, Pennsylvania, killing everyone on board.[9]

When Atta flew American Airlines Flight 11 into the North Tower of the World Trade Center, the airplane cut through seven floors, killing everyone on the aircraft and hundreds of people in the building.[10] All stairwells were effectively cut off or destroyed, leaving hundreds of people trapped on the upper floors of the burning building. As United Airlines Flight 175 hit the South Tower of the World Trade Center, the aircraft was banking and cut through nine floors.[11] Everyone on board the airplane was killed, but since rescue efforts from the crash of Flight 11 had included evacuation of the South Tower, several hundred individuals were waiting to leave the building when Flight 175 hit. Still, many people were killed or severely injured when the second plane hit, but the angle at which Flight 175 hit the South Tower had left one stairwell open to evacuate upper floors. The "most complicated rescue operation in [New York City] history" became a salvage operation when both towers of the World Trade Center collapsed.[12]

The damage to the Pentagon was also extensive. It was estimated that when American Airlines Flight 77 hit the building it was traveling at 520 miles per hour. The crash killed all sixty-four individuals on board the airplane, and one hundred and twenty-five people inside the Pentagon; a hundred and sixty other individuals were seriously injured.[13] Between the time Flight 11 took off and Flight 93 crashed in rural Pennsylvania—a span of just over two hours—the attacks of September 11 killed more than 3,000 individuals, making it the deadliest terrorist attack in history. The attacks were not only devastating because of the sheer number of deaths and amount of destruction that occurred, but the terrorists also targeted prominent symbols of American economic and military strength. Flight 93 failed to reach its target, so its final destination is not definitively known. However, subsequent investigations into the lives of the hijackers and interrogations of captured al-Qaeda operatives suggest Flight 93 was to crash into Capitol Hill—a symbol of American government.[14]

The immense scope of 9/11 produced a flood of questions, analyses, and speculation that have been discussed in the mainstream media, academic books and articles, and, of course, government agency reports including the official report by the National Commission on Terrorist Attacks Upon the United States (i.e., the 9/11 Commission).[15] Many questions deal with issues such as how the elaborate plot developed, how the hijackers were able to enter the United States, why law enforcement and government agencies were unable to prevent the attacks, and what measures can be taken to prevent another attack of this magnitude. While these and other questions will be debated for years to come, most fall into one of two general categories. Some questions take a retrospective review of how the 9/11 plot developed and was carried out; others are prospective (or future-oriented) and ask how future attacks can be prevented.

It has been firmly established that the nineteen hijackers were members of the terrorist organization known as al-Qaeda and that they received training, financing, and support from the diffuse terrorist network headed by Osama bin Laden and his second-in-command, Ayman al Zawahiri. In February 1998, bin Laden issued a fatwa—a religious ruling or command based on interpretation of Islamic law—that declared war against Americans.[16] Despite the fact that bin Laden is not an officially trained Islamic scholar and therefore not qualified to issue a fatwa, the declaration claimed that "to kill Americans and their allies, both civil and military, is an individual duty of very Muslim. . . . And to obey God's command to kill the Americans and plunder their possessions where he finds them and whenever he can."[17]

This open declaration of war went largely unnoticed by most Americans, and the U.S. government gave limited attention to al-Qaeda as a serious threat to the United States until after 9/11. While there were several attacks against U.S. targets overseas—including the bombing of the *U.S.S. Cole* and of the U.S. Embassies in Africa—the possibility of an al-Qaeda attack on American soil had not been given the consideration it deserved prior to 9/11.

Of course, retrospective analyses are fraught with complications. Some social science research has indicated that most acts of violence, particularly targeted violence, are preventable because they follow a pattern of observable and understandable thinking and behavior on the part of those who commit these kinds of acts.[18] On the other hand, attempts to develop methods for predicting future events based on an analysis of past events is prone to an error in judgment and decision-making known as "hindsight bias." This bias is based on the proverbial notion that "hindsight is 20-20," and that by looking at past events it is possible to identify certain events that could have predicted a known outcome. In reality, events often can not be predicted with complete accuracy. A review of the September 11 attacks has the advantage of hindsight, yet some post-9/11 reactions (e.g., certain provisions of the U.S. Patriot Act) came about as a result of the belief that certain details of the attacks could not have been known without stronger law enforcement tools to identify and detain potential terrorists.

The 9/11 Commission found that many things were clearly known—or should have been known—about the plot before it occurred. For instance, a meeting between a CIA official and an FBI agent addressing the investigation into the bombing of the *U.S.S. Cole* revealed that Khalid al Mihdhar, one of the hijackers on American Airlines Flight 77 that flew into the Pentagon, was an al-Qaeda operative.[19] In subsequent meetings between the CIA and FBI, however, important information about the travel patterns of Mihdhar were not communicated. By the time the FBI discovered that Mihdhar had entered the United States, it was a month before the September 11 attacks. It is quite likely that if the CIA and FBI had shared information, Mihdhar would have been identified and perhaps apprehended, which could have shed light on plans for the September 11 attacks. In addition, an FBI agent in Phoenix, Arizona had sent a memo to FBI headquarters in July 2001 concerning his belief that bin Laden was sending operatives into the United States to train at aviation schools and to use aircraft in terrorist attacks.[20] Although the agent's memo and recommendation to assemble lists of aviation schools and to obtain visa information on individuals attending the schools were not acted upon, the 9/11 Commission concluded that the September 11 plots would probably not have been uncovered even if the FBI agent's suspicions had been investigated thoroughly. Nevertheless, action on the memo might have sensitized the FBI to take another of their agent's concerns more seriously.

In August 2001, the FBI's Minneapolis Field Office began an investigation into Zacarias Moussaoui, who had come under suspicion for undergoing light training at an Oklahoma aviation school and another school in Minnesota.[21] Moussaoui was known to have strong jihadist beliefs, no interest in learning to become a commercial pilot, and minimal knowledge of flying, particularly with respect to taking off and landing an aircraft. The FBI in Minnesota arrested Moussaoui for overstaying his visa, and during deportation proceedings, sought a warrant from FBI headquarters to search Moussaoui's computer. Unfortunately, the request was denied because senior officials believed there was insufficient probable cause to undertake the search. Of course, in the wake of the September 11 attacks, it is generally believed that Moussaoui was the twentieth hijacker and may have been selected to be on board United Airlines Flight 93—the only airplane in the September 11 attacks with four hijackers and the one that failed to reach its target.

These specific instances of 9/11 perpetrators coming under suspicion by government intelligence and law enforcement agencies represent just a few of many details that are generally believed to be errors in judgment or missed opportunities. Yet the assessment of what the attacks mean for America's future remains an equally pressing concern. The United States as a nation, and its citizens in particular, have shown remarkable resilience in dealing with the devastating attacks and moving forward. But questions remain about what al-Qaeda is, its reasons for attacking the United States, and what its capabilities and intentions are for carrying out attacks in the future.

There is considerable disagreement among academic, government, law enforcement, and intelligence experts about exactly what al-Qaeda represents.[22] Although many of al-Qaeda's senior leaders have been captured or killed by counterterrorism measures in the wake of the September 11 attacks, the organization still poses a substantial threat to the security of the United States and its allies around the world. The primary reason that al-Qaeda and jihadist terrorists continue to operate is because they represent an ideology and movement that is able to operate without a clear hierarchical leadership like traditional terrorist organizations. As one noted terrorist expert has observed, "al-Qaeda's resiliency (and longevity) is not predicated on the total number of jihadists that it may have or have not trained in the past, but on its continued ability to recruit, to mobilize, and to animate both actual and would-be fighters, supporters, and sympathizers."[23]

Therefore, the scope of the 9/11 attacks demonstrate not only the level of commitment al-Qaeda and its followers have in destroying the United States, but it also reveals how patient planning, diffuse and decentralized organization of terrorist cells and operatives, and the willingness of terrorists to die for their cause present a very dangerous and long-term threat to the United States. In this respect, the attacks represent a clear turning point in the history of terrorism on American soil.

There is much that can be learned by continuing to study the events of 9/11 and the circumstances that led up to the attacks of that day. However, several questions are likely to persist and may never be answered fully. Like the assassination of John F. Kennedy, which has been examined and re-examined with varying degrees of resolution to certain issues, September 11 will be studied for many years. It is important to keep in mind, however, that some approaches to looking at the events of 9/11 are likely to produce few, if any, useful results. As historical events chronicled in this book have shown, some terrorist attacks have been studied with an eye toward identifying broad conspiracies. Some of these views have found their way into the post-9/11 analysis, such as theories that speculate—by merely asking rhetorical questions about what was known or should have been known and without any concrete evidence—that the U.S. government had somehow perpetrated the attacks as a pretext to beginning military actions overseas. Baseless claims such as these provide nothing of value to our study of September 11 and should be dismissed outright in favor of constructive analysis that will help us learn from the tragic events.

On the other hand, there appears to be ample room for undertaking a critical review of how organizational, governmental, and systematic failures to identify information possibly led to the failure of law enforcement and intelligence agencies to prevent the attacks. For example, it is clear that the CIA and FBI failed to connect the dots among various clues and information that was known about al-Qaeda in the months, and even years, leading up to the attacks. There was "a considerable amount of alarming information" that al-Qaeda was planning attacks within the United States—information that became available as a result of the *U.S.S. Cole* bombing, African embassy cases, and even the 1993 World Trade Center bombing and the subsequent arrest of the perpetrators of those attacks.[24] While not bearing full responsibility for failures leading up to 9/11, the FBI was nevertheless criticized by the 9/11 Commission as a law enforcement agency because it "lacked the ability to know what it knew."[25] This finding is but one of many that a retrospective study of September 11 reveals and that can be used to correct inefficiencies in counterterrorism efforts so that future attacks may be prevented.

Of course, it would be a major error in judgment to presume that all future terrorist attacks can be prevented merely by correcting what was wrong prior to 9/11. As a terrorist movement, al-Qaeda will change its procedures and its operatives, modify its strategies to overcome security measures, and continue to target prominent sites in the United States. A particularly useful recommendation that has been advanced is separating intelligence and law enforcement roles, particularly in the domestic United States. Whereas law enforcement officers are primarily oriented to look at past events—investigating crimes, collecting evidence, and making arrests—intelligence officers look to future events. They collect information, analyze it for trends and potential threats, and strive to prevent attacks before they occur. In this regard, it is important for the United States to confront how intelligence will be collected in domestic situations, while the rights and liberties that are part of the foundation of our democracy are preserved. Although there are no easy answers to these questions, careful analysis and cordial debate (as well as well-informed legislation), rather than political maneuvering based on emotional reaction to catastrophic events, will move us in the right direction.

The U.S.A. Patriot Act of 2001 is a case in point. This massive piece of legislation was passed by sweeping approval of both the House of Representatives and the Senate and signed into law by President Bush less than seven weeks after the September 11 attacks[26]. Much has been written about the Patriot Act, with its supporters claiming that the legislation provided the necessary strengthening of laws to fight terrorism and its detractors asserting it tramples on civil liberties. Given the extremely broad scope of the Patriot Act—with its 161 sections and over 300 pages of text—it makes little sense to decide whether one is "for" or "against" the controversial legislation. Some provisions of the law, particularly those that affirm the need to avoid prejudice against Muslim Americans or those that strengthen border protections and facilitate existing law enforcement practices, are clearly needed. On the other hand, some provisions, such as those that make it easier for law enforcement officers to engage in electronic surveillance of American citizens without a warrant or probable cause, deserve increased scrutiny. In short, the challenge in analyzing the Patriot Act is to identify those provisions that are necessary and effective, while separating out those that may not be effective and that may actually change the nature of America by reducing freedoms. There are no easy answers to some of these questions. However, a balanced approach to discussing not only the Patriot Act, but also the events of September 11 and what we can learn from them, is needed if we hope to move forward productively in our efforts to combat terrorism.

ARE YOU AFRAID?

THE ANTHRAX LETTERS

*You can discover what your enemy fears most by observing
the means he uses to frighten you.*

—Eric Hoffer[1]

EXACTLY ONE WEEK AFTER THE ATTACKS OF SEPTEMBER 11, 2001, TWO
envelopes containing a granular substance were sent from Trenton, New
Jersey to the New York City offices of NBC News and the *New York Post*.[2]
In addition to the unusual substance, each envelope contained a handwritten letter dated "9-11-01" with the following message: "This is next. Take
penacilin (*sic*) now. Death to America. Death to Israel. Allah is great."[3]
Within ten days of the letters being opened, an editorial assistant at the *New
York Post* developed a blister on her finger, a postal maintenance worker in
Trenton developed a strange skin lesion, a Trenton postal carrier also developed a lesion, and an assistant to NBC News anchor Tom Brokaw noticed
a strange lesion near her collarbone. All four individuals subsequently tested
positive for a bacterial anthrax infection.

The letters sent from Trenton were the first known incidents in a series
of bioterrorist attacks that added further panic to the heightened anxieties
brought about by the events of September 11. In Boca Raton, Florida, a
photo editor working for the tabloid paper *The Sun* began to feel ill on
September 30. He was experiencing high fever, confusion, and vomiting. By
the time he was diagnosed with an anthrax infection, his condition had
deteriorated, and he died on October 5 despite efforts to treat him with
antibiotics.[4] When investigators from the Centers for Disease Control
attempted to identify the source of the editor's infection, they tested the
offices of American Media, Inc. (AMI), where both *The Sun* and the
National Enquirer are published.[5] Anthrax spores were found on the editor's
computer keyboard and in the mailroom at the AMI offices. The source of

the infection was generally believed to be letters sent to the tabloid publisher, and the AMI office building was subsequently evacuated and secured.[6] Although bizarre and threatening letters were common occurrences, given the sometimes controversial subject matter published in the company's tabloid newspapers, a fan letter to the actress/singer Jennifer Lopez bearing the star of David and sent to AMI is believed to be the source of a white powdery substance. On October 8, a mailroom worker at AMI tested positive for inhalation anthrax, and by October 13, another six workers had tested positive. The massive contamination led to employees being given treatment with the antibiotic ciprofloxacin, the recommended treatment for anthrax infection[7].

Aside from the anthrax-laced letters mailed from Trenton and handled through the mailroom at AMI, the case was complicated by other letters that were initially believed to contain anthrax but which turned out to be hoaxes. For instance, NBC and the *New York Post* received letters containing a harmless powder. On October 12, Judith Miller, a reporter with *The New York Times* who has written extensively about bioterrorism, received a letter postmarked from St. Petersburg, Florida. When she opened the letter, it sprayed her with a powdery mist.[8] The substance turned out to be harmless, but the incident was regarded as part of an anthrax threat that was growing in scope.

Letters containing phony anthrax threats were common prior to 9/11. In 1999, for example, the FBI received 180 anthrax threat hoaxes.[9] Many fake anthrax attacks in the years leading up to 9/11 were attributed to individuals making threats to magazine publishers, courthouses, and abortion clinics that were intended to create panic and instill fear, rather than kill anyone. But the confirmed anthrax infections in New York, New Jersey, and Florida constituted terrorism perpetrated through the U.S. mail.

As anthrax contamination was being investigated at the offices of AMI, NBC, and the *New York Post*, the case expanded when another target emerged—the U.S. government. On October 9, two letters were mailed from Trenton, New Jersey to the offices of South Dakota Senator Tom Daschle and Vermont Senator Patrick Leahy. Both letters bore the same fictitious return address, "4th Grade Greendale School, Franklin Park, NJ 08852," and contained the same ominous message dated "09-11-01": "You can not stop us. We have this anthrax. You die now. Are you afraid? Death to America. Death to Israel. Allah is great."[10]

Whereas the letters sent to New York City and Florida contained anthrax spores that were unrefined and resulted in cutaneous infections, the letter sent to Senator Daschle's office was different. When it was opened, the envelope released a cloud of fine dust, suggesting the anthrax was weaponized. In the manufacture of biological weapons, weaponization refers to a process whereby anthrax spores are made into very small particles that do not develop a charge of static electricity, will not lump together, and float in the air, making inhalation of the substance more likely.[11] Investigators found the anthrax dust emitted from the Daschle letter was very effective. The particles were so small, they were typical of the most effective method for weaponizing anthrax in the United States. This optimal method is secret and undertaken through a process involving a series of patented procedures generally believed to be unknown in any other country.[12] Although the weaponized nature of the anthrax suggested the perpetrator came from within the United States, there was one other fact that made this possibility even more likely. The type of anthrax used in all the attacks was identified by a specific bacterial version known as the Ames strain, a name used for identification purposes in research laboratories. Only about twenty laboratories in the world were known to have access to this strain.[13]

When the letters were processed through the mail system in Washington, D.C., anthrax spores were pressed through the envelopes and contaminated machinery and other mailings. On October 20, the office building where mail is processed for members of Congress tested positive for anthrax, and the next day, a Washington postal worker died from inhalation anthrax.[14] Whereas previous anthrax contamination was cutaneous, the scope of the problem was widening. The Daschle letter indicated that inhalation of anthrax spores from a weaponized version of the biological agent was posing a much more dangerous threat. By October 22, the anthrax contamination in Washington had grown as another postal worker presented to an area hospital with flu-like symptoms and died in the evening from what was later determined to be anthrax infection[15]. Two more postal workers were hospitalized, prompting the testing of more than 2,000 employees of the U.S. Postal Service.

Almost as abruptly as delivery of the anthrax letters began, the mailings ended. The last in the series was a hoax letter mailed to the offices of Senator Daschle on November 15, and the letter to Senator Leahy containing anthrax was found on November 16.[16] In the two-month period following the September 11 attacks, a total of four letters containing anthrax were identified, and a fifth delivered to the offices of AMI in Florida was believed to have been thrown away after it was opened. During this period, there were anywhere from three to five hoax letters, and each contained threatening statements and a harmless powder that contained no anthrax or other harmful agents.[17] Despite being able to identify the specific anthrax strain used in the attack, the weaponized preparation of the material contained in some of the letters, and specific laboratories where access to the material was possible, investigators were unable to identify someone responsible for the attack. The inability to bring the investigation to a successful conclusion prompted rampant speculation about who might have been responsible for the attacks.

Given the timing of the anthrax letters, one theory suggested that al-Qaeda hijackers who carried out the September 11 attacks also sent the anthrax letters as part of an extended terrorism campaign against the United States. Several pieces of circumstantial evidence lend credence to the theory. For instance, it is known that some of the hijackers had explored the possibility of obtaining crop dusters, which could have been used to spread deadly pathogens on populated areas.[18] Furthermore, a pharmacist in Florida later recognized two of the hijackers—Mohamad Atta and Marwan al-Shehhi—as individuals who came to his pharmacy looking for treatment of skin irritation on the hands. An emergency room physician in Florida also treated an individual who was later identified as a 9/11 hijacker for symptoms consistent with cutaneous anthrax exposure. Still, the apartments, automobiles, and belongings of the hijackers were tested for anthrax contamination and revealed no evidence that they had handled or been exposed to anthrax. Moreover, if the al-Qaeda hijackers had been responsible for the anthrax letters, they would have needed others to help them, since the first letter was postmarked one week after all hijackers died in the September 11 attacks.[19]

One of the more widely accepted theories about the letters was that they were sent by an individual within the United States who had a domestic, rather than foreign or international, terrorist agenda. The Federal Bureau of Investigation issued a behavioral profile of the unknown individual who had sent the anthrax letters. Using what little was known about the individual—that his or her selected method for terrorizing the U.S. population was the lethal biological agent anthrax—the FBI profile speculated that the perpetrator was most likely an adult male employed in a setting (e.g., laboratory) where he was comfortable working with hazardous material, who had access to and a working knowledge of anthrax, and who was rational and organized in his thinking.[20] The FBI profile also presumed, based on the original mailing of the letters, that the perpetrator was familiar with the Trenton, New Jersey area and had selected his victims deliberately, not randomly, since the proper address had been used for each addressee. According to the behavioral profile, the perpetrator was also thought likely to avoid confrontation with others, to prefer being alone, and to have strong feelings of contempt against the media and the U.S. government.

The highly generalized nature of the profile appeared to be straightforward deductions from what was known about the anthrax letters. Yet the profile did not render any useful leads or breaks in the case. In fact, the FBI identified a list of "persons of interest" who fit aspects of the profile. One individual identified as a person of interest, Dr. Stephen J. Hatfill, had a history of doing anthrax-related work for the U.S. Army Medical Research Institute of Infection Diseases (USAMRIID) and reportedly had knowledge of anthrax weaponization procedures.[21] Despite Hatfill's public defense of himself as someone with no knowledge of the anthrax letters, the FBI persisted in its investigation but never found evidence pointing to anyone on its list of suspects in the anthrax attacks.

Behavioral profiles have generally been touted as investigative techniques that can assist police in their efforts to identify unknown perpetrators of crimes by identifying likely suspects, narrowing leads, and assisting with effective interrogation of suspects. However, they have rarely been successful in solving perplexing crimes by themselves. Instead, it is solid police work that often leads to breaks in a case and the discovery of new evidence that leads to an arrest. Despite several theories about domestic versus al-Qaeda-linked terrorists as the perpetrators of one of the more terrifying bioterrorist attacks on American soil, the case remains unsolved, and investigators appear no closer to solving the case than they were when the letters first appeared.

Aside from questions about who mailed the anthrax letters in the wake of the September 11 attacks, one thing remains clear. Bioterrorism became a very real threat to every American citizen. A common scene observed by many in the wake of the attacks was their daily postal carrier wearing rubber gloves to prevent the possibility of exposure to harmful biological or chemical agents being transported through the U.S. mail system. Like the airliners used by the 9/11 hijackers, the U.S. postal system is an important part of the social and economic infrastructure of American society used by terrorists to kill citizens, disrupt the daily lives of Americans, and create mass fear, regardless of how far removed citizens may have been from the risk of exposure.

The highly weaponized nature of the anthrax used in the attacks pointed to someone with detailed technical knowledge of how to manufacture an effective biological agent that could kill. Moreover, the timing of the attacks added fuel to the fires of the lingering fears and anxieties created by the attacks of September 11. In many ways, 9/11 and the anthrax letters together mark both an end to the era of what-if scenarios in counterterrorism and the beginning of an era in which a new form of terrorism—one where the risk of catastrophic destruction and the use of weapons of mass destruction—has found its way onto American soil.

EPILOGUE

You see that flag, Mr. Reid? That's the flag of the United States of America. That flag will fly there long after this is all forgotten.
—William Young, U.S. District Judge[1]

WHILE IT MAY SEEM ENTICING TO END THIS CONCISE HISTORY WITH A DRA-matic statement about a new era of catastrophic terrorism, perhaps it better befits our discussion to first review what, if anything, we might learn from the survey of cases that have been discussed. An initial observation is that these cases are not discrete incidents with no connection to one another. Rather, the history covered in this book began in the latter half of the nineteenth century and ends in what noted terrorism researcher David Rapoport has called the era of "modern terror."[2]

Professor Rapoport observed that modern terrorism is characterized by four waves of violence, each characterized by a particular motive or method of expression. The first of these waves grew out of Russia in the 1880s and within a few decades spread throughout the world.[3] Spurred by anarchists who refined the use of explosives and related tactics, the terrorist in this first wave sought to overthrow organized government and attempted to give greater power to the labor class. Around 1920, anarchism gave way to a second wave of terrorism that Rapoport characterized as anti-colonial.[4] A number of regions around the world—including Northern Ireland, Israel and Palestine, and South America—saw political violence by terrorist groups seeking to revolt against imperialism and colonization. After about forty years, the anti-colonial wave was replaced by a period characterized by a "New Left."[5] According to Rapoport, this third wave was prompted by global concerns—particularly the Vietnam war—and was associated with both radicalism and nationalism. Finally, the New Left era gave way to a fourth wave of modern terrorism motivated by religion. This wave began at the time of the Iranian revolution in 1979, and is likely to continue for approximately another two decades. Whether this fourth wave will, in fact, dissipate or be replaced by a new wave of terrorism remains to be seen.

The history of terrorism on American soil mirrors these four waves of terrorism. Beginning with the Haymarket bombing in 1886 and spanning the assassination of William McKinley and bombings of 1910 (*Los Angeles Times* building), 1919 (anarchists), and 1920 (Wall Street), the United States experienced a rash of attacks motivated by anarchists and their teachings. After the assassination attempt on President-elect Franklin D. Roosevelt in 1933, the threat of anarchist violence faded. During the next wave of terrorism, attacks on American soil reflected an anti-colonial trend. The assassination attempt on Harry S. Truman and the shooting attack at the U.S. House of Representatives were both carried out by Puerto Rican nationalists protesting U.S. control over the island territory. Many of the terrorism attacks on racial minorities, including the infamous bombing of the 16th Street Baptist church, although not motivated purely by anti-colonialists, were similarly motivated by fear over encroachments of various social and ethnic groups into the sovereignty of the social majority. During the third wave of New Left violence, attacks on American soil were carried out by groups like the Weather Underground. Finally, recent trends in terrorism on American soil have reflected strong religious themes. Cases chronicled in this book include the assassination of Rabbi Meir Kahane, assassinations and bombings at abortion clinics by religiously inspired terrorists, shooting attacks carried out by individuals consumed with hatred toward the United States because of its foreign policies in the Middle East, and, of course, the 1993 World Trade Center bombing and the attacks of September 11, 2001.

Within the terrorism literature, there is ongoing debate about whether there is a "new terrorism" that represents a more dangerous threat than older forms of political violence.[6] Some researchers have observed that within the last decade, terrorist attacks around the globe have become deadlier, while other researchers believe concern over the use of weapons of mass destruction by terrorists is shrouded in hysteria and rhetoric that overstates the real threat. Whether the notion of a new terrorism is valid, a second observation that follows from a collective reading of the cases in this book is that terrorism is not a new phenomenon in the United States. Since the time of post-Civil War reconstruction through the beginning of the twenty-first century, the United States has seen a steady stream of terrorist violence on its soil. The long history of terrorism in America and the interest that both domestic and international terrorist organizations have in attacking U.S. interests point to the fact that the cases in this book represent neither the entire history of U.S. terrorism nor the end of terrorism's legacy. Like many other nations and regions around the world, the United States is a nation that has terrorism as part of its past, present, and future.

A third observation about the cases in this book is that, while terrorism is not a new phenomenon, the threat has intensified in recent years and attacks have become increasingly deadly. The attacks on American soil with the highest number of fatalities—the Oklahoma City bombing and the September 11 attacks—occurred recently and within a span of six years. Moreover, the thwarted suicide bombers in New York City and the anthrax attacks merely underscore concerns prompted by 9/11 that the terrorists of today are not only willing to die for their cause but are also willing to seek out and use weapons of mass destruction that have the potential to kill large numbers of people. The threat of suicide attackers also demonstrates that deterrence through harsh criminal punishment will have little, if any, impact on reducing the threat of terrorism and our efforts to combat the problem need to become preemptive and preventive. We need to increase the sophistication of our intelligence-gathering capabilities to identify threats before they arise.

A fourth observation about these cases is that terrorism on American soil takes many forms and is carried out by individuals and groups with different motives or agendas. Although the United States is currently involved in a major confrontation with al-Qaeda and its operatives, the fact remains that terrorism on American soil is not solely the work of Middle Eastern terrorists. Over the last century and beyond, the United States has confronted threats from domestic terrorist groups like the Earth Liberation Front, racist groups like the KKK, left-wing organizations like the Weather Underground, and more loosely organized movements like anarchism. While there is much we can learn from each of the cases outlined in this book, it is important to recognize that terrorism is not a uniform phenomenon and counterterrorism is not a "once size fits all" process. Each individual or group must be understood and confronted based on the unique nature of the threat it poses.

Another interesting observation is that terrorists have been viewed as criminals inconsistently throughout history. The terrorist acts of some individuals, like the assassins Leon Czolgosz and Giuseppe Zangara and bombers Ted Kaczynski and Eric Rudolph, were investigated as crimes, and each was convicted and sentenced to either death or life in prison. Other terrorist perpetrators, like Lolita Lebron and remnant members of the Weather Underground, either received pardons or minimal sentences for their activities. Some cases, like the 1993 World Trade Center bombing and the thwarted suicide bombers in New York City, represent examples of investigative police work at its finest. Other cases, like the Wall Street bombing of 1920 and the post-9/11 anthrax attacks, frustrated law enforcement authorities for years and remain unsolved. The fact that terrorism is a concept shrouded in controversy and one that lacks a universal definition has hindered efforts to develop consistent policies for developing intelligence on emerging threats, investigating certain crimes as acts of terrorism, and adjudicating and punishing suspected and convicted terrorists. It behooves American citizens to demand firm, fair, and strict laws that will clarify, rather than cloud, the way terrorism is confronted.

Finally, the cases in this book provide an eclectic collage of terrorism on American soil. While many of these cases are tragic in that they involve the loss of innocent lives and horrific destruction, they also provide a reason both to admire the strength of the American spirit and remain hopeful for the nation's future. The Wall Street bombing of 1920 did not cause a massive decline in the stock market or prompt a major economic downturn. William McKinley's assassination and the attacks on the Congress did not disrupt the workings of the United States government. Attacks on racial minorities and the deaths of the young girls in the bombing of the 16th Street Baptist Church did not prevent civil rights legislation from being enacted or progress toward racial fairness from continuing. Oklahoma City and New York City have shown remarkable resilience in their response to the devastating attacks that each endured. In short, Americans have shown a profound capacity to respond well in the aftermath of terrorist attacks and to continue their daily lives, even in the face of persistent threats.

If the cases in this book have been intriguing, educational, or in some way helpful in offering insight into the history of terrorism on American soil, then so much the better. However, they underscore the sentiments expressed by U.S. District Judge William Young cited at the beginning of this epilogue. Long after the plots, attacks, and perpetrators in these cases have been forgotten or enshrined in infamy, the American flag continues to wave. In this specific regard, the legacy of terrorism on American soil is not only cause for admiration but also a reason for optimism about our future.

ENDNOTES

INTRODUCTION

1. "Bin Laden's Message," *BBC News,* November 12, 2002, http://news.bbc.co.uk/1/low/world/middle_east/2455845.stm (accessed April 28, 2004).
2. Ibid.
3. Ibid.
4. The reference to Hulegu Khan and the historical significance of the reference was provided by terrorist researcher and expert Brian Michael Jenkins. I am grateful to Mr. Jenkins for providing these details; see also "Hulagu Kahn," *Wikipedia,* http://en.wikipedia.org/wiki/Hulegu_Khan, (accessed March 6, 2006).
5. John Horgan, *The Psychology of Terrorism* (New York: Routledge, 2005), 30.
6. A copy of the al-Qaeda training manual can be found in the online library at the National Memorial Institute for the Prevention of Terrorism at http://library.mipt.org.
7. Bernard Lewis, *The Assassins: A Radical Sect in Islam* (New York: Basic Books, 1967), 11-12.
8. Ibid., 12.
9. Some assassinations are not included in this book because they either have motives that were clearly not political (e.g., the assassination of President James Garfield who was killed by a mentally ill individual with a personal, and possibly delusional grudge), unknown (e.g., the assassination of John F. Kennedy by Lee Harvey Oswald), or atypical or bizarre (e.g., the assassination attempt on presidential candidate George Wallace or the assassination attempt on Ronald Reagan).
10. J. Reid Meloy and James E. McEllistrem, "Bombing and Psychopathy: An Integrative Review," *Journal of Forensic Sciences* 43 (1998): 556-562.
11. Horgan, *The Psychology of Terrorism,* 116.
12. One kidnapping case that is not included in this book that is often cited among examples of terrorist violence in the United States is the abduction of Patty Hearst. This case was not included because it was discussed elsewhere in one of my other publications. See Charles P.

Ewing and Joseph T. McCann, *Minds on Trial: Great Cases in Law and Psychology* (New York: Oxford University Press, 2006).

13. William Langewiesche, "The Crash of Egypt Air 990," *The Atlantic Monthly*, November, 2001, http://www.theatlantic.com (accessed May 27, 2003).

14. Alex P. Schmid and Albert J. Jongman, *Political Terrorism: A New Guide to Actors, Authors, Concepts, Data Bases, Theories, and Literature* (New Brunswick, NJ: Transaction Publishers, 2005), 5.

15. Federal Bureau of Investigation, *Terrorism 2000/2001* (Washington, DC: Federal Bureau of Investigation, 2000/2001), iii.

LOST CAUSE TERRORISM
The Assassination of Abraham Lincoln

1. Elizabeth Frost-Knappman and David S. Shrager, *A Concise Encyclopedia of Legal Quotations* (New York: Barnes & Noble Books, 1998), 281.

2. H. Donald Winkler, *Lincoln and Booth: More Light on the Conspiracy* (Nashville, TN: Cumberland House, 2003), 13.

3. Donald W. Hastings, "The Psychiatry of Presidential Assassination: Part 1: Jackson and Lincoln," *Applied Therapeutics* November, 1965: 993–1015.

4. Robert A. Fein and Bryan Vossekuil, "Assassination in the United States: An Operational Study of Recent Assassins, Attackers, and Near-lethal Approachers," *Journal of Forensic Sciences* 44 (1999): 321-333.

5. Winkler, *Lincoln and Booth*, 61.

6. Edward Steers, Jr., *Blood on the Moon: The Assassination of Abraham Lincoln* (Lexington, KY: The University of Kentucky Press, 2001), 29.

7. Ibid., 27.

8. Ibid, 34.

9. Ibid, 35.

10. Ibid., 31.

11. Ibid., 32.

12. Ibid., 36.

13. Ibid., 71.

14. Ibid., 80.

15. Mudd's recollections are tainted by the fact that he tried to distance himself from Booth after the assassination in order to protect himself. Surratt also had a motive to minimize his connection to Booth. What

Booth said and what was agreed to during this meeting is based on later testimony or public statements by Mudd and Surratt. Their recollections could be based on their desire to distance themselves from Booth to avoid prosecution as co-conspirators.

16. Winkler, *Lincoln and Booth*, 34.

17. Ibid., 35.

18. Ibid., 48.

19. Andrew Jackson had been the target of an assassination attempt by a mentally ill individual who was committed to an institution for the criminally insane. Jackson helped to fend off his would-be attacker after two pistols misfired.

20. Steers, *Blood on the Moon*, 26.

21. Ibid., 87.

22. Winkler, *Lincoln and Booth*, 66.

23. Ibid.

24. Ibid., 107.

25. See Winkler, *Lincoln and Booth* and Steers, *Blood on the Moon* a full discussion of the details of the related attacks on Johnson and Seward.

26. Ibid.

BEGINNING THE DYNAMITE ERA
The Haymarket Bombing

1. Robert I. Fitzhenry, ed., *The Harper Book of Quotations*, 3rd ed. (New York: Harper Collins, 1993), 301.

2. Paul Avrich, *The Haymarket Tragedy* (Princeton, NJ: Princeton University Press, 1984), 61.

3. John Most, "The Case for Dynamite," in *Voices of Terror: Manifestos, Writings and Manuals of al-Qaeda, Hamas, and Other Terrorists from Around the World and Throughout the Ages*, ed. Walter Laqueur (New York: Reed Press, 2004), 340-343, 340.

4. "Haymarket Affair Chronology," *The Haymarket Affair Digital Collection* http://www.chicagohistory.org/hadc/chronology.html (accessed December 16, 2005).

5. Avrich, *The Haymarket* Tragedy, 189-190.

6. Ibid., 190.

7. Ibid. The text of the flier, as reproduced here, is in abbreviated form. Nevertheless, this abridged version conveys the views and opinions that Spies wished to convey.
8. Ibid., 200.
9. "Haymarket Affair Chronology."
10. Avrich, *The Haymarket Tragedy*, 208.
11. Ibid.
12. Ibid., 234.
13. Ibid., 235.
14. Ibid., 440.
15. "Haymarket Affair Narrative," *The Haymarket Affair Digital Collection* http://www.chicagohistory.org/hadc/intro.html (accessed December 16, 2005).
16. "Haymarket Affair Chronology."
17. Avrich, *The Haymarket Tragedy*, 265.
18. "Haymarket Affair Chronology."
19. Avirch, *The Haymarket Tragedy*, 375.
20. Corinne J. Naden, *The Haymarket Affair: Chicago, 1886: The "Great Anarchist" Riot and Trial* (New York: Franklin Watts, 1968), 49.
21. John Most, "Action as Propaganda," in: Laqueur, *Voices of Terror*, 108.

A FALSE SENSE OF COMMUNITY
The Assassination of William McKinley

1. Elizabeth Frost-Knappman and David S. Shrager, *A Concise Encyclopedia of Legal Quotations* (New York: Barnes & Noble Books, 1998), 19.
2. Eric Rauchway, *Murdering McKinley: The Making of Theodore Roosevelt's America* (New York: Hill and Wang, 2003), 6.
3. Ibid.
4. James C. Fisher, *Stolen Glory: The McKinley Assassination* (La Jolla, CA: Alamar Books, 2001), 55.
5. Philip H. Melanson, *The Secret Service: The Hidden History of an Enigmatic Agency* (New York: Carroll & Graf, 2002), 24.
6. Ibid., 26.
7. Ibid., 27.
8. Fisher, *Stolen Glory*, 55.
9. Ibid.
10. Ibid., 58.

11. Ibid., 59.

12. Ibid., 46.

13. Ibid.

14. Ibid., 60.

15. There has been lingering controversy over the medical care McKinley received for his injuries. A distinguished Buffalo gynecologist was the physician who ultimately operated on the President because one of the nation's imminent surgeon's, Dr. Roswell Park who was based in Buffalo, was several miles away and unavailable at the time. Some people who have studied the McKinley assassination argue that had Park been available, McKinley would have survived his attack. Historian Jack Fisher, who is also a physician, has carefully studied the case and outlines his opinions in his book on the subject, *Stolen Glory: The McKinley Assassination*. Fisher concludes that McKinley's injuries were so severe that it is unlikely any surgeon of the day could have saved the President's life. However, McKinley's life would most likely be saved if his injuries had occurred today.

16. Rauchway, *Murdering McKinley*, 16-17.

17. D. E. Haines, "Spitzka and Spitzka on the Brains of the Assassins of Presidents," *Journal of the History of Neuroscience* 4 (1995): 236-266.

18. Rauchway, *Murdering McKinley*, 20-27.

19. Ibid., 19.

20. Controversy continued over the course of Czolgosz's trial, execution, and autopsy. In order to avoid morbid curiosity and attempts to re-examine the assassin, his body was dissolved in acid, and subsequent attempts to check on the accuracy of his autopsy report have not been possible. Also, questions have been raised about the adequacy of his legal defense. Some have speculated that Czolgosz was, in fact, insane. One hypothesis offered by historian Eric Rauchway in his book *Murdering McKinley* is that Czolgosz may have suffered from mental illness brought on by syphilis. These and other points of contention are not relevant to the issue of McKinley's assassination as an act of terrorism and therefore I have not discussed them in any detail. However, my own study of the case has led me to the conclusion that in all likelihood Czolgosz was sane at the time he shot McKinley.

21. See the work of psychiatrist Vernon L. Briggs discussed in James W. Clarke, *American Assassins: The Darker Side of Politics* (Princeton, NJ: Princeton University Press, 1982), 41.

22. Donald W. Hastings, "The Psychiatry of Presidential Assassination, Part II: Garfield and McKinley," *Applied Therapeutics*, December (1965): 1113-1123, 1131.

23. Clarke, *American Assassins*, 42.

24. Ibid., 42.

25. Rauchway, *Murdering McKinley*, 166.

26. Ibid., 98.

27. Ibid., 108. Rauchway notes that police withheld food, burned Goldman's eyes with bright light and threatened her but she never confessed to playing any role in the assassination.

28. Jerrold M. Post, Kevin G. Ruby, and Eric D. Shaw, "The Radical Group in Context: 1. An Integrated Framework for the Analysis of Group Risk for Terrorism," *Studies on Conflict and Terrorism* 25 (2002): 73-100, 88.

Stop the Presses
The Los Angeles Times Bombing of 1910

1. Elizabeth Frost-Knappman and David S. Shrager, *A Concise Encyclopedia of Legal Quotations* (New York: Barnes & Noble Books, 1998), 281.

2. The notion of terrorism as "theater" is from the work of terrorism expert Brian Michael Jenkins, discussed in Bruce Hoffman, *Inside Terrorism* (New York: Columbia University Press, 1998), 38.

3. Simon Reeve, "One Day in September," in *Confronting Fear: A History of Terrorism*, ed. Isaac Cronin (New York: Thunder's Mouth Press, 2002), 210-226.

4. "The Bombing of the *Los Angeles Times*," *Los Angeles Fire Department Historical Archive*, http://www.usc.edu/isd/archives/la/scandals/times.html (accessed November 14, 2003).

5. Jeffrey D. Simon, *The Terrorist Trap: America's Experience with Terrorism* 2nd ed. (Bloomington, IN: Indiana University Press, 2001), 40.

6. Ibid., 40-41.

7. "Indict Seven for Los Angeles Plot," *The New York Times*, January 6, 1911, 1.

8. Simon, *The Terrorist Trap*, 41.

9. William W. Robinson, *Bombs and Bribery: The Story of the McNamara and Darrow Trials Following the Dynamiting in 1910 of the Los Angeles Times Building* (Los Angeles: Dawson's Book Shop, 1969).

10. Ibid.

11. "Indict seven," 1.

12. Robinson, *Bombs and Bribery.*

13. "Union Leaders Arrested for Bomb Outrage," *The New York Times,* April 23, 1911, 1.

14. Ibid.

15. Robinson, *Bombs and Bribery.*

16. Ibid.

17. Ibid.

18. Ibid.

19. Ibid., 16.

20. Ibid., 19.

21. Ibid.

22. Ibid.

23. Ibid.

24. Geoffrey Cowan, "A Man for Some Seasons: Clarence Darrow," *The American Lawyer,* December 6, 1999, http://www.law.umkc.edu/faculty/projects/ftrials/DarrowCowan.html (accessed June 1, 2004).

25. Jacob Stein, "Great Closing Arguments," *FindLaw's Legal Commentary* http://writ.findlaw.com/commentary/20000612_stein.html, (accessed June 18, 2004).

AN ECLECTIC CRIMINAL
The Case of Erich Muenter

1. http://www.quoteland.com (accessed on April 24, 2006).

2. "Bomb Rocks Capitol," http://www.senate.gov/artandhistory/history/minute/Bomb_Rocks_Capitol.htm, (accessed June 7, 2005).

3. Ibid.

4. George DeWan, "His Calling Cards Were Guns," *Newsday.com* http://www.newsday.com/community/guide/lihistory, (accessed June 7, 2005).

5. Ibid.

6. Ron Chernow, *The House of Morgan: An American Banking Dynasty and the Rise of Modern Finance* (New York: Grove, 2001), 197.

7. DeWan, "His Calling Cards Were Guns."

8. Ibid.

9. Ibid.

10. "Holt's Past Dark to Wife," *The New York Times*, July 6, 1915, 4.

11. "Professors Kept Muenter Secret," *The New York Times*, July 6, 1915, 1.

12. "Muenter Unaided Dr. MacDonald Says," July 25, 1915, 8.

13. Ibid.

14. "Muenter's Acid Bomb Myth," *The New York Times*, July 8, 1915, 2.

15. DeWan, "His Calling Cards Were Guns."

16. Ibid.

A QUESTION OF INNOCENCE
The San Francisco Preparedness Day Bombing

1. Elizabeth Frost-Knappman and David S. Shrager, *A Concise Encyclopedia of Legal Quotations* (New York: Barnes & Noble Books, 1998), 244.

2. Ibid., 153.

3. Estolv E. Ward, *The Gentle Dynamiter: A Biography of Tom Mooney* (Palo Alto, CA: Ramparts Press, 1983), 9.

4. Curt Gentry, *Frame-Up: The Incredible Case of Tom Mooney and Warren Billings* (New York: W. W. Norton, 1967).

5. Ward, *The Gentle Dynamiter*, 33.

6. Ibid., 34.

7. Ibid., 40.

8. Ibid., 36.

9. Edward T. O'Donnell, "87 Years Ago: The Preparedness Day Bombing," *The Irish Echo*, November 17-23, 2004, http://www.irishecho.com/nespaper/story, (accessed November 18, 2004), 1.

10. Ibid.

11. Ibid., 2.

12. Ibid.

13. Gentry, *Frame-up*, 14.

14. Ibid., 15.

15. Ibid.

16. Ibid., 16.

17. Ibid., 29-30.

18. Ibid., 22-23.

19. Ibid.

20. Ibid., 29.

21. Ward, *The Gentle Dynamiter*, 78.

22. O'Donnell, "87 Years Ago," 2.

23. *In re Mooney*, 10 C.2d 1 (Cal. Sup. Ct., 1937), 10.

24. Ibid.

25. Ibid., 19.

26. Ibid., 35.

27. O'Donnell, "87 Years Ago," 2.

28. *In re Mooney*, 86.

29. O'Donnell, "87 Years Ago," 2.

30. Ibid.

OUTRAGE
The Anarchist Bombings of 1919

1. Elizabeth Frost-Knappman and David S. Shrager, *A Concise Encyclopedia of Legal Quotations* (New York: Barnes & Noble Books, 1998), 306.

2. Paul Avrich, *Sacco and Vanzetti: The Anarchist Background* (Princeton, NJ: Princeton University Press, 1991), 52-53.

3. Ibid., 53.

4. Curt Gentry, *J. Edgar Hoover: The Man and the Secrets* (New York: W. W. Norton, 1991), 75.

5. Avrich, *Sacco and Vanzetti*, 153.

6. Ibid., 150.

7. Ibid., 148.

8. Ibid., 150.

9. Ibid., 152.

10. Ibid., 151.

11. Ibid.

12. Ibid., 152.

13. Gentry, *J. Edgar Hoover*, 76.

14. The content of the "Plain Words" flyer is presented in condensed format; a complete version can be examined in Avrich, *Sacco and Vanzetti*, 81. The original contains a number of grammatical and syntactical errors that are preserved here to maintain the original tone of the document.

15. Avrich, *Sacco and Vanzetti*, 154.

16. Ibid., 153-154.

17. Ibid., 155.
18. Gentry, *J. Edgar Hoover*, 76.
19. Ibid., 85.
20. Avrich, *Sacco and Vanzetti*, 156.
21. Ibid., 95.

PROPAGANDA BY THE DEED
The Wall Street Bombing of 1920

1. Platt, *Respectfully Quoted: A Dictionary of Quotations* (New York: Barnes & Noble Books, 1993), 356.
2. Paul Avrich, *Sacco and Vanzetti: The Anarchist Background* (Princeton, NJ: Princeton University Press, 1991), 205.
3. Ibid.
4. William Bryk, "Big Bang on Wall Street" *New York Press*, 14 (2002), http://www.nypress.com (accessed April 16, 2002), 1-3.
5. Ibid.
6. Ron Chernow, *The House of Morgan: An American Banking Dynasty and the Rise of Modern Finance* (New York: Grove Press, 2001), 212.
7. Ibid.
8. John Brooks, *Once in Golconda: A True Drama of Wall Street, 1920-1938* (New York: Dutton, 1985), 6.
9. Avrich, *Sacco and Vanzetti*, 205.
10. Bryk, "Big Bang on Wall Street," 2.
11. Avrich, *Sacco and Vanzetti*, 206.
12. "Luigi Gallaeni (1861-1931)," http://www.radio4all.org/anarchy/galleani.html (accessed April 17, 2002).
13. Alan Dershowitz, *America on Trial: Inside the Legal Battles that Transformed Our Nation* (New York: Warner Books, 2004), 251-255.
14. Avrich, *Sacco and Vanzetti*, 206.
15. Edmund Gilligan, "The Wall Street Explosion Mystery" *The American Mercury*, September 1938, 63-67, 66.
16. Fran Jurga, "Historical Precedent: Horses and Terrorists in New York City," http://horses.about.com/library/uc-feature20.htm (accessed April 17, 2002).
17. Gilligan, "The Wall Street Explosion Mystery," 66.

18. Jennet Contant, *Tuxedo Park: A Wall Street Tycoon and the Secret Palace of Science that Changed the Course of World War II* (New York: Simon & Schuster, 2002), 35.

19. "Wall St. Explosion Laid to Gelatin," *The New York Times*, October 16, 1920, 16.

20. "Fisher Had Made Prophecy in Toronto and Declared Millionaires Should Be Killed," *The New York Times*, September 17, 1920, 1.

21. Ibid.

22. Nathan Ward, "The Fire Last Time: When Terrorists First Struck New York's Financial District," *American Heritage* 52 (2001), http://www.americanheritage.com/AMHER/2001/08/fire.shtml (accessed April 16, 2002).

23. Avrich, *Sacco and Vanzetti*, 206.

24. "Wall Street Bomb Suspect Caught," *The New York Times*, October 4, 1920, 1.

25. Ibid.

26. Ibid.

27. Ibid.

28. "Zelenska Accused Under Commerce Act," *The New York Times*, October 6, 1920, 16.

29. Avrich, *Sacco and Vanzetti*, 205.

30. Ibid.

31. Ibid., 207.

32. Ibid., 245.

33. In footnote 32 on page 245 of his book, *Sacco and Vanzetti*, Avrich states that he has it from a "reliable source" and believes the identity of Buda as the Wall Street bomber to be true. Given the extensive nature of Avrich's research and writings, his assertion is credible.

34. Bill Torpy, "Echoes of a Blast: Before There was a September 11, There was a Sept. 16, 1920," *Atlanta Journal-Constitution*, December 14, 2001, http://www.accessatlanta.com/ajc/opinion/1201/1920bomb/1216bombing.html (accessed April 16, 2002).

35. Michael Coote, "The Ghosts of 1920 Com Back to Haunt the New Millennium," *National Business Review Personal Investor*, October 5, 2001, http://www.stockchat.co.nz/features/nbr/article.php/ecc01714 (accessed April 15, 2002).

36. Ibid.

Rush to Justice
The Case of Giuseppe Zangara

1. *Frank v. Mangum*, 237 U.S. 309 (1915), 347.
2. Balise Picchi, *The Five Weeks of Giuseppe Zangara: The Man Who Would Assassinate FDR* (Chicago: Academy Chicago Publishers, 1998), i.
3. Ibid., 4.
4. Ibid., 15.
5. Ibid., 21.
6. Transcript of the interview under the title "Sworn Statement of Joseph Zangara" available at http://www.fbi.gov.
7. Picchi, *The Five Weeks of Giuseppe Zangara*, 52.
8. "Sworn Statement of Joseph Zangara," 2.
9. Ibid., 106.
10. Ibid., 110.
11. Picchi, *The Five Weeks of Giuseppe Zangara*, 163.
12. Ibid., 189.
13. Ibid., 191.
14. James W. Clarke, *American Assassins: The Darker Side of Politics* (Princeton: Princeton University Press, 1982), 168.
15. Picchi, *The Five Weeks of Giuseppe Zangara*, 243-244.
16. Ibid.
17. Clarke, *American* Assassins, ,166.

Doomed from the Start
The Nazi Sabotage Plot of 1942

1. Elizabeth Frost-Knappman and David S. Shrager, *A Concise Encyclopedia of Legal Quotations* (New York: Barnes & Noble Books, 1998), 3.
2. Gary Cohen, "The Keystone Kommandos," *The Atlantic Monthly* February, 2002, http://www.theatlantic.com (accessed May 27,2003).
3. Alex Abella and Scott Gordon, *Shadow Enemies: Hitler's Secret Terrorist Plot Against the United States* (Guilford, CT: The Lyons Press, 2002), 5.
4. Ibid., 4.
5. Ibid., 18.
6. Ibid., 21-22.
7. Ibid., 46.
8. Ibid., 9.

9. Cohen, "The Keystone Kommandos," 5.

10. Ibid., 8.

11. Dasch's true intentions were outlined in the statement he subsequently gave to the FBI and in his memoirs and summarized in Abella and Gordon, *Shadow Enemies.*

12. Ibid., 74.

13. Cohen, "The Keystone Kommandos," 8.

14. Ibid., 9.

15. George Lardner, "Nazi Saboteurs Captured! FDR Orders Secret Tribunal," *The Washington Post,* January 13, 2002, W12.

16. Abella and Gordon, *Shadow Enemies,* 125.

17. Lardner, "Nazi Saboteurs Captured."

18. Abella and Gordon.

19. Ibid.

20. Lardner, <u>supra</u> note 17.

21. *Ex Parte Milligan,* 71 U.S. 2 (1866).

22. *Ex Parte Quirin,* 317 U.S. 1 (1942).

23. Abella and Gordon, *Shadow Enemies,* 236.

24. Ibid.

25. For a discussion of these issues, see John Dean, "Appropriate Justice for Terrorists: Using Military Tribunals Rather Than Criminal Courts," *Findlaw's Legal Commentary,* September 28, 2001, http://writ.findlaw.com/dean/20010928.html (accessed May 29, 2003) and John Dean, "The Critics are Wrong: Why President Bush's Decision to Bring Foreign Terrorists to Justice Before Military Tribunals Should Not Offend Civil Liberties," *Findlaw's Legal Commentary,* November 23, 2001, http://writ.findlaw.com/dean/20011123.html (accessed May 29, 2003).

Drawing Attention to the Cause
The Assassination Attempt on Harry S. Truman

1. Robert I. Fitzhenry, ed., *The Harper Book of Quotations* 3rd ed. (New York: Harper Collins, 1993), 338.

2. George Fetherling, *The Book of Assassins: A Biographical Dictionary from Ancient Times to the Present* (New York: John Wiley & Sons, 2001), 104.

3. Elbert B. Smith, "Shoot-out on Pennsylvania Avenue," *American History,* June, 1998,

http://americanhistory.about.com/library/prm/blpennsylvania1.htm
(accessed November 11, 2004).

4. James W. Clarke, *American Assassins: The Darker Side of Politics* (Princeton, NJ: Princeton University Press, 1982), 65.

5. Ibid.

6. Ibid.

7. Ibid.

8. Ibid., 66.

9. Ibid.

10. Ibid.

11. Ibid., 67.

12. Smith, "Shoot-out on Pennsylvania Avenue," 3.

13. From Collazo's testimony at his trial; see Clark, *American Assassins*, 69.

14. Smith, "Shoot-out on Pennsylvania Avenue," 4.

15. Elbert B. Smith, "Shoot-out on Pennsylvania Avenue-Part 2," *American History*, 2002, http://americanhistory.about.com/library/prm/blpennsylvania2.htm (accessed November 18, 2004).

16. Ibid., 2.

17. Clark, *American Assassins*, 71.

18. Ibid., 72.

19. Ibid.

20. Elbert B. Smith, "Shoot-out on Pennsylvania Avenue-Part 3," *American History*, 2002, http://americanhistory.about.com/library/prm/blpennsylvania3.htm (accessed November 18, 2004).

21. Ibid.

22. Ibid.

23. Ibid., 3.

24. Clark, *American Assassins*, 75.

25. Ibid.

26. Ibid.

27. There are several theories about the assassination of John F. Kennedy that suggest there was another shooter. One of these theories claims, for example, is that there was a gunman on the grassy knoll who fired the fatal head wound that killed Kennedy. I do not wish to explore any of these theories in this book. My statement that the Truman assassination

attempt was the only one involving two gunman is based on the fact that it is the only case where two gunmen could be confirmed.

A SECOND WAVE OF FOREIGN POLICY PROTESTS
The 1954 Attack on the House of Representatives

1. Elizabeth Frost-Knappman and David S. Shrager, *A Concise Encyclopedia of Legal Quotations* (New York: Barnes & Noble Books, 1998), 91.

2. Simon, J. D. (2001). *The Terrorism Trap: America's Experience with Terrorism (2nd ed.)*. Bloomington, IN: Indiana University Press, p. 52.

3. Lolita Lebron. *Nationmaster.com* http://www.nationmaster.com/encyclopedia/Lolita-Lebron (accessed February 4, 2005).

4. Manuel Roig-Franzia, "A Terrorist in the House," *Washington Post*, February 22, 2004, W12.

5. Ibid.

6. Ibid.

7. Ibid.

8. Ibid.

9. Ibid.

10. Ibid.

11. Ibid.

12. Ibid.

13. Ibid.

14. Walt Sheppard, "Suicide Watch: Author Irene Vilar's Memoir Confronts Death, Depression and Puerto Rican Nationalism," *Syracuse New Times* October 16, 1996, http://newtimes.rway.com/1996/101696/cover.htm (accessed May 10, 2005).

15. Ibid.

16. Simon, *The Terrorist Trap*, 53.

17. Roig-Franzia, "A Terrorist in the House."

18. Ibid.

19. Ibid.

20. Ibid.

21. Simon, *The Terrorist Trap*, 53.

FIRST IN FLIGHT
America's First Airline Hijacking

1. *The Columbia World of Quotations*, http://www.bartleby.com (accessed on April 24, 2006).
2. Bruce Hoffman, "Rethinking Terrorism and Counterterrorism Since 9/11," *Studies in Conflict and Terrorism* 25(2002): 303-316.
3. Jeffrey D. Simon, *The Terrorist Trap: America's Experience with Terrorism* 2nd ed., (Bloomington, IN: Indiana University Press, 2001), 46.
4. Ibid., 79.
5. "Hijacker: Cuba Suspected Spying," *The Miami Herald*, November 7, 1975, 1B, 2B.
6. "1st Hijacker's Story Checked," *Miami News*, November 26, 1975, 1.
7. "4 Hijackers Agree; They Regret Crimes," *The New York Times*, August 21, 1980, A19.
8. "Hijacker," 1B.
9. Ibid.
10. "4 Hijackers," A19.
11. Ibid.
12. "1st Hijacker," 1.
13. Simon, *The Terrorist Trap*, 79.
14. Ibid., 80.
15. Timothy Naftali, *Blind Spot: The Secret History of American Counterterrorism* (New York: Basic Books, 2005), 19-20.
16. Ibid., 20.
17. Simon, *The Terrorist Trap*, 97.
18. Ibid., 98.
19. Naftali, *Blind Spot*, 42.
20. Ibid.
21. Ibid., 46.

JUSTICE DELAYED
Bombing of the Sixteenth Street Baptist Church

1. *The Quotations Page*, http://www.quotationspage.com (accessed on April 24, 2006).
2. *Brown v. Board of Education*, 346 U.S. 483 (1954).

3. See generally, David M. O'Brien, *Constitutional Law and Politics (Volume 2): Civil Rights and Civil Liberties* 6th ed. (New York: W. W. Norton, 2005).

4. Gus Martin, *Understanding Terrorism: Challenges, Perspectives, and Issues* (Newbury Park, CA: Sage, 2003), 329.

5. Ibid.

6. "16th Street Baptist Church Bombing," *Wikipedia*, May 24, 2005, http://www/en.wikipedia.org/wiki/16th_Street_Baptist_Church_bombing (accessed June 9, 2005).

7. Frank Sikora, *Until Justice Rolls Down: The Birmingham Church Bombing Case* (Tuscaloosa, AL: University of Alabama Press, 1991), 29.

8. Ibid., 6.

9. Ibid.

10. Ibid., 7.

11. Dale Russakoff and Melanie Peeples, "Ex-Klansman Cherry Convicted of Murder," *Washington Post*, May 23, 2002), A1.

12. Sikora, *Until Justice Rolls Down*, 3.

13. Ibid., 4.

14. Ibid.

15. Ibid., 9.

16. Ibid., 11.

17. Ibid.

18. Ibid., 15.

19. Ibid., 14.

20. Ibid.

21. Ibid., 20.

22. Ibid., 69.

23. "Birmingham Church Bombing Timeline," *CNN.com/Law Center*, April 9, 2001, http://archives.cnn.com/2001/LAW/04/09/birmingham.bomb.timeline (accessed June 9, 2005).

24. Sikora, *Until Justice Rolls Down*, 41.

25. Ibid., 45.

26. Ibid., 47.

27. Ibid., 139.

28. Ibid., 140.

29. "Bombing Timeline."

30. Sikora, *Until Justice Rolls Down*, 156.

31. "Bombing Timeline."

32. Curt Gentry, *J. Edgar Hoover: The Man and the Secrets* (New York: W. W. Norton, 1991), 442.

33. Ibid., 412.

34. Ibid., 683.

35. Dale Russakoff and Melanie Peeles, "Ex-Klansman Cherry Convicted of Murder: 4 Black Girls Died in 1963 Bombing of Church," *Washington Post*, May 23, 2002, A1.

36. Jessica Reaves, "In Birmingham, a Question of Mental Unfitness," *Time*, April 16,
   http://www.time.com/time/nation/printout/0,8816,106531,00.html (accessed June 9, 2005).

37. "16th Street Baptist Church Bombing," *Wikipedia*, http://en.wikipedia.org (accessed June 9, 2005).

AN UNSHAKABLE OBSESSION
The Assassination of Robert F. Kennedy

1. Elizabeth Frost-Knappman and David S. Shrager, *A Concise Encyclopedia of Legal Quotations* (New York: Barnes & Noble Books, 1998), 250.

2. James W. Clarke, *American Assassins: The Darker Side of Politics* (Princeton, NJ: Princeton University Press, 1982), 76.

3. George Fetherling, *The Book of Assassins: A Biographical Dictionary From Ancient Times to the Present* (New York: John Wiley & Sons, 2001), 335.

4. Robert Blair Kaiser, *"R.F.K. Must Die!" A History of the Robert Kennedy Assassination and its Aftermath* (New York: E. P. Dutton & Co., 1970), 26.

5. Ibid., 28–29.

6. Thomas F. Kranz, "Robert F. Kennedy Assassination Report to the Los Angeles County Board of Supervisors," March, 1977, http://www.fbi.gov (accessed May 23, 2004), 9.

7. Dan E. Moldea, *The Killing of Robert F. Kennedy: An Investigation of Motive, Means, and Opportunity* (New York: W. W. Norton, 1995), 27.

8. Kaiser, *R.F.K. Must Die*, 203.

9. Ibid.

10. Ibid., 204.

11. Moldea, *The Killing of Robert F. Kennedy*, 102.

12. Ibid., 103.

13. Krantz, "Robert F. Kennedy Assassination Report," 14.

14. Ibid., 15.

15. Ibid.
16. Kaiser, *R.F.K. Must Die*, 440.
17. Ibid.
18. Ibid., 443.
19. Ibid.
20. Ibid., 476.
21. Moldea, *The Killing of Robert F. Kennedy*, 122.
22. Ibid.
23. Ibid.

A YEAR OF LIVING DANGEROUSLY
The Bombing Attacks of 1975

1. *The Columbia World of Quotations*, http://www.bartleby.com (accessed April 24, 2006).
2. George Fetherling, *The Book of Assassins: A Biographical Dictionary from Ancient Times to the Present* (New York: John Wiley & Sons, 2001), 153.
3. Ibid., 251.
4. Selwyn Raab, "F.A.L.N. Terrorists Tied to 10 Bombings in Region," *The New York Times*, February 7, 1975, 68.
5. Ibid.
6. Ibid.
7. Timothy Naftali, *Blind Spot: The Secret History of American Counterterrorism* (New York: Basic Books, 2005), 102.
8. Selwyn, "F.A.L.N. Terrorists."
9. "A Chronology of Weather Underground Communiqués," (Washington, DC: Federal Bureau of Investigation) http://www.fbi.gov (accessed March 15, 2005).
10. Ron Jacobs, *The Way the Wind Blew: A History of the Weather Underground* (London: Verso, 1997), 201.
11. John Springer, "LaGuardia Christmas Bombing Remains Unsolved 27 Years Later," *CNN.com*, December 24, 2002, http://cnn.law.com (accessed May 31, 2004).
12. Ibid., 2.
13. Ibid., 3.
14. Ibid.
15. Phillip Jenkins, *Images of Terror: What We Can and Can't Know About Terrorism* (New York: Aldine de Gruyter, 2003), 35.

16. Ibid., 36.

FAKE BOMBS
The Hijacking of TWA Flight 355

1. *The Quotations Page*, http://www.quotationspage.com (accessed on April 24, 2006).
2. Jeffrey D. Simon, *The Terrorist Trap: America's Experience with Terrorism* 2nd ed. (Bloomington, IN: University of Indiana Press, 2001), 111.
3. Ibid.
4. Ibid.
5. Richard Brockman, "Notes while being hijacked," *The Atlantic Monthly*, December, 1976, http://www.theatlantic.com (accessed May 31, 2004), 1.
6. Ibid., 2.
7. "Julienne Busic: An ASI Exclusive Interview," *Aviation Security International* http://www.asi-mag.com/editorials/busic.htm (accessed February 4, 2005), 2.
8. Ibid., 2.
9. Simon, *The Terrorist Trap*, 112.
10. Ibid.
11. Ibid.
12. Ibid.
13. Ibid., 113.
14. Ibid.
15. Ibid.
16. Ibid., 117.
17. Brockman, "Notes While Being Hijacked," 7.
18. Ibid., 9.
19. Ibid., 10.
20. "Julienne Busic Interview," 3.
21. David Binder, "A Strange bond: Officer's Widow and Air Hijacker" *The New York Times*, December 19, 1994), B1.
22. Ibid.
23. Ibid.
24. Ibid.
25. Ibid.
26. "Julienne Busic Interview," 4.

27. Binder, "A Strange Bond," 4.
28. Timothy Naftali, *Blind Spot: The Secret History of American Counterterrorism* (New York: Basic Books, 2005), 97.
29. "Julienne Busic Interview," 5.

Spillover Effect
The Assassination of Orlando Letelier

1. Robert I. Fitzhenry, ed., *The Harper Book of Quotations* 3rd ed. (New York: Harper Collins, 1993), 226.
2. Gus Martin, *Understanding Terrorism: Challenges, Perspectives, and Issues* (Thousand Oaks, CA: Sage, 2003), 218.
3. Ibid., 219.
4. Peter Kornbluh, *The Pinochet File: A Declassified Dossier on Atrocity and Accountability* (New York: The New Press, 2004), 349.
5. John Dinges and Saul Landau, *Assassination on Embassy Row* (New York: Pantheon, 1980), 24..
6. Kornbluh, *The Pinochet File*, 349.
7. Donald Freed and Fred Landis, *Death in Washington: The Murder of Orlando Letelier* (Westport, CT: Lawrence Hill & Co, 1980), 227.
8. Kornbluh, *The Pinochet File*, 1.
9. Ibid., 11.
10. Ibid., 524–525n49.
11. Ibid.
12. Dinges and Landau, *Assassination on Embassy Row*, 83.
13. Ibid., 87n.
14. Ibid., 208.
15. Ibid., 174.
16. Ibid., 178.
17. Ibid., 208.
18. Ibid.
19. Kornbluh, *The Pinochet File*, 352.
20. Dinges and Landau, *Assassination on Embassy Row*, 208.
21. Ibid., 212.
22. Kornbluh, *The Pinochet File*, 352.
23. Ibid.
24. Ibid.
25. Ibid., 331.

26. Ibid., 332.

27. Ibid., 404.

28. Dinges and Landau, *Assassination on Embassy Row*, 93.

29. Kornbluh, *The Pinochet File*, 412.

30. Ibid., 471-475.

31. Ibid., 179.

32. Ignacio Badal, "Pinochet Spy Chief Imprisoned in Landmark Case," *Yahoo! News*, January 28, 2005) http://news.yahoo.com/news (accessed January 28, 2005).

33. Alfonso Chardy, "Chilean Could be Pinochet Witness," *The Miami Herald*, October 13, 2003, http://www.miami.com/mlk/miamiherald/news/local (accessed November 14, 2003).

34. Kornbluh, *The Pinochet file*, xi

35. Ibid., 466.

36. Ibid., 476.

37. Badal, "Pinochet Spy Chief Imprisoned."

BACKLASH
An Alleged Plot to Kidnap the Governor of Minnesota

1. *The Quotations Page*, http://www.quotationspage.com (accessed on April 24, 2006).

2. "US 9/11 Revenge Killer Convicted," *BBC News*, October 1, 2003, http://newsvote.bbc.co.uk/mpapps/pagetools/print/news.bbc.co.uk/2/hi/americas/3154170stm (accessed April 8, 2005).

3. Ibid.

4. "The Hostage Crisis in Iran," *The Jimmy Carter Library*, November 20, 2002, http://jimmycarterlibrary.org/documents/hostages.phtml (accessed April 7, 2005).

5. Ibid.

6. Hank Klibanoff, "Iranian Students Feel US Backlash: They Face Job Bias, Demonstrations and a Deportation Order," *The Boston Globe*, December 18, 1979, http://nl.newsback.com/nl-search/we/archives (accessed February 7, 2005).

7. Ibid.

8. Ibid.

9. Ibid.

10. Marisa Helms, "Former Governor Honored at 80th Birthday Celebration," *Minnesota Public Radio News*, September 19, 2003, http://news.minnesota.publicradio.org/features/2003/09/19 _helmsm_quie (accessed on February 7, 2005).

11. "Four Iranians Accused with Sudanese of Plot to Kidnap Gov. Quie," *The New York Times*, November 10, 1979, 6.

12. "Sudanese Released in Kidnap Plot," *The New York Times*, November 11, 1979, 14."

13. Ibid.

14. Kilbanoff, "Iranian Students."

15. Ibid.

16. "Iranians Freed After Arrest for Alleged Kidnapping Plot," *The New York Times*, November 14, 1979, A9.

17. Ibid.

18. "Incident Profile: Other Group Attacked Government Target," *MIPT Terrorism Knowledge Base* http://www.tkb.org/Incident.jsp?incID=2527 (accessed on December 3, 2004).

GROUP REMNANTS
The U.S. Capitol Bombing of 1983

1. *The Columbia World of Quotations*, http://www.bartleby.com (accessed on April 24, 2006).

2. "U.S. Capitol Often a Target of Violence," *The Shawnee News-Star*, July 25, 1998, http://www.news-star.com/stories/072598/new_shoot4.html (accessed June 3, 2005).

3. Ibid.

4. "3 Radicals Agree to Plead Guilty in Bombing Case," *The New York Times*, 1990, B8.

5. Philip Shenon, "U.S. Charges 7 in the Bombing at U.S. Capitol," *The New York Times*, May 12, 1988), A20.

6. *United States v. Whitehorn et al.*, Criminal No. 88-9145, Indictment, June 3, 1987, http://www.tkb.org (accessed October 25, 2005).

7. "Group Profile: May 19 Communist Order," *MIPT Terrorism Knowledge Base*, http://www.tkb.org (accessed October 24, 2005).

8. Jeremy Varon, *Bringing the War Home: The Weather Underground, the Red Army Faction, and Revolutionary Violence in the Sixties and Seventies* (Berkley: University of California Press, 2004), 298.

9. Ibid.

10. Ibid.

11. Ron Jacobs, *The Way the Wind Blew: A History of the Weather Underground* (London: Verso, 1997), 182.

12. Varon, *Bringing the War Home*, 299.

13. "3 Radicals Agree," B8.

14. Ibid.

15. Indictment, 1.

16. Indictment, 2.

17. "3 Radicals," B8.

18. "Radical Gets 20-Year Term in 1983 Bombing of U.S. Capitol," *The New York Times*, December 8, 1990), 14.

19. Jonathan Serrie, "Students 'Duke it Out' With Controversial Speaker," *FOXNews.com*, January 27, 2003, http://www.foxnews.com (accessed October 24, 2005).

Influencing an Election
America's First Modern Bioterrorist Attack

1. Robert I. Fitzhenry, ed., *The Harper Book of Quotations*, 3rd ed. (New York: Harper Collins, 1993), 508.

2. W. Seth Carus, *Bioterrorism and Biocrimes: The Illicit Use of Biological Agents Since 1900* (Washington, DC: Center for Counterproliferation Research, National Defense University, 1998) www/ndu.edu/center counter/Full_Doc.pdf (accessed March 5, 2004), 56.

3. T. J. Torok, R. V. Tauxe, R. P. Wise, J. R. Livengood, R. Sokolow, S. Mauvais, K. A. Birkness, M. R. Skeels, J. M. Horan, and L. R. Foster, "A Large Community Outbreak of Salmonellosis Caused by Intentional Contamination of Restaurant Salad Bars," *JAMA* 278(1997): 389.

4. Carus, *Bioterrorism and Biocrimes*, 51.

5. Douglas Martin, "Guru's Commune Roiled as Key Leader Departs," *The New York Times*, September 22, 1985, 26.

6. "Former Aides to Guru in Oregon Plead Guilty to Numerous Crimes," *The New York Times*, July 23, 1986, B9.

7. Carus, *Bioterrorism and Biocrimes*, 51.

8. Ibid.

9. Ibid.

10. Ibid.

11. Ibid., 52.

12. Details of the plot were outlined by David Berry Knapp, who went by the cult name of KD, and who provided detailed information to the FBI. A transcript of the interrogation is contained in FBI files and has been described in detail by Carus, *Bioterrorism and Biocrimes*. The narrative that follows is based primarily on Carus' analysis.

13. "Former Aides to Guru," B9.

14. Torok et al., "A Large Community Outbreak."

15. Jessica Stern, *The Ultimate Terrorists* (Cambridge, MA: Harvard University Press, 1999), 67.

16. Carus, *Bioterrorism and Biocrimes*, 52-53.

17. "Former Aides to Guru," B9.

18. Stern, *The Ultimate Terrorists*, 185n52.

A MEETING OF THE TERRORIST MINDS
The Case of Yu Kikumura

1. Elizabeth Frost-Knappman and David S. Shrager, *A Concise Encyclopedia of Legal Quotations* (New York: Barnes & Noble Books, 1998), 59.

2. Vikran D. Amar, "Are the U.S. Sentencing Guidelines Judicial or Legislative?" *Findlaw's Writ*, September 17, 2004
http://www.corporate.findlaw.som/script/ (accessed January 5, 2005).

3. Ibid.

4. *Blakely v. Washington*, 542 U.S. 296 (2004).

5. Sherry F. Colb, "A Significant Decision That May Not Matter: The Supreme Court Holds That Only Juries, Not Judges, Can Make the Factual Determinations That Increase Sentences," *Findlaw's Writ* June 29, 2004 http://www.corporate.findlaw.com/scripts/ (accessed January 5, 2005).

6. Tony Mauro, "Supreme Court: Sentencing Guidelines Advisory, Not Mandatory," *Law.com* http://www.law.com/jsp (accessed January 13, 2005); see also Laurie P. Cohen and Gary Fields, "High Court Declares Guidelines on Sentencing Violate Rights," *Wall Street Journal*, January 13, 2005, 1A, 8A.

7. *United States v. Kikumura*, 698 F. Supp. 546 (D.N.J. 1988), 548.

8. Ibid.

9. Ibid., 548.

10. Ibid., 547.

11. Jonathan R. White, *Terrorism: An Introduction* 4th ed. (Belmont, CA: Wadsworth, 2003), 180.

12. Ibid., 180-181.

13. Jeffrey D. Simon, *The Terrorist Trap: America's Experience With Terrorism* 2nd ed. (Bloomington, IN: Indiana University Press, 2001), 6-7.

14. *United States v. Kikumura*, 706 F. Supp. 331 (D.N.J. 1989), 335.

15. Ibid., 338

16. Ibid., 336.

17. Ibid.

18. Ibid., 337.

19. Simon, *The Terrorist Trap*, 197.

20. Ibid., 199.

21. *United States v. Kikumura* (1989), 339.

22. Ibid., 337.

23. Ibid.

24. *United States v. Kikumura*, 918 F.2d 1084 (3rd Cir., 1990).

25. *United States v. Kikumura* (1989), 337.

26. Ibid.

27. *United States v. Kikumura* (1988), 552.

28. *United States v. Kikumura* (1989), 333.

29. Ibid., 334.

30. Ibid., 335.

31. *United States v. Kikumura* (1990), 1095.

32. Ibid.

33. *United States v. Kikumura* (1989), 346.

34. *United States v. Kikumura*, 947 F.2d 72 (3rd Cir., 1991), 82.

35. Ibid., 75.

36. Ibid.

37. "The FBI Laboratory: An Investigation Into Laboratory Practices and Alleged Misconduct in Explosive-related and Other Cases," (Washington, DC: Federal Bureau of Investigation, n.d.) http://www.criminaljustice.org/MEDIA/fbilabreport/ (accessed December 31, 2004).

38. *Kikumura v. Hurley*, 242 F.3d 950 (10th Cir., 1999).

FLASHPOINT
The Assassination of Rabbi Meir Kahane

1. Robert I. Fitzhenry, ed., *The Harper Book of Quotations* 3rd ed. (New York: Harper Collins, 1993), 158.
2. Judith T. Baumel, "Kahane in America: An Exercise in Right-wing Urban Terror," *Studies in Conflict & Terrorism* 22(1999): 311-329.
3. Ibid., 314.
4. Ibid., 316.
5. John Kifner, "In Israel, Kahane's Ideas Have Taken on a Life of Their Own," *The New York Times*, November 11, 1990, E2.
6. Leonard Buder, "Prison for Ex-J.D.L. Chief in Bombing," *The New York Times*, October 27, 1987, B3.
7. John Miller, Michael Stone, and Chris Mitchell, *The Cell: Inside the 9/11 Plot, and Why the FBI and CIA Failed to Stop It* (New York: Hyperion, 2002), 38.
8. Ibid., 39.
9. Ibid.
10. Seamus McGraw, "A Lone Gunman," *Court TV Crime Library*, 2004 http://www.crimelibrary.com/terrorists_spies/terrorists/elsayid_nosair/index.html (accessed June 1, 2004).
11. Miller et al., *The Cell*, 39.
12. Ibid.
13. Ibid., 40.
14. Ibid.
15. John Kifner, "Kahane Suspect is a Muslim with a Series of Addresses," *The New York Times*, November 7, 1990), A1.
16. Ibid.
17. Ibid.
18. Ibid.
19. Seamus McGraw, "The Road to Terror," *Court TV Crime Library*, 2004 http://www.crimelibrary.com/terrorists_spies/terrorists/elsayid_nosair/4.html (accessed June 1, 2004).
20. Miller et al., *The Cell*, 66.
21. Ibid.
22. Ibid., 67.
23. Ibid., 47.
24. Ibid., 115.

INTERNATIONAL MANHUNT
The Case of Mir Aimal Kasi

1. Kasi's name is spelled differently across various sources. Sometimes his middle name is spelled "Amal" and his last name is spelled "Kansi." In two legal documents—appellate court decisions dealing with his criminal case—his name appears as "Mir Aimal Kasi." I chose to use this spelling throughout the case discussion.
2. Elizabeth Frost-Knappman and David S. Shrager, *A Concise Encyclopedia of Legal Quotations* (New York: Barnes & Noble Books, 1998), 204.
3. *Kasi v. Commonwealth of Virginia*, 508 S. E. 2d 57 (Va. 1998) http://www.courts.state.va.us/opinions/opnscvtx/1980797.txt (accessed May 23, 2005).
4. Steve Coll, *Ghost Wars: The Secret History of the CIA, Afghanistan, and bin Laden, from the Soviet Invasion to September 10, 2001* (New York: Penguin, 2004), 371.
5. Ibid., 246.
6. Ibid.
7. *Kasi v. Commonwealth* (1998).
8. Coll, *Ghost Wars*, 246.
9. Ibid.
10. *Kasi v. Commonwealth* (1998).
11. Ibid.
12. Coll, *Ghost Wars*, 246.
13. Ibid.
14. *Kasi v. Commonwealth* (1998).
15. Ibid.
16. Ibid.
17. Coll, *Ghost Wars*, 371.
18. Ibid., 373.
19. *Kasi v. Angelone*, No. 02-2 (4th Cir. 2002) http://caselaw.lp.findlaw.com/scripts/ (accessed May 20, 2005).
20. Coll, *Ghost Wars*, 374.
21. Ibid.
22. Ibid.
23. *Kasi v. Commonwealth* (1989).
24. Richard A. Clarke, *Against All Enemies: Inside America's War on Terror* (New York: Free Press, 2004), 151.

25. Ibid.
26. See *Kasi v. Commonwealth* (1989) and *Kasi v. Angelone* (2002) for a full discussion of the legal issues.
27. *Kasi v. Commonwealth* (1989).
28. *Kasi v. Angelone* (2002).
29. "Pakistani Man Executed for CIA Killings," *CNN.com*, November 15, 2002) http://archives.cnn.com/2002/LAW/11/14/cia-killings.execution/ (accessed May 26, 2005).
30. Ibid.
31. Ibid.
32. Ibid.
33. Ibid.

A Needle in a Haystack
Investigating the 1993 World Trade Center Bombing

1. Cited in John Horgan, *The Psychology of Terrorism* (New York: Routledge, 2005), 3. This statement was issued by the Provisional IRA after it had attempted to assassinate British Prime Minister Margaret Thatcher in a bombing of the 1984 conference of the British Conservative Party.
2. Simon Reeve, *The New Jackals: Ramzi Yousef, Osama Bin Laden and the Future of Terrorism* (Boston: Northeastern University Press, 1999), 140.
3. Ibid.
4. Ibid.
5. Ibid.
6. Ibid., 138.
7. Ibid.
8. Robert E. Precht, *Defending Mohammad: Justice on Trial* (Ithaca, NY: Cornell University Press, 2003), 13.
9. Ibid., 14.
10. Jim Dwyer, David Kocieniewski, Deidre Murphy, and Peg Tyre, *Two Seconds Under the World* (New York: Crown, 1994), 166.
11. Ibid., 167.
12. Dwyer et al., *Two Seconds Under the World*, 167.
13. Precht, *Defending Mohammad*, 63.
14. Ibid.
15. Ibid.

16. Ibid., 92.

17. Reeve, *The New Jackals*, 6.

18. Ibid.

19. Ibid., 8.

20. Ibid., 10-12.

21. Ibid.

22. Ibid.

23. Ibid., 15.

24. Dwyer et al., *Two Seconds Under the World*, 25.

25. Reeve, *The New Jackals*, 24.

26. Ibid., 26.

27. Ibid., 31.

28. Ibid., 28.

29. Ibid., 31.

30. Ibid.

31. Dwyer et al., *Two Seconds Under the World*, 196-197.

32. Ibid., 196.

33. Ibid., 197.

34. Precht, *Defending Mohammad*, 165.

35. Reeve, *The New Jackals*.

36. National Commission on Terrorist Attacks Upon the United States. *Final Report of the National Commission on Terrorist Attacks Upon the United States (authorized edition)* (New York: W. W. Norton, 2004), 72. (hereinafter *9/11 Commission Report*)

37. Ibid., 72.

38. Reeve, *The New Jackals*, 109.

39. Ibid.

OVERZEALOUSNESS
The Case of the Sheik and His Lawyer

1. Elizabeth Frost-Knappman and David S. Shrager, *A Concise Encyclopedia of Legal Quotations* (New York: Barnes & Noble Books, 1998), 79.

2. New York State Bar Association, *The Lawyer's Code of Professional Responsibility* (Albany, NY: New York State Bar Association, 1990), 49.

3. National Commission on Terrorist Attacks Upon the United States, *Final Report of the National Commission on Terrorist Attacks Upon the*

United States (authorized edition) (New York: W. W. Norton, 2004), 72. 9hereinafter *9/11 Commission Report*).

4. "Abdel-Rahman, Omar Ahmad Ali: Key Leader Profile," *MPIT Terrorism Knowledge Base* http://www.tkb.org (accessed November 9, 2005).

5. Ibid.

6. *9/11 Commission Report*, 72.

7. Robert E. Precht, *Defending Mohammad: Justice on Trial* (Ithaca, NY: Cornell University Press, 2003), 42–43.

8. *United States v. Rahman, et al.* Indictment (No.: S3 93 Cr. 181), http://www.tkb.org (accessed November 9, 2005).

9. Precht, *Defending Mohammad*, 42.

10. Elaine Cassel, "The Lynne Stewart Guilty Verdict: Stretching the Definition of "Terrorism" to its Limits," *FindLaw's Legal Commentary* February 14, 2002, http://writ.corporate.findlaw.com (accessed November 2, 2005).

11. Ibid.

12. *United States v. Sattar*, 314 F.Supp. 2d 279 (S.D.N.Y. 2004).

13. Ibid.

14. Ibid.

15. Cassel, "The Lynne Stewart Guilty Verdict," 2.

16. Elaine Cassel, "The Lynne Stewart Case: When Representing an Accused Terrorist Can Mean the Lawyer Risks Jail, Too," *FindLaw's Legal Commentary*, October 8, 2002, http://writ.corporate.findlaw.com (accessed June 18, 2004).

17. Cassel, "The Lynne Stewart Guilty Verdict," 1.

18. Ibid., 2.

19. Ibid.

20. Ibid., 3.

21. Ibid.

22. *United States v. Sattar*, (2004).

23. Cassell, "The Lynne Steward Guilty Verdict," 1.

24. Mark Hamblett, "Lynne Stewart Holds Up in Closing Testimony of Terrorism Case," *Law.com*, 2004, http://www.law.com (accessed December 30, 2004).

25. Ibid.

26. Ibid.

27. Cassell, "The Lynne Stewart Guilty Verdict," 4.

THOU SHALT KILL
The Paradox of a Religiously Motivated Assassination

1. Elizabeth Frost-Knappman and David S. Shrager, *A Concise Encyclopedia of Legal Quotations* (New York: Barnes & Noble Books, 1998), 168.
2. Jessica Stern, *Terror in the Name of God: Why Religious Militants Kill* (New York: Harper Collins, 2003), 7.
3. Cynthia C. Combs, *Terrorism in the Twenty-first Century* 3rd ed. (Upper Saddle River, NJ: Prentice Hall, 2003), 164.
4. Abby Goodnough, "Florida Executes Killer of an Abortion Provider," *The New York Times*, September 4, 2003 http://www.nytimes.com/2003/09/04/national/04EXEC.html (accessed September 4, 2003).
5. Ibid.
6. Paul J. Hill, "Should We Defend Born and Unborn Children With Force?" http://www.webcom.com/~pinknoiz/right/knowenemy.html (accessed September 4, 2003).
7. Ibid.
8. Ibid.
9. Ibid.
10. John-Thor Dahlburg, "Killer of Abortion Doctor Faces His Execution Date," *Press & Sun Bulletin*, September 2, 2003, 1A, 5A.
11. Tom Burghardt, "Introduction to Paul Hill's Text," 2004 http://www.webcom.com/~pinknoiz/right/knowenemy.html (accessed September 4, 2003).
12. Confirmatory bias is a term used by psychologists to describe an error in cognitive processing that individuals sometimes commit when they search for, and use, only evidence that will support a pre-existing notion or belief, while ignoring or discounting evidence that tends to disconfirm or disprove that notion or belief.
13. Dahlburg, "Killer of Abortion Doctor," 1A.
14. Ibid.
15. Goodnough, "Florida Executes Killer," 1.
16. Ibid.

Reverberations
The Political Context of a New York City Homicide

1. *The Quotations Page,* http://www.quotationspage.com (accessed on April 24, 2006).
2. Yhudit Barsky. "The Brooklyn Bridge Shooting: An Independent Review and Assessment." (New York: The American Jewish Committee, n.d.) http://www.ajc.org/inthemedia/publications (accessed February 14, 2005), 2.
3. Francis X. Clines and Joe Sexton, "What Are You, Rashid?" *The New York Times,* March 14, 1994, B1, B4.
4. Barsky, "The Brooklyn Bridge Shooting," 2.
5. Ibid.
6. Ibid.
7. Ibid.
8. Clines and Sexton, "What Are You Rashid?" B4.
9. Samuel M. Katz, *Jihad in Brooklyn: The NYPD Raid that Stopped America's First Suicide Bombers* (New York: New American Library, 2005), 46.
10. Ibid.
11. Barsky, "The Brooklyn Bridge Shooting," 3.
12. Ibid.
13. Katz, *Jihad in Brooklyn,* 62.
14. Joe Sexton, "Indistinct Picture of Shooting Suspect," *The New York Times,* March 4, 1994, B2.
15. Clines and Sexton, "What Are You, Rashid?" B4.
16. Ibid.
17. Sexton, "Indistinct Picture," B2.
18. "Bridge Gunman is Called Angry But Sane," *The New York Times,* November 29, 1994, B7.
19. Barsky, "The Brooklyn Bridge Shooting," 6.
20. Ibid.
21. Ibid., 7.
22. Barsky, "The Brooklyn Bridge Shooting," 11.
23. Ibid.
24. Ibid.

CONSPIRACY THEORIES
The Oklahoma City Bombing

1. Stephen Jones and Peter Israel, *Others Unknown: Timothy McVeigh and the Oklahoma City Bombing Conspiracy* (New York: Public Affairs, 2001), xiii-xiv. McVeigh's lead defense attorney, Stephen Jones, stated that the convicted Oklahoma City bombing suspect once made this statement during their conversations together.
2. Lou Michel and Dan Herbeck, *American Terrorist: Timothy McVeigh & the Oklahoma City Bombing* (New York: Harper Collins, 2001), 48.
3. Ibid., 37, 40.
4. Ibid., 40.
5. Ibid., 38-39.
6. Ibid., 39.
7. Ibid., 56.
8. Ibid., 58, 60.
9. Ibid., 80.
10. Ibid., 96, 101.
11. Ibid., 99.
12. Jones and Israel, *Others Unknown*, 68.
13. Ibid.
14. Ibid., 74.
15. Although McVeigh's attorney, Stephen Jones casts doubt on this assertion, the notion that McVeigh believed the orders originated from the Oklahoma City federal building comes from an assertion of Michael Fortier; see Jones and Israel, *Others Unknown*, 74.
16. C. J. M. Drake, "The Role of Ideology in Terrorists' Target Selection," *Terrorism and Political Violence* 10(1998): 53-85, 78.
17. Michel and Herbeck, *American Terrorist*, 205.
18. Edward T. Linenthal, *The Unfinished Bombing: Oklahoma City in American Memory* (New York: Oxford, 2001), 7.
19. *United States v. McVeigh and Nichols*, Indictment No. CR-95-110, (1995, Dist. Ct. of W. Oklahoma), http://www.tkb.org (accessed January 16, 2006).
20. Michel and Herbeck, *American Terrorist*, 226.
21. Ibid., 231.

22. Oklahoma Today Magazine, *The Official Record of the Oklahoma City Bombing: 9:02 a.m., April 19, 1995* (Oklahoma City: Oklahoma Today Magazine, 2005), 13.

23. Ibid., 96.

24. Michel and Herbeck, *American Terrorist*, 239.

25. Ibid., 240.

26. Ibid., 250.

27. Ibid., 256.

28. Jayna Davis, *The Third Terrorist: The Middle East Connection to the Oklahoma City Bombing* (Nashville, TN: WND Books, 2004), 52.

29. Ibid.

30. Michel and Herbeck, *American Terrorist*, 293.

31. Ibid., 341.

32. Ibid., 365.

33. Jones and Israel, *Others Unknown*, xv.

34. Ibid., 201.

35. Davis, *The Third Terrorist*, 240.

36. Ibid., 241.

37. Ibid., 243.

38. Jones and Israel, *Others Unknown*, 172.

39. Ibid., 171.

40. I am relying on the chapter "The Defense of One Known to be Guilty" in Jones and Israel, *Others Unknown*, 48-64.

41. Julie DelCour, "Timothy McVeigh Receives the Death Penalty," in *The Official Record of the Oklahoma City Bombing*, 164.

COMPULSORY NONSUIT
The Case of the Unabomber

1. Green v. United States, 365 U.S. 301, at 309-310 (1961).

2. Alston Chase, *Harvard and the Unabomber: The Education of an American Terrorist* (New York: W. W. Norton, 2003), 48-49..

3. "The Unabomber: A Chronology," *Court TV Online* http://www.courttv.com/trials/unabomber/chronology/chron_before.html (accessed October 1, 2002).

4. Ibid.

5. Chase, *Harvard and the Unabomber*, 110 (italics added). See also paragraph #18 of "Industrial Society and It Future," (i.e., "The Unabomber

Manifesto") http://www.thecourier.com/manifest.htm (accessed September 13, 2002).

6. Ibid.

7. Ibid.

8. Chase, *Harvard and the* Unabomber, 52

9. Ibid.

10. Ibid.,42.

11. "The Unabomber: A Chronology."

12. Michael Mello, *The United States of American Versus Theodore John Kaczynski: Ethics, Power and the Invention of the Unabomber* (New York: Context Books, 1999), 71.

13. Ibid., 54.

14. Ibid., 89.

15. *Dusky v. United States*, 362 U.S. 402, 80 S.Ct. 788 (1960).

16. "Psychiatric Competency Report of Dr. Sally C. Johnson," dated September 11, 1998, filed in *United States v. Kaczynski*, CR. No. S-96-259 GEB (E.D. Cal., 1998).

17. Ibid.

18. Ibid.

19. Ibid.

20. Ibid.

21. *Godinez v. Moran*, 113 S.Ct. 2680 (1993).

22. Mello, *The United States*, 99.

23. Chase, *Harvard and the Unabomber*, 342.

24. From a statement dated January 26, 1998; see Mello, *The United States*, 140.

REGIONAL MANHUNT
The Case of Eric Rudolph

1. Elizabeth Frost-Knappman and David S. Shrager, *A Concise Encyclopedia of Legal Quotations* (New York: Barnes & Noble Books, 1998), 206.

2. Matthew Vita, "A Look at the Four Bombing Attacks," *Washington Post*, June 1, 2003, A11.

3. Henry Schuster Charles Stone, *Hunting Eric Rudolph: An Insider's Account of the Five-Year Search for the Olympic Bombing Suspect* (New York: Berkley, 2005), 13.

4. Ibid., 14.

5. Vita, "A Look at the Four Bombing Attacks," A11.

6. Ibid.

7. Ibid.

8. Schuster and Stone, *Hunting Eric Rudolph*, 28.

9. "Why the Government Considered Jewell a Suspect," *CNN.com*, October 28, 1996, http://www.cnn.com/US/9610/28/jewell.suspect/index.html (accessed May 19, 2003).

10. Schuster and Stone, *Hunting Eric Rudolph*, 33.

11. Ibid., 34.

12. Ibid., 35.

13. Ibid.

14. "Eric Rudolph Timeline," *Washingtonpost.com*, May 31, 2003, http://www.washingtonpost.com/ac2 (accessed June 2, 2003).

15. Ibid.

16. Schuster and Stone, *Hunting Eric Rudolph*, 54-55; I have retained punctuation, capitalization, and grammatical errors (e.g., "there") as written in the original source to provide a degree of authenticity in the quotation.

17. "Eric Rudolph Timeline."

18. Schuster and Stone, *Hunting Eric Rudolph*, 74.

19. Ibid., 77.

20. "Eric Robert Rudolph: Loner and Survivalist," *CNN.com*, December 1, 2003, http://www.cnn.com/2003/US/05/31/rudolph.profile/index.html (accessed March 11, 2005).

21. Schuster and Stone, *Hunting Eric Rudolph*, 142-143.

22. "Loner and Survivalist."

23. Schuster and Stone, *Hunting Eric Rudolph*, 301.

24. "Eric Rudolph Reaches Plea Deal in Bombings," *USAToday.com*, April 8, 2005, http://www.usatoday.com/sports/olympics/ 2005-04-08-rudolph-guilty-plea_x.htm?csp=34 (accessed April 11, 2005).

25. Ibid.

A FINGER ON THE TRIGGER
America's First Suicide Terrorist Bombers

1. Robert I. Fitzhenry, ed., *The Harper Book of Quotations* 3rd ed. (New York: Harper Collins, 1993), 160.
2. Bruce Hoffman, "The Logic of Suicide Terrorism," *The Atlantic Monthly*, June, 2003, 42-43.
3. David Von Drehle, "U.S. Fears Use of Belt Bombs," *Washington Post*, May 13, 2002, A1.
4. Ibid.
5. Ibid.
6. Samuel M. Katz, *Jihad in Brooklyn: The NYPD Raid that Stopped America's First Suicide Bombers* (New York: New American Library, 2005), 77-78.
7. Ibid., 108.
8. Ibid., 110.
9. Ibid., 113.
10. Ibid., 129.
11. Ibid.
12. Ibid.
13. Ibid., 132.
14. Ibid., 220.
15. *United States v. Khalil*, Docket Nos. 98-1723(L), 99-1134, (2nd Cir., 1999) http://caselaw.lp.findlaw.com (accessed February 10, 2005).
16. Katz, *Jihad in Brooklyn*, 251.
17. Office of the Inspector General, "Bombs in Brooklyn: How the Two Illegal Aliens Arrested for Plotting to Bomb the New York Subway Entered and Remained in the United States," (Washington, DC: U.S. Department of Justice Office of the Inspector General Special, March 1998) http://www.usdoj.gov.oig/brookb/brbtoc.htm (accessed January 28, 2002), Executive Summary, 3.
18. Ibid., Part IIB, 4-5.
19. Ibid.
20. Ibid., Part IIF(2), 4.
21. Ibid., Executive Summary, 5.
22. Ibid.
23. Ibid., 6.
24. Ibid.
25. *United States v. Khalil* (1999).

26. Ibid.
27. "Letter to Hon. Reena Raggi, U.S. District Judge for the Eastern District of New York," December 1, 1998 http://www.mipt.org (accessed February 10, 2005).
28. *United States v. Khalil* (1999), 11.
29. Ibid.
30. Ibid.
31. Katz, *Jihad in Brooklyn*, 301.
32. Ibid., 288.

OUT OF THE BLUE
Shooting Attack at the Empire State Building

1. Elizabeth Frost-Knappman and David S. Shrager, *A Concise Encyclopedia of Legal Quotations* (New York: Barnes & Noble Books, 1998), 252.
2. Peg Tyre, "Gunman Shoots 7, Kills Self at Empire State Building," *CNN Interactive*, February 27, 1997)
http://www.cnn.com/US/9702/24/empire.shooting
(accessed February 17, 2003).
3. Frank Bruni, "A Fables View Yields to Panic and Horror," *The New York Times*, February 24, 1997,
http://query.nytimes.com/search/restricted/article
(accessed April 7, 2003).
4. Matthew Purdy, "The Gunman Premeditated the Attack, Officials Say," *The New York Times*, February 25, 1997,
http://query.nytimes.com/search/restricted/article
(accessed April 7, 2003).
5. Frank Bruni, "A World Remade by Empire State Gunfire," *The New York Times*, May 18, 1997,
http://query.nytimes.com/search/restricted/article
(accessed April 7, 2003).
6. D. Van Natta, Palestinian, 69, Carried Travel Papers and a Gun. *The New York Times*, February 24, 1997,
http://query.nytimes.com/search/restricted/article
(accessed April 9, 2003).
7. Ibid.
8. Matthew Purdy, "Empire State Gunman's Not: Kill 'Zionists,'" *The New York Times*, February 26, 1997,

http://query.nytimes.com/search/restricted/article
(accessed April 7, 2003).

9. Ali Abu Kamal, "Charter of Honour,"
    http://www.thesmokinggun.com/longhand/empirestate.shtml
    (accessed April 7, 2003). The charter has been reproduced with gram-
    mar, spelling, and punctuation that is as close to the original as possible;
    a few proper names have been edited out.

10. Purdy, "The Gunman."

11. N. R. Kleinfield, "From Teacher to Gunman: U. S. Visit Ends in Fatal
    Rage," *The New York Times*, February 25, 1997,
    http://query.nytimes.com/search/restricted/article
    (accessed April 7, 2003).

12. Ibid.

13. Ibid.

14. Ibid.

15. Ibid.

16. Ibid.

17. Purdy, "The Gunman."

18. Ibid.

LEADERLESS RESISTANCE
The Arson Fires of Vail Ski Resort

1. Robert I. Fitzhenry, ed., *The Harper Book of Quotations*, 3rd ed. (New
    York: Harper Collins), 227.

2. G. Davidson Smith, "Single Issue Terrorism" [Commentary No. 74],
    (Ottawa, Canada: Canadian Security Intelligence Service, 1998),
    http://www.fas.org/irp/threat/com74e.htm (accessed June 1, 2004), 1.

3. Rachel Monaghan, "Single-Issue Terrorism: A Neglected
    Phenomenon?" *Studies in Conflict & Terrorism* 23(2000): 255-265.

4. Simson L. Garfinkel, "Leaderless Resistance Today," *First Monday*
    8(2003) http://firstmonday.org/issues/issue8_3/garfinkel/index.html
    (accessed July 26, 2005).

5. Ibid.

6. Ibid.

7. Garfinkel, "Leaderless Resistance," 3.

8. Smith, "Single-Issue Terrorism," 2.

9. Daniel Glick, *Powder Burn: Arson, Money, and Mystery on Vail Mountain* (New York: Public Affairs, 2001), xv.

10. Ibid., 104.

11. Ibid., xvi.

12. Ibid., 48.

13. Ibid., 24.

14. Ibid., 5.

15. Craig Rosebraugh, *Burning Rage of a Dying Planet: Speaking for the Earth Liberation Front* (New York: Lantern Books, 2004), 61.

16. Ibid., 60.

17. Ibid., 132.

18. Glick, "Leaderless Resistance," 134.

19. Rosebraugh, Burning Rage," 60.

20. See Garfinkel, "Leaderless Resistance," 9.

21. Ibid.

22. Ibid.

23. Ibid., 11.

24. Rosebraugh, *Burning Rage*, 237.

25. Jonathan R. White, *Terrorism and Homeland Security* 5th ed. (Belmont, CA: Thompson, 2006), 6.

26. Garfinkel, "Leaderless Resistance," 9.

27. Ibid.

28. Ibid.

OPPORTUNITIES LOST AND FOUND
The Attempted Millenium Bombing

1. Elizabeth Frost-Knappman and David S. Shrager, *A Concise Encyclopedia of Legal Quotations* (New York: Barnes & Noble Books, 1998), 108.

2. H. Bernton, M. Carter, D. Heath, and J. Neff, *The Terrorist Within: The Story Behind One Man's Holy War Against America* (Seattle, WA: The Seattle Times, 2002) http://seattletimes.nwsource.com/news/nation-world/ terroristwithin/ (accessed January 17, 2003). (Hereinafter, *The Terrorist Within*), Chapter 12, 1.

3. Ibid.

4. Ibid., 2.

5. *The Terrorist Within*, Chapter 2, 1.

6. Ibid., 3.
7. *The Terrorist Within*, Chapter 4, 3.
8. *The Terrorist Within*, Chapter 6, 1-2
9. *The Terrorist Within*, Chapter 7, 1.
10. Ibid.
11. Bruce Hoffman, "The Leadership Secrets of Osama bin Laden," *The Atlantic Monthly*, April 2003, 26-27.
12. *The Terrorist Within*, Chapter 8, 1.
13. Ibid.
14. Ibid., 2-3.
15. Ibid., 3.
16. *The Terrorist Within*, Chapter 10, 1-3.
17. Ibid.
18. *The Terrorist Within*, Chapter 11, 1-3.
19. Ibid.
20. *The Terrorist Within* Chapter 16, 1-3.
21. Ibid.

Connecting the Dots
September 11, 2001

1. http://www.quoteland.com, (accessed on April 24, 2006).
2. National Commission on Terrorist Attacks Upon the United States, *9/11 and Terrorist Travel: A Staff Report of the National Commission on Terrorist Attacks Upon the United States* (Franklin, TN: Hillsboro Press, 2004), 3.
3. Ibid., 4
4. National Commission on Terrorist Attacks Upon the United States, *The 9/11 Commission Report: Final Report of the National Commission on Terrorist Attacks Upon the United States (authorized edition)* (New York: W. W. Norton, 2004), 32. (hereinafter *9/11 Commission Report*).
5. *9/11 Commission Report*, 32.
6. *9/11 Commission Report*, 33.
7. *9/11 Commission Report*, 226.
8. *9/11 Commission Report*, 33.
9. Ibid.
10. *9/11 Commission Report*, 285.
11. *9/11 Commission Report*, 293.

12. Ibid.

13. *9/11 Commission Report*, 314.

14. Yosri Fouda and Nick Fielding, *Masterminds of Terror: The Truth Behind the Most Devastating Terrorist Attack the World Has Ever Seen* (New York: Arcade Publishing, 2003), 128.

15. See *9/11 Commission Report*. The Commission was a bipartisan panel with an extensive staff that published its findings of the U.S. government's official investigation into the attacks of September 11.

16. *9/11 Commission Report*, 47.

17. As cited by Gerald Posner, *Why American Slept: The Failure to Prevent 9/11* (New York: Random House, 2003), 133.

18. See, for example, Robert A. Fein and Bryan Vossekuil, "Assassination in the United States: An Operational Study of Recent Assassins, Attackers, and Near-Lethal Approachers," *Journal of Forensic Sciences* 44(1999): 321-333.

19. *9/11 Commission Report*, 266.

20. Ibid., 272.

21. Ibid., 273.

22. Bruce Hoffman, *Al-Qaeda, Trends in Terrorism and Future Potentialities: An Assessment* (Santa Monica, CA: RAND, 2003), 3.

23. Ibid., 9.

24. Stephen J. Schulhofer, *Rethinking the Patriot Act: Keeping America Safe and Free* (New York: The Century Foundation Press, 2005), 18.

25. *9/11 Commission Report*, 77.

26. Schulhofer, *Rethinking the Patriot Act*, 3.

ARE YOU AFRAID?
The Anthrax Letters

1. Elizabeth Frost-Knappman and David S. Shrager, *A Concise Encyclopedia of Legal Quotations* (New York: Barnes & Noble Books, 1998), 140.

2. "Chronology of Anthrax Events," *Sun-Sentinel.com*, 2003, http://www.sun-sentinel.com/news/local/southflorida/sfl-1013anthraxchronology.story?coll=sfla-home-headlines (accessed July 18, 2003).

3. Robert Graysmith, *Amerithrax: The Hunt for the Anthrax Killer* (New York Berkley, 2003), 54.

4. "Chronology."

5. Martha Thompson, *The Killer Strain: Anthrax and a Government Exposed* (New York: Harper Collins, 2003), 7.

6. Ibid., 81.

7. Ibid., 12, 14.

8. Graysmith, *Amerithrax*, 60.

9. Ibid., 71.

10. Ibid., 96, 104.

11. Barbara Hatch Rosenberg, *Analysis of the Anthrax Attacks* (Federation of American Scientists) http://www.fas.org/bwc/news/anthraxreport.htm (accessed July 18, 2003), 10.

12. Ibid., 10.

13. Ibid., 9.

14. Ibid., 4.

15. Ibid.

16. Ibid., 5.

17. Ibid., 6.

18. William J. Broad and David Johnston, "Report Linking Anthrax and Hijackers is Investigated," *The New York Times*, March 23, 2002, http://www.ph.ucla.edu/epi/bioter/antrhaxhijackerslink.html (accessed May 2, 2003).

19. Ibid.

20. Critical Incident Response Group, *Linguistic/Behavioral Analysis of Anthrax Letters*, (Washington, DC: National Center for the Analysis of Violent Crime, November 9, 2001, http://www.fbi.gov/anthrax/amerithrax.htm (accessed May 2, 2003).

21. Thompson, *The Killer Strain*, 38-39.

EPILOGUE

1. *United States v. Richard Colvin Reid*, Statement at Judgment (U.S. District Court, District of Massachusetts, January 30, 2003). This statement was made at the end of Justice Young's sentencing of Richard Reid to life in prison for attempting to blow up a passenger airliner by concealing a bomb in one of his shoes. Before leaving the courtroom, a defiant Reid responded that, "That flag will be brought down on the day of judgment and you will see in front of your Lord and my Lord and then we will know.

2. David C. Rapoport, "The Four Waves of Modern Terrorism," in eds. Audrey K. Cronin and James M. Ludes, 46-73 *Attacking Terrorism: Elements of a Grand Strategy* (Washington, DC: Georgetown University Press, 2005), 46.

3. Ibid., 47.

4. Ibid.

5. Ibid.

6. See Walter Laqueur, *No End To War: Terrorism in the Twenty-First Century* (New York: Continuum, 2004), 145.

ABOUT THE AUTHOR

Joseph T. McCann is a licensed psychologist and attorney in Binghamton, New York with many years of clinical and forensic experience in a variety of consulting and professional roles. He is a clinical psychologist at United Health Services Hospitals, a Clinical Assistant Professor of Psychiatry at SUNY Upstate Medical University, and a member of the adjunct faculty at Binghamton University (SUNY), where he teaches a course on the psychological and legal aspects of terrorism. He maintains an active program of research, teaching, and writing on terrorism and forensic psychology. Among his several books is the recently published volume *Minds on Trial: Great Cases in Law and Psychology* (co-authored with Charles P. Ewing; Oxford Press).

Sentient Publications, LLC publishes books on cultural creativity, experimental education, transformative spirituality, holistic health, new science, ecology, and other topics, approached from an integral viewpoint. Our authors are intensely interested in exploring the nature of life from fresh perspectives, addressing life's great questions, and fostering the full expression of the human potential. Sentient Publications' books arise from the spirit of inquiry and the richness of the inherent dialogue between writer and reader.

We are very interested in hearing from our readers. To direct suggestions or comments to us, or to be added to our mailing list, please contact:

SENTIENT PUBLICATIONS, LLC
1113 Spruce Street
Boulder, CO 80302
303-443-2188
contact@sentientpublications.com
www.sentientpublications.com